THE DAY WE
LOST THE H-BOMB

THE DAY WE
LOST THE H-BOMB

COLD WAR, HOT NUKES, AND
THE WORST NUCLEAR
WEAPONS DISASTER
IN HISTORY

BARBARA MORAN

PRESIDIO
PRESS

BALLANTINE BOOKS | NEW YORK

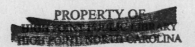

Published in the United States by Presidio Press, an imprint of The Random House Publishing Group, a division of Random House, Inc., New York.

PRESIDIO PRESS and colophon are trademarks of Random House, Inc.

LIBRARY OF CONGRESS CATALOGING-IN-PUBLICATION DATA
Moran, Barbara.
The day we lost the H-bomb : cold war, hot nukes, and the worst nuclear weapons disaster in history / Barbara Moran.
p. cm.
Includes bibliographical references and index.
ISBN 978-0-89141-904-4 (hardcover : alk. paper)
1. Aircraft accidents—Spain—Palomares—History—20th century.
2. Hydrogen bomb—United States—History—20th century. 3. Airplanes, Military—Accidents—United States—History—20th century. 4. Search and rescue operations—United States—History—20th century. 5. Nuclear accidents—Spain—Palomares Region—History—20th century. I. Title.
TL553.5.M579 2009
363.12'493—dc22   2009005359

Printed in the United States of America on acid-free paper

www.presidiopress.com

2 4 6 8 9 7 5 3 1

FIRST EDITION

Book design by Laurie Jewell

CONTENTS

MARCH

APRIL

PROLOGUE

Francisco Simó Orts stood on the deck of his fishing boat, squinting at the Spanish coastline. It was midmorning and the sky was a brilliant blue, the bright sun blazing as it climbed toward noon. Simó, tall and square-shouldered with a head of thick dark hair, looked more like a movie star than a shrimp fisherman. Like a bronzed Kirk Douglas, said a reporter much later, playing the role of captain. He even had the perfect dimple in his chin.

Despite his marquee looks, Simó was indeed just a fisherman, and at the moment he was deciding whether to lift his shrimp nets from the sea. Having worked the waters off southeastern Spain since he was a boy, he was a seasoned sailor and, at the age of thirty-eight, also a shrewd and prosperous businessman. Simó owned two sturdy fishing boats with the latest sounding gear and was known as a big man around town. And his town, the coastal village of Aguilas, was no backwater. It was a growing seaside resort with a whiff of worldliness, a bit out of character for this part of rural Spain. Aguilas even had a four-story building—more than other nearby towns could say.

But even in this rising city, Simó's self-confidence set him apart. His family had originally come from Catalonia, an independent-minded region on the northeastern coast of Spain. Even today, people from there think of themselves as Catalonian first and Spanish second, if at all. They prefer speaking Catalan to Spanish and are widely known for their business sense. Simó, by all accounts, had inherited the enterprising spirit of his ancestors. He had that quality that admiring Americans call "hustle." The other fishermen in Aguilas, not altogether kindly, called him "El Catalan."

On this particular Monday, January 17, 1966, Simó had left Aguilas at dawn and trundled some forty miles down the Spanish coast to the shrimp banks off the small town of Palomares. Simó's boat dropped her nets and puttered slowly, scooping shrimp from the sea. The ship, named *Manuela Orts Simó* after Simó's mother, sailed parallel to the shore, about five miles off the coast. A bit farther out to sea was Simó's other boat, the *Agustín y Rosa,* steered by his older brother Alfonso. Closer to shore chugged the *Dorita,* captained by another Aguilas fisherman named Bartolomé Roldán Martínez. By 10:22 a.m., the three boats had been trawling for two hours and were preparing to raise their nets. Simó looked at the desert hills on the shoreline to get his bearings. He had learned to find his position by certain landmarks, and he knew the coastline by heart. Lining up a particular mountain with an abandoned chimney, for instance, and a familiar building with a certain hill, allowed him to establish his location precisely. Now he stood on his swaying boat, looking at the scrubby brown hills around Palomares and the bright, cloudless sky above. Then he saw an explosion.

High above the hills, an orange fireball flashed in the blue sky, followed by a deep, thunderous rumble. A rain of debris showered the Spanish countryside, and black smoke rose from the town of Palomares. Moments later, Simó saw five parachutes floating out to sea. They drifted for long minutes, hanging in the sky. Two chutes hit the ocean close to shore, near the *Dorita.* Another sailed high over Simó's head and landed far out to sea. And two splashed down near Simó— one about twenty-five yards toward shore, another about seventy-five yards seaward. Before they hit the water, Simó got a good look at them. Each seemed to carry a grisly cargo. The closer parachute seemed to hold a half a man, with his guts trailing from his severed torso. The other seemed to carry a dead man, hanging still and silent. Hoping the dead man might simply be unconscious, he steered his boat to the spot where his chute had hit the sea. But when Simó arrived, the dead man had already disappeared under the waves, parachute and all. Simó glanced at the coast and noted his position. Then he turned his boat to the *Dorita,* sailing as fast as his trailing shrimp nets would allow.

JANUARY

1.

Mighty SAC

Twenty-four hours earlier, across the ocean, Captain Charles Wendorf sat in Saint Luke's Methodist Church in Goldsboro, North Carolina, teaching his weekly Sunday school class to a group of lanky teenagers. Thirty years old, blue-eyed, and athletic, Wendorf sported a blond buzz cut and a relaxed confidence that belied his years. Wendorf had it all—a wife, three kids, a house, and a great job flying B-52 bombers. He also held a deep, earnest faith in God, America, and the U.S. Air Force, a faith tempered by an easy, self-deprecating manner and a gentle sense of humor. He had the disarming habit of starting sentences with the phrase "Well, I guess . . ." When asked if the kids in his Sunday school class looked up to him, a hotshot pilot, he chuckled and said in his aw-shucks way, "Well, I guess I suppose they did."

When the class finished, Wendorf got into his car with his wife, Betty, for the drive back to their home on Seymour Johnson Air Force Base. It was early in the afternoon. Wendorf had to be at squadron headquarters for a preflight briefing at 3:30 p.m., and he wanted to get home in time for a quick nap. In the car, Betty spoke up. She had a bad feeling about tonight's flight and wished Charlie could get out of it. Wendorf reassured his wife; he had flown this mission more than fifty times before, it was perfectly routine, there was nothing to worry about. She dropped the subject. There was no point in arguing; they both knew that the Air Force always won.

Wendorf had been in the Air Force his entire adult life, starting with ROTC when he was a student at Duke. He had entered flight training right after graduation and earned his wings in October 1959. His Air Force supervisors called him a born pilot. Wendorf had spent the last five and a half years behind the controls of B-52s, logging 2,100 flying hours in that plane alone. Initially disappointed to be assigned to the lumbering B-52, rather than a glamorous fighter plane, he eventually came to believe it far more challenging to manage a seven-man crew than a fighter plane and rose to become the youngest aircraft commander in the Strategic Air Command (SAC), his part of the Air Force. He also came to love his plane. "The airplane is huge, it's mammoth," he said. "But if you could fly that airplane like I could, you could thread a needle with it."

Wendorf got home from church around 2 p.m. and took his nap. When he woke up, he put on his olive green flight suit, grabbed his flight gear and briefcase, and headed to squadron headquarters. There, he checked his box for messages, found nothing, and met up with the rest of his crew for the preflight briefing. On this mission, Wendorf would be sharing pilot duties with two other men. His copilot was twenty-five-year-old First Lieutenant Michael Rooney. Only four years junior to Wendorf, Rooney had a hard-partying lifestyle that made him seem younger. One writer described the pilot as a jolly bachelor who enjoyed chasing skirts in nearby Raleigh. Rooney said the writer should have included Durham, Charlotte, and Goldsboro as well. His bachelor status made him a fish out of water in SAC, where most of the airmen were married with kids. SAC wives like Betty Wendorf fussed over the young man, inviting him for dinner and stuffing him with home-cooked food. Rooney's close friendship with the Wendorf family led to a lot of easy banter between the two men. Rooney had graduated from the University of North Carolina at Chapel Hill, a longtime rival of Wendorf's Duke, and for the two pilots, trashing the other's alma mater was an endless source of amusement.

Like many young men, Rooney had joined the Air Force with dreams of becoming a fighter pilot. His grades in flight school had put that dream out of reach, at least temporarily. He respected the B-52 but didn't enjoy flying it; it was too much like driving a truck.

That morning, while Wendorf was teaching Sunday school, Rooney, a practicing Catholic, went to Mass. ("I may have been doing something wild the night before," he said, "but I'm not telling.") Then he changed into uniform and drove his big, white 1963 Chevy Impala convertible to headquarters. The parking lot was nearly empty that Sunday, so he parked illegally in a senior officer's spot. He figured he'd be back before the officer showed up for work.

The third pilot that day was Major Larry Messinger, at forty-four the oldest and most experienced member of the crew and less inclined to joking around. He was on board as the relief pilot, standard practice for long flights. Messinger had served in the Air Force for more than twenty years, collecting a cluster of medals along the way. When the United States entered World War II, he signed up for the Army Air Forces right away and was soon rumbling over Germany in a B-17 bomber. On his sixth mission, while bombing an oil refinery, he took fire and lost an engine. Headed for a crash landing in a wheat field, his plane's left wing caught a wire strung between two telephone poles. The B-17 cartwheeled end over end, finally crashing on its back. Messinger and the copilot were suspended upside down, hanging from their seat belts. They unfastened their belts and dropped into the wreckage, finding themselves in the no-man's-land between the German and American lines. Badly injured, the two men struggled to the U.S. side and huddled on the front lines with the Seventh Armored division for a week before they were airlifted out. Messinger spent two months in an English hospital before getting back into the air, flying twenty-nine more missions before the end of the war. He later flew B-29s over Korea, where he "got shot up a bunch of times but never shot down." In his two combat tours, he flew seventy missions. Now he worked as an air controller at Seymour Johnson, filling in as a relief pilot when needed. Tall and trim, he had a long face and serious, steady eyes.

After the briefing, the three pilots walked out onto the tarmac, looked over their B-52, and then went to the bomb bay to inspect the four hydrogen bombs they'd be carrying that day. Each bomb packed 1.45 megatons of explosive power, about seventy times as much as the bomb that destroyed Hiroshima. Rooney put a hand on each of them and gave a good tug, just to make sure they were locked in tight. Then the pilots climbed inside the plane with the rest of the crew to begin the systems check. They found two small problems: the UHF radio wasn't working right, and neither was one of the oil pressure gauges.

By the time these were fixed, the crew was running eleven minutes late. The plane lumbered down the long runway and crept into the air, just after 6 p.m. Once they were airborne, Wendorf lit up a cigarette and settled in for the ride.

It was a perfectly ordinary Sunday in Cold War America. The big news stories were an army coup in Nigeria that had left two government ministers dead and a proposed $3 billion spending hike for President Lyndon Johnson's Great Society programs. Also, Secretary of State Dean Rusk, facing a failed "peace offensive" in Vietnam, told reporters that the U.S. government would consider "all necessary military measures" against Communist aggression in Southeast Asia. News analysts were trying to figure out exactly what that meant. And 35,000 feet above it all, Wendorf turned his plane east and headed toward Russia.

Over the next twenty-three hours or so, Wendorf and his crew, in tandem with another B-52, planned to fly across the Atlantic, circle over the Mediterranean, and then—unless they heard otherwise—turn around and come home. Wendorf's flight, part of a program called airborne alert, was a key activity of the Strategic Air Command, the nuclear strike component of the U.S. Air Force. In 1966, most Americans still assumed that the United States and the USSR stood, at all times, on the brink of nuclear war. Many believed—with an unshakable, almost religious fervor—that it was SAC, and these highly visible bomber flights, that kept the Soviets in check.

SAC's growth over the two previous decades had been explosive. In 1945, when America had dropped "Fat Man" and "Little Boy" on Hiroshima and Nagasaki, SAC didn't exist and the United States owned exactly two atomic bombs. By 1966, SAC was the most powerful force in military history. The primary guardian of America's nuclear arsenal, it controlled the bulk of the nation's 32,193 nuclear warheads, as well as 674 bombers, 968 missiles, and 196,887 people. The commander of SAC directed the Joint Strategic Target Planning Staff, which selected America's nuclear targets. SAC supplied much of the military intelligence and got the lion's share of the United States' defense money. To many inside and outside the military, SAC seemed all-powerful and unstoppable. Their influence was so great that it seemed perfectly reasonable—even necessary—for pilots to fly toward Russia, during peacetime, with four hydrogen bombs in their plane.

The story of the Strategic Air Command—its origin, mission, and philosophy—lay at the heart of the Cold War. And the story of SAC, and thus the story of Charles Wendorf's ill-fated flight, began during World War II, before humans had invented nuclear bombs, before people dreamed of nuclear war, and before the U.S. Air Force even existed. World War II launched the Air Force into being and spawned the atomic weapons that made it preeminent among the services. The war also shaped the military ideas of a tough young general named Curtis Emerson LeMay, teaching him the lessons he needed to turn SAC into the most powerful fighting force the world had ever seen.

At dusk on March 9, 1945, on an airstrip on the South Pacific island of Guam, an American B-29 Superfortress sped down a runway and lifted off just as the sun dropped below the horizon. One minute later, another B-29 followed, its four churning propellers roaring it into the sky. Again and again, American bombers took off from two runways in Guam, one minute after another for almost three hours. At the same time, bombers lifted off from nearby Saipan and Tinian. By 8:10 p.m., 325 American planes were flying toward Tokyo, filling the sky in a massive, roaring herd. That night, the bombers would make history in the deadliest bombing raid of World War II. This mission over Tokyo would cement the future of the Air Force and the legend of Curtis LeMay.

The bombing raid was a gamble. LeMay, a tough, reticent, thirty-eight-year-old general, was well known for his ability to solve problems and whip struggling outfits into shape. He had done it earlier in the war in Europe and China, and now he was in charge of the ailing 21st Bomber Command in Guam. LeMay had been running the show since January, but so far he hadn't fared much better than his predecessor, who had been fired. LeMay knew that if he didn't get results soon, he would be sent packing as well.

LeMay's assignment in Japan was the same one he had had in Europe: bomb the enemy's factories, gas depots, and ports and destroy its ability to wage war. But Japan had thrown him a few curveballs. First, the weather over the country was terrible for bombing—clouds covered the major cities almost every day, making accurate visual targeting nearly impossible. And at 35,000 feet, the powerful jet stream blew bombers (and bombs) off course and forced planes to use an inordinate amount of fuel. Each four-engine B-29 needed twenty-three tons of fuel just to get from Guam to Tokyo and back, leaving room for only three tons of bombs. In his first two months in the Pacific, LeMay had learned these facts the hard way, through a series of embarrassing missions where his bombers hit only a few targets by chance.

Sensing impatience from Washington, LeMay devised a daring plan for the March 9 mission. He would send the bombers in at night at a low altitude—under 10,000 feet—to avoid the jet stream and surprise the Japanese. If a bomber didn't have to fight the jet stream, LeMay calculated, it would use about two and a half tons less fuel. And he could save an additional two tons by stripping the planes of most of their guns, gunners, and ammunition. These two changes—flying at low altitudes and basically unarmed—would allow each plane to double its payload and drop bombs more accurately. It would also put the pilots at greater risk from Japanese antiaircraft fire, but LeMay concluded that it was a fair gamble. The Japanese air defenses were weaker than those he had seen in Europe. He thought his pilots could pull it off.

LeMay was used to tough decisions, but this was one of the toughest. If this strategy worked, it could shorten the war and maybe prevent an invasion of Japan. But if he had miscalculated, he would be sending hundreds of young men on a suicide run. On the night of March 9, after seeing the planes off, the mission weighed heavy on his mind. At about 2 a.m., an Air Force PR officer named St. Clair McKelway found LeMay sitting on a wooden bench beneath the mission control boards. "I'm sweating this one out," LeMay told McKelway. "A lot could go wrong. I can't sleep. I usually can, but not tonight."

LeMay knew that there was much at stake: his reputation, the lives of all those men, possibly the outcome of the war. But something else hung in the balance, too—the future of an independent Air Force.

When World War II began, there was no such thing as the U.S. Air Force. Planes and pilots served under the U.S. Army Air Forces (USAAF), which provided firepower, transport, and supplies—what's called tactical support—to Army troops on the ground, where the real fighting was going on. The airplane was just another tool for ground warfare, and it had no mission or role beyond what the Army assigned it.

To airmen, however, the airplane wasn't just a glorified school bus or food truck, it was a machine that could change the face of warfare. But they knew airpower could never reach its full potential under

Army generals. They wanted their own service, with their own money, their own rules, and airmen in charge. To make a legitimate claim for independence, they had to prove that they were indeed different and offered a valuable skill that the Army and Navy lacked. That skill, most agreed, was long-range strategic bombing.

Strategic bombing can be a bit hard to distinguish from tactical bombing, because the two often overlap. But in general it means dropping bombs on key bits of enemy infrastructure—oil refineries, engine plants, important bridges—that aren't directly involved in a current battle but greatly affect the enemy's ability to fight. In 1921, an Italian general named Giulio Douhet first defined strategic bombing in his book *The Command of the Air*. Douhet's idea gained popularity between World War I and World War II but faced some resistance. For Douhet, strategic bombing meant that an entire country was fair game; planes could target hospitals and food depots as legitimately as airstrips and factories. There were few safe havens, no noncombatants. Bombing city centers could crush the will of the civilian population, argued Douhet, forcing enemy leaders to surrender quickly and leading to less bloodshed in the end. American airmen, wary of civilian casualties, advocated bombing specific targets to disable the enemy's economy. Even so, critics called such tactics uncivilized, immoral, and un-American. Outside airpower circles, the idea fizzled.

Then came World War II, and the Army Air Forces saw their chance. They argued for the opportunity to bomb German train yards and oil refineries, and they got it. And it was true that the airplanes offered something that Navy ships and Army tanks couldn't: only airborne bombers could fly deep into Germany, destroy German factories, and break the German war machine. That is, if the bombers could actually get to Germany and manage to hit anything.

In the early days of World War II, an assignment to a bomber crew was nearly a death sentence. The lumbering B-17 Stratofortresses flew in large, rigid formations, easy targets for enemy fighters and flak. Bombers flying from England to Germany sometimes had fighter escorts, but the fighters had such a short range that they usually turned back at the border of Germany, leaving the bombers to face the most risky portion of the journey alone. Bomber groups sometimes lost half—or more—of their planes on raids over Germany. In one infamous circumstance, the 100th Bomber Group lost seven planes over Bremen on October 8, 1943. Two days later, it lost twelve of its remaining thirteen planes over Munster. Bomber crews were more likely than foot soldiers to be killed, wounded, or captured. Twice as many air officers died in combat as those on the ground, despite their smaller numbers. An airman in a World War II bomber had a shorter life expectancy than an infantryman in the trenches of World War I.

After reading accounts of air battles, such statistics seem less surprising. On August 17, 1943, German fighters attacked a division of American B-17 bombers over Belgium. An observer in one of the rear planes later described the battle:

> A stricken B-17 fell gradually out of formation to the right, then moments later disintegrated in one giant explosion. As the fighters kept pressing their attacks, one plane after another felt their fury. Engine parts, wing tips, even tail assemblies were blasted free. Rearward planes had to fly through showers of exit doors, emergency hatches, sheets of metal, partially opened parachutes, and other debris, in addition to human bodies, some German, some American, some dead, some still alive and writhing. As more German fighters arrived and the battle intensified, there were so many disintegrating airplanes that "sixty 'chutes in the air at one time was hardly worth a second look." A man crawled out of the copilot's window of a Fortress engulfed in flames. He was the only person to emerge. Standing precariously on the wing, he reached back inside for his parachute—he could hardly have gotten through the window with his chute on—used one hand to get into the harness while he clung to the plane with the other, then dove off the wing for an apparently safe descent, only to be hit by the plane's onrushing horizontal stabilizer. His chute did not open.

The passage comes from *Iron Eagle,* Thomas Coffey's biography of Curtis LeMay. LeMay, head of the 4th Bombardment Wing in England at the time, flew in the lead bomber. Until his superiors forbade it, LeMay often accompanied his men on bombing missions, a habit that inspired deep trust and loyalty among his flyers. LeMay also inspired fear, or at least trepidation. Stocky, square-jawed, and perpetually chewing a cigar, he was a tough guy who looked the part. He scowled often and spoke little. Decades after the war, LeMay's gruff demeanor and blunt, often tactless public statements would make him the object of widespread derision and caricature. But here, in World War II, he was in his element. He got things done.

LeMay hated the thought of being unprepared, of losing men and bombers because of poor training or sloppy mistakes. When he arrived in England, he was alarmed by the rabble the Army gave him—rookie airmen who could barely fly a plane or bomb a target. These kids would die unless he whipped them into shape. And whip them he did. His men called him "Iron Ass" for his relentless training regimen— exhausted pilots would return from a bombing run ready for bed, only to be ordered back in the plane to practice bad-weather takeoffs. Bombardiers had to memorize stacks of photographs in preparation for future missions. LeMay worked as hard as his troops, becoming a brilliant strategist. During his time in Europe, he devised new flying formations and bombing techniques that saved bombers and helped pick off German factories. On August 17, 1943, the day of the mission described in the passage above, the surviving B-17s flew to Regensburg and dropped 303 tons of bombs on a Messerschmitt aircraft plant, one of the most accurate strategic bombing runs of the war.

By the time LeMay arrived in Guam, the AAF bombing campaign against Japan seemed a pretty dismal failure. The Navy, not the AAF, deserved the credit for gains in the Pacific, having crushed the Japanese fleet, mined the Japanese harbors, and captured valuable islands. The Navy brass, riding high, were even eyeing the powerful new B-29 bombers, plotting to steal them from the Army and incorporate them into the Navy. If LeMay didn't get some results soon, Washington might scrap the strategic bombing campaign altogether. Failure in Japan would seriously jeopardize the case for an independent Air Force.

Luckily, LeMay had a new weapon at his disposal, one that would alter the fate of strategic bombing in Japan: napalm, a jellied gasoline that stuck to almost anything and burned slow and steady. In a city like Tokyo, where about 98 percent of the buildings were made of wood, incendiary bombs promised massive destruction. When his 325 planes left Guam, Saipan, and Tinian on March 9, most carried six to eight tons of napalm "bomblets," designed to scatter when dropped and ignite buildings at a number of points.

LeMay put a trusted brigadier general named Thomas Power in charge of the raid. Power was to lead the planes to Tokyo, drop his bombs, and then circle at 10,000 feet to observe the rest of the operation. At around 2:30 a.m., Power, circling Tokyo, sent his first message to LeMay: "Bombing the primary target visually. Large fires observed, flak moderate. Fighter opposition nil." Soon, messages arrived from other bombers reporting "conflagration."

The raid devastated Tokyo. The flaming napalm stuck to the flimsy wooden houses, starting small fires that quickly spread into giant firestorms. The flames burned so brightly that the bomber pilots could read their watch dials by the glow. The blaze burned nearly seventeen square miles of the city to cinders, destroying 18 percent of its industry. Somewhere between 80,000 and 100,000 people died, burned to death when their hair, clothes, and houses caught fire or suffocated when the firestorm sucked away oxygen. The smell of burning flesh hung in the air for days.

The carnage sparked little sympathy in America. "When you kill 100,000 people, civilians, you cross some sort of moral divide," said the historian Edward Drea. "Yet at the time, it was generally accepted that this was fair treatment, that the Japanese deserved this, that they had brought this on themselves." If LeMay had any moral qualms about the slaughter, he never acknowledged them. For him, it was an obvious trade: Japanese lives for American. "No matter how you slice it, you're going to kill an awful lot of civilians. Thousands and thousands. But if you don't destroy the Japanese industry, we're going to have to invade Japan," he wrote in his autobiography, *Mission with LeMay*. "We're at war with Japan. We were attacked by Japan. Do you want to kill Japanese, or would you rather have Americans killed?"

When the B-29s returned from Tokyo on the morning of March 10, LeMay ordered them to get back into the air that evening and bomb Nagoya, Japan's second largest city. But after a look at the exhausted crews, he postponed the Nagoya raid for twenty-four hours. Over ten days, LeMay's B-29s firebombed aircraft plants in Nagoya, steel mills in Osaka, and the port of Kobe, destroying thirty-three square miles of those cities. He bombed Japan until he ran out of bombs and started again when the Navy brought him more. Throughout April, May, and June 1945, LeMay's bombers pounded the cities of Japan. By summer, LeMay announced that strategic bombing could probably force Japan's surrender by October.

The end came even sooner. On August 7, 1945, U.S. forces dropped an atomic bomb named "Little Boy" on the city of Hiroshima. Nine days later, they dropped a second, "Fat Man," on Nagasaki. That evening, Japan surrendered. The war was over.

The Japanese surrender confirmed one of LeMay's long-standing beliefs: the value of massive, overwhelming force. In his eyes, the widespread bombing had shortened the war and saved lives. "I think it's more immoral to use less force than necessary than it is to use more," he wrote. "If you use less force, you kill off more of humanity in the long run, because you are merely protracting the struggle." It was far more humane, he argued, to cut off a dog's tail with one quick flick of the knife than to saw it off one inch at a time.

On September 2, LeMay attended the Japanese surrender ceremonies on board the USS *Missouri* in Tokyo Bay. As he stood on the ship's crowded deck, thinking of the Americans who had died and "where I'd gone wrong in losing as many as we did," a roar filled the air. Four hundred sixty-two B-29s flew overhead in a massive, deafening salute. To LeMay, the atomic bombs had been impressive but anticlimactic. In his opinion, those B-29s had won the war.

In the months after VJ Day, LeMay and his fellow air generals toured the United States, drumming up support for an independent Air Force. Despite his initial ambivalence, LeMay soon realized that the atomic bomb was a major boon for his cause. In LeMay's biggest raid over Japan, hundreds of planes had dropped thousands of bombs, adding up to the power of about 3,000 tons of TNT. A single atomic bomb, dropped onto Hiroshima by a single plane, exploded with *five times* that power—the equivalent of 15,000 tons of TNT. One bomb could now destroy a city. Whoever controlled this new weapon owned the future of war.

The Army Air Forces had a head start. The early atomic bombs were far too big and heavy (the bomb dropped on Nagasaki weighed 10,000 pounds) to be launched by a soldier, tank, or battleship. Only a few, specially modified B-29s could actually drop one of these behemoths on a target. Some airpower advocates gleefully claimed that the atomic bomb had made the Army and Navy obsolete. The famed pilot Jimmy Doolittle said that the Navy's only purpose now was ferrying supplies, the Army's only job to occupy a country after bombers had crushed it into submission. LeMay wasn't quite so harsh but argued that this new atomic age required a strong, vigilant Air Force to protect America. "Being peace-loving and weak didn't stop us from getting into a fight," he told the Wings Club in October 1945. "Maybe being strong and ready will do it."

Congress, the president, and even the Army agreed that World War II and the atomic bomb had enhanced the status of airpower. With the Army's blessing, the AAF broke free. In September 1947, the U.S. Air Force became an independent service.

The Air Force started life with three distinct commands. The Tactical Air Command (TAC) handled fighter planes and tactical support, the Air Defense Command (ADC) defended America against air attack, and the Strategic Air Command (SAC) took care of the bombers and atomic weapons. Most of the new Air Force generals believed that strategic bombing had won them independence, and they saw SAC as the key to the Air Force's future. In the postwar scramble for planes, bases, and personnel, SAC grabbed the lion's share.

Not that there was much to grab. After the war ended, President Harry Truman rapidly demobilized the military, reducing defense spending from 40 percent of the gross national product in 1944 to a mere 4 percent by 1948. He slashed Air Force personnel from a high of 2.4 million to only 300,000 by May 1947. He sent soldiers home to their regular jobs and ordered planes and jeeps sold for scrap. Records were dumped into boxes and thrown away. "We just walked away and left everything," said Leon Johnson, a bomber pilot who became an influential Air Force general. "We started from nothing, from nothing, to rebuild the Air Force."

For several years after the war, SAC floundered under limited budgets and weak leadership. But by 1948, there was a sense of urgency; the uneasy postwar alliance between the Soviet Union and the United States was rapidly crumbling. The two countries had never shared an easy friendship, even while allies in World War II, but now the relationship was worsening by the day. The Communists were gobbling up territory in Eastern Europe, and their hunger for more seemed insatiable. Then, in 1948, the tension reached a new height, focused on the German city of Berlin.

After World War II, Germany had been divided into four sectors, under American, French, British, and Soviet control. Deep within the Soviet sector, the city of Berlin was subdivided into four sectors. The Soviets had long bristled at this arrangement, and in June 1948 they ramped up their efforts to assert themselves in the city by blocking all road, rail, and barge traffic to the western sectors of Berlin, leaving the Berliners marooned without adequate food or fuel. The United States responded with a massive airlift, hauling tons of milk, flour, medicine, and coal into the starving city. But Western leaders feared that the Berlin blockade was merely a prelude, that the USSR would soon try to push beyond Berlin and deep into Western Europe. If the Soviets made a move, Washington might need the bumbling Strategic Air Command to intervene. On October 19, 1948, SAC got a new commander: Curtis LeMay.

LeMay, who had been running the Berlin airlift, started his new job by visiting SAC headquarters at Andrews Air Force Base near Washington, D.C. The situation shocked him. "Not one crew—not one crew—in the entire command could do a professional job," he said. "Not one of the outfits was up to strength—neither in airplanes nor in people nor anything else." LeMay grew annoyed when people at SAC told him that "everything was rosy." He knew that pilots had been running practice bombing raids and asked about their accuracy. The commanders bragged that bombardiers were hitting targets "right on the button."

> They produced the bombing scores, and they were so good I didn't believe them. . . . I found out that SAC wasn't bombing from combat altitudes, but from 12,000 to 15,000 feet. . . . It was completely unrealistic. It was perfectly apparent to me that while we didn't have much capability, everyone thought we were doing fine.

LeMay saw history repeating itself. SAC was just like the ragtag bomber groups he had initially commanded in Europe. But this time, America faced an even bigger threat: the Soviet Union would undoubtedly have its own atomic bomb soon. LeMay felt a tremendous sense of urgency. "We had to be ready to go to war not next week, not tomorrow, but this afternoon, today," he said. "We had to operate every day as if we were at war."

With Air Force leadership backing him, LeMay sprang into action. Seven days after taking command, LeMay put Tommy Power, his old friend from the Pacific, into the deputy commander slot. Power was not well liked (even LeMay said he was a "mean sonofabitch"), but he got things done. LeMay replaced virtually all SAC's commanders and headquarters staff with his pals from the Pacific bombing campaign. Their first mission was to prepare at least one group for atomic combat. They started with the 509th Bomber Group at Walker Air Force Base in Roswell, New Mexico. The Army had created the 509th for the sole purpose of dropping the atomic bombs on Hiroshima and Nagasaki. Now it was the only group even close to atomic readiness. LeMay's staff stocked their warehouses with supplies and made sure that the planes had parts, guns, and gas. They weeded through personnel, replacing dead wood with crack crews.

LeMay worked nearly every day, from eight in the morning until well into the evening, and his housecleaning touched every corner of SAC. "My goal," he said later, "was to build a force that was so professional, so strong, so powerful, that we would not have to fight. In other words, we had to build this deterrent force. And it had to be good." He argued to Air Force leaders that SAC must be their top priority in funding, research, planes, and personnel. Aided by his reputation and zeal and the growing Soviet threat, LeMay convinced them to give him carte blanche. He created a recruitment and screening system that filled SAC's ranks with bomber crews handpicked for their self-discipline and maturity. He arranged for new housing to be built so the airmen would have decent places to live. He made his leaders write detailed manuals for every job and train the airmen relentlessly. SAC developed elaborate war strategies, which it planned to change every six months. It built a million-dollar telephone and teletype system to link all SAC bases with the new headquarters at Offutt Field in Omaha, Nebraska. In six months, LeMay had turned SAC around and landed on the cover of *Newsweek*. Underneath his scowling portrait ran the headline "Air General LeMay: A Tough Guy Does It Again." Inside the magazine, a glowing article called LeMay a genius and described how he had turned SAC from a "creampuff outfit" into an atomic force with real teeth. "When LeMay first came in, we were nothing but a bunch of nits and gnats," one young officer told *Newsweek*. "Today, we're a going concern."

LeMay had done more than shape SAC up; he had created a religion. The gospel he preached was a simple parable: the schoolyard bully and the gentle giant. The Soviets were the schoolyard bullies, aiming to seize Europe, crush America, and spread communism throughout the world. SAC was the gentle giant, the muscle-bound kid who stuck up for the skinny geeks and pimply weaklings, the kid who didn't want to hurt anyone but could knock you out with one punch if he had to. The Strategic Air Command, and no one else, stood as America's shield and protector.

In the years to come, LeMay would never waver from this core message. Increasingly, those who doubted this truth or questioned its morality were labeled fools, cowards, or Commies.

The year 1952 began the golden age of SAC. The command had a clear mission, a strong leader, and the American public on board. In the early 1950s, the Bomb loomed over everything. Those were the years when schoolchildren ducked under their desks for atomic air-raid drills and teachers handed out dog tags so they could identify students after a nuclear blast. The year 1952 also brought a new president—Dwight Eisenhower—who announced that strategic airpower and nuclear weapons were now the nation's top defense priority.

Disgusted by the slogging stalemate of the Korean War, Eisenhower viewed nuclear deterrence as a far cheaper way to keep the nation safe and oversaw a massive buildup of SAC and the nation's nuclear stockpile. He also believed that there could be no such thing as a "limited" nuclear war. Because such a war would destroy both countries, if not the world, it had to be prevented at all costs. Eisenhower had joined LeMay's church of deterrence: America could prevent nuclear war only by showing spectacular strength.

Eisenhower's philosophy led to a windfall for the nuclear military, especially the Air Force. Between 1952 and 1960, the Air Force received 46 percent of America's defense money. SAC more than doubled its personnel in five years, from 85,473 in 1950 to 195,997 by 1955. During those five years the bomber fleet also grew dramatically, from 520 to 1,309. In 1951, SAC had thirty-three bases, including eleven outside the continental United States. By 1957, SAC operated out of sixty-eight bases. Thirty of these were spread around the world, in North Africa, Canada, New Zealand, England, Guam, Greenland, and Spain. Although other services had nuclear weapons by the mid-1950s—Army soldiers could fire small nuclear artillery shells, and the Navy could launch cruise missiles from submarines—SAC ruled the nuclear kingdom. "SAC was still the big daddy," said

Jerry Martin, command historian for the U.S. Strategic Command. "They had the nuclear hammer."

On March 19, 1954, at the height of this expansion, SAC hosted a classified briefing at its headquarters in Omaha. Major General A. J. Old, director of SAC operations, spoke to about thirty military officers from various service branches, regaling the crowd with charts, graphs, and maps detailing SAC's capabilities. Afterward, LeMay answered questions for a half hour.

Sitting in the audience that day was a Navy captain named William Brigham Moore. Moore took detailed notes at the meeting and later wrote a memo describing it for his director. The top secret memo, declassified in the 1980s, gives a small but rare glimpse inside SAC at the apex of its power.

According to Moore, Old told the crowd that SAC had several hundred strike plans. Then he described SAC's optimum strike plan, what defense insiders called the "Sunday Punch." With enough warning time, SAC could send 735 bombers flying toward the Soviet Union. The bombers, approaching from many different directions, would hit the Soviets' early warning screen simultaneously and overwhelm their defenses. Old estimated that the planes could drop somewhere between 600 and 750 bombs. "The final impression," wrote Moore, "was that virtually all of Russia would be nothing but a smoking, radiating ruin at the end of two hours."

General Old concluded the meeting by raising an issue that would come to dominate SAC policy, the concept of "alert time." Old framed it this way: If the Soviets launched a surprise attack against the United States, would SAC have enough time to load its planes and get them off the ground before Russian bombs blew them to bits? With two hours' warning, he said, Russian bombs could destroy about 35 percent of the command. But if the Soviets sneaked in a total surprise attack and caught SAC with its pants down, the bombs could decimate the command, obliterating 90 percent of its infrastructure. "The amount of alert time," concluded Moore, "is the most important factor as far as SAC is concerned."

The concept of alert time had been cooked up by defense analysts at the RAND Corporation, a California think tank sponsored by the Air Force. In the early 1950s, RAND analysts became convinced that SAC bases, especially those overseas, were vulnerable to a surprise attack. SAC leaders soon realized that these vulnerabilities could work in their favor. For SAC to survive an all-out surprise attack and retaliate in kind, it would need a striking force at least double the size of the Soviets'. Building such a force would require a massive influx of funding. SAC could ask for the sky.

On April 30, 1956, Curtis LeMay sat at a long table in the Capitol building, facing a row of somber senators. LeMay had flown to Washington to testify before the Senate Armed Forces Subcommittee about the strength of SAC's bomber fleet and its vulnerability to surprise attack. The hearings had been in the making for about a year. Senate Democrats had accused President Eisenhower of pinching military funds excessively in order to balance the budget. With a presidential election looming, the subcommittee had called for hearings to examine, specifically, Eisenhower's Air Force policies. The sessions, which became known as the Congressional Air Power Hearings of 1956, brought the question of SAC's vulnerability to the American public and made "bomber gap" a household term.

Worrisome intelligence had trickled in from Russia over the past year. One incident in particular had caused grave concern. The previous summer, the Soviets had invited a number of U.S. Air Force attachés to an air show near Moscow. The day of the air show had started pleasantly enough—one news report describes the attachés sitting under colored umbrellas, drinking beer, and chatting with other foreigners. Then came the air parade, which included Soviet Bison bombers, four-engine jet planes suspected to have intercontinental range. At the time, Air Force Intelligence guessed that the Soviets had about twenty-five Bisons, maybe up to forty. But at the air show, the Americans saw ten Bisons flying overhead, then another nine, then yet another nine. There were twenty-eight planes in all, just at the parade.

The Air Force representatives realized—or rather, thought they did—that they had grossly underestimated the size of the Soviet bomber force. Returning home, they fed the information to Air Force intelligence, who figured that twenty-eight Bisons in the air meant the Soviets must have fifty-six already finished. Adding in what they knew about Soviet factory space and learning curves, intelligence analysts predicted that by 1959 the Soviets could have five hundred to eight hundred Bisons.

We know today, and some suspected even then, that the Soviets had nowhere near that number of long-range bombers. In fact, the Soviets had only ten Bisons at the time, and those had rolled off the assembly line just weeks before the air show. Analysts later speculated that the Soviets had fooled the American attachés by flying the same planes over the viewing area again and again.

The suspected Soviet bomber strength became public knowledge during Curtis LeMay's testimony before the Senate subcommittee. LeMay's testimony was a bit odd—because the hearings involved issues of national security, the senators had given LeMay written questions and he read the censored answers. (One reporter speculated that Air Force PR had dreamed up this tactic to keep LeMay from shooting his mouth off.) Despite the stilted setting, LeMay got his point across. Looking "guarded" and "somber," he told the senators that the Russians were beating America in the bomber race. SAC's new long-range B-52 bomber, he said, had a serious engineering flaw: a flywheel in the B-52's alternator had a nasty habit of breaking off. The defect had already caused one crash and led to serious production delays. Boeing had delivered seventy-eight B-52s so far, and SAC had returned thirty-one to the shop. This left SAC with only forty-seven of the new long-range bombers. The Air Force guessed that the Soviets already had about a hundred.

LeMay's testimony on this "bomber gap" made front-page headlines, and Americans reacted with dismay. How did Russia get ahead of us? Both houses of Congress demanded that the president add an additional billion dollars to the Air Force budget. (The budget already included $16.9 billion for the Air Force, $10 billion for the Navy, and $7.7 billion for the Army.) Eisenhower, sensing trouble, cautioned against getting caught up in a "numbers racket" and trying to match the Russians plane for plane. He pointed out that the United States had a massive fleet of midrange bombers stationed all over the globe, not to mention the most powerful navy in the world. When the full story came out, he said, the American public would "feel a lot better."

The president's soothing words calmed the storm for a few weeks. The House of Representatives passed Eisenhower's budget as it stood, without additional funds for the Air Force. Then LeMay returned for one more Senate hearing. It was his "guess," he said on May 26, that the Soviets could destroy the United States in a surprise attack by 1959. From 1958 on, he said, the Russians would be "stronger in long-range airpower than we are, and it naturally follows that if [the enemy] is stronger, he may feel that he should attack."

It's impossible to tell if LeMay believed his own rhetoric. Some considered him a cynical opportunist, using spotty intelligence and scare tactics to build SAC into an empire at the expense of the other services. One anonymous administration spokesman told *Time* magazine that "Curt LeMay thinks only of SAC." But many believed him a patriot defending his country against an ominous enemy. Most Americans assumed that the Communists were hell-bent on world domination and would like nothing better than to bomb America into a nuclear wasteland. If the United States gave them an inch or fell behind at all, they would try it.

At the conclusion of the airpower hearings, the Senate sided with LeMay. Over Eisenhower's objections, Congress gave the Air Force an additional $928.5 million to bulk up against the Soviet threat. SAC could move its mission forward.

To counter the threat of a surprise attack, SAC started experimenting with a program called "ground alert" in November 1956. In this system, maintenance crews kept a handful of SAC bombers poised on the airstrip, filled with fuel and bombs. Flight crews lived and slept in nearby barracks. They could leave the barracks while on alert duty but never wander more than fifteen minutes away from their planes. Frequent drills kept the airmen in line. When the alarm—a blaring klaxon that could wake the dead—sounded, the crews ran to their planes at full speed, as if Curtis LeMay himself were chasing them. The first plane took off within fifteen minutes; the others followed at one-minute intervals. On October 1, 1957, ground alert became official SAC policy.

The new system came just in the nick of time. Three days later, on October 4, the Soviets launched *Sputnik,* the first man-made satellite to orbit the earth. *Sputnik* by itself was no threat to the United States. Barely bigger than a basketball, it contained scientific instruments to measure the density of the atmosphere. But *Sputnik* hadn't climbed into orbit by itself; the Soviets had shot it up there with a rocket. And if Soviet rockets could shoot satellites into space, they could certainly shoot nuclear missiles at the United States. "Soon they will be dropping bombs on us from space like kids dropping rocks onto cars from freeway overpasses," said Senator Lyndon Johnson. SAC's new ground alert seemed like a brilliant, prescient move. By the following year, SAC had reorganized its structure to keep one third of the bomber force on alert at all times.

That same year, SAC began testing another program, called "airborne alert." Instead of holding bombers ready on the ground, this program kept loaded SAC bombers in the air at all times, flying in prearranged orbits that approached Soviet airspace. Proponents argued that airborne alert gave SAC added security. "Any Soviet surprise attack," wrote one reporter, "would find the 'birds' gone from their nests." Airborne bombers, closer than planes on the ground to Soviet targets, also posed a more powerful deterrent. With those bombers in the sky, the Soviets would think twice before trying any funny business.

Tommy Power told Congress about the new program in 1959, after he had finished initial testing. Airborne alert was ready to go, but SAC needed more money. "I feel strongly that we must get on with this airborne alert," Power told Congress in February. "We must impress Mr. Khrushchev that we have it, and that he cannot strike this country with impunity."

Power's arguments did not convince Eisenhower. It would be "futile and disastrous," said the president, to strive for constant readiness against any Soviet attack. It was madness to sit around thinking, every minute of the day, that bombs were about to fall on Washington. Airborne alert, he implied, promoted just that type of thinking.

Eventually the two sides reached a compromise. Eisenhower gave SAC permission to start an airborne alert training program, just in case America ever needed such a system in place. On January 18, 1961, Power publicly announced that airborne alert had begun. Reports said that SAC now kept at least twelve bombers in the air at all times; the exact number remained classified. SAC named the program "Chrome Dome," probably because most of the bombers' flight paths arched over the Arctic Circle, drawing a cap over the top of the world. Power refused to confirm or deny if the flights carried nuclear bombs (they did), but an Air Force spokesman said that "the training is conducted under the most realistic conditions possible." The flights were still called "indoctrination" or "training" flights because they wouldn't actually be dropping bombs on the USSR—unless, of course, an order came through from the president, and then, in an instant, a training flight would become a bombing mission.

By the time the first Chrome Dome mission went up, LeMay had moved on. In 1957, he had been promoted to Air Force vice chief of staff. Tommy Power was now in charge of the thriving Strategic Air Command. LeMay left Power a force of 1,655 bombers, 68 bases, and 224,014 men. In his nine years at SAC, LeMay had transformed the force from a national joke into a nuclear powerhouse.

Over the next seven years, Power carried the torch through changing times. As engineers made nuclear weapons smaller and lighter and missiles more reliable, other services—especially the Navy, with its nuclear submarines—began to get a larger share of the nuclear pie. By the 1960s, the United States had a nuclear "triad" of long-range land-based missiles, manned bombers, and submarine-launched missiles. SAC controlled everything but the subs and wanted to keep it that way. But as missiles grew more sophisticated and accurate, some asked whether bombers were becoming obsolete. Robert McNamara, who became secretary of defense in 1961, was seen as a missile man, hostile to the continued reliance on manned bombers. But Power, who had circled the burning Tokyo and seen the devastating power of bombers firsthand, argued that the manned bombers, which he called the "backbone of SAC's deterrent strength," would always have a role in nuclear strategy. SAC, he insisted, must continue to demonstrate its power through programs like airborne alert. In order to deter nuclear war, said Power, the Soviets had to see America's strength and know that America stood ready to use it.

2.

The Accident

At midmorning on January 17, 1966, Captain Wendorf and his crew approached their midair refueling point over southeastern Spain. In the cockpit, Wendorf and Larry Messinger piloted the plane. Twenty feet behind them, facing backward, sat two men side by side: First Lieutenant George Glesner, an electronic warfare officer in charge of defending the B-52 (and arming the nuclear bombs), and the gunner, Technical Sergeant Ronald Snyder. Between the pilots and the defensive team a short ladder led down to a cramped, windowless compartment where Major Ivens Buchanan, the radar officer, and First Lieutenant Stephen Montanus, the navigator, sat facing forward. Mike Rooney, taking a break from his copilot duties, sat in the jump seat a few feet behind Buchanan and Montanus, reading a novel called *Thy Tears Might Cease,* by the Irish writer Michael Farrell.

The lower compartment, where Rooney sat, was about the size of a big closet—twelve feet long, three feet wide, and barely high enough to stand up in. Crew members called it "the box"—once they were strapped in, they couldn't tell whether it was day or night. At the back of the box crouched a chemical toilet. With the lid down and a cushion on top, it doubled as Mike Rooney's jump seat. Retired Chrome Dome airmen love to talk about the toilet. More precisely, they love to explain, in great detail, the proper eating strategy for long flights. Steak, bread, and hamburgers were okay; chili or anything "foreign" was off limits. The goal was to avoid having a bowel movement for the duration of the flight. This was partly out of deference to the unfortunate airmen stuck a few grim feet away from the toilet. But crews also had a custom that the first man to do his business in the "honeypot" earned the unsavory job of cleaning it once they got home.

So far, the trip had been uneventful in all respects. Wendorf, during his break, had time to nap, eat some fruitcake, and smoke a cigarette. The crew expected an easy journey back to North Carolina and needed just one final refueling to get home. The KC-135 tanker that would fill the bomber's fuel tanks had already left the SAC airfield near Morón, Spain, and was circling in the air waiting for the bomber. When the two planes were about twenty-one miles apart, the tanker began its "roll-out," a long, curving maneuver that placed it directly in front of the bomber. Soon the bomber pilots could see the tanker about two miles in front of them and a thousand feet above. Messinger, at the B-52's helm, began to close the distance.

Messinger was about to attempt one of the marvels of modern flight—a midair refueling. In the early days of aviation, flying long distances meant packing your plane with fuel. During its historic flight across the Atlantic, *The Spirit of St. Louis* carried extra fuel under the wings and a main tank so big it partially blocked Charles Lindbergh's view. Army pilots of the early twentieth century, dreaming of long-range bombing, knew that Lindbergh's strategy would never work for them. Where would they put the bombs? In military lingo, planes with limited range are said to have "short legs." To give planes longer legs, the airmen needed a way to refuel them in the air.

The earliest attempts at midair refueling were just stunts—a daredevil "wing walker" crawling onto the top wing of a biplane with a can of gasoline strapped to his back, leaping onto the wing of a passing plane, and pouring the sloshing gas into the fuel tank. After World War I, the idea stumbled forward for a few decades but never really caught on. Designers found other ways to make planes fly farther, such as larger fuel tanks, more efficient engines, and lighter materials. But with the rise of the Strategic Air Command, midair refueling suddenly became crucial. When Curtis LeMay took over SAC in 1948, he had hundreds of bombers under his command, but none that could take off from America with nuclear bombs, drop them in the heart of the USSR, and get back to safety. All his war plans required planes to attack the Soviet Union from forward bases, mostly in Europe and the Pacific. Analysts pointed out that any forward base within striking distance of the Soviet Union was also vulnerable to Soviet attack. What SAC really needed was a way to fly from the United States to the USSR and back without having to land for gas. By the early 1950s, midair refueling was a SAC priority.

SAC tried a number of refueling methods and tanker-bomber combinations, but each had its shortcomings. One of the biggest problems was speed matching. In 1951, SAC started flying a piston-engine tanker called the KC-97. SAC paired this slow tanker, which had a maximum speed of only 375 mph, with the B-47 jet bomber, which could fly up to 600 mph. Both planes, when linked for refueling, had to fly at exactly the same speed, slowing the bomber dangerously close to a stall. To avoid this sticky situation, pilots invented a daring maneuver: the two planes linked at a high altitude and then dove in tandem so the less powerful tanker could match the jet bomber's speed. This technique was imperfect, to say the least, and SAC pilots eagerly awaited jet-to-jet refueling. In 1957, they finally got it. On the receiving end was the B-52. On the tanker side was the KC-135 Stratotanker, equipped with a Boeing innovation called the flying boom. In 1966, the KC-135 and its flying boom were the state of the art in midair refueling, and they remain so today.

The boom is an aluminum tube 33 feet, 8 inches long and about 2 feet in diameter. The far end is bulbous, giving the contraption the look of a giant metal Q-tip. Near the tip, two four-foot wings stick off either side of the boom. These wings were Boeing's big innovation— "ruddervators" that allow the boom operator to fly the pipe into position, a bit like sticking your hand out the window of a moving car and swimming your fingers up and down. Tucked inside the boom is a 12-foot, 3-inch telescoping nozzle that shoots in and out at the boom operator's command. The fuel travels through the nozzle to the receiving plane.

To prepare for refueling, a boom operator, or "boomer," walks to the back of the KC-135 and hops down into a small, coffin-shaped room called the boom pod. The pod is about three feet across, three feet high, and ten feet long. At the end of the pod, giving a view out the back, is a window about three feet wide and two feet high. On both sides of this main window are small side windows, and directly below it is an instrument panel. A long, padded cushion, shaped a bit like a fully reclined dentist's chair, fills the rest of the pod. The boomer lies on this cushion stomach down, hands on the controls, looking out the back window.

The job of boom operator is widely regarded as the best enlisted job in the Air Force, because it's challenging and well paid and earns a lot of respect. "In what other job," runs a popular joke among boomers, "do you get two officers to drive you to work?" (Pilots usually reply that the boomer has it easy, because "he gets to lie down on the job and pass gas.")

To hook up, the tanker holds its position as the receiving plane slowly approaches from behind and below. The boomer extends the telescoping nozzle about ten feet out the end of the boom and watches the other plane approach. (Human depth perception falls off after about twenty feet—to the untrained eye, the ten-foot nozzle looks as if it extends a foot or less.) The boomer guides the receiving plane toward the boom by lights on the tanker's belly, shining a steady "F" for "forward" until it hovers about ten feet away. The receiving plane crawls closer at about one foot per second, making sure its large bow wave doesn't knock the tanker out of position.

The receiving plane finally stops closing the gap about two feet from the end of the nozzle and "parks" it in the air, exactly matching the tanker's speed and heading. The boomer lines up the boom with the tiny, four-inch hole in the roof of the receiving plane. Then, when the boom and the hole are aligned, the boomer presses a button and the last two feet of the nozzle shoot out the end of the boom and slap into the hole. It looks and sounds like a giant iguana shooting its tongue out to snag a fly. The nozzle locks into place, and the gas begins to pump.

After the "thwock" of the connection, the tanker's belly lights glow a steady green if the receiving plane is correctly situated. The boom can swing in a circle about 20 degrees up, 40 degrees down, and 10 degrees left and right. The receiving plane must fly within this cone-shaped "envelope" to stay connected to the boom.

Pumping the gas is a complicated job, and it falls to the tanker's copilot. Offloading 7,500 gallons of fuel can drastically alter the tanker's center of gravity, unless the copilot continually monitors and regulates the fuel levels in each tank. Pumps connect the KC-135's ten fuel tanks, allowing the copilot to shuttle fuel among them and keep the plane on an even keel.

It's a balancing act, and there's plenty that can go wrong. If the tanker's pumps go haywire and pump with too much pressure, they can blow the receiving plane backward off the boom. If the two planes disconnect too quickly, the tanker can spray jet fuel all over the receiver's windshield, creating a smeary mess. Or the two planes could collide, causing everything from a crunched boom to a fiery crash. Refueling gets more dangerous when bad weather hits, or when a tired or inexperienced pilot is flying the receiving plane. Even under ideal conditions, things can quickly go awry.

On January 17, 1966, Wendorf's bomber would refuel over the scrubby hills between the villages of Cuevas and Palomares, in what was known as the Saddle Rock Refueling Area. Saddle Rock was one of the best places in the world for midair refueling, as the dry desert air kept the sky bright and clear and there were no busy cities or airports below. Wendorf liked refuelings—they were an interesting break from the long and tedious flights where he spent most of his time "boring holes" through empty space. But Wendorf had already handled one refueling on this trip, and as a courtesy common on such flights, he asked Messinger to take the second. For Messinger, refueling was one of his least favorite parts of the job. Unlike Wendorf, Messinger hated flying the B-52. "It was a dog," he said. "No fun to fly and hard to work. It was like driving a Mack truck." B-52 pilots say that flying the plane is challenging because it is relatively unresponsive. "First you tell the plane to turn, then it thinks about it for a minute, *then* it makes the turn," said one veteran B-52 pilot. "And once it goes, it doesn't want to stop."

Refueling any plane requires the pilot to make continuous, minute adjustments. Accordingly, refueling can be one of the toughest things B-52 pilots have to do. They rely on little tricks to align themselves correctly with the tanker. For instance, when a small black UHF antenna on the tanker's belly appears to line up with a certain white stripe, the bomber is at the proper 30-degree angle for receiving fuel. Once connected, if the bomber's copilot can see the boomer's face through a certain high corner window, the B-52 is flying safely inside the envelope.

Throughout the approach and refueling, Messinger would have to keep his right hand on the eight throttles and his left hand on the yoke, both moving constantly. He couldn't take his eyes off the tanker plane for a second. Because of the danger, both crews wore full safety gear—helmet, gloves, and parachute—for the entire rendezvous and fuel exchange. The whole process normally took thirty minutes to an hour. Even with two decades of flying under his belt, Messinger still found refueling a sticky business. By the end, he was usually drenched with sweat.

Pilots usually refer to the B-52 by the nickname "BUFF." Depending on whom you ask, this stands for either "Big Ugly Flying Fellow" or, less politely, "Big Ugly Fat Fucker." The B-52 entered the fleet in 1955, underwent multiple modifications, and by 1966 was the workhorse of SAC's bomber force. The "ugly" bit notwithstanding, most pilots regard the BUFF with fond nostalgia—a dependable old bird that always got you home.

A B-52 is the size of a Boeing 707, with elegant wings, tapered and graceful as a hawk's, stretching ninety feet from top to tip. When the plane is sitting on the ground, the wings, laden with fuel tanks and four engines each, droop almost to the tarmac. They would drag on the ground if not for the small wheels on each wingtip. Once the plane gets moving, the wings rise. With a seventeen-foot deflection in either direction, they can move seventeen feet upward and seventeen feet downward. As a result, the wings can "flap" up to thirty-four feet during turbulence.

Saving weight was a major issue for the B-52. When they built the plane, pilots say, they crammed it full of gas and bombs and threw some people in as an afterthought. The G model that Wendorf and Messinger flew had a takeoff weight of 488,000 pounds, almost 40,000 pounds heavier than previous models, even though the designers had lopped nearly eight feet off the horizontal stabilizer. Yet the engines offered barely more thrust. During the Cold War, SAC stuffed the G models so full of bombs and fuel that they usually topped the takeoff weight sitting in the chocks. To help the plane take off, engineers devised a technique called "water augmenting" the engines, pushing the limits of technology in pursuit of SAC's Cold War mission.

During takeoff, B-52 pilots injected 10,000 pounds of water into the back sections of each engine. The water cooled the engine blades, allowing them to spin faster without melting or disintegrating. The water also added mass to the exhaust, creating more lift. Often the B-52 remained well above its takeoff weight as it zoomed down the runway. But during the trip, the plane consumed 4,000 to 5,000 pounds of fuel and 10,000 pounds of water. That weight loss, along with the extra 2,550 pounds of thrust, allowed the bomber to crawl into the sky.

The water-augmented thrust lasted exactly ten seconds. When the airborne plane reached about a thousand feet, it lost power and took a sudden dip. The dip usually caused utter panic in first-time pilots, much to the amusement of old-timers.

At 10:20 a.m. on January 17, 1966, the sky in Saddle Rock shone a bright, clear blue. The bomber and tanker cut their speed and began their approach. In the B-52, Messinger sat on the left, in the pilot's seat; Wendorf sat in the copilot's seat to the right. Rooney was downstairs reading. The B-52 was 31,000 feet in the air and about 150 feet below the tanker when Messinger sensed that something was wrong.

"We came in behind the tanker. We were a little bit fast, and we started to overrun him a little bit," Messinger said. "There is a procedure they have in refueling where if the boom operator feels that you're getting too close and it's a dangerous situation, he will call, 'Breakaway, breakaway, breakaway.' " Messinger remembers overrunning the tanker a "wee bit" but nothing serious. "There was no call for breakaway, so we didn't see anything dangerous about the situation," he said. "But all of a sudden, all hell seemed to break loose."

What happened next is disputed. Wendorf says he still had his eye on the tanker when he heard an explosion coming from the back of the B-52. The plane pitched down and to the left. Fire and debris shot into the cockpit, and the plane began to come apart.

The other pilots agree that the accident began with an explosion in the back of the B-52. But the official accident report tells a different story. Investigators concluded that the B-52 overran the KC-135 and then pitched upward and rammed the tanker. The collision ripped the tanker's belly open, spilling jet fuel through the plane, onto the bomber, and into the air. A fireball quickly engulfed both planes.

Rooney and Wendorf suspect that fatigue failure—a problem in the B-52—caused a portion of the tail section to break off. Flying debris sparked an explosion in one of the gas tanks, and the plane came apart. After the initial explosion, the bomber may have rammed the tanker—

everything happened so quickly that the pilots can't be sure. But they insist that the explosion came first and that it came from the back of the bomber.

We may never know conclusively whether a collision or an explosion triggered the accident. After a crash, it is Air Force custom to bury the wreckage. Because this accident occurred on foreign soil, SAC dumped the debris into the ocean. The one surviving member of the investigation board has refused to speak publicly about the accident.

Regardless of how it started, the first explosion grew into a massive fireball that enveloped the KC-135 tanker. The tanker had no ejection seats; the four men aboard were incinerated. More explosions began to rip both planes into large chunks and flaming fragments, flinging four hydrogen bombs into the sky.

In the cockpit of the B-52, the force of the explosion pitched Wendorf forward. He hit his face on the steering column and blacked out for a few seconds. When he came to, the cockpit was hot. The ejection hatch next to him had been blown, and Messinger and his seat were gone. The plane was tumbling downward, and the excruciating g-forces crushed Wendorf into his seat. He was bent over and unable to move, his left hand stuck, immobile, on the throttle.

"To eject from a plane," Wendorf said, "you have to be upright in your seat, with your back straight, elbows in, and your feet together. If you are not within the confines of your seat, you are going to lose whatever is hanging out there." Wendorf remembers taking a long look at his left arm, stuck on the throttle. He felt as if he had all the time in the world to make a decision, and finally he did. "I knew I was going to lose my arm," he said. "But I thought it was better to lose that than lose everything." With intense effort, he forced his right hand to pull the ejection trigger on the arm of his seat and shot into the sky.

Rooney, sitting in the lower compartment with his nose buried in his book, had removed his gloves to better turn the pages. He heard the explosion and looked up. Through the hatch he saw fire and debris shooting forward from the back of the plane. The gunner and the electronic warfare officer, sitting just to the rear of the hatch, were probably killed instantly. Buchanan, in the lower compartment with Rooney, turned around to see what was going on. Rooney gave him a thumbs-down, signaling that he should eject. Buchanan pulled the ejection handle and shot down out of the plane. His ejection seat, designed to automatically separate from him and activate the parachute, didn't work. He raced toward the ground stuck in his seat, his parachute stubbornly shut. He reached back and started to haul his chute out of the pack, foot by foot. It finally snapped open just before he hit. He crashed into the ground, still trapped in his seat, and survived with major burns and a broken back.

As Rooney unbuckled himself, the plane pitched violently to the left, flinging him into the radar with such force that his helmet split. He crumpled, badly stunned, as the plummeting plane careened into a left-handed spin. Montanus ejected. His ejection seat, like Buchanan's, malfunctioned. Montanus didn't make it.

Rooney was now the only living person left in the plane. A few feet away gaped the hole in the floor where Buchanan and Montanus had been sitting. The g-forces crushed Rooney to the floor, just as they had pinned Wendorf to his seat. Barely able to move, he looked out the hole at the brown earth and blue sky. The hole was only a few feet away, but it seemed an impossible distance. "I'm saying to myself, either I get out of here or I'm going to die," Rooney recalled. He dragged himself across the wall toward the hole. He reached the hatch and grabbed its sharp edge, giving his gloveless hands a vicious slice. Pulling himself halfway out, he stuck there, pinned in place by the fierce wind. Then the plane shifted and suddenly he was free, hurling through the hole and into the sky.

Rooney tumbled through the air as hot chunks of debris hissed by. A flaming engine pod passed so close that it singed the hair off his arms and neck. When he was clear of the disintegrating plane, he pulled his rip cord. As his chute caught the wind and floated him gently over the water, he pulled his gloves over his cold, bleeding hands and inflated his life vest. He splashed down about three miles out to sea. He unstrapped a Buck knife from his boot and cut himself free from his parachute. Then, bobbing in the waves, he prayed for help.

Charles Wendorf was knocked unconscious when he ejected from the plane and woke with a jerk when his parachute opened automatically at 14,000 feet. With a sudden burst of cheer, he realized that he was still alive, with his left arm intact. He took stock of the situation: though happily still attached, his left arm seemed badly broken, with a bone sticking out of the wrist. His helmet was gone, and there was a bloody tear on his left leg where a pocket used to be. With a shock of dismay, Wendorf realized that the pocket had held his wallet. "Shoot," he remembers thinking, "now I'm going to have to get a new driver's license." Then he had another realization—his parachute didn't seem to be working so well. And he smelled smoke.

Looking up, Wendorf put it all together. Part of his chute was on fire, and the rest was tangled and flapping wildly. He saw his boxy survival kit caught in the lines, preventing the chute from opening fully. "I tried to reach up with my left arm, but it wasn't working," he said. "So I reached up with my right arm and shook out the lines." A few shakes put out the fire and untangled the lines. The parachute opened and slowed his fall. Wendorf breathed a bit easier.

Floating out over the sea, Wendorf saw several small fishing boats below. When he got closer to the sea, he tried to steer for one of them. But as he pulled the riser, he accidentally collapsed his chute and plummeted into the cold water. He swam to the surface, buoyed by the rectangular survival kit that was somehow tucked under his right arm. He inflated his life preserver and floated in the water, waiting for help. Like Rooney, he had landed about three miles out from shore. The two men had hit the water astonishingly close to each other but didn't know it. The waves rolled too high for them to see very far. Within ten minutes, the fishing boat *Dorita* was chugging toward Wendorf. The crew threw him a life ring and pulled him on board. Wet and shivering uncontrollably, Wendorf was stripped of his clothes and wrapped in blankets. As he lay on the deck, he glimpsed Rooney, bobbing on the waves as the boat approached. Rooney had been in the water for about an hour, growing increasingly frustrated that he had survived a plane crash but was now going to die of hypothermia. The fishermen pulled Rooney aboard; he was bleeding badly from a gash in his leg. As they wrapped him in blankets and gave him hot coffee, Francisco Simó—the fisherman who had tried and failed to rescue the unconscious man—approached in the *Manuela Orts*. The captains agreed that the *Dorita* should hustle the injured men back to shore while Simó looked for more survivors. Simó headed toward his brother, who was steering the *Agustín y Rosa* toward a floating parachute some five miles distant. The *Dorita* headed to Aguilas.

As they motored toward shore, Rooney and Wendorf lay on the deck, shivering under a pile of blankets. Wendorf turned to Rooney and tried to make a joke. "The only thing that could complete this day," he said, "is if this was a Russian trawler." Rooney doesn't remember laughing.

The shore was crowded with curious onlookers. In his excitement, the *Dorita*'s captain crashed into the dock, giving the passengers a good knock and badly damaging the boat. Two bread trucks were waiting nearby to take the injured airmen to the local infirmary. Rooney remembers lying on a wooden bench in the back as the truck struggled up a windy mountain road. "Every time I looked up, the driver's looking back at me to see how I'm doing," Rooney said. "And I'm turning to him saying 'Look at the goddam road!' I've already been in a plane crash and a boat wreck, and if they get me in a car wreck, that's going to be three strikes and I'm out."

Larry Messinger had a longer journey to safety. As he ejected from the exploding B-52, he knocked his head hard enough to make him woozy. Disoriented, he pulled his rip cord immediately, opening his parachute at 31,000 feet. "I shouldn't have done that," Messinger recalled. "I should have free-falled and the parachute would open automatically at fourteen thousand feet. But I opened mine anyway, because of the fact that I got hit in the head, I imagine."

Messinger, fighting the strong wind, drifted out to sea. Helplessly, he watched the coastline dwindle as he sailed farther and farther over the Mediterranean, miles past the spot where Wendorf and Rooney landed. Finally he splashed into the sea, about eight miles from land. Messinger inflated his life raft and climbed in. He floated for about forty-five minutes, riding huge swells and shivering from the cold. Eventually two fishing boats approached. Simó's brother, in the *Agustín y Rosa,* got to him first. The crew pulled him aboard, stripped off his soaking wet clothes, and wrapped him in a blanket. Then they gave him a shot of brandy and headed to shore.

When Air Force officials visited his bed in the Aguilas infirmary, Messinger remembered something important. Drifting over the ocean below his parachute, he had seen something odd in the water below, off to the side. It was a huge ripple on the surface of the sea, "like when you drop something in the water and it makes a big circle," he said. Messinger told the officials about the huge circle in the water. As far as he knows, they never did a thing about it.

That evening, a helicopter took the survivors to nearby San Javier. There they boarded a plane for the U.S. air base in Torrejón, near Madrid. The next day, the accident board convened at the air base. The investigators questioned the men separately and told them not to discuss the accident among themselves. Wendorf recalls no one asking him about the four nuclear bombs missing from his plane, and he didn't venture any guesses. The interrogation continued for two days. Then the investigators took the survivors' statements and left.

The survivors stayed at Torrejón Air Base for two weeks to recuperate. One day, a week or so after the accident, Wendorf, Messinger, and some other Air Force personnel were shooting the bull. They started talking about the accident, trying to remember how many parachutes they had seen after ejecting from the plane. As Wendorf replayed the scene in his mind, he recalled seeing a couple of survival chutes and then remembered something else. Survival chutes, which carry people, are orange and white, so they can be easily found. Bomb chutes are more of an off-white or dirty yellow. Wendorf had seen an off-white chute. Suddenly he realized that it must have been one of the bombs falling to the ocean. Messinger, startled, told him about the giant circle he had seen on the water.

The two men looked at each other. Each one went into a separate room. Someone ran and got a couple of maps of the Spanish coastline. Separately, each man marked the map where he thought a bomb might have hit the water. When they compared marks, they were about a mile apart.

An Air Force aide took the maps and "ran off like he discovered gold," said Wendorf. A couple of days later, the survivors boarded a plane home to North Carolina. Rooney had bought a new copy of *Thy Tears Might Cease* but decided not to read it in the air.

At 7:05 a.m. Washington time on January 17, just about the time that Spanish fishermen were plucking Wendorf, Messinger, and Rooney from the cold Spanish sea, Lyndon Johnson sat in his bedroom eating a breakfast of melon, chipped beef, and hot tea. A messenger from the White House Situation Room walked in and handed the president his daily security briefing. The first page of the memo offered dismal news from Vietnam: a series of Viet Cong attacks against government installations; a mine explosion under a bus that had killed twenty-six civilians; a deadly raid on an infantry school. The second page held only one item: an early report of the accident, peppered with inaccuracies. It read:

B-52 CRASH

A B-52 and a KC-135 Tanker collided while conducting a refueling operation 180 miles from Gibraltar. The B-52 crashed on the shore in Spain and the Tanker went down in the sea. Four survivors have been picked up, and three additional life rafts have been sighted. The B-52 was carrying four Mark 28 thermo-nuclear bombs. The 16th Nuclear Disaster team has been dispatched to the area.

President Johnson picked up the phone and asked for Bob McNamara.

The First Twenty-four Hours

Manolo González Navarro believed in fate. He believed in visions. As a boy, he had sometimes seen a plane flying far overhead—a strange and wonderful sight. Since that time he had experienced a specific, recurring premonition. In it, he saw an airplane crash and went to look at the wreckage. Over the years, the thought came again and again, until it seared into his mind's eye with the permanence of memory.

González did not find the premonition disturbing; he simply accepted it. But even he would have to admit that the vision was an odd one, given that he had grown up in the tiny farming village of Palomares, far from any airport or air base. In recent years, however, he had had a daily, fleeting encounter with the U.S. Air Force. Each morning, just after 10 a.m., a set of American jets passed high over his town. They had not inspired his vision, but they would certainly fulfill it.

At 10:22 a.m. on January 17, 1966, González was sitting on his motorcycle talking to his father. The white contrails marking the paths of the American planes appeared overhead, just as they did every morning, and the two men looked up. They saw the contrails in the sky and then an explosion.

Fiery debris rained onto Palomares. A section of landing gear smashed through a transformer in the center of town, cutting off electricity to a handful of homes. The B-52's right wing crashed into a tomato field, the fuel inside igniting and blazing orange. The tanker's jet engines, filled with fuel, screamed down to earth, thudded into the dry hills, and burst into flame. Black smoke hung in the air; twisted shards of metal lay everywhere.

González and his father watched in horror. Immediately Manolo's thoughts turned to his young wife, Dolores. Five months pregnant with their first child, she was teaching at a local school that morning. Worried that debris would hit the school, he sped to his wife on his motorcycle.

Dolores had just opened the school doors when the windows started to rattle. At first she thought a small earthquake was shaking the building. Then one of the students shouted that fire was falling from the sky. Everyone ran to the windows, watching the fire and smoke. Soon the storm passed, leaving the school unscathed. A passel of worried mothers arrived to collect their children, and Manolo roared up on his motorcycle. He made sure that his wife wasn't hurt, then rode off to see if anyone else needed help.

González dropped off his motorcycle, climbed into his Citroën pickup truck, and rumbled off to the hills surrounding the town. The village had no paved roads, making travel slow and dusty. Even the main road into town was hard-packed dirt. Not that it mattered— usually nobody was rushing to get in or out. Palomares was just a tiny farming village in the back of beyond. It didn't even appear on most maps of Spain.

Palomares sat on the southeastern coast of Spain, about forty miles south of Cartagena. To the south lay the Costa del Sol, booming with foreign tourists and high-rise hotels. To the north stretched the Costa Blanca, also popular with European travelers. Between them lay a Costa without a catchy name and the town of Palomares. Palomares had a beach, the Playa de Quitapellejos, but its sand was hard-packed and windswept, unattractive to both tourists and townspeople. The town itself rested on a gentle rise about a half mile inland.

Despite their proximity to the Mediterranean, the villagers of Palomares worked the land, rather than the sea. Around the town lay the evidence of their labor—flat plains furrowed with farmers' fields. On either side of the fields, mountain ranges ran down toward the sea. The "mountains" were actually large hills, deep brown from a distance and desert tan up close, thick with scrubby gray-green bushes, prickly pear cactus, and tall, spiky agave. The landscape looked remarkably like the American Southwest—so much so, in fact, that areas nearby had served as sets for spaghetti westerns. A few years earlier, Clint Eastwood had graced the desert to film his hit movie *Per un Pugno di Dollari,* better known to American audiences as *A Fistful of Dollars.*

For the most part, the 250 or so families living in Palomares farmed the land or raised sheep. In ancient times, people had mined and smelted ore from the nearby hills. But the mines had been tapped out long ago, and farming now seemed the only real option. But it was not an easy one. The town lay in the Almería desert, the most arid region of Europe. The region is so parched that when people speak of a "river," they actually mean a dry riverbed. In the rare cases where a river runs with water, locals call it a *río agua.* At the time of the accident, the last measurable rain had fallen in Palomares on October 18, 1965, about three months earlier.

Faced with these tough conditions, forward-thinking farmers had formed an irrigation cooperative about a decade before. With money borrowed from local banks, the men had sunk nearly a hundred wells and created a pumping and irrigation system to water the dusty fields. They also started using chemical fertilizers. These upgrades allowed the farmers of Palomares to scrape together some respectable crops, including wheat, beans, alfalfa, and, most important, tomatoes. In Palomares, tomatoes ruled the roost. They were the town's crown jewels, its salvation. Under the relentless desert sun, they grew into magnificent, succulent red orbs, prized throughout Europe. In 1965, the town sold 6 million pounds of tomatoes to cities in Spain, Germany, and England.

Tomatoes had given the tiny, isolated town a measure of prosperity. Though most villagers still lived in small, low houses attached to animal pens, they kept the outside walls neatly whitewashed and the inside rooms brightened with electric lights. The townspeople had enough money to support seven general stores and three taverns. Some villagers still rode donkeys, but others had made the leap to motorized transport. All told, the residents owned fourteen cars and trucks, a handful of tractors, and a lot of scooters. Exactly eight television sets flickered their blue glow in Palomares. Most homes had radios. Few, however, had indoor plumbing. The nearest phone, in the town of Vera, was fifteen miles away.

Manolo González was more privileged than most of his fellow townspeople. His father, a prosperous landowner, was known as the "Mayor of Palomares." Palomares didn't actually have a mayor, but the elder González worked for the post office in Cuevas de Almanzora, about fifteen miles away. Since Cuevas was the seat of local government and González was the senior civil servant in town, any local administrative duties naturally fell to him. His son Manolo had inherited some of this status. A cheerful, outgoing man, Manolo trained as an electrician and never had to work the fields. He and Dolores were good-looking and youthful, more middle-class than peasant farmer. They lived in a house adjoining the school. The house had a bathroom with a small sink and toilet but no running water. Like almost everybody else in Palomares, Dolores had to carry water from a nearby well.

González drove his little Citroën down rutted tracks past fields of ripening tomatoes and headed to the nearby hills. He had seen an orange-and-white parachute falling to earth and wanted to investigate. When he arrived at the chute, he saw an ejection seat nearby, with a man still strapped to it. The seat had toppled forward and arched over the limp body. Another villager had already reached the man and started to cut the straps with a pocketknife. Together, González and the other man tipped the seat back and looked at the man. It was Ivens Buchanan, the B-52 radar operator who had ejected from the bomber and pulled his parachute out by hand. Still alive but barely conscious, Buchanan shivered violently. He said nothing except "I'm cold, I'm cold."

González drove the injured man to the medical clinic in nearby Vera. Then he sped back to Palomares to see what else he could do.

Wendorf's bomber had not been alone in the sky at the time of the crash. It had flown the entire route in tandem with another B-52 from Seymour Johnson Air Force Base. For the first third of the flight, Wendorf's plane had taken the lead. The two planes had planned to switch places after their turn around the Mediterranean. But after the first refueling, because of a minor radar malfunction in Wendorf's plane, he had relinquished the lead to the other bomber.

When Wendorf's plane exploded, the other bomber, with its own companion tanker plane, was a couple of miles ahead, completing its own midair refueling. This gave the boom operator—the only man with a backward-facing window—a view of the explosion. The boomer shouted the news to the cockpit, and the tanker crew radioed the news to their base in Morón. At 10:27 a.m., the Morón Command Post radioed the Sixteenth Air Force headquarters at Torrejón Air Base near Madrid with the first news of the crash. The call sign for the undamaged tanker was "Troubador One Two":

> **Morón:** We just received a call from Troubador One Two. He reports smoke and flames aircraft behind him, and he has no contact with aircraft. We're getting coordinates now.
>
> **Torrejón:** Roger, thank you very much.
>
> **Torrejón:** (Two minutes later) Was that in his aircraft or in the aircraft behind him?
>
> **Morón:** That was the aircraft behind him. Troubador One Two says they have not made contact with the number two bomber. Reported sighted smoke and flames behind their refueling formation.

The tanker, after finishing the refueling, wheeled back to survey the scene. Flying at 4,000 feet, the crew reported what appeared to be the tail section of the B-52 in a dry riverbed, burning wreckage about a mile inland, and still more aircraft debris farther toward the hills. Meanwhile, Morón reported the incident to SAC:

> **Morón:** Believe possible mid-air collision KC-135 and airborne alert B-52. It is not confirmed at this time. Was reported from Troubador One Two. The boomer sighted a burning aircraft spinning behind him in the formation. They have been unable to contact either the bomber or the tanker. The KC-135 from Morón Tanker Task Force . . . The B-52 from Seymour. Of course, weapons aboard.

As the news crisscrossed Spain and the Atlantic, the phone rang on the desk of a twenty-nine-year-old Air Force lawyer named Joe Ramirez. Ramirez worked in the staff judge advocate's office at the U.S. Air Force base at Torrejón. The person on the phone told Ramirez to get over to headquarters on the double.

Ramirez grabbed a notebook, told his boss about the call, and hustled across the street to headquarters. In the war room, things were humming. "The general was there, and people were running around back and forth," said Ramirez. "We had sketchy information at the time, but I did learn that there had been a crash between a B-52 bomber and a KC-135 tanker." Ramirez knew that those were big planes and that the tanker had been full of fuel. A crash between them could be catastrophic.

Ramirez had never heard of Chrome Dome and had never seen a nuclear weapon. He worried more about damage from falling aircraft debris. He learned that the crash had happened over a remote part of Spain and was told to be ready to fly down there soon, probably within an hour, to help assess the damage on the ground. Ramirez went back to his office, grabbed a "claims kit" full of forms, and called his wife. He told her that there had been a crash and he had to go somewhere in southern Spain but would probably be back that evening or the next day. Around 12:30 p.m., he boarded a cargo plane with thirty-five other members of the disaster control team and headed for a town that nobody had ever heard of. He still had the keys to the family car in his pocket.

Though Joe Ramirez probably couldn't tell a nuclear bomb from a hot-water heater, he proved to be one of the Air Force's most useful men in Palomares. As a lawyer, he was used to gathering spotty information from witnesses. In addition, Ramirez was the only airman deployed to Palomares that day who spoke Spanish fluently.

Ramirez had grown up in a small south Texas town, and his parents spoke both Spanish and English at home. His father was a tall, handsome man who had taught himself auto mechanics and eventually ran his own garage. Though Joe and his brother spent plenty of time working in the shop—the two of them could overhaul an engine in a day—their father pushed them to excel in school, telling them that education was the ticket to getting out of south Texas and seeing the world. Buoyed by his teachers and his close-knit family and encouraged by success in language arts and public speaking, Ramirez went to college and then law school, joining Air Force ROTC along the way.

Ramirez loved the Air Force. Soon after he was commissioned, he and his young wife, Sylvia, were stationed at Homestead Air Force Base, a SAC base outside Miami. Homestead often hosted Latin American politicians and dignitaries, and Ramirez was regularly asked to deliver briefings to top Spanish-speaking officials. He and Sylvia were often invited to important formal dinners, seated between Latin American generals and governors, and asked to make conversation and translate. This was heady stuff for the young couple, who were almost always the lowest-ranking people in the room. Because they spoke Spanish—and because he and Sylvia were gracious, charming, and discreet—the couple were given an entrée into a different world.

Ramirez enjoyed his work, but by 1965 he and Sylvia had two children, with another on the way. With college tuition looming ahead, he had been thinking about going into private practice. To entice him to stay, the Air Force offered him a plum posting at Torrejón Air Base. Joe and Sylvia, who had never been to Europe, decided to take them up on it.

Joe, Sylvia, and the two kids arrived in Madrid in the summer of 1965 and had a dramatic welcome to Spain. They flew overnight and arrived, exhausted, in the early afternoon. The Air Force had arranged for them to stay in a hotel in the center of town, on the main avenue called, at the time, Avenida del Generalissimo. They arrived at the hotel, climbed up to their room, closed the blinds, and collapsed into bed.

Shortly before 5 p.m., Ramirez woke up. Careful not to disturb his sleeping wife and children, he tiptoed to the windows and peeked through the shutters. He was on a high floor and could see the roof of the adjoining building. Looking in that direction, he was startled to see uniformed men in strange black hats, armed with machine guns, running around on the roof. He looked across the street and saw more men, also heavily armed, on rooftops across the way. "My God!" Ramirez remembers thinking. "We've landed in the middle of a coup!"

He woke Sylvia, then called the reception desk and asked what was going on. They said not to worry, it was just a soccer game. This didn't make a lot of sense until the desk clerk explained further: Generalissimo Francisco Franco, the ruler of Spain, loved soccer and would be attending today's match at the nearby stadium. The armed men were members of the Guardia Civil, Franco's paramilitary police force. The guardias civiles on the rooftops were advance guards. If you look out the window, said the clerk, you'll see the generalissimo himself in a few minutes. And sure enough, a bit later came the motorcade, with motorcycles and an escort car and Franco himself, with all the pomp and clatter befitting a military dictator. And watching from a hotel window high above was a young American family, enjoying the spectacle below.

About twenty minutes before 2 p.m. on the day of the accident, less than four hours after the bomber and tanker had exploded in the sky, the plane carrying Joe Ramirez and the rest of the disaster control team landed at a Spanish air base in San Javier, north of Cartegena. They were met there by General Delmar Wilson, who had flown down from Torrejón with his staff a bit earlier and had circled above the wreckage on the way.

Wilson was the commander of the Sixteenth Air Force, the SAC wing that supervised Torrejón and the other Spanish bases. He was a steady, capable leader, with the expected look of an Air Force general: tall, silver-haired, trim, and distinguished. More than one person described him as "straight out of Central Casting."

Wilson also had a unique link to the nation's nuclear history. Late in World War II, the Air Force had created the 509th Composite Group, a special unit of B-29s on Tinian Island that would drop the atomic bombs on Japan. Wilson, then a young colonel, was Curtis LeMay's liaison to the Atom Bomb Project. But since the project was top secret, LeMay couldn't actually tell Wilson why he was sending him to Tinian. When Wilson arrived, the staff at Tinian wasn't thrilled to have him there. "They looked on me as a spy for LeMay," he said. "They ignored me." Eventually a Navy captain took pity and clued Wilson in, starting off by asking "Have you ever heard of an atom?"

Now, two decades later, Wilson had a big atomic problem on his hands. He had seen the tail section from the B-52 slumped in a dry riverbed and other wreckage spread over a wide area of desert, farms, and hills. Somewhere among that debris were four hydrogen bombs. At San Javier, he learned that three of the injured airmen lay in hospital beds in a town called Aguilas. He decided that he and his close advisers would visit them first. Wilson briefed the assembled disaster control team and sent them to Palomares, with orders to assemble at the tail section later.

Ramirez climbed into the lead car of the caravan. Until now, most of Ramirez's legal work at Torrejón had involved young American servicemen who had gotten themselves into trouble, usually involving large American cars, narrow Spanish roads, and cheap alcohol. He had never investigated an accident of this magnitude, and on the long drive to Palomares, he had plenty of time to fret. He knew that the tanker had been filled with fuel and the bomber loaded with weapons. Had the wreckage set a town on fire and killed hundreds? Would the ground be littered with charred bodies? Would the townspeople attack them in a furious mob? Ramirez looked out the window at the desert landscape and worried.

After a couple of hours of driving, the caravan pulled into Vera to get gas and ask for directions to Palomares. Ramirez asked the locals for news from the village and was relieved to hear that there were no tales of widespread death and destruction. Still, he was anxious.

The group finally pulled into Palomares about an hour and a half before sundown. Outside the village, Ramirez saw a dirt road leading up a hill past a whitewashed wall and a lot of activity in the area just beyond. With a handful of others, he approached the wall, which bordered a cemetery. He saw smoldering debris, burned branches, and a man's hand lying on the ground, severed at the wrist and swollen from the fire. A number of villagers approached, with Manolo's father, the Mayor of Palomares, among them. When they realized that Ramirez could speak Spanish, they clustered around him, excited and agitated.

"What I noticed immediately," said Ramirez, "was that there was no hostility." Instead, there was a massive gush of sympathy and concern. The villagers wanted to help. They wanted to tell what they had seen. They wanted to know how the accident had happened, if the dead airmen had any children. They pointed out a row of simple wooden caskets on the dirt road by the cemetery and explained that they had collected charred remains and placed them inside.

Ramirez questioned the assembled villagers: "Anybody killed or injured on the ground?" he asked. No, no, no, no. "Any animals?" No, no, no, no. "Any homes destroyed?" No, no, no, no. Ramirez was amazed. "You could see still smoldering debris in backyards, in alleys, in dirt roads, in a ditch, in a field, all around. But none on any structure." January 17 was the feast day of Saint Anthony the Abbot, the patron saint of the village. Many said that the saint had sheltered Palomares from ruin. The local priest disagreed. "This miracle is too big for any one saint," he said. "It was the work of God himself."

A member of the Guardia Civil approached and spoke to Ramirez. He had seen something odd in the nearby hills. *"Parece un torpedo,"* he said in Spanish—it looks like a torpedo. Ramirez, by now knowing that nuclear weapons had been aboard the B-52 but not sure what one looked like, asked the guardia, *"Donde?"* Where?

Pulling himself away from the crowd, Ramirez found an Air Force colonel and told him about the torpedo. The colonel's ears perked up. Ramirez ran to find the guardia who had told him about it, and the three of them set off to search the hills.

Night had fallen by then. The colonel and the guardia each had a tiny flashlight; Ramirez had none. The three men walked into a rocky, uninhabited area outside Palomares. As they stumbled through the hills, the two feeble flashlight beams barely pierced the darkness. They could see rocks and scrub a few yards ahead, but the rest of the world was black.

The guardia led them toward the spot where he thought he had seen the torpedo. But all the dirt paths and beige rocks looked the same at night. The three men trudged through the hills for an hour or so, going over the same ground again and again—they thought—as the guardia grew steadily more embarrassed. Finally, the colonel called it quits for the night. The men headed back to the village.

One of Ramirez's fellow servicemen had more luck that day. A sergeant named Raymond Howe spent the afternoon locating major pieces of aircraft debris and checking them for radioactivity, including a big piece of the tanker fuselage that had fallen near the cemetery, and the B-52's tail section, which had landed nearly upright in a dry riverbed that led to the sea. Both tested negative. As dusk fell, Sergeant Howe was still poking around, asking if anyone had seen other major pieces of debris. One of the guardias civiles motioned him back toward the dry riverbed, near the mangled tail section. There, on the bank of the riverbed, about two hundred yards from the sea, lay a bomb.

The bomb was torpedo-shaped and dull silver in color, twelve feet long and twenty inches around. It had a nine-inch gash in its rounded nose, and three of its four tail fins had shorn away. The tail plate, a flat piece of metal that sealed the parachute compartment at the rear end of the bomb, had also torn away, and one of the parachutes lay spilled nearby. The ready/safe switch—part of the arming mechanism—was in the "safe" position. Except for the cosmetic damage, the bomb seemed intact. Howe checked for radiation and found none. He called some EOD—Explosive Ordnance Disposal—men, who also checked for radiation and rendered the bomb safe. Howe posted some Air Force guards around the weapon. It became known as bomb number one, because it was the first one the Americans found.

The "H" in "H-bomb" stands for hydrogen, the smallest atom in the universe and the simplest of the elements. The hydrogen nucleus consists of one solitary proton, which is circled by one electron—its own tiny, whirring solar system. Hydrogen makes up most of the gas in the universe and most of the mass of stars, and is found in all living things on Earth.

Hydrogen has an isotope—a sort of half sister—called deuterium. Though nearly identical to hydrogen, deuterium has a small but critical difference: its nucleus carries one proton *and* one neutron. For this reason, deuterium is often called "heavy hydrogen." It is this tiny extra neutron that makes the hydrogen bomb possible.

In 1934, a physicist named Ernest Rutherford and two of his colleagues were working in England and discovered something curious about deuterium. When Rutherford sped up two deuterium atoms and smashed them together, they fused and became a new element: helium. This surprised Rutherford, because the deuterium atoms, each with one positively charged proton in its nucleus, had an immense repulsive force and should have stayed apart. Yet accelerating or heating the atoms gave them enough extra energy to overcome their repulsion and fuse together. Because the reaction required acceleration or heat to fuse the nuclei, Rutherford called it a thermonuclear reaction. He called the whole process hydrogen fusion.

Oddly, the fused helium nucleus weighed slightly less than the two separate deuterium nuclei. The missing mass, Rutherford discovered, had been converted into energy. A lot of energy. Theoretically, each gram of deuterium, when fused, would release energy equivalent to 150 tons of TNT. This is about 100 million times as much firepower as a gram of ordinary chemical explosive. To put this into perspective, the firepower of Curtis LeMay's biggest raid on Japan, involving hundreds of planes and thousands of bombs, would have required only 20 grams of deuterium, about the weight of a robin's egg. The bomb dropped on Hiroshima: just 100 grams, equivalent to two jumbo chicken eggs. The numbers scale up quickly as the analogy moves on to heavier forms of produce. Twenty-six pounds of deuterium—the weight of about half a sack of potatoes—would yield 1 million tons of TNT. That yield—one megaton—is about seventy times the power of the bomb dropped on Hiroshima. It was also close to the yield of bomb number one, which Sergeant Howe had found on the soft bank of the dry Almanzora River.

Back in the 1930s, when Rutherford discovered fusion, however, the idea of a fusion bomb seemed nearly impossible. Rutherford needed a massive amount of energy to fuse just *two atoms*. It seemed unlikely that humans could find a source of energy hot enough to trigger a large-scale thermonuclear reaction and fuse a few kilograms of heavy hydrogen. Then came the atom bomb.

Atom bombs—the type of bombs dropped on Hiroshima and Nagasaki—work through fission, splitting the atom, rather than fusion. Every atom (except for hydrogen) has a nucleus made up of protons and neutrons, like a ball of marbles stuck together with glue. This nuclear glue has a name: binding energy. Because protons, with their positive charge, want to repel one another, it takes a lot of binding energy to hold a nucleus together, especially a big one. Nuclear fission splits the nucleus of an atom, breaking the marbles apart and releasing the nuclear energy in the form of heat, light, and radiation.

Some elements, namely those with more than 209 protons and neutrons, are so big that no amount of glue can hold their nucleus together. These heavy elements are naturally unstable and regularly shed bits of themselves, or "decay," to become smaller and more stable. Scientists call these unstable elements "radioactive." Probably the two most famous radioactive elements are those used in the atomic bombs of World War II, uranium and plutonium (or, more specifically, their highly fissionable isotopes, uranium-235 and plutonium-239). Scientists found that they could speed the disintegration by bombarding the uranium and plutonium nuclei with neutrons. When they did this, the nuclei split and released two or three neutrons and more energy. If additional uranium or plutonium atoms were nearby, the neutrons could blast their nuclei apart as well, releasing more neutrons and causing more fission. This reaction will eventually peter out, unless there is enough radioactive material placed closely enough together to sustain the reaction. If a "critical mass" of uranium or plutonium—about 110 to 130 pounds of uranium-235 or 13 to 22 pounds of plutonium-239—can be piled together, the number of neutrons released will increase in each generation. This leads to a chain reaction of atom splitting and a nuclear explosion.

Plutonium is more radioactive than uranium and more difficult to handle. But during World War II, uranium manufacturing moved slowly. The Manhattan Project scientists would have enough uranium-235 for only one weapon by 1945. If they wanted more bombs, they would have to build them from plutonium.

To build the bomb, metallurgists took a mass of plutonium and cast it into a hollow sphere. Then engineers created a shell of high explosive around the plutonium. In theory, if they detonated the high explosive from many different points at the same time, it would implode, crushing the plutonium into a solid ball. Hopefully, the squeezed plutonium ball would achieve critical mass and lead to a nuclear explosion. Few Manhattan Project scientists believed this design could work. "No one had ever used explosives to assemble something before," Richard Rhodes explained in *Dark Sun,* his history of the hydrogen bomb. "Their normal use was blowing things apart." Such a precise, perfectly timed explosion seemed implausible. The Navy captain in charge of explosives research said that the task was like trying to implode a beer can "without splattering the beer."

But the implosion bomb did work, first at the Trinity test near Alamogordo, New Mexico, on July 16, 1945, and then over Nagasaki on August 9, 1945. The bomb over Nagasaki, "Fat Man," reportedly used about 13.7 pounds of plutonium, for a yield of 23 kilotons. It was about 17.5 times as efficient as the Hiroshima bomb.

Even before the Trinity test, at least one Manhattan Project physicist was already looking ahead. Edward Teller had taken charge of the implosion group in January 1944, but increasingly he turned his thoughts to fusion. Maybe, he thought, the immense heat of a fission bomb could ignite a lump of deuterium, making a fusion bomb possible.

Teller, it turns out, was right. Finally, here was a source of energy powerful enough to trigger a fusion reaction. But the engineering problems were daunting, making an imploding beer can seem like child's play. Engineers had to design a bomb that could contain a fission explosion long enough to trigger fusion, then keep the fusion going long enough to get a good yield before the whole bomb assembly disintegrated. Yet by 1952 they had figured it out. On November 1 of that year, the United States exploded a hydrogen bomb on Eniwetok Atoll, about three thousand miles west of Hawaii. The test, code-named "Mike," yielded 10.4 megatons, nearly seven hundred times the power of the Hiroshima bomb. Mike vaporized the island of Elugelab and killed everything on the surrounding islands, leaving a crater more than a mile wide. If it had been dropped on New York City, it would have obliterated all five boroughs. For the physicist Herbert York and many others, the Mike test heralded the beginning of a more dangerous world: "Fission bombs, destructive as they might have been, were thought of [as] being limited in power. Now, it seemed we had learned how to brush even these limits aside and to build bombs whose power was boundless."

The hydrogen bomb lying in the riverbank outside Palomares was called a Mark 28. The Mark 28 could be assembled in five different variants for a range of configurations and yields. This particular Mark 28 was a torpedo-shaped cylinder that weighed about 2,320 pounds. The bomb had entered the arsenal in 1958, and by May 1966, the United States had produced 4,500 of them.

The exact inner workings of the Mark 28 are still classified, but it is possible to make some educated guesses about what lay inside. The bomb contained a fission trigger, which was a plutonium core surrounded with reflective material (probably uranium) to contain the explosion, and high explosive to start the implosion. This "primary," as it was called, was probably about a foot in diameter and vaguely resembled a soccer ball. Like a soccer ball, the primary had a pattern of twenty hexagons and twelve pentagons, forming a sphere. Each of these hexagons or pentagons, designed to focus explosive power inward, was called a lens. Each lens was filled with high explosive and attached to a detonator wire. When detonated simultaneously they imploded, crushing the plutonium inside into a critical mass and igniting a fission explosion.

If the high explosive didn't detonate simultaneously, the plutonium would not be evenly compressed; there would be no critical mass and no nuclear explosion. Such a precise detonation could happen only when a bomb was armed—not the case with the bombs of Palomares. This is not to say that detonating the high explosive is a good thing. Plutonium is highly radioactive, and an explosion could scatter it for miles.

The rest of the Mark 28 bomb contained a secondary fusion bomb and probably a third fission bomb to keep the fusion reaction moving. All the various sections (as well as batteries and electronics) were probably supported by a dense plastic foam. When the primary implodes, the fission emits radiation that causes a series of reactions. In a few hundred microseconds or less, the massive energy crushes a cylinder full of deuterium, sometimes called the "pencil." Inside the pencil, a plutonium "spark plug" explodes, releasing X-rays and gamma radiation. The radiation shoots outward, reacting with the plastic foam, which swells or explodes and further crushes the deuterium in the pencil. All this complicated engineering implodes and explodes within the blink of an eye, and the result is nuclear fusion. The Mark 28 was a deadly weapon and top secret—not the type of thing the United States wanted to leave lying around southern Spain, where anybody could see it, photograph it, or pick it up and cart it away.

As the sun rose on January 18, the Air Force searchers in Palomares began to gather for the day's work. For everyone, it had been a long night.

After landing at San Javier, General Wilson had taken a small party and driven about two hours up the coast to visit Rooney, Messinger, and Wendorf in Aguilas. He spoke to them about the accident and arranged for their transportation to Torrejón. Afterward, Wilson and his men drove back to Palomares and convened at the B-52 tail section. The general took a quick look around and listened to the early reports.

The charred remains of the dead airmen had been brought to Cuevas de Almanzora, the local government seat. In Cuevas, a priest had said a Mass for the men. Later in the afternoon, authorities laid the wooden caskets in the reception room of the town hall and surrounded them with burning candles. Townspeople filed by to pay their respects.

That evening, General Wilson drove to Cuevas to claim the bodies. Somehow, the townspeople and guardias civiles who had gathered the remains had determined that there were eight bodies, rather than seven, and distributed the remains into eight coffins. Wilson met with the authorities in Cuevas and explained that there had been eleven airmen on the planes and that four had survived, leaving seven deceased. After some bureaucratic struggle, the Spaniards allowed Wilson to sign for seven bodies. Late that night, a baker's delivery van—the only appropriate vehicle available—carried the remains to San Javier. From there they were flown to Torrejón for identification and then home to America.

After completing this somber duty, General Wilson and his entourage drove back to Palomares to meet with the rest of the disaster control team. Most of the team—and, it seemed, most of the villagers—had crammed into a bar in the center of town. Amid the clamor, Wilson sorted through the day's good and bad news. The good news was pretty good: searchers had found one bomb intact with no leaking radiation. There seemed to be no one hurt in the village, and certainly no widespread death and destruction. The locals seemed willing to help, and at least thirty-eight guardias civiles had already arrived to aid with searching and security.

The bad news: seven men were dead; two planes lay shattered across the Spanish countryside; there were no accurate maps of Palomares; there was no secure communication link to Torrejón; and there were still three bombs missing.

Wilson had sent a message to Torrejón earlier in the day by using a helicopter radio to talk to a KC-135, which relayed the message to Morón and then sent it on to Madrid. But the chopper was gone and he needed to talk to headquarters. The Air Force team set up a single sideband radio, and Wilson ordered more men, better maps, food, water, and a secure communications link. Because anyone could easily tap into the radio channel, Wilson used the code name "Warner," which would stick for the rest of the mission. He also sent a messenger to Vera to find a telephone and call Madrid with the news of bomb number one.

When Wilson's message arrived in Torrejón and Morón around midnight, available airmen were rousted from their barracks and ordered onto buses. Most carried only the clothes on their backs and maybe a blanket. Two convoys left Torrejón by 3 a.m., with 175 men on six buses and an ambulance trundling along with the group. Two additional convoys left Morón by around 4 a.m., with 126 men on six buses. The convoy from Morón also included an ambulance, as well as one van and one truck carrying bedding, food, water, and radios.

In Palomares, Ramirez and the rest of the disaster control team set off to find somewhere to spend the night. Ramirez and a handful of others drove to Cuevas, where, they were told, the Guardia Civil had made some arrangements. The group bumped along over the dark, unfamiliar roads, and eventually found Cuevas and the office of the Guardia Civil. Ramirez, the designated spokesman for the group, pounded on the door and woke up the guardia. The bewildered soldier had no idea who these Americans were or why they were waking him up in the middle of the night asking for somewhere to sleep. Ramirez explained the situation. "It doesn't have to be a hotel," he said. "Anyplace where we can get a bed." The guardia suggested a couple of boardinghouses, and the Air Force men fanned out across the dark town to see what they could find. Ramirez wound up in an old house and spent the night in a cold, sagging bed, happy to have a blanket and a roof over his head.

In the morning, Ramirez and the rest of his group headed back to Palomares and gathered at the tail section in the riverbed. By 7:30 a.m., they were joined by a seven-man disaster control team from SAC headquarters, who had left Omaha a few hours after the accident and traveled all night. The busloads of men from Morón and Torrejón wouldn't arrive until early afternoon.

The small teams moved out from the tail section and began searching nearby for the missing bombs, in the hope that they had landed near bomb number one. Aircraft debris—scraps of metal, shards of plastic—lay scattered all around. Radar-jamming chaff resembling silver tinsel hung from the trees. The teams walked slowly, scanning the ground and marking searched areas with string or toilet paper tied to bushes and poles.

At 9 a.m., helicopters arrived from Morón and began reconnaissance flights. At 10 a.m., a chopper pilot sent word that he saw a metal tube in the rocky hills behind the cemetery, about a mile west of the village. Ramirez and others went to look. There, in the same area he had explored the previous night, Ramirez saw a circular crater, twenty feet across and six feet deep. In the middle of the crater sat a parachute and a bomb. Or rather, part of a bomb.

Bomb number two was in bad shape. Some of the high explosive around the primary had detonated, digging the crater and exploding weapon fragments up to a hundred yards in all directions. What was left in the crater was the secondary—the fusion section of the bomb. Fragments of metal, parts of switches, and connecting rings lay all around. The ready/safe switch lay among the wreckage but was so damaged that its position was unreadable. Ten pounds of high explosive littered the area in small pieces and slivers. The afterbody—the tail section of the bomb, which held the parachutes—had been blasted apart from the rest and lay a hundred yards away. Next to the crumpled afterbody sprawled a ribbon parachute. The chute looked beat up, like a fishing net washed up on a beach after a storm. Another parachute, still tightly packed in its canvas bag, stuck halfway out of the afterbody. The nuclear core, or pit, was nowhere in sight.

Ramirez didn't know it, but the area around bomb number two was highly contaminated with plutonium. Although there had been no nuclear explosion, some of the high explosive lenses had detonated from the force of the impact, scattering radioactive plutonium across the countryside. It was, in effect, a dirty bomb. "I didn't know how an H-bomb worked," said Ramirez. "But we had been told that if there was radioactivity, it would be low and not harmful. It's alpha type [that] we could brush off or wash off."

The "alpha type" radiation that Ramirez had been warned about can be either harmless or lethal, depending on where it goes. Alpha particles—two protons and two neutrons—are given off by radioactive plutonium and uranium as they decay into more stable elements. These particles are relatively large and slow, so they can't travel very far or push their way through obstacles. An alpha particle shot into the air won't usually travel much farther than an inch and can be blocked by a sheet of paper.

If alpha particles land on human skin, they won't penetrate the dead layer of cells on the surface and will sit there until scrubbed off.

When, however, alpha particles get into the bloodstream—usually because someone inhales them—they can be lethal. The large particles barge through the body's cells like a bull through a china shop, breaking DNA and causing genetic mutations that can lead to cancer. They are especially dangerous when inhaled into the delicate tissue of the lungs. There, alpha particles can come into direct contact with cells, wreaking havoc.

Ramirez, standing on the edge of the crater, didn't know any of this. He called to the rest of the crew, and they came running over. One man got to work with something that looked like a Geiger counter. Ramirez stayed out of the way.

If he had looked up into the sky right around that time, Ramirez would have seen two thin vapor trails appear far overhead, converge, and separate. The morning's Chrome Dome rendezvous went off without incident. The Cold War was proceeding on schedule.

Around 10:30 a.m., just after Ramirez found bomb number two, other airmen spotted a third. Bomb number three lay in a plowed field at the base of a wall, near the house of a shopkeeper named José López Flores, "Pepe" to his friends. At least three different stories tell who found this bomb and how. The first story says that the Guardia Civil had told Sergeant Howe—the first airman to see bomb number one the previous day—about a bomb lying near a garden wall, which Howe then tracked down. The second story tells of an unidentified airman, stopping to urinate near a stone wall, who happened to look left and saw a bomb protruding from a crater.

Both of the stories were hogwash to Pepe López himself, who knew that *he* had found the bomb the previous day. After the two planes collided in the sky, López heard a blast and ran outside. His aged uncle lay in the dust, knocked to the ground by the shock of the explosion. He helped the old man up, made sure he was okay, and led him back into the house. Then he went off to explore the damage. Walking over to the stone wall, he saw a half-burned parachute. A small brush fire burned nearby, and López smelled acrid smoke, the way a gun smells after a shot has been fired. Taking a closer look, the shopkeeper saw a bulky shape under the parachute. Worried that it might be a dead or injured pilot, he rushed to pull the parachute aside.

Removing the parachute, he found a "monster of a bomb" busted open like a watermelon. "I knew it was a bomb, because when it fell from the airplane it cracked open," he said later. "It was cracked open in the back part where the metal is white and I could see inside, the powder. I immediately knew this was a bomb. There was some fire burning around it and I stamped it out, because of course I knew it wasn't safe to have a fire around a bomb."

According to some accounts, Pepe López also gave the bomb a good kick, for reasons known only to him. Later, when he told the men at the bar what he had done, they laughed. "If that bomb had gone off," they said, "Pepe would be a little speck of dust in New York."

The bomb lay in its crater by the wall until the Americans found it the following day. As López had observed, the weapon was badly damaged. Like bomb number two, some of its high explosive had detonated, gashing a crater in the dirt and scattering shards of weapon in all directions. Some major parts were fairly intact: the secondary lay in the crater, which measured four feet across and three feet deep; the afterbody was dented but still in one piece. But the rest of the weapon case and innards were badly broken up. A bottle of tritium—a radioactive isotope of hydrogen that boosts the fission reaction—was found mashed and ruptured about 1,500 feet away. Eighty pounds of high explosive and plastics lay within a hundred feet of the crater, and weapon parts were scattered up to four hundred yards away. SAC's final report of the accident said that most of the weapon was so mangled "that you couldn't tell what it was or where it came from."

Despite the conditions of bombs numbers two and three, the U.S. Air Force felt optimistic. Just a day after the accident, searchers had found three of the four bombs. No one on the ground had been harmed, and the villagers, far from turning into an angry mob and demanding vengeance, were friendly and anxious to help. The Air Force was still missing one bomb, as well as a combat mission folder and a box containing top secret codes and documents, but men were combing the area and more searchers were on the way.

There was some contamination to clean up, but even that didn't seem too bad. A situation report was sent to the secretary of defense, the White House, and others. Its tone was cautiously optimistic. The memo explained that high explosive had detonated in two bombs, which "could involve local plutonium scattering with related radiation hazard." However, if the detonation had been small enough, there might have been no plutonium scattering at all. "It is not believed," said the memo, "that there is any basis for undue concern over the low order detonation of the two weapons." And, to the great relief of everyone concerned with U.S.-Spain relations, the memo reported, "Impact on populace practically nil."

4.

The Ambassador

On the morning of the accident, the one person most concerned with Spanish-American relations sat at lunch in Madrid, stoically fulfilling one of his more mundane job requirements. Being an American ambassador had its moments. Sometimes the nights were filled with glitz and glamour: dining at elegant tables, sipping champagne, conversing with kings. Other days swelled with political intrigue: wheeling and dealing, carving treaties, molding history alongside statesmen. But much of the time, the job sagged under the weight of duty. Today the ambassador was spending the afternoon at a luncheon for the American Management Association in Madrid: sitting in a banquet hall, steeling himself for a dismal lunch, and discussing President Johnson's recent efforts to reduce the United States' dollar outflow. That was where Angier Biddle Duke, the U.S. ambassador to Spain, was trapped on January 17, 1966. Then something caught his eye.

Duke sat with five other men at the head table, on a dais at the front of the banquet hall. As he listened to a speech by the Spanish industry minister, he saw someone familiar standing in the wings. Duke glanced over, then looked back to the speaker. Then he did a double take. Joseph Smith, a young Foreign Service officer from the embassy, stood on the side of the stage, trying desperately to get his boss's attention. Duke quickly excused himself and joined Smith in the wings. The two men went somewhere quiet to talk. Smith, the manager of the embassy's political-military affairs, said he had received a call at 11:05 a.m. informing him that two American military planes had crashed; there were several survivors and one plane had carried unarmed nuclear weapons.

The ambassador listened to the news. He asked Smith a couple of questions, then decided to head back to the embassy. The two men slipped out of the hall and climbed into the ambassador's limousine. After a block or two, Duke changed his mind, redirecting the driver to the Spanish Foreign Ministry.

Ten minutes later Duke and Smith went inside the ministry and spoke to an usher. Duke asked to speak with Ángel Sagáz, the director of North American affairs, but Sagáz was out of the office. So was his deputy, the foreign minister himself, and almost everyone else, as far as they could tell. Many were attending a funeral for a colleague's mother; the rest were eating lunch.

The two Americans finally made contact with an undersecretary for foreign affairs, a man Smith regarded as "not particularly friendly" and "not terribly fond of Americans." It was not ideal, but Duke had to make *some* diplomatic contact with the Spanish government. So the ambassador, doing his best to be charming, told the dour undersecretary everything he knew about the crash. The undersecretary seemed very serious and quite concerned. He asked the Americans a lot of questions, most of which they couldn't answer. After a short discussion, the ambassador said he needed to return to the embassy to gather more information. He promised to keep the Spanish government informed.

If America had to choose someone to deliver bad news to a grumpy foreign official, Angier Biddle Duke was the perfect man for the job. "Angie," as everyone called the ambassador, was charming and urbane, with flawless manners, a voice smooth as velvet, and a way of easing uncomfortable situations. He never lost his temper. "Even," said his wife, "when people were behaving badly."

Duke had been born and bred into gentility, with a family tree reaching and branching through a century of American aristocracy. His grandfather Benjamin Duke helped found the American Tobacco

Company, a Duke family business that dominated the cigarette industry until it was trust-busted in 1911. Grandfather Duke also helped
found Duke University. On the other side of the family, Angie could
list ancestors such as Nicholas Biddle, the first editor of Lewis and
Clark's journals, and Brigadier General Anthony Drexel Biddle, Jr.,
deputy chief of staff to Eisenhower during World War II.

As ambassador to Spain in 1966, Angie was in his early fifties but
still tall and trim from regular exercise. He had a long, aristocratic
face and combed his thinning hair straight back from his high forehead. He dressed elegantly, in finely tailored clothes. Angie evoked an
earlier age, a time when people dressed up to fly on planes, wore hats
and gloves in public, and wrote notes on personalized stationery. He
was, above all, civilized.

Yet for all his connections, Angie's upbringing had left him inse-
cure. His mother, Cornelia Drexel Biddle, had married his father,
Angier Buchanan Duke, when she was only sixteen. The marriage had
failed, and the two had divorced when Angie was six years old.
Angie's father had died two years later but had disinherited his two
sons, cutting them off from his share of the Duke tobacco fortune.
Angie's mother was so furious that she changed her sons' names to incorporate her own: Angie, christened Angier Buchanan Duke, Jr., became Angier Biddle Duke. Despite the disinheritance, Angie inherited
enough from his grandfather that he never actually had to work for a
living. But as an adult he invested poorly and was never quite as rich
as everyone thought. Joseph Smith recalled that Duke never had any
cash on hand to pay for restaurants and lodging. Smith would also receive letters from luxury hotels around Spain, saying that the ambassador's checks had bounced.

For a role model, Angie turned to his uncle Tony Biddle, a globe-
trotting diplomat. As a teenager, he regularly visited Uncle Tony in
Oslo, once attending a hunting party in Austria that his uncle hosted
for the king of Spain. The visit with the royal family made a strong
impression on him, especially the evening conversations about Central Europe and the rise of Hitler. Angie, dazzled by the dignitaries,
the serious talk, and the importance of it all, began to contemplate a
career in diplomacy. He attended Yale, studying Spanish and history
on a "prediplomatic" track. But after two and a half years, he dropped
out, married the first of his four wives, and never went back to school.
He regretted the decision for the rest of his life. Throughout his ca-

reer, he remained painfully embarrassed that he had never earned a college degree.

After Yale, Angie floundered. He spent his twenties traveling the world, working briefly at a sports magazine, and toying with business. He divorced his first wife and married his second. Eventually, World War II gave him some direction. He enlisted in the Army before Pearl Harbor, then attended Officer Candidate School, becoming a second lieutenant in January 1942. It was a proud moment for the flighty young man with no college degree: for the first time in his life, he had actually accomplished something. He served much of his tour in the Washington war room of Secretary of War Henry Stimson. There, as the lowest-ranking officer, Angie read incoming cables and updated battle maps with colored pushpins. Sometimes he stood at the maps with a pointer as generals discussed battle plans. He remained in the Army for five years, retiring with the rank of major.

After the war Angie drifted again until fate pushed him back toward foreign affairs. In 1948, he was conducting an auction at a golf tournament. In the audience that day was an investment banker named Stanton Griffis. Griffis was impressed by the young man's poise and, speaking with him afterward, discovered Angie's interest in diplomacy. Griffis had served as ambassador to Poland and was expecting another appointment if Harry Truman got elected. Griffis knew that any embassy posting would involve a heavy load of socializing, and, as a widower in his sixties, he wasn't up to the task. Angie and his young wife, however, would be perfect. Angie lit up at the proposition, but with no college degree, he wasn't qualified to take the Foreign Service exam. Griffis pulled some strings, Angie took the exam, and in 1949, Angier Biddle Duke began his diplomatic career as special assistant to Stanton Griffis, the new ambassador to Argentina. When Griffis was appointed to Spain in 1951, after the United States had resumed diplomatic relations with the country, he took Angie with him. The following year, President Truman named Angier Biddle Duke ambassador to El Salvador. Only thirty-six years old, he was the youngest U.S. ambassador in history.

Ambassador Duke poured his abundant energy into the new job. He desperately wanted to make his mark on foreign policy and worked hard to understand key issues and participate in important decisions. But, to his continued dismay, most of his colleagues considered him more adept at parties than policy. The American press called Angie a "tobacco-rich playboy," and one colleague described him as an "amiable lightweight." Yet he was much loved in the countries he served. One Salvadoran reporter wrote, "He has dedicated more sewers, slaughterhouses, and clinics than half a dozen politicians." When Eisenhower, a Republican, won the 1952 election, Angie hoped to remain at his post in El Salvador, but the political winds blew him out of his beloved government job. He plugged away on international refugee issues for the next eight years, then worked on the John F. Kennedy campaign. When Kennedy won the 1960 election, Duke expected another posting, hopefully as ambassador to Spain. Instead, the new president called him in late December and asked him to serve as his director of protocol.

Angie balked at the offer. He wanted to shape foreign policy, not arrange table settings like some glorified Emily Post. But Kennedy, with Secretary of State Dean Rusk, convinced him that the job was critical to the administration's foreign policy goals, and Angie finally accepted. Soon he and his third wife—a Spanish aristocrat he had met while stationed in Spain—were up to their ears in diplomatic minutiae. Duke ensured that the rooms of one foreign dignitary were stocked with his favorite brand of soda crackers; that another had an informative visit to the Tennessee Valley Authority. He sent birthday greetings from the president and answered queries on the correct way to display the American flag. He introduced new ambassadors to Kennedy and arranged the seatings and menus for state dinners. He attended about a dozen cocktail parties a week, a half-dozen dinners, and two or three luncheons. With his elegance and boundless energy, Duke excelled at the job. In 1964, *The New Yorker* ran a long, flattering profile of Duke. At one point, it caught him in a moment of despondency. "I'm lost," he told the magazine. "I'm lost and of no importance." Then, after a moment, he brightened. "But there are compensations," he said. "It's satisfying to be as close as I've been to the sources of world power."

After President Kennedy was killed, President Johnson kept Angie on as director of protocol. But Duke craved something more substantive. In early 1965, Johnson gave Angie his dream job: ambassador to Spain. Duke's third wife, the Spanish aristocrat, had died in a plane crash in 1961, and he had remarried for a fourth and final time the following year. So in 1965, he, his wife, Robin, and their children from previous marriages packed up and moved to Madrid.

Ironically, once he got to Spain, Angie felt marooned. For years, he had stood at the side of the president. Maybe he had just been an observer, but he had been at the center of the Washington whirl, meeting kings, chatting with Jackie Kennedy, watching history being made. Now he was stuck in the backwaters of Europe. "When I got there, I found that I was moving from the center of the action into the countryside," he said years later. "Fankly, to move to a dictatorship after the hurly burly of the White House years, in many ways was disappointing."

Nonetheless, Duke, patriotic and dedicated, threw himself into his new job with characteristic vigor. Spain had changed enormously since Duke's last posting in the early 1950s. But the embassy's main policy goals had changed very little. As ambassador, Duke had to maintain the solid working relationship between the U.S. and Spanish governments. There was only one reason the United States cared at all about its relationship with Spain: the military bases. In 1966, the U.S. and Spanish governments jointly held four major military bases in Spain. The Air Force operated three bases: Torrejón, near Madrid; Morón, outside Seville; and Zaragosa in northeastern Spain. The Navy ran a Polaris submarine base on the southern coast at Rota, near Cádiz. Connecting these four bases, cutting across the center of Spain, stretched a 485-mile-long pipeline that supplied the bases with petroleum. The American military presence also peppered the rest of Spain. The Air Force ran a small air base at San Pablo and a fighter base at Reus, about ninety miles southwest of Barcelona. The Navy stored oil at a supply center in northwestern Spain and kept oil and ammunition in a depot at Cartagena. The U.S. military also operated seven radar sites across the country.

George Landau, who worked at the embassy with Duke and became the State Department's director for Spanish and Portuguese affairs in 1966, called the Spanish bases the "crown jewels" of America's foreign military bases. Strategically located at the entrance to the Mediterranean, they were a key component of the military's nuclear deterrent strategy. The Sixteenth Air Force, headquartered at Torrejón, oversaw the bases in Spain (and Morocco until 1963) and was the largest SAC force overseas. SAC stocked the Spanish bases with tanker planes and medium-range bombers, critical for both its strip alert and airborne alert programs. The bases also offered numerous amenities: servicemen could live there on the cheap, the sky beamed blue and clear almost every day, and the Spanish government—at least in the early days—rarely hassled the Americans about anything. "The Pentagon was absolutely enamored with Spain," said Landau. "They thought it was the wherewithal for everything."

The base agreement that existed in 1966 would expire in just two years, and American officials were starting to negotiate terms for a new agreement. The American military had a good thing going in Spain and wanted the situation to remain as it was. But the Spanish government had grander goals. "Spain wanted to be a part of Europe, a world power," said the embassy staffer Joseph Smith. "The original base agreement made it clear that Spain was a junior partner. They wanted the United States to acknowledge Spain as something bigger. . . . They wanted to change from a purely military relationship to one that involved politics on the highest level." The U.S. Embassy in Spain had a finite number of diplomatic chits; diplomats had to spend and save them wisely, always with an eye toward the upcoming base renegotiations. The bases, according to Landau, were not the embassy's top concern, they were the only concern. If not for the bases, the United States would have never reached out to Spain's military dictator, General Francisco Franco, at a time when Western Europe still regarded him with scorn.

Generalissimo Francisco Franco, chief of state, president of the Council of Ministers, and caudillo of Spain by the grace of God, didn't look the part of an iron-fisted terror. He was short and tubby, his soft face dominated by wide brown eyes with long eyelashes that gave him a decidedly feminine appearance. When he spoke, words tumbled out in a high-pitched squeak. Angie Duke described him as "the most uncharismatic dictator you ever saw in your life." Franco had "a white face, mottled, jowled, fishy eyes, a very limp handshake, a big pot belly. Yet at the same time, he had quite an impressive personality. He had enormous reserves of power inside of him."

Franco had led the right-wing Nationalists to victory during the Spanish Civil War of 1936–1939. Both sides had committed horrendous atrocities against civilians, and Franco emerged from that bloody conflict with a reputation for coldhearted brutality. During the war, Franco ordered the slaughter of anyone who opposed him or posed a threat: schoolteachers, trade unionists, prisoners, wounded troops. He refused to hear any appeals for clemency.

Franco idolized Adolf Hitler and Benito Mussolini, and his side received massive military assistance from them during the war. But when World War II began just six months after the end of the Spanish Civil War, he had little to offer his friends. The civil war had devastated Spain. Most of the country's industry lay in ruins. About half a million Spaniards had been killed or had died of disease and malnutrition. Another half million had fled the country, and those who remained faced widespread poverty and hunger. Spain was a broken country, and Franco was in no position to support the Axis powers when World War II broke out. Throughout the war, Spain remained officially neutral.

The Allies worked hard to maintain Spain's neutrality. Britain knew of Franco's infatuation with Hitler and Mussolini—the British ambassador reported that Franco kept signed photos of the two dictators on his desk. But the British also knew that they couldn't afford to lose Gibraltar, the tiny British stronghold jutting off southern Spain that served as their gateway to the Mediterranean. They, along with the United States and other allies, sent Spain petroleum, cotton, food, and other materials under the condition that the country remain neutral. Franco eagerly accepted the goods while keeping his eye on the changing winds of the war. Once the United States entered the fray and the tide began to turn against the Axis powers, Franco started to hedge his bets. "Henceforth," said one historian, "his energies were to be devoted almost impartially to working both sides of the street while keeping Spain untouched by war."

Meanwhile, Franco continued his brutal behavior within Spain. Between 1939 and 1945, the Franco government executed thousands of political opponents; one study says the death toll may have reached 28,000. The government imprisoned hundreds of thousands more and sentenced them to hard labor. Franco, threatened by ethnic groups like the Basques and Catalans, banned the Basque and Catalan languages, folk music, and traditional dance. The government muzzled the press and stifled all political opposition. Only Catholics were allowed to build churches and practice their religion openly.

Franco's internal policies, and his waffling during the war, disgusted the Allies. After the war, the victors paid him back. The fledgling United Nations excluded Spain from membership. Then, at its second meeting, the U.N. General Assembly adopted a resolution recommending that all members recall their ambassadors from Madrid.

On March 4, 1946, the United States, France, and Great Britain signed a Tripartite Declaration to the Spanish people, warning that they would not gain full relations with the three countries as long as Franco remained in power. In 1949, when NATO was formed, Spain was kept out. Finally, and perhaps most devastating, the Allies excluded Spain from the Marshall Plan, the massive aid program that helped rebuild Europe after the war.

Spain crawled forward in virtual isolation for several years, its only foreign relations with the dictatorships of Portugal and Argentina. The country lagged behind the rest of Europe, its economy and industry struggling, its people—for the most part—desperately poor. But Franco, dictator for life, knew he could wait out any storm. Historians tell a famous anecdote about the dictator's legendary patience. As the story goes, Franco kept two boxes on his desk. One was labeled "Problems That Time Will Solve"; the other, "Problems That Time Has Solved." Franco's career involved shifting papers from the first box to the second.

And indeed, time—and the advent of the Cold War—did solve the problem of Spain's isolation. In the late 1940s, as the situation between the United States and the USSR grew increasingly tense, "more weight was given to the help Spain might furnish in the next war than to any hindrance she had offered in the last," according to the historian Arthur Whitaker. Franco had long been a virulent anti-Communist, and in the new world of nuclear deterrence, Spain's strategic location looked increasingly useful. Furthermore, the idea of giving aid to Spain now seemed more acceptable: American Catholics were lobbying their congressmen to give economic aid to the starving country. Franco encouraged the warming Spanish-American relations. In July 1947, he told a reporter that the United States could obtain the use of Spanish bases if it tried hard enough. The Pentagon pushed for bases, and President Truman didn't put up much resistance. "I don't like Franco and I never will," he said. "But I won't let my personal feelings override the convictions of you military men." In late 1950, Congress appropriated $62.5 million in aid for Spain. In 1951, Stanton Griffis—with Angie Duke in tow—arrived in Spain to fill the long-vacant post of ambassador. That summer, American military officials started talking to Franco about military bases in Spain as Great Britain watched in annoyance. "The strategic advantages which might accrue from associating Spain with western defense," said the British foreign secretary in the summer of 1951, "would be outweighed by the political damage which such an association might inflict." American military officials waved such protests aside. They wanted those bases.

On September 26, 1953, the United States signed three agreements with Spain that together became known as the Pact of Madrid. The United States would give Spain military aid—$226 million in the first year alone—in exchange for the use of three existing air bases at Morón, Torrejón, and Zaragosa. The United States would expand and update the bases, as well as build a new Navy base at Rota and other facilities. The United States and Spain would operate the bases jointly, but the Americans would run the show. The pact would remain in effect for ten years—until 1963—and then could be extended in five-year increments. Because the pact was an executive agreement, not a treaty, it did not require congressional approval. Military necessity had trumped the ideals of freedom and democracy. A *New York Times* editorial called the deal "a bitter pill." "Let us hope," it said, "that the medicine will not do more harm than good."

By 1959, the base renovations were virtually complete and 20,000 American troops had moved in. In December of that year, as a symbol of the two countries' new partnership, President Eisenhower visited Madrid. It was the first visit to Franco by any Western head of state since he took power. Eager to advertise his new alliance with the United States, Franco ordered Spain to welcome the president with open arms.

When Eisenhower's plane landed at Torrejón, the president smiled, walked down the steps, and greeted Franco with a firm handshake. Traditionally, greeting a Latin leader requires an *abrazo,* or formal embrace. But the U.S. government had decided that Franco, a dictator, would receive only a handshake, and Eisenhower hewed to the policy. But the visit went exceptionally well. A crowd of 500,000 Spaniards crammed the president's motorcade route into Madrid, lining the sidewalks fifteen and twenty deep, waving flags and cheering "Ike! Ike!" as church bells pealed a welcome. (Of course, they cheered the president's nickname in Spanish—"Eekay! Eekay!"— much to Eisenhower's amusement.) In deference to the president's grueling travel schedule, Franco arranged for dinner to be served at 8:45 p.m., unusually early for Spain. At dinner, the two generals offered warm toasts to each other's countries, commenting on the shared history and goals of the United States and Spain. When they parted the next day, the president and the generalissimo exchanged not one but two *abrazos*. Franco, rejected by most of the world, had been embraced by the world's greatest power.

Buoyed by American money and the stamp of American approval that encouraged foreign investors to move in, Spain slowly began to climb out of poverty. In the late 1950s and early 1960s, Franco, now in his late sixties, allowed a handful of forward-thinking ministers in his cabinet to modernize the economy. They slashed the budget, devalued the peseta, and opened the country to foreign goods. At the same time, the standard of living in Western Europe surged. Europeans had money to burn, and suddenly foreign money and tourists began flowing into Spain. Construction gear and cranes popped up all over the country, and modern dams and skyscrapers stretched into the sky. Between 1960 and 1965, the gross national product of Spain climbed by an astonishing 65 percent. During that same time, 36 million tourists spent $3.5 billion in Spain, $1.1 billion in 1965 alone. That same year Spain hit another milestone: the per capita income reached $500 a year, meaning that the United Nations no longer classified Spain as a "developing country."

The Spain that Ambassador Duke saw in 1966 was a far cry from the broken, impoverished country he had seen in 1951 with Stanton Griffis. But the country remained a land of deep contrasts, at once utterly modern and shockingly primitive. The Spanish magazine ¡Hola!, somewhat akin to *Life* magazine in the United States, provides an insightful glance into Spanish society at the time. The issues in early 1966 offered endless fluff and photos covering the comings and goings of the rich and famous: royal weddings, debutante balls, and Jackie Kennedy's ski trips with John-John and Caroline. Photos showed women wearing the latest fashions and hairstyles, sandwiched between full-color ads for TVs, dishwashers, and Johnnie Walker Red Label.

This modern, high-fashion Spain was a world away from the hard-scrabble desert of Palomares, where indoor plumbing was still a luxury. The modern beach resort of Marbella, with its high-rise hotels, manicured golf courses, and glassy apartment buildings, was just a couple hundred miles down the coast from Palomares. Yet it seemed like another planet. It was hard to imagine the tomato farmers of Palomares lounging by the pool, sipping iced cocktails, and flipping through ¡Hola! for news of Mia Farrow's daring new haircut.

So great was the divide between these two Spains that ¡*Hola!* never mentioned the Palomares incident. Angier Biddle Duke, however, fit perfectly into its pages, appearing in two articles in early 1966. One showed him and Robin gazing at a painting as they inaugurated a new American cultural center in Madrid. The other included a two-page photo spread of a hunting trip with the ambassador, various government ministers, and Generalissimo Franco himself. Duke posed with a shotgun, sharing a drink with Franco around the bonfire. He looked perfectly at home amid wealth and power. And that was a good thing for him. The ambassador would need every bit of his charm and connections in early 1966; the accident in Palomares would ruffle a lot of feathers, and Angie would have to smooth them.

In the days immediately following the accident, the main concern of the Spanish government—and of Duke—was keeping a lid on the press. The Spanish government wanted the word "nuclear" kept out of the news entirely, lest the public learn about nuclear overflights, radioactivity, or possible contamination. The accident was an unfortunate plane crash, no more. But the international press had quickly gotten wind of the accident, and reporters were already sniffing around. Both the U.S. and Spanish governments agreed to tell them as little as possible in the hope they would go away. On the day of the accident, at 9:45 p.m. in Madrid, the U.S. Information Service, the Department of Defense, and the State Department released a joint statement about the accident to UPI, the Associated Press, Reuters, ABC, and *Stars and Stripes*. It read, in its entirety:

> A B-52 bomber from the 68th Bomb Wing, Seymour Johnson AFB, N.C. and a KC-135 tanker from the 910th air refueling squadron, Bergstrom AFB, Texas, crashed today southwest of Cartagena, Spain, during scheduled air operations. There are reports of some survivors. An Air Force accident investigation team has been dispatched to the scene. Additional details will be made available as the investigation progresses.

Over the next couple of days, Duke kept an eye on the papers as the story bubbled through the international press. The embassy sent a steady stream of reports back to Washington. On the days following the accident, short, straightforward stories ran in British and American newspapers. A few papers speculated that the planes might have been carrying nuclear weapons. At the same time, the Spanish press ran newspaper, television, and radio stories without any critical comment, treating the accident as simply an unusual news event.

By Wednesday, January 19, two days after the accident, the story seemed to be fizzling out, much to the relief of Spanish and American officials. On that day and the next, Duke sat down to discuss the situation with his key contact in the Spanish Foreign Ministry, Ángel Sagáz, who ran the North American section. At the meetings, Sagáz seemed calm but concerned about repercussions if the Spanish public discovered that nuclear-armed American bombers regularly flew over Spain. "Sagáz also mentioned, without great stress, that sensational stories about missing bombs and radiation could excite Spanish public," Duke reported in a cable to the secretary of state.

At one point during the meetings, the Americans asked to issue a statement of gratitude for Spain's help in the search-and-rescue effort. Sagáz and other Spanish officials shot the idea down. The story was already dying in the press, they said, and they certainly didn't want it resurrected. Duke pushed the point: if, by some chance, the story rekindled, it would be good to have a statement ready. Sagáz agreed, and Duke drafted a seven-paragraph statement providing some basic details of the crash and thanking Spanish officials for their help.

Although the meeting went well, hints of trouble emerged. Some lower-level Foreign Office officials expressed surprise that these risky refueling operations were taking place over land. Around the same time, Spanish Vice President Agustín Muñoz Grandes met with U.S. Air Force General Stanley Donovan, head of the Joint U.S. Military Group and Ambassador's Duke's chief military contact, to suggest that the refuelings take place over water, rather than Spanish territory. Muñoz Grandes also posed an uncomfortable question: Did the United States have any nuclear devices stored on Spanish territory? Although the U.S. military had stored nuclear weapons in Spain since 1958, its policy was strict and unyielding: never tell anyone exactly where the weapons were. "The subject was still very touchy," said the former embassy staffer Joseph Smith. "It doesn't surprise me that Muñoz Grandes didn't know—or didn't know for certain." General Donovan was a blunt, plainspoken man who emulated Curtis LeMay, in both his cigar-chomping demeanor and his direct speech. "He was not dumb," said Smith. "I can't believe that Donovan would have told him anything."

Despite these diplomatic bumps, Duke told Washington that tension remained low and both sides were cooperating. Military and government officials in Madrid felt good about the situation. On January 19, a secret cable to the Joint Chiefs of Staff in Washington rang with optimism: "American Embassy officials report Spanish Foreign Office is of the opinion that coverage has reached its peak and will now decline," it read. "Queries from American news bureaus in Madrid have diminished appreciably."

The optimism would not last. A young reporter named Andró del Amo was about to upset Ambassador Duke's delicately balanced diplomacy. The previous evening, del Amo, a twenty-five-year-old UPI reporter, had left for Palomares with Leo White, a London *Daily Mirror* reporter, to investigate the scene firsthand.

They drove all night, arriving at the dirt road into Palomares about 6:30 a.m. on Wednesday, January 19. As they headed into town, they saw some wreckage—what looked like airplane engines—lying on a hillside. They stopped the car, took some photos, and continued on. In the center of town, they saw some guardias civiles on patrol, but nobody gave the two reporters a second glance. Del Amo asked a villager where he could find the Americans and was directed toward the camp in the dry riverbed. The most complete account of what happened next is recorded in Tad Szulc's book *The Bombs of Palomares:*

> Driving up the road, del Amo suddenly slammed on his brakes. As he said later, he became "very excited" by what he saw. Long lines of American airmen in fatigues or bright yellow coveralls were moving through the fields, beating the bushes, tomato vines, and clumps of vegetation with long sticks and canes. They were doing it with extreme thoroughness, del Amo thought, as they slowly advanced almost shoulder to shoulder. Other airmen, closer to the road, were checking the ground with portable instruments del Amo and White assumed to be Geiger counters.

The two men continued on to the camp and saw a frenzy of activity. The tail section of the B-52 still sat in the riverbed, with the blue Air Force buses that had carried the airmen from Morón and Torrejón scattered around it. American officers, airmen, and guardias civiles buzzed around the camp. In the center of activity stood General Wilson in his blue greatcoat, issuing orders and receiving reports. The two reporters asked some questions but received little information. But del Amo had enough for an initial report. He drove to Vera to call in his first story to Madrid. After lunch, the two reporters returned to the riverbed camp to track down the Sixteenth Air Force's information director, Colonel Barnett Young, who told them that the airmen in the fields were simply looking for wreckage. When the reporters asked if the planes had carried nuclear weapons, Young "exploded with anger," according to del Amo, shouting, "This is not a place for scandal stories or outrageous hypotheses!" Young warned the reporters to stop nosing around.

As the two reporters headed back toward the village, a young Air Police trooper flagged down their car. Readying themselves for another confrontation, the reporters were struck instead by a bolt of luck. Looking desperate, the airman asked if either of the men spoke Spanish. Del Amo replied that he did. "Great," the air policeman said. "There's a fellow in that bean field, and I've got to get him out of there." Del Amo said he would be happy to translate.

The two reporters trudged into the bean field, and Del Amo translated the airman's message, telling the farmer that he had to leave the field because of dangerous radioactivity. On the way back to the car, del Amo asked the airman if the Air Force was worried about the bombs. Their conversation, recorded in *The Bombs of Palomares,* would break the Palomares story wide open:

"How do you know about the bombs?" the airman asked, suddenly suspicious.

"Hell," del Amo told him, "I've just come back from the camp."

The air policeman was reassured. "Well, they found three of them very shortly after the crash, but they're worried because they haven't found the other one," he said. They reached the car, and he pointed to the sites where the three bombs had been found. "One was in the river bed where the camp now is," he explained. "The second bomb was near that white house over there, you see? And the third one way over in those hills in front of you. Now they're all worried about the fourth bomb."

Del Amo sped back to Vera. He called the Madrid bureau and told it about the four bombs, radioactivity, and a missing nuclear weapon— everything the governments wanted to keep covered up.

That evening, in Madrid, Duke got wind of del Amo's dispatch. At 9:46 p.m., he sent a terse cable to Washington: "Have just learned local UPI correspondent filed story today on B-52/KC-135 accident to effect three atom bombs recovered from wreckage but one still missing and that hundreds of US troops combing countryside with Geiger counters." He added, "Foregoing may lead to escalation of media treatment and rapid change in present circumstances."

The following morning, January 20, 1966, *The New York Times* ran the UPI story on page one. The headline read, "U.S. Said to Hunt Lost Atom Device." The article began:

> United States Air Force men today were reported searching the Spanish countryside for an atomic device that was understood to be missing after the collision of a B-52 nuclear bomber and a jet tanker Monday during a refueling mission.
>
> United States officials in Madrid and here in Southeastern Spain refused to confirm or deny that a nuclear bomb was carried by the B-52, which crashed into the KC-135 jet tanker near here.
>
> But they gave every sign they were looking for one. Hundreds of American servicemen were searching the crash scene, some of them armed with Geiger counters. Palomares is a village a little more than a mile inland on Spain's southeastern coast, about 95 miles east of Granada.
>
> When asked what the Geiger counters were being used for, Col. Barnett Young, chief information officer for the 16th Air Force at Torrejón Air Force base, near Madrid, asked in return, "what do you normally use Geiger counters for?"

The article, which went on to describe the massive search under way near Palomares, made no splash in Spain on January 20. Exercising its iron grip on the press, the Spanish government allowed no major foreign newspapers into the country that day. When Foreign Minister Fernando Castiella summoned Duke to a meeting that evening, they spent most of the time discussing the long-contested territory of Gibraltar and barely mentioned Palomares.

But the storm had only been delayed. The following day, the UPI article landed on Franco's desk, sent by the Spanish Embassy in Washington. The generalissimo was not pleased.

Shortly after noon on January 21, the Spanish foreign minister called Duke to report that Franco had read the UPI article and was extremely concerned. Ángel Sagáz, the director of North American affairs, was on his way to the U.S. Embassy to discuss the situation.

Sagáz arrived at the embassy agitated and upset. Franco fired people at will, and Sagáz undoubtedly felt the gun sights turning in his direction. This was a crisis. He gave Duke an earful: Who were these "United States officials" mentioned in the article? And what were these other reports, citing "Spanish inhabitants of the accident area" who had complained about nuclear overflights? If this turned into a radiation scare, it could wreck the tourism industry. He thought that the United States and Spain had been working together to contain the press, but since that obviously wasn't the case, the Spanish government might take matters into its own hands. Maybe it would convene its own press conference, to at least spin the story in Spain's favor.

Duke, the man who could calm kings, responded. He understood why Sagáz was upset. This was a delicate situation of great concern to both governments. Both needed to remain calm and work together. He had no idea who the "United States officials" were—certainly, neither he nor anyone under his control had spoken to the UPI reporter, but he would get to the bottom of it. In the meantime, U.S. Air Force General Stanley Donovan, Duke's chief military contact, was visiting Palomares and expected to return at any moment. When Donovan got back, they would get an up-to-date situation report and then decide what to do next. Everything would be fine if they stuck together. Sagáz calmed down and agreed to wait for further reports from the scene.

After the meeting, Duke got to work. Donovan gave him the rundown on Palomares: the fourth bomb was still missing, but the Air Force was following every lead; experts had identified several small radioactive areas, which were now closed off and awaiting remediation; the Air Force was buying affected plants and livestock; medical teams were examining people in the area who might have been exposed. The residents of the area seemed a bit fearful, but there was no mass panic.

Spanish medical teams, nuclear experts, and civil authorities were on the scene and cooperating. The situation seemed under control. However, a growing crowd of international press was swarming the area, including UPI, *Paris Match,* CBS-TV, and some British media.

Duke next called the UPI bureau chief, Harry Stathos, to give him a piece of his mind. He refuted the "United States officials" quoted in the article and asked where he had found that information. The shaken Stathos started to backpedal. He said he had gotten the information thirdhand and apologized for filing the story without double-checking with the embassy.

It was about 7:30 in the evening on January 21, the Friday after the accident. Duke called Sagáz with a summary and offered to send an embassy officer with a full report, which Sagáz quickly accepted. The officer who briefed Sagáz reported that he listened intently, especially to the story of the UPI bureau chief. It seemed that Sagáz wanted that part of the story particularly clear to report to his superiors. The embassy assured Sagáz that it was open to any Spanish suggestions on how to handle the situation but believed they should continue working together closely. Sagáz agreed. The crisis of the day was over.

But the larger crisis was not. The Spanish government would not be soothed as easily as Sagáz. The next morning, General Donovan met with Spanish Vice President Muñoz Grandes to give him the latest news from Palomares. Muñoz Grandes did not appear upset, but he responded with a demand: nuclear flights over Spanish territory must be stopped until further notice.

The demand did not appear to originate from Muñoz Grandes. A military man, he had always been cooperative and friendly toward the Americans, "the only friend we really had," according to George Landau. Most likely the ban had come from the civilian side of the Spanish government, or maybe Franco himself. And it probably had little to do with Spain's concern for its people; the government might simply have been arming itself with a bargaining chip for the 1968 base renegotiations.

Muñoz Grandes's decree meant little for the Chrome Dome route over Spain. Though some reports claimed that SAC dropped the route, U.S. Embassy staffers say the flights continued but started refueling over water. But the decree also had another implication: no more nuclear *logistics* flights either. The United States couldn't fly nuclear bombs over Spain just to get them somewhere else, such as to storage depots in Germany, for instance. Most viewed these curbs as simply an inconvenience: planes could be rerouted over oceans or other countries. But others saw clouds gathering on the horizon. What if other European countries—Britain, France, Germany—fearing a Palomares accident of their own, started asking questions? What if they demanded that the United States remove nuclear bombs from their bases, nuclear subs from their waters, nuclear-armed planes from their skies? If Spain's decision caused a domino effect, the United States' nuclear strategy could be curtailed. Everything in Spain had to be patched up as quickly as possible. Over the next few months, Ambassador Duke constantly received a question from Defense: When can we get the overflights reinstated?

Duke foresaw other troubles ahead, and not just from the Spanish government. The story had broken open, and hordes of international journalists were massing on Spain's southern shore. Despite Duke's best efforts, Palomares was swelling into an international news event. He braced himself for a long struggle, concluding his January 22 dispatch to Washington with a warning and a plea:

Believe we must be prepared for continued and possibly increased media treatment of accident until fourth bomb located and removed. If much more time elapses without success in search, we may be faced with practical necessity admitting officially one bomb still missing. This in turn carries obvious dangers including potentially triggering off further GOS [government of Spain] official statements possibly including public reference to Spanish demand that refueling and/or overflights nuclear-armed aircraft be stopped. It therefore clearly of utmost urgency that no effort be spared locate fourth bomb with minimum delay. Urge all necessary US resources be provided for search.

5.

Parachutes

Joe Ramirez pushed aside the ropes of plastic beads that dangled in place of a door and stepped into the tavern. The small room was dominated by an L-shaped bar. In late afternoon, the tavern was not crowded. Ramirez ordered a drink and stood at the counter near the door. Soon he spied the man he had come looking for: the mayor of Herrerias—also the owner of the bar. The mayor walked over and joined him for a drink. They began to talk.

Ramirez had spent the last few days in Palomares translating, answering questions, and following leads. He had come to this small tavern in the tiny mountain town of Herrerias to track down an especially promising story. A local man had approached Ramirez in the Air Force camp and said, "I understand you're looking for *un artefacto*." *Artefacto,* Spanish for "artifact" or "device," had somehow become the favored euphemism for "missing nuclear bomb." The man pointed to a tiny village perched high in the mountains. "The mayor of that little village has a brother who's a shepherd," he said, "and he grazes his flock on this mountain, the one between us and the sea." The shepherd, he continued, had seen the planes explode and the debris fall; he might have some important information to share.

Ramirez got permission to check it out. He commandeered a vehicle and, with an Air Force lieutenant colonel, drove the narrow, unpaved road to Herrerias. They arrived just before dark, tracked down the mayor in the tavern, and asked if the story was true. The mayor, a gregarious man, said that he did have a brother, a shepherd who lived on the mountain and had seen the accident. Ramirez asked to speak with him, but the mayor replied that this would be difficult: his brother was deaf and dumb. To complete the picture, the mayor added, *"Le llaman Tarzan."* They call him Tarzan.

As the men continued to talk, word spread through town that two Americans had holed up in the bar, and curious villagers began to fill the room. Then an unexpected visitor loomed in the tavern doorway: Tarzan himself. The mayor grabbed his brother's arm and dragged him over to the two Air Force officers. Using sign language, he explained why the Americans had come. Tarzan hulked over the men but was shy and offered little information. Painstakingly, they dragged his story out. The lieutenant colonel, who spoke only English, asked a question; Ramirez translated it into Spanish for the mayor, who then asked his brother in sign language. Tarzan's answer traveled back through the same slow route. Over several hours, the officers learned that the shepherd had seen, among the falling debris, a large white double parachute with an object dangling underneath. This sounded promising. At the end of the interview, the lieutenant colonel had one final question: "Ask him if he'll go with us in a helicopter tomorrow."

They didn't need a translator to understand the shepherd's reply. Tarzan was emphatic: No! No way was he getting into some flying contraption with these Americans! The mayor signed to his brother some more, cajoling and convincing, and told the officers not to worry. They should show up in the helicopter tomorrow morning; Tarzan would be ready.

The next morning around 10 a.m., Ramirez sat in a helicopter hovering above Herrerias, looking down at the village square. The villagers had gathered in a circle to watch the whirring machine, and the chopper's wash swirled them with dust. As the helicopter set down, Ramirez saw the mayor tugging his brother forward. Hopping out amid the churning dust, Ramirez handed the mayor a helmet fitted with a radio and microphone. The mayor beamed with pleasure, trying on the helmet and strutting for his constituents. Then Ramirez, the mayor, and the reluctant shepherd piled in the chopper and lifted into the sky.

Once airborne, the lieutenant colonel asked where the shepherd had been working at the time of the accident. By the time the question and answer traveled back and forth, the group had overshot the point by several miles. This would never do. The lieutenant colonel ordered the pilot to hover until they established where the shepherd had been standing and where he had seen the parachute and object fall. Information in hand, they headed back to the village. Pleased with the whole adventure, the mayor leapt out of the chopper with a flourish. His brother just looked relieved to be back on solid ground.

Returning to camp, Ramirez gave the new information to his superiors, who dispatched a search team to the shepherd's hills. Less than a week into the search, the Air Force was still chasing every lead. Searchers, scouring the area, had found the combat mission folder. The heat of the explosion had melted the folder's plastic coverings together, sealing the top secret codes securely inside. Searchers also found the box containing additional classified documents, still locked tight. These finds gave the Air Force some measure of relief. But there was still no sign of bomb number four. Some people began to suspect that the bomb might have exploded in the air, buried itself underground, or fallen into the sea. But it had been only a few days, and the chances remained high that bomb number four had fallen on land near the other three. Perhaps Tarzan's clue marked the spot. A team headed to the mountains to search the area. They returned without the bomb.

By January 20—the Thursday after the accident—General Wilson realized that finding the bomb and cleaning up the mess would take longer than he originally thought, and he relayed the news to SAC headquarters in Omaha. General John D. Ryan, who had succeeded Tommy Power as SAC's commander in chief, directed Wilson to use all available resources to find the missing bomb. "Until every avenue of search is exhausted," he said, "we do not have much of a leg to stand on."

Hundreds of searchers had arrived from Morón and Torrejón the day after the accident and were camping in the dry riverbed near the B-52's tail section. The first night, the men slept in the open air or under the buses. The next day, as tents and gear arrived, the men set up a rudimentary camp. They called the area "Camp Wilson." Conditions were rough. Phil Durbin, an airman who arrived from Torrejón, re-members the desert nights as cold and damp. He and his friends, seeing a small wooden bridge in the nearby hills, tore it down and burned it for warmth. Robert Finkel, a squadron commander, slept under a bus with his head in a cardboard box to keep the sand out of his face. The men ate cold C-rations out of metal cans. There were no bathrooms or showers except the Mediterranean Sea.

After a few days of searching with no maps or strategic plan, Wilson's men got organized. Bombs numbers one, two, and three had fallen in a jagged line along the doomed planes' flight path, with bomb number one near the water, bomb number three about a mile inland, and bomb number two a mile or so inland from that. Wilson assumed—or at least hoped—that they would find bomb number four somewhere along the same path. Each day, coordinators—soon supplied with photomosaic maps from U.S. Air Force reconnaissance planes—mapped out areas to search. At daybreak, the searchers rumbled out in buses to their as-signed patch of desert scrub or tomato farm. The men spread out in a line and walked shoulder to shoulder, eyes glued to the ground, looking for any sign of the bomb. After a certain amount of trudging under the merciless desert sun, the men "wheeled" the line and walked back to their starting point.

If the searchers saw anything of interest, they marked it with a flag on a pole, a piece of string, or a bit of colored toilet paper. If they found small bits of metal, they placed them in bags for inspection back at camp. Durbin found a chunk of the boom nozzle nearly as long as his arm. Nobody knew which piece of scrap might lead them to bomb number four. Those who thought the bomb had disintegrated in midair found some evidence for their theory: a reservoir—a piece of a bomb mechanism—lying 1,500 feet from bomb number three. Perhaps it was a remnant of the missing weapon. The Air Force sent the scrap to Los Alamos for identification. The verdict: the reservoir was just another piece of bomb number three.

More clues appeared. That first week, a searcher found a round metal plate with two sides squared off. Experts identified it as a tail closing plate—the part that fits on the end of a bomb and holds the parachutes in place. They also discovered that it had come from bomb number four—the first identifiable bit of the weapon that anyone had found. But the plate was found about a hundred yards from the B-52's tail section, an area that the Air Force had already searched exhaustively. Surely it should have been seen earlier. Had someone put it there? For days, the Air Force asked around. Finally they found the local man who had had originally discovered the tail plate. He had been away at his mother's funeral. He said he had seen the plate fall on the day of the accident, picked it up, and given it to a member of the Guardia Civil, who had dropped it near the tail section. New information in hand, the Air Force stepped up the search in an area closer to the shoreline and shipped the tail plate back to the United States for examination.

Only a handful of people in the United States knew the full significance of this particular piece of metal, and they worked in a jumble of drab government buildings at Sandia National Laboratories in Albuquerque, New Mexico. The engineers at Sandia didn't design nuclear warheads; that job belonged to the physicists at Los Alamos. However, they engineered just about every other part of America's nuclear bombs: the casing, the fusing mechanism, the arming and safing devices, and the parachutes. They knew the Mark 28 inside and out.

Sandia in the 1960s was a secret paradise for the slide rule set. Every engineer who worked there had graduated in the top of his or her college class. They had cutting-edge equipment, seemingly endless funding, and a fairly loose rein. They also worked with a deep sense of mission. Nuclear weapons, most of them believed, kept their country safe from the Soviets. Sandia engineers considered themselves to be not only the elite of Albuquerque but indispensable to the defense of the United States.

On this mission, Sandia's marching orders trickled down from the top. As soon as President Johnson heard news of the crash, he called Secretary of Defense Robert McNamara. He first asked McNamara if the bombs might explode. When McNamara assured him that they would not, the president told him to "do everything possible to find them." Word was passed to Jack Howard, McNamara's assistant secretary of defense for atomic energy. A few days later, Howard dialed his friend Alan Pope, the director of Aero Projects at Sandia. He told Pope that bomb number four remained at large and asked for help in finding it. Right away, Pope called Randy Maydew, the manager of Sandia's Aerodynamics Department. Maydew put down the phone, scrambled into the office, and got to work.

High-energy and hyperactive, Maydew, like many engineers, was a man of compulsive habits. Every morning, he sweated through a half-hour regimen of floor exercises; every Saturday, he wrote in his journal; every Sunday, he attended church. He liked to move fast and get things done quickly, and when he got the call about Palomares, he headed straight to Sandia and gathered a small team. They sat down to crunch some numbers and see if they could pinpoint the location of the missing bomb, or at least make an educated guess. The engineers knew the altitude, heading, and speed of the planes at the time of collision and had their own data on the aerodynamics of the bomb. They also had a state-of-the-art supercomputer, the IBM 7090, at their disposal. But they weren't sure exactly where the accident had taken place and had only sketchy, conflicting meteorological data. Furthermore, they didn't know if the bomb was intact or broken to bits or which, if any, of the bomb's parachutes had deployed.

The parachute question was critical. Stuffed into its back end, the Mark 28 carried a complicated multiparachute system that allowed pilots to drop nuclear bombs from a variety of altitudes. Pilots could, for instance, speed into enemy territory under the radar, drop bombs at an extremely low altitude—below 500 feet—and still clear out before the bomb exploded.

Sandia had developed this "laydown system" in the 1950s to help American planes evade Soviet air defenses, which had been specifically designed to shoot down small numbers of aircraft carrying nuclear weapons. According to intelligence experts, the Soviet defense missiles could hit planes flying as high as 60,000, maybe 80,000, feet. But the system could not hit very-low-flying planes, especially if they whizzed by faster than the speed of sound. However, a pilot dropping a nuclear bomb from a low altitude would surely be caught in the deadly blast—unless there was a way to delay the explosion. The Air Force called Sandia.

In 1953, Randy Maydew's boss asked him to work on the project. The Air Force, at that time, wanted to drop nuclear bombs from 2,000 feet, at speeds greater than Mach 1. (Later, they requested drops under 200 feet.) The only way to do this and give the pilot time to escape, Maydew figured, was to slow the bomb down with parachutes. Knowing nothing about parachutes, he surveyed the literature and found that no parachute in the world could withstand the stress of being blown open at the speed of sound. So the Sandia engineers set out to design one that could. Along the way, they came up with other ways a weapon could survive a low-altitude drop: a bomb with a spike on its nose that stuck in the ground like a dart; a bomb with a metal honeycomb tip that could endure a bruising dent in the nose. In a couple of years, Sandia gave the Air Force plans for a laydown weapon. Maydew, meanwhile, became an expert on high-performance parachutes.

The Mark 28 bomb missing in Palomares packed an elaborate four-parachute system into its hind end. In a low-altitude drop, when the system worked correctly, three nylon parachutes would open in sequence—an elegant bit of fancy footwork in the sky. Soon after a bomb fell from the belly of a plane, a ring of explosive bolts fired on the back of the bomb, knocking the tail plate off. The inside of the tail plate had an eyebolt in the center, tied to a lanyard. The lanyard attached to a four-foot-diameter guide parachute. When the tail plate fell, it pulled the small chute out behind it. The pilot chute, in turn, heaved out a sixteen-foot-diameter ribbon parachute. This sixteen-foot chute slowed the bomb for two to three seconds, then cut itself loose. As it drifted away, it yanked another pack out of the bomb, pulling the cover off a sixty-four-foot chute. The sixteen-foot chute floated away, carrying the empty bag, as the larger chute finished the job. This monstrous canopy opened and slowed the bomb to about twenty-eight feet per second by the time it hit the ground, giving the pilots time to get away. To complicate matters for the bomb search, the Mark 28 was also designed to free-fall from a high altitude. In that case it would release only a small, thirty-inch chute, which would stabilize the bomb as it sailed down to its target.

Because bomb number four had been torn from its rack in an explosion, any—or none—of the parachutes might have opened. The three bombs found on land only emphasized the range of possibilities. The first bomb, which had hit the ground at about 140 feet per second, had deployed the sixteen-footer but nothing else, but that had been enough to keep the bomb intact. The second bomb had landed without deploying any chutes, smashing into the ground at about 325 feet per second. This high-speed impact had detonated the high explosive, scattering plutonium dust, case fragments, and remnants of parachute over the Spanish countryside. The third bomb had deployed the sixteen-foot chute, but because the chute was damaged, it hadn't supplied enough drag. The bomb had hit the ground at about 225 feet per second, igniting its high explosive and scattering radioactive debris.

There were hundreds, maybe thousands, of possible scenarios for bomb number four. But despite the dearth of data, the Sandia engineers made some quick calculations over the weekend. Since bomb number four's tail plate had come off, it seemed likely that at least one of its parachutes had popped out behind it. *If* the big, sixty-four-foot chute had deployed right after the explosion, and *if* the wind had been blowing out to sea, and *if* the gusts had been strong enough, the engineers thought, the bomb could have splashed into the Mediterranean. Only one of many possibilities, it was an early hint that the bomb might not be on land. On Monday, one week after the accident, Sandia told the Pentagon that the bomb might have gone into the sea. A few days later, Sandia's computer spit out an estimated location: 37° 13.9′ N, 01° 42.3′ W. This was not good news; according to this calculation, the bomb had plunked far out in the Mediterranean, closer to Africa than to Spain.

On January 27, General Wilson requested that Randy Maydew or his boss, Alan Pope, fly to Spain. Wilson was building an advisory team to help define the search area, and he wanted someone from Sandia on board. Having experts on site, he had decided, would be better than "furnishing data to unseeing computers." As the engineers in Albuquerque continued to hog the IBM 7090 for their calculations (ultimately generating a three-foot stack of paper printouts), Maydew prepared to jet off to Spain. As he was packing, a fellow engineer dropped by his office with a gift: a forked stick, like those used by diviners to search for hidden water.

While Maydew and his team were crunching numbers in Albuquerque, Joe Ramirez had been chasing leads up and down the coast of southern Spain. Soon he would have to begin the sticky work of settling claims, but for now, all focus remained on the search. Ramirez had another lead that seemed even more promising than Tarzan. One morning, a Spanish naval officer had shown up at camp with some pieces of aircraft debris he had collected at sea. He told Ramirez that some bigger pieces were still sitting on his ship and asked if the Americans could send someone to pick them up. Ramirez grabbed an air-

President Kennedy, General Curtis LeMay, and General Tommy Power. LeMay transformed SAC from a "creampuff outfit" to the most powerful military force in history. *Official United States Air Force photograph, provided by the U.S. Strategic Command History Office*

A KC-135 tanker refueling a B-52 bomber. In 1966, the Strategic Air Command kept bombers in the air at all times, loaded with nuclear weapons, in anticipation of a Soviet surprise attack.

Official United States Air Force photograph, provided by the U.S. Strategic Command History Office

The village of Palomares in 1966. *Courtesy of Lewis Melson*

Found on the day of the accident on the bank of a dry river, the first bomb was largely intact. *Courtesy of Sandia National Laboratories*

Some of the high explosive in bomb number two detonated, exploding weapon fragments up to 100 yards in all directions. The surrounding area was highly contaminated. *Courtesy of Sandia National Laboratories*

Pepe López pulled the parachute aside to find bomb number three. "I immediately knew this was a bomb," he said. As in bomb number two, high explosive had detonated, scattering radioactive debris. *Courtesy of Sandia National Laboratories*

By February, hundreds of Americans were scouring the Spanish countryside for the missing bomb. When searchers found debris, they marked it with a colored flag or a bit of toilet paper. *Courtesy of Sandia National Laboratories*

Admiral William S. Guest (white hat) briefs Ambassador Angier Biddle Duke (right) at Camp Wilson. Duke clashed with the military over the secretive press policy. *Rare Books, Manuscripts, and Special Collections Library, Duke University*

Duke speaks with Palomares resident Antonio Sabiote Flores during a visit to the village, as Admiral Guest (left) and General Delmar Wilson (right) look on. *Rare Books, Manuscripts, and Special Collections Library, Duke University*

The Air Force collected aircraft debris in a pile near Camp Wilson. Here it is loaded onto a barge to be dumped at sea. *U.S. Naval Historical Center photograph*

Workers cleared a dense thicket of tomato stakes so fields could be decontaminated. The Air Force bought the tomatoes and fed them to airmen.
Courtesy of Lewis Melson

To dilute plutonium in the soil, the Americans agreed to plow or water more than five hundred acres of land. *Courtesy of Lewis Melson*

The most contaminated dirt was packed into 4,810 barrels for shipment to the Savannah River nuclear processing center in South Carolina.

Courtesy of Sandia National Laboratories

Manolo González (right) and Joe Ramirez (standing left) with a photomosaic map used for claims work.

Courtesy of Joe Ramirez

Alvin being lifted from the *Fort Snelling*'s well deck. The sub had completed only one mission prior to Palomares.
U.S. Naval Historical Center photograph

Alvin pilots Bill Rainnie, Mac McCamis, and Val Wilson.   *Woods Hole Oceanographic Institution*

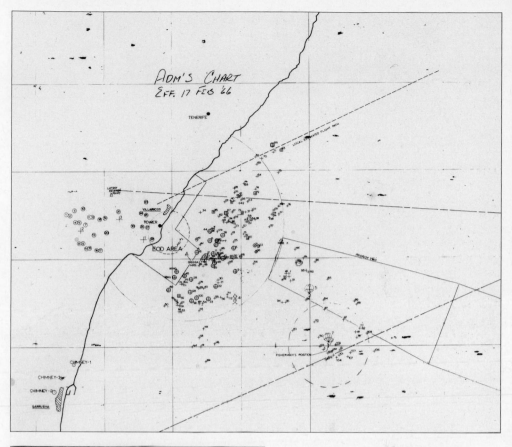

Admiral Guest outlined four search areas, encompassing twenty-seven square miles of ocean. The area to search was larger than Manhattan.

Courtesy of Lewis Melson

Aluminaut under water. Larger and less maneuverable than *Alvin*, *Aluminaut* could stay submerged for up to seventy-two hours.

Courtesy of Georgianna Markel

Francisco Simó Orts, the Spanish fisherman who saw a "dead man" on a parachute fall into the sea. Guest centered a high-priority search area on Simó's sighting.

Courtesy of Sandia National Laboratories

Lieutenant Commander DeWitt "Red" Moody, an EOD expert who joined Guest's inner circle.

Official U.S. Navy photograph, courtesy of D. H. "Red" Moody

Brad Mooney, a thirty-five-year-old Navy lieutenant, was a veteran of the *Thresher* search and understood the submersibles' capabilities.

Courtesy of Brad Mooney

Ambassador Duke (right) and Manuel Fraga Iribarne waving to photographers during their famous swim. The publicity stunt made papers around the world; *Variety* dubbed it the "Best Water Show since Aquacade."

Rare Books, Manuscripts, and Special Collections Library, Duke University

On March 15, 1966, *Alvin* took this photo at about twenty-five hundred feet below the surface. "How do you know it's not a parachute full of mud?" asked Guest. *U.S. Naval Historical Center photograph*

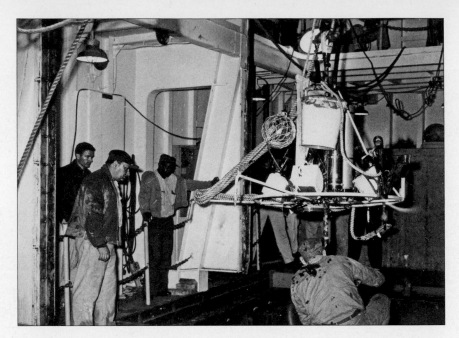

To retrieve the bomb, Red Moody helped construct POODL. One Navy man called it a "kludge." *U.S. Naval Historical Center photograph*

CURV, a torpedo-recovery device, used a specially designed grapnel to attach lines to the parachute. *Courtesy of Sandia National Laboratories*

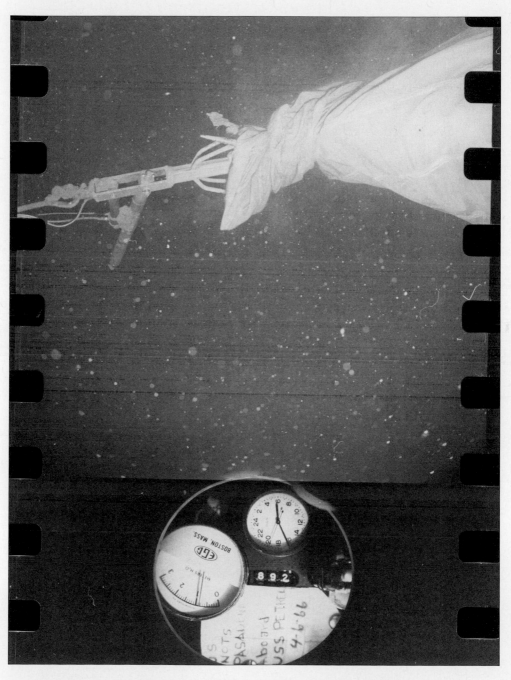

CURV twists a grapnel into the parachute. *U.S. Naval Historical Center photograph*

April 7, 1966. The log of the USS *Petrel* reads, "0846: Weapon on deck with parachute." *U.S. Naval Historical Center photograph*

An EOD technician begins to render the bomb safe. Everything went smoothly until the team reached the battery.

U.S. Naval Historical Center photograph

General Wilson (left, hands on knees), Red Moody (center), Cliff Page, and Admiral Guest examine bomb number four. Lieutenant Walter Funston, who safed the bomb, is in the foreground. CURV is in the background. *U.S. Naval Historical Center photograph*

Aerial shot of the USS *Petrel* during the press review. The bomb and CURV are visible on the fantail as *Alvin* and *Aluminaut* pass by. This was the first time that the United States displayed a nuclear weapon in public. *Courtesy of Brad Mooney*

man and headed to Garrucha, a fishing port just south of Palomares, where the Spanish navy ship was anchored.

After finding the ship and collecting the debris, Ramirez stopped to chat with some of the Spanish officers. One of them asked Ramirez if he had spoken to the fishermen who had rescued the bomber pilots. No, said Ramirez. He hadn't even heard about the fishermen. The navy officer told him that they lived in Aguilas, a port city thirty miles up the coast from Palomares.

The paved road to Aguilas, winding along the beautiful Spanish coastline, proved far less grueling than the narrow path to Tarzan's mountain home. Ramirez and a major from Camp Wilson arrived in the evening and found the port authority office on the second floor of a small, two-story building. The port captain greeted them warmly and asked them to wait while he called the fishermen. He told Ramirez their names: Francisco Simó Orts and Bartolomé Roldán Martínez.

As the winter night deepened, the officers chatted with the port captain, waiting for the fishermen. Around 8 p.m., Simó and Roldán arrived. The fishermen, especially Simó, impressed Ramirez. Businesslike and straightforward, Simó—who did most of the talking—clearly understood the sea. "He did not appear to me to be a charlatan," said Ramirez. "Whatever he said, he meant. There was no fooling around."

Simó told Ramirez about that bright morning on his shrimp boat, about the explosion and the many parachutes. Ramirez, who had just recently learned that some nuclear bombs have parachutes, asked the fisherman to describe them. Simó did. And then he said something that Ramirez found strange: he apologized for not saving the other flyer. "What other flyer?" asked Ramirez, puzzled. He knew that all the airmen had been accounted for. Simó explained that he had seen all the airmen drifting down to the sea, and he knew they were alive because their arms and legs were moving. But this other person, the man who had fallen near him, hadn't been moving at all, so he must have been unconscious or maybe dead. Simó apologized profusely for not having reached the motionless man in time. When the flyer hit the water, he said, he had turned his boat and tried to rescue him. But his nets had still hung deep, and had slowed the boat; the man had sunk before he arrived.

Simó added one more twist: another, smaller parachute had fallen near his fishing boat. "I saw a parachute smaller than the others, which carried what seemed like the chest of a man," said Simó. "I didn't see legs or a waist. Something was hanging from the bottom." Then Simó added a gory detail: what he had seen dangling from the torso, he said, were the man's intestines.

Ramirez didn't know what to think. Simó insisted that he had seen a dead man—maybe two—but that couldn't be true. Or could it? Had Ramirez been misinformed about the number of airmen in the planes? Or could Simó have seen the bomb dangling from a parachute? Ramirez wasn't sure. "I came out of that meeting convinced that there was something substantive there," he said. "But I knew that someone with more knowledge than I had to talk to him." Ramirez wrapped up the meeting and asked if the fishermen could show the Americans where the parachutes had fallen. Of course, they said.

Ramirez reported this latest bit of news back to Camp Wilson. A day or two later, on January 22, he found himself on the USS *Pinnacle* with Simó, Roldán, and a handful of U.S. Navy officers. The *Pinnacle,* along with the USS *Sagacity,* both minesweepers, had arrived the previous day to search the area with mine-detecting sonar. The Navy officers asked Simó to show them where he had seen the larger parachute enter the water. He guided them to the spot without a compass, using only his seaman's eye to align various landmarks on shore. When the *Pinnacle* arrived at the specified point, their sonar got two hits. The water was just over two thousand feet deep.

The *Pinnacle* then moved away, and the officers, testing Simó's navigation skills, asked him to guide them back. Simó fixed the position again. The *Pinnacle* found the same two sonar hits. Then the Navy officers asked Simó and Roldán to show them another area where debris had fallen. The fishermen guided the Navy men to the spot. More hits blipped onto the *Pinnacle*'s sonar. The Navy men were impressed by the fishermen's navigation skills, but the sonar hits were vague. One report described them as both "sharp and hazy" and guessed that they could be "either a school of fish or a parachute partially filled with air bubbles." Nonetheless, the blips were duly noted, and the Spanish fishermen returned to shore.

On the evening of Simó's boat ride, in Washington, President Johnson sat down in the White House screening room to watch a movie with several guests, including Lady Bird, Secretary of Defense Robert McNamara, and McNamara's wife. The movie was the new James

Bond thriller *Thunderball,* released a few weeks earlier and now at the top of the box office. In the film, an international ring of evildoers called "SPECTRE" hatches a sinister plan. An agent of SPECTRE, disguised as a NATO commandant, hijacks a fighter plane loaded with two nuclear bombs, kills the crew with poison gas, and crash-lands the plane in the ocean. After the plane settles gently to the bottom, a group of scuba divers appears, driving a futuristic underwater craft that looks like a giant orange stingray. The divers snatch the nuclear bombs and squirrel them away aboard a pleasure craft. SPECTRE demands £1 million in flawless diamonds, or it will detonate the bombs in a city. James Bond, braving spear guns, shark attacks, and a duplicitous redhead, saves the day.

During the week after the Palomares accident, everyone was talking about the movie. When Jack Howard called Alan Pope at Sandia, he told the engineer that the nation was facing a real-life *Thunderball.* And now a handful of people, led by a Spanish fisherman, an Air Force lawyer, and a few computer nerds, was starting to realize that a real nuclear weapon might now be lost under a real sea. And early reports noted that real Soviets—not the caricatured evildoers of SPECTRE— were circling in the waters. The bomb saga was about to shift from the parched Almería desert to the cold Spanish sea. James Bond, sadly, was nowhere in sight.

6.

Call In the Navy

Red Moody sat in the cockpit of a KC-135, looking out the window at the driving snow and thanking his lucky stars he was a diver, not a pilot. He and his dive team had been scheduled to land at Andrews Air Force Base that morning, but a snowstorm had buried the runways and air traffic control had diverted the plane to Dulles. Sitting in the jump seat just behind the pilots, Moody listened now as they discussed whether they could land in a blizzard with thirty-five-knot gusts. The pilots decided to go for it. Moody watched, with alarmed fascination, as the pilots cranked up the power and turned the plane almost sideways to approach the runway. Down they went, the snow whirring and whistling by the windows, Dulles barely visible below. Wheels touched tarmac, and the plane skidded out straight. Moody and the divers in the back breathed a sigh of relief.

Moody had been up for hours, ever since the late-night call from the duty captain at the Chief of Naval Operations (CNO). On January 22, still less than a week after the accident, Assistant Secretary of Defense Jack Howard had called the Navy. The following day, the CNO had established a task force, known as Task Force 65, to help the Air Force recover its lost bomb. Then the Navy had ordered men and ships to Spain. Lieutenant Commander Moody oversaw a group of Navy divers in

Charleston, South Carolina, who specialized in explosive ordnance disposal, or EOD. Moody's divers handled all sorts of dangerous jobs: they defused floating mines, found missiles lost in offshore testing ranges, and tracked down planes that crashed into swamps. The duty captain called Moody around midnight on January 22 and asked when Moody could get a dive team to Palomares. Moody said they'd be at the airport, with their gear, by 9 a.m.

After surviving their landing at Dulles, the divers sacked out while the maintenance crews scrambled to find fuel for the plane. The snow slowed everything down, and the divers were stuck at Dulles for hours. They finally took off for Spain that evening and landed at Torrejón the following day. They ate lunch, flew to southern Spain, and took a bus to a small Spanish town. By this point Moody and his divers had been awake for nearly forty-eight hours.

After a few hours of sleep, Moody went out to find a local tavern. As he drank at the bar, a man in a business suit sat down next to him and introduced himself as Captain Page. Cliff Page, it turned out, had just been appointed chief of staff to Admiral William S. Guest, the man who would oversee Task Force 65. The two men chatted for a while. Then Page asked Moody why his divers were still here, zonked out in the hotel, instead of reporting for duty at Camp Wilson. Red bristled at the question but played it cool. He patiently explained that his men had been awake for almost two days and were in no condition to dive. They would get a decent night's sleep and report for duty the next day. Page backed off quickly and offered to arrange a bus for the divers in the morning. Moody accepted.

On Tuesday, January 25, Red Moody, eleven divers, and about 14,000 pounds of diving gear arrived at Camp Wilson to join the growing Navy contingent. Four U.S. Navy minesweepers, an oceanographic ship, and a destroyer already sailed offshore, with a handful of tankers, tugs, and other ships on the way. A small team of EOD divers from Rota, led by Lieutenant Oliver Andersen, was setting up shop on the beach when Moody's team joined them. A young ensign followed on Moody's heels. "His sole purpose in life," recalled Andersen, "was to follow behind Red and write down everything that was happening." Andersen, curious, asked the kid for his notebook and flipped through it. "Closer we get to the scene," the ensign had written, "the more outstanding the confusion."

Moody spoke with an Air Force colonel to get a rundown of the situation. Afterward, Moody and Andersen talked for a few minutes, sharing what little information they had. Then Moody made an announcement: he was heading out—uninvited—to the USS *Macdonough,* the admiral's flagship, to see what the Navy brass could tell him. Commandeering an inflatable seven-man rubber boat, he left Andersen in charge of his divers and puttered out into the waves.

DeWitt "Red" Moody was a tall, fit, broad-shouldered man with a commanding presence and a thick Texas accent. Everyone called him "Red" because he had once sported a full head of copper-colored hair. Now, at age thirty-eight, most of his hair was long gone, his forehead rising high and bald as a bullet above his face. The nickname, however, had stuck.

Moody was a freshman in high school when the United States entered World War II, too young to join the military. He waited, impatiently, and then enlisted in the Navy in 1944, the day after his seventeenth birthday. He went to sonar school and served in the Pacific on the USS *Strong* but saw little action. When the war ended, he decided to stay in the Navy. He came from a broken family with little money, and the Navy offered him a camaraderie and security he had never experienced before. Stationed on an aircraft carrier, he met some Navy EOD divers and saw them at work. The men impressed him with their teamwork and "can-do" attitude. He decided that diving was the job for him.

EOD divers are a special breed. The job throws them into dirty, difficult situations with no obvious solution. They must solve problems in a limited amount of time—before their air runs out or something explodes—so they get used to working quickly with improvised tools. Because divers need to make snap decisions, the relationship between officers and enlisted men differs from that in other parts of the Navy. Divers speak out, show little deference, and are willing to accept ideas from the lowest man on the totem pole.

Moody excelled in this world. EOD diving became his life. After eleven years, he earned an officer's commission, one of the rare "mustang" officers in the Navy who had risen from the ranks of the enlisted. At the time of the Palomares crash, he was overseeing a team of forty-seven at his headquarters in Charleston. When an accident happened, Moody usually dispatched a three-man team to cover it. Sometimes, after a high-profile accident, he sent a larger team and went along himself. This was one of those occasions.

Red Moody steered his rubber boat alongside the *Macdonough,* chuckling to himself as he wondered what the sailors on the destroyer thought of his tiny raft bobbing in the waves. Moody jumped on board, introduced himself to the deck officer, and asked to speak with Admiral Guest. But the ship's executive officer had left word: anybody coming to see the admiral had to go through him first. The deck officer sent a messenger off to find the XO while Moody cooled his heels. After some time the messenger returned, empty-handed.

The deck officer started to send the messenger off in another direction when Moody spoke up. "I've been waiting here for quite a while," he said. "I'll just go with him." No, no, no, said the deck officer. Bad idea. You really ought to wait here. But Red Moody was done waiting. "You tell the exec where I am if you find him," he said and took off with the messenger. A few minutes later, the two men were climbing the ladder by the wardroom—the officers' mess. Moody suspected that Admiral Guest might be inside. He told the messenger to go on ahead. "You go find the XO," he said. "I'll be in here."

Moody slipped into the wardroom and saw a clutch of Navy officers, including Admiral Guest, huddled over a secret message from Washington. He moved closer to listen to the discussion. The message listed various pieces of gear that were being sent to aid the search. There was something called OBSS—ocean bottom scanning sonar—a Decca navigation system, and a couple of underwater vehicles. All the gear was familiar to Moody. In fact, it had been destined for a diving mission in the Gulf of Mexico, where one of Moody's teams needed it to recover a Bullpup missile from the Air Force test range off Elgin Air Force Base. But the Navy had diverted the equipment to the more critical mission in Spain. After listening for a few minutes to the officers puzzling over this list of strange machines, Moody realized that they didn't know much.

He piped up. "Excuse me," he said, "but that equipment was actually slated for one of my operations down in the Gulf of Mexico." As the group grew silent, Moody explained what each piece of equipment did, how it worked, and what to use it for. He stayed for lunch. Then, around 2 p.m., he asked permission to leave. Permission was granted. Red Moody jumped into his little rubber boat and went away.

The next day, Admiral Guest paid a visit to Camp Wilson. The admiral approached the beach in a small barge, which couldn't land on shore. Moody sent a rubber boat to pick up the admiral and bring him to the beach. Admiral Guest hit the sand and greeted Moody. "Did you get my message?" he asked. "You're now on my staff." Moody hadn't received any such message but told the admiral he was up for the job. Great, said Admiral Guest. When will you be ready? Now, said Moody. Admiral Guest looked at the diver, surprised. "What about your gear?" he asked. "I got people can get my gear for me, Admiral. If you want my services, you got it."

Admiral Guest was headed to a briefing with General Wilson and asked Moody to go along. Red dropped everything and joined him. From that day on, Moody remained close to the admiral. "We seemed to have a special affinity for each other, because he knew I was ready to go," Moody said. "He also knew I would not BS him. I would tell him the way I thought it was."

Guest needed all the help he could get. He had been thrown into this operation just a few days earlier—yanked from his post in Naples by an early-morning phone call—and was still trying to get the lay of the land. Guest was a no-nonsense man, hardworking, heavy-smoking, and blunt. He demanded full dedication from his staff and had little patience for slackers. A small man, he was known to some as "Little Bulldog," less for his growl than for his tenacious grip.

Guest came from a long line of military men, most of whom had served in the U.S. Army cavalry. When Guest received an appointment to the Naval Academy rather than West Point, his father devised a scheme by which the young officer could transfer to the Army after graduation to carry on the family tradition. Guest, who had fallen in love with the Navy, refused his father's offer. The elder Guest, a wealthy man, told his stubborn son that if he stayed in the Navy, he would disinherit him. Admiral Guest thought it over and refused the offer again. His father stayed true to his word; according to family lore, the two men did not speak again. When Guest's father died, he left his son one dollar.

During World War II, Guest flew a dive-bomber in the Pacific and achieved a spectacular fighting record. He was the first carrier-based aviator to sink an enemy ship in that war, a feat that won him the Navy Cross, the second highest honor in the Navy. (The only higher award is the Medal of Honor.) During the rest of his service in World War II, Guest won the Air Medal, a Gold Star, the Legion of Merit, and the Bronze Star. The Navy also awarded him several Purple

Hearts, which he never wore. After the war, he climbed the Navy hierarchy, becoming a rear admiral in 1962.

In Palomares, Guest hit the ground running, establishing a high-probability search area on the day he arrived, January 24. At the time, he already knew about the Spanish fishermen. But he also knew that the Air Force had found three bombs on land and that Navy divers and minesweepers were picking up debris and sonar hits near shore. It seemed clear that if bomb number four had fallen into the water, it had landed either in the area described by Simó and Roldán or in the shallow debris field adjacent to the beach.

However, at this early stage in the game, Guest couldn't afford to leave anything out. On a map, Guest found the point where the fishermen had plucked Larry Messinger from the sea. Guest knew that Messinger had opened his parachute immediately after ejection. If the bomb had done the same, he reasoned, it probably wouldn't have floated much farther than the airman. From Messinger's landing point, he drew two straight lines to shore, one reaching far north of Palomares, the other far south. This created a triangular-shaped search area encompassing every piece of debris, every sonar hit, and every parachute observed to have fallen into the ocean. The search area was massive: a giant pie-shaped wedge stretching from the Spanish shoreline to a point in the sea. The wedge measured just over fifty square miles, more than double the size of Manhattan. Guest knew he had to narrow it down. This was just too much ocean to search.

Oliver Andersen, left in charge of the divers by Red Moody, was doing his part to cover some ground. His divers, equipped with scuba gear, could make quick dives to 100 or 150 feet—maybe 200 feet, if they really pushed it—and spent much of the early search doing just that. Navy minesweepers collected sonar hits and handed the information to Andersen's divers, who made quick "bounce" dives to see if the contact might be the bomb. The divers found a lot of debris in the first couple of weeks: fuselage sections, tubing, an instruction manual, a survival kit bag, a wing section, wiring, fuel cells, and a flashlight. No bomb.

After a week, Andersen decided that they needed a more systematic plan. He found the coordinates of the three bombs that had fallen on land and drew a line from those into the ocean, hoping that bomb number four had landed along the same path. Then he picked points to the north and south, farther than he thought the bomb could have drifted. Having no decent maps, he used a handheld compass to mark bearings and sketch out a search area. Then his divers methodically began to swim the full shoreline, back and forth, out to where the water was about eighty feet deep.

Underwater searching is complicated, since divers can't see far and their time beneath the surface is limited. So they use something called a "jackstay." The setup for a jackstay search is simple. A line is attached to a "clump," a weight that sits on the bottom, underneath the water. The other end of the line is attached to a buoy that floats on the surface. Then a second line and buoy are attached to a second clump. Finally, the two clumps, resting on the bottom, are joined together by a "distance line." The distance line can be any length, depending on visibility and the size of the area to be searched.

To run a jackstay search, a diver swims down to a clump, puts a hand on the distance line, and swims to the other clump. (The search can also be done with two divers swimming on opposite sides of the distance line.) While swimming, the diver feels the way in front of him, hoping to find the object he's looking for. "You're basically searching like a blind man," explained Master Diver Ron Ervin. Lights are not usually useful because of the silt, unless you find an object and want to take a close look.

After the diver swims the distance line and reaches the other end, he picks up the clump and walks, say, ten steps with it in a certain direction. (He's not exactly walking, though—it's more of a half stumble, half crawl, tripping over the fins on his feet.) Then he sets the clump down, taking care to keep the line taut so he stays on course, and swims the line back to the other end. The process continues, the diver slowly covering the search area.

Divers who search for lost objects are perpetually annoyed by people who expect the search to go faster. As Ervin explained, "It's not like walking through a parking lot. You have very little visibility—you're really just putting out your hands and hoping you run into it. If the thing has any surface area, it's going to float off, and if there's current, it's going to go even further. It's like trying to look for something on land and having someone pushing you all the time."

"That's what pisses you off," said Ervin. "When people who never dive are saying 'I dropped it right there, why can't you find it?' Or even worse, 'I could have found it myself by now.' " It makes you want to say, 'Okay, go ahead. I'm taking my toys and going home.' "

In Palomares, Andersen's divers had few toys to begin with. At one point early on, the divers needed a way to see how far they were from shore. They didn't have enough line to reel off five hundred yards here and five hundred yards there. So they used toilet paper. "We found out that a roll of toilet paper was about yea so long," said Andersen. "One guy would walk over to the beach and he would hold on to a roll of toilet paper, and we would get in our boat and we'd steam out at right angles to that little beach mark until we ran out of the roll of toilet paper." At that point, Andersen dropped a buoy, marking that they were exactly one roll of toilet paper from shore. It wasn't precise, but it was better than nothing.

Back aboard the USS *Macdonough* and cruising far offshore, Admiral Guest was quickly realizing the enormity of his task. For one thing, the Costa Bomba—as people had quickly started to call this stretch of Spain—was an enigma: nobody knew much about the underwater terrain or currents, and there were no decent charts of the offshore waters. Guest had one large-scale Navy chart of the area, drawn in 1935 from old Spanish charts and slightly revised in 1962. A note on the chart read, "Some features on this chart may be displaced as much as one-half mile from their true position." Navigators soon found that this caveat was the rule rather than the exception. Someone dug up another chart that actually showed Palomares, as well as nearby Villaricos and Garrucha, but it contained so little sounding data or landmarks that navigators found it equally useless. One Navy captain named Lewis Melson had the foresight to grab an issue of *National Geographic* featuring Spain as he left for Palomares. For a while, the *National Geographic* pullout map was the best the task force had.

This would never do. Admiral Guest told the Navy he needed some real charts. On January 27, the USS *Kiowa* arrived with a device called the Decca hi-fix. The hi-fix involved three radio transmitters set up on shore. The transmitters broadcast overlapping radio waves, creating a "net" that could be read by a ship's receiver. The ship could use the radio waves to calculate its location, but only relative to the transmitters. The Navy had a grander plan: once the system was operational, the USNS *Dutton,* an oceanographic survey ship, would use the Decca net to create proper charts.

The plan made perfect sense, but it soon butted up against military bureaucracy. When the Decca hi-fix arrived in Palomares, it sat in its crates. Nobody knew how to set it up. Even worse, some of the Decca technicians were foreign nationals, from the United Kingdom, Canada, Australia, and Holland, whom the Navy wouldn't allow on site without clearance. It would be several weeks before technicians got the system up and running, several more before the *Dutton* could deliver accurate charts to Admiral Guest.

Salvage operations never run smoothly, and Admiral Guest was not a salvage expert. He was an aviator whose brain brimmed with knowledge of fighter planes and aircraft carriers. And this particular salvage operation was tougher than most, both physically and politically. The United States had lost a top secret nuclear weapon somewhere over the territory of a key Cold War ally. There was a chance that the twelve-foot bomb had fallen somewhere into the vast, dark Mediterranean Sea, a terrain filled with unknown canyons and currents. General Wilson had sent hundreds of men walking across the Spanish desert to look for the bomb, but Admiral Guest could do no such thing. If the bomb had fallen into the deep ocean, Guest had few means to search for it, much less pick it up. The bomb might as well have been on the moon.

The impossibility of the search was surpassed only by the metaphors dreamed up to describe it. Guest himself said it was "like going up here in the hills behind Palomares at midnight on a moonless night, and taking a hollow can and putting it over one eye, and covering the other eye and taking a pencil flashlight and starting to look through 120 square miles of area in these hills. It's not easy." One diver described it as "throwing a needle into a swimming pool and then blindfolding a guy and telling him to go pick that needle up." *Time* magazine compared it to "finding a needle in a haystack—or perhaps in a hayfield."

But a SAC colonel perhaps put it best. "This must be the devil's own work," he said. "If someone had sat down to figure out the hardest way to lose a hydrogen bomb, he could not have come up with anything more devilish."

FEBRUARY

7.

Villa Jarapa

By early February, the residents of Palomares who walked to the edge of their village and looked down toward the Mediterranean saw a curious sight. On the windswept Playa de Quitapellejos, edged up against the sea, sat a full-blown military camp. "The once-deserted Mediterranean coast at Palomares," said *Life* magazine, now "looks like a World War II invasion beachhead."

Around the time that Joe Ramirez was visiting Tarzan the Shepherd, General Wilson decided that his men should not be camping in a dry riverbed. A flash flood—though a remote possibility—could easily wreck the camp. Even worse, airmen tromping around in the soft sand released an awful lot of dust—possibly contaminated—into the air. Looking around, Wilson decided that the barren, hard-packed playa near Palomares would serve his needs. He ordered a section of the beach leveled, and on Friday, January 21, Camp Wilson moved to its new home.

By February 1, Camp Wilson served as home and office to more than seven hundred people, who lived and worked in seventy-five canvas tents. General Wilson had his own command center, the walls hung with photomosaic maps and status boards listing aircraft movements, available vehicles, and the number of working radiation monitors. Air

Force staff manned the command post twenty-four hours a day, seven days a week. General Wilson held a briefing every morning at 9 a.m., where staff presented summaries of the last twenty-four hours and plans for upcoming projects. Every day, Wilson sent a report to SAC Commander General Ryan in Omaha, summarizing the search and cleanup activities.

To deliver mail and supplies, Wilson established a daily courier nicknamed the "Red-Eye Special." The courier, either a truck or a helicopter, left Camp Wilson around 5 a.m. with a list of needed supplies. The courier made its way to San Javier, handed over the shopping list, and picked up the goods that had arrived from Torrejón, Morón, or elsewhere in Europe the previous day.

The Air Force sequestered all the enlisted men in Camp Wilson and told them to avoid contact with the villagers. Officers had a looser rein, however, and a few were lucky enough to find berths in town or at a seaside hotel within driving distance. Robert Finkel, the squadron commander who had slept with his head in a cardboard box, roomed above a gas station. The quarters had no shower but sported a bathtub with enough hot water for one bath. Finkel and his roommates rushed to get home at the end of each day—only the first arrival got the hot water; it was cold baths for the rest. Joe Ramirez, also rooming happily above a gas station, didn't mind the cold showers as much as the meager breakfasts. One day, he complained about his grumbling stomach to a Spanish agricultural expert, who gave the young lawyer some life-altering advice. He told Ramirez to ask for a *bocadillo de lomo de cerdo*—a grilled pork sandwich—for breakfast. Ramirez took his advice, and after that his outlook improved considerably.

Even for the enlisted men, camp life had its pleasures. Gone were the days of sleeping under buses and choking down cold C-rations. Though not luxurious, Camp Wilson offered amenities that even the villagers on the hill didn't have. Medical personnel ran a dispensary to treat sprains, blisters, and chest colds. A steady supply of water from the Navy allowed full laundry and bath facilities. The cooking staff set up an outdoor cafeteria that served three hot meals a day.

The Air Force provided entertainment as well: it borrowed a movie screen and projector from the Navy, so the men could sit on the sand and watch films at night. During the day, if the men had time and energy to spare, they played beach volleyball or touch football. The tough ones could swim in the sparkling but chilly sea.

Someone at Camp Wilson even designed a semiofficial emblem. It pictured a camp tent perched on the edge of the sea with a broken arrow—the military term for this kind of nuclear accident—in the sky overhead. Airmen took to wearing the emblem on black berets, the favored hat of the local Spanish men.

The villagers of Palomares, from their vantage point above the playa, watched the scene below with interest. To them, the rows of flapping canvas tents looked less like a military invasion than a curious patchwork quilt laid out by the sea. Among themselves, they called Camp Wilson "Villa Jarapa." *Jarapa* is a regional word that doesn't translate exactly into English. It's something like a crazy quilt or a colorful rug woven from scraps and rags.

Judging by the size and scope of Camp Wilson, an observer could tell there was more going on than a simple search for debris. Everyone knew, and the press had widely reported, that the Americans were searching for a missing H-bomb. But, much to the frustration of the gathering hordes of international reporters, the military remained tight-lipped. It admitted that the crashed planes had carried nuclear armaments but said nothing about radioactive contamination or missing bombs. According to the Air Force, the seven hundred men at Camp Wilson were simply cleaning up accident debris. The Navy was ordered to refer all news queries to the Air Force. "There are no denials. There are no confirmations," said CBS News reporter Bernard Kalb. "Only 'no comment' again and again." Kalb reported airmen wearing masks and radiation badges but could squeeze no information out of the Air Force, even after villagers told him where the first three bombs had been found. A rumor circulated that *Paris Match* was offering a week in Paris for information on the search. "So stringent is the official secrecy," reported *Newsweek*, "that for once the men in the Pentagon have refrained from coming up with a catchy name for an operation, preferring to let this one go discreetly unidentified."

Press briefings were maddening. *New York Times* reporter Tad Szulc described a typical exchange:

Reporter: Tell me, any sign of the bomb?

Air Force Spokesman: What bomb?

Reporter: Well, you know, the thing you're looking for . . .

Air Force Spokesman: You know perfectly well we're not looking for any bomb. Just looking for debris.

Reporter: All right, any signs of the thing that you say is not the bomb?

Air Force Spokesman: If you put it that way, I can tell you that there is no sign of the thing that is not the bomb. . . .

Even the Spanish reporters, no strangers to official secrecy, were impressed. They started calling Air Force spokesman Barnett Young "Señor No Comment."

The information vacuum quickly filled with misinformation and propaganda. London papers reported that Palomares had been sealed off and evacuated. The *Sydney Sun* ran a story under the headline "Death Rain from an H-Bomb." Radio España Independiente (REI), the Spanish-language Communist radio station, leapt in with both feet. Almost every day, beginning on the day of the accident, REI broadcast news of Palomares. This was no small achievement, given that it usually had no actual news to report. Sometimes the coverage simply reminded listeners that a nuclear bomb was missing and called, vehemently, for the Yankee imperialists to get out of Spain and Vietnam. But sometimes reports carried lengthy features, such as poems and songs sent in by listeners, interviews with authorities on radiation, and surveys of local farmers. (All of whom, of course, wanted the Yankee imperialists to get out of Spain and Vietnam.)

The REI stories, reporting mass hysteria and poisoned produce, sounded shrill and absurd to many. But in the absence of real information, they held power and resonance. Palomares was fertile ground for propaganda. Many of the villagers were illiterate, and the Americans told them little. For many of them, news came from gossip, and gossip often started with the radio. The radio said that the bombs had contaminated Almería with dangerous radiation, and the Americans offered little information to counter that. In fact, some Americans were walking around in masks, gloves, and sterile suits, talking about radioactivity and alpha particles. No wonder many of the villagers soon became worried.

• • •

At Camp Wilson, life for most of the enlisted men settled into a routine. The men woke at dawn, climbed into buses, and bumped across the countryside. At the appointed patch of desert, they stumbled out of the bus for another day of searching. According to the SAC final report, "It was a long, and a very trying and tiring task. Day after day, the entries in the daily operations log at the accident site simply stated: 'Ground search continued.' " Walter Vornbrock, the base comptroller at Torrejón who helped organize the search parties, estimated that searchers covered about thirty-five square miles on foot, much of it two or three times. Despite the drudgery, the SAC report said, about 20 percent of the men "found they liked the outdoor life and volunteered to remain." Of course, this meant that 80 percent did not.

Colonel Alton "Bud" White, the director of civil engineering for the Sixteenth Air Force, arrived in Palomares on January 22 to start clearing aircraft debris from the fields and hills around the village. White had two flatbed trucks from Morón and Torrejón and soon added seven Spanish dump trucks to his fleet. Because most of the Air Force personnel were searching for bomb number four, White hired ten Spanish laborers. The Spanish were, however, leery of picking up chunks of radioactive debris. Ever since the accident, Spanish and American officials had been chasing them out of the tomato fields, warning them about *radioactividad*. The families of the ten laborers, alarmed about their new jobs, persuaded some of them not to return. Of the ten men that Bud White hired, only five came back the next day. Those five figured that if the Air Force guys were picking up debris, it couldn't be that dangerous.

White soon supplemented his labor pool with forty-two fishermen from the nearby village of Villaricos. The Spanish navy had declared their fishing grounds off-limits, not out of fear of possible contamination but because their boats might interfere with the search for aircraft debris in the water. The fishermen, according to White, proved "a pretty tough crew." They were used to hard labor, long days, and handling rough fishing nets with their bare hands. White put them on the payroll, and they stayed for the entire operation.

White and his crew worked from dawn until dark. In just nine days, they cleared about 150 tons of scrap metal from the mountains and valleys around Palomares, heaping it on a junk pile just down the beach from Camp Wilson.

His men having cleared the bulk of the debris, White prepared to return to Madrid. That same day, General Wilson and the Spanish military liaison, Brigadier General Arturo Montel Touzet, arranged an assembly at the small movie house in the center of Palomares to calm the fears of the villagers.

Wilson and Montel spoke to a crowd of about 250 heads of local families. The Air Force banned members of the press from attending, physically barring at least one at the door. Speaking through a translator, Wilson thanked the villagers for their help and thanked God that nobody in Palomares had been injured. "On behalf of my Government, I would like to publicly express my most heartfelt appreciation to each and every one of you," said Wilson. "As Comrades-in-Arms in the defense against Communism, I know that the mutual admiration and high respect existing between the people of our two countries will continue in the future as in the past." Wilson assured the villagers that the Air Force would clear the land of debris and pay the villagers for damages. He avoided mention of nuclear weapons, lost bombs, or radioactivity.

Wilson knew, however, that he had a major contamination problem on his hands. When Bud White reported that his team had cleared the major debris and his job was done, he was surprised—and a bit shocked—to learn that he was not going back to Madrid but would instead take over the "detection and decontamination division," tracking down and cleaning up the scattered plutonium. White knew next to nothing about radiation. He had grown up on a farm and held a degree in agriculture. But the next day, he took charge of the cleanup effort.

White did have some expert help. A team of scientists from the Spanish nuclear agency, Junta de Energía Nuclear (JEN), had been in Palomares since a day or two after the accident. Emilio Iranzo, one of the Spanish scientists, said that when he arrived and learned that two of the bombs had broken open, he worried that they would have to evacuate the village. But after some quick air measurements, the Spanish scientists decided that the air contamination was not bad enough to warrant an evacuation. Then they tested the crops and soil and found that much of the land had received a fine dusting of alpha particles. They ordered the villagers to stop harvesting tomatoes, and the Guardia Civil enforced the rule. The villagers watched in dismay as their tomatoes ripened, rotted, and fell off the vine.

Now White's job was to calculate how far contaminated dust had spread from the two broken bombs and to map the contamination. Starting at each bomb's impact point, White drew a series of lines leading away from the crater, each line angling about fifteen degrees from the next. White's team, using a handheld alpha-measuring device called a PAC-1S, walked along each line, measuring the alpha contamination until it reached zero. They used this information to draw "zero lines"—giant squiggly circles around the contaminated areas.

Work proceeded slowly. Because alpha radiation travels such a short distance in air, PAC-1S operators—most of whom were trained on the spot—had to hold the face of the counter close to the ground to get a reading. But the PAC-1S had been designed for laboratory use; the measurement face was thin and fragile as paper and tore easily on the jagged rocks.

Despite the equipment problems, White and his team managed to run zero lines around the two bomb craters and the town itself. Their results were daunting. The contaminated area inside the circles included about 640 acres of hillside, village, and farmland. Of the 640 acres, 319 were cultivated farmland. In Oklahoma, 319 acres might add up to a couple of flat, level fields of soybeans—a tractor could plow it under in two or three days. But in Palomares, farmers had chopped the land into a patchwork of 854 separate plots, almost all of them smaller than four acres, some smaller than an acre. To separate their tiny, uneven fields, villagers had built stone walls and tangled cactus fences. Through this maze ran irrigation ditches, carrying water to the ripening tomatoes. In some fields, the crops stood thick; the tomato plants, especially, climbed high and sagged under their heavy fruit. The U.S. and Spanish governments wanted this maze of land cleared—and somehow cleaned of radioactivity—by April 1, so farmers could plant their next rotation of crops. "In twenty-four years of Air Force experience," said Bud White, "I have never, never had a challenge like this one."

While Bud White worked on a cleanup plan, something had to be done about the tomatoes. In Palomares, farmers used thin, flexible, six-to-eight-foot poles to support their tomato plants, forming dense thickets in the fields. The majority of poles and plants showed no contamination. But plutonium dust had settled in the soil around the plants, so the Air Force decided to clear the fields to the ground. "The only way you could treat that land," said White, "was to get rid of those cane poles, because you couldn't get the plow in there."

The job of chief tomato plant chopper fell to Bob Finkel. His superiors gave him a handful of men and a bucketful of machetes. Every day, he faced a new patch of tomatoes. From dawn until dusk, he and his men hacked tomato plants until the fields lay clear. Someone nicknamed the group "Finkel's Farmers," but he thought they looked more like a chain gang. By the end of a day in the blazing sun, Finkel and his crew were filthy with sweat and dirt and sticky with rotten tomatoes.

Finkel's Farmers piled the cane poles and green plants at the far end of each field for mulching and disposal. The ripe tomatoes, on the other hand, were gathered into gleaming red heaps. One news reporter wrote that most of the crop was dumped at sea, in an operation quickly dubbed "the Boston Tomato Party." But residents of Camp Wilson knew that many ended up in the mess hall.

As a gesture of goodwill, and to help support the desperate tomato farmers, the Air Force had decided to buy the contaminated tomatoes, wash off any alpha contamination, and feed them to the airmen. At the peak of the harvest, it bought 250 pounds of tomatoes a day. "Anywhere you turned around, there was a bucket of tomatoes," said Walter Vornbrock. "We could eat tomatoes all day and all night, for that matter. If you loved them, you were in Heaven."

A bit farther down the beach from Camp Wilson, somewhat aloof from the Air Force men, sat the Navy divers' tent, sometimes marked by a cardboard sign over the door reading "EOD Command Post." The divers took pride in being a bit rougher, a bit wilder, than their Air Force brethren. "The Air Force is okay," said Gaylord White, a diver who came to Palomares from Rota. "I mean, they live in nice, clean, dry places; they eat good food. But we're not used to that crap."

Noting strong winds on the beach, the divers set up their tent, holding the corners down with concrete clumps—the ubiquitous diving tools used to secure buoys and search lines—then watched smugly as other tents blew down. Inside the tent, the divers built a wooden workbench for mapping out search patterns. Underneath the desk, they dug a deep hole and buried an empty oil drum with the top cut off. They filled the drum with beer, fitted a plywood lid on top, and covered it with sand. Anyone inspecting the scene would see a diver scribbling at his workbench and never suspect that his feet rested on a buried drum of beer. "Leave it to divers," said White. "They'll find a way."

On the afternoon of February 2, Ambassador Duke flew to San Javier with his special assistant, Tim Towell, and General Donovan. The group spent the night in San Javier, then flew by helicopter to Camp Wilson to meet General Wilson and Admiral Guest. It was the ambassador's first visit to Palomares, but not his first report from the scene. Right after the accident, Duke had sent Towell and another embassy staffer, Joe Smith, to the village to survey the scene. After chatting with some locals in a bar, they had tracked down General Wilson, who was not thrilled to see them. Wilson viewed the accident as a simple military operation and saw little need for diplomats, diplomacy, or making nice with Spanish officials. "Just go in, put a clamp on the area, clean it out, and then get out of there," said Smith, describing Wilson's view. "I think they saw me being there, especially the fact that I spent a lot of time in the village . . . that that was not particularly a good thing," he added. Towell was more blunt. "General Wilson was totally dismissive of these civilian wimps from the State Department," he said. "He didn't want to play with a bunch of pointy-headed sissies. This was a job for real men."

Smith and Towell stayed for a couple of days, eventually convincing Wilson to hold a sanitized briefing for the local military governor, which Wilson did reluctantly. "If you take care of sovereign people and deal with them in a respectful way, it advances the United States national interest," said Towell. "You're not just being Mr. Nice Guy." Wilson, however, was searching for a missing H-bomb and contending with possibly massive plutonium contamination; he had little energy to devote to diplomacy. Smith and Towell returned to Madrid and told Duke what they had seen. Their report did not please the ambassador. He decided to visit Palomares himself.

At Camp Wilson, Duke met General Wilson and Admiral Guest for a briefing on the search for the missing bomb and the ongoing cleanup work. Then the ambassador visited the crash site, the junk pile, and the nearby fishing village of Villaricos. He also spent time in Palomares speaking to villagers. Duke took notes on the visit. Of General Wilson, he wrote, "His mission—to leave Spain as we found it before the accident." Below, he wrote, "delighted to learn that there is no danger whatsoever to public health. However, whole operation will continue for at least another month." Under the name of Admiral Guest, he listed the array of high-tech gear being used. He also scribbled the words *Alvin* and *Aluminaut*—the names of two minisubmarines that would soon arrive on scene to search the deep water. Most of the notes, however, related to the situation in Palomares. Farmers were working, but only in certain fields; fishermen could fish, but not in the search area; and villagers were filing claims for losses. At the top of the final page, he wrote the words "Local Morale" and underlined them. Underneath he wrote:

The population was fretting at not receiving information, and subject to rumors while idle. Now they appear to be more satisfied that they know what is going on after meeting with Genls Wilson and Montel—some have already gone back to work. Some will be picked up by the 16th. Foreign radio news was a disquieting factor, but some of the absurdities, which they could verify, tended to reassure them. Anxious that no outside labor be brought in. They are anxious to help and work.

On the back of the final page, Duke scribbled one last thought: "The people of Palomares," he wrote, "have been propelled into the Atomic Age."

Duke returned to Madrid with several new priorities. First, he had to ensure that the people of Palomares received quick, fair compensation to restore trust and keep the situation calm. Second, he had to convince the Spanish and U.S. governments to be more open with the news media.

Duke had already complained to Washington about the secrecy surrounding the operation. On January 27, he had sent a cable to the secretary of state outlining the problem. The press, he noted, had been able to "piece together essentially correct stories and TV coverage despite tight security and lack official statements." Reporters, smelling a big story and a cover-up, would not simply disappear. American officials should give them controlled information, rather than just wishing them away. "Although number pressmen on scene has declined, introduction of exotic equipment and buildup at sea has rekindled high interest; many planning return to scene shortly."

Without Washington's approval, Duke took matters into his own hands. A few hours after his return from Palomares, he called a press conference at his residence in Madrid. Though he didn't admit that the United States had lost a hydrogen bomb, he explained the goal of the operation—to leave Spain as it had been before—and said that work would continue until the job was done. He gave a detailed description of the sea search, discussing the new equipment arriving in Spain and promising to try to get some unclassified photos released. The newsmen appreciated the meeting, savoring the first solid news from Palomares. Washington was less enthusiastic. The next day, the Pentagon gave Duke a wrist slapping for ignoring its "no comment" policy. Duke, convinced his actions served America's best interest, took it in stride.

The day after the press conference, approximately six hundred people gathered outside the U.S. Embassy to protest nuclear overflights, U.S. bases in Spain, and the United States in general. The protest surprised no one; leaflets had been circulated in Madrid, announcing the place and time. Security guards shut the embassy gates as hundreds of riot police gathered outside.

At the time, it was illegal to assemble in Spain without a permit. But when the protestors—mostly students—arrived, the police let them march up and down the street for a bit, burning newspapers and chanting "Yanquis, no! Bases, no!" and other anti-American slogans. Soon, however, the police charged in, beating the protestors with wooden clubs until the crowd dispersed.

Ambassador Duke watched the scene from the fifth floor of the embassy. The protest was a minor one, but it must have reinforced his feelings about the situation in Palomares. The accident offered a rich propaganda opportunity for those who wanted the U.S. military out of Spain. Defusing the tension was going to require some creative diplomacy. But there was only so much Duke could do. The shouting wouldn't end until someone found the missing bomb.

8.

Alvin and the Deep, Dark Sea

Mac McCamis had a problem. *Alvin,* the miniature submarine he piloted, was acting up. *Alvin* and her crew had arrived at Rota Naval Air Station in Spain, about 350 miles down the coast from Palomares, after a grueling trip on a prop plane from the United States. *Alvin* was a curious-looking little sub, twenty-two feet long, with a white bulbous body and a fiberglass "sail" towering over the hatch. To fit her on the cargo plane, the crew had separated *Alvin* into several large pieces and strapped the parts onto wooden pallets. Now they had reassembled the sub and were attempting a test dive—or rather a test *dunk*—off a pier at Rota. A crane slowly lowered the rotund, three-man submersible into the water as the crew watched. Water soon covered three-quarters of *Alvin;* only the top still bobbed on the surface. Suddenly, a battery shorted out. The crew sighed. One of them signaled the crane to lift *Alvin* from the water and lower her back onto the pier.

Mac and another *Alvin* pilot named Valentine Wilson had flown with *Alvin* on the plane from the United States, and the ride had been bone-jarring. During the flight, Wilson swore he could have stood still and passed a rod under his feet, the vibrations jolted him so far up off the floor. Mac figured the same vibrations must have shaken something loose in *Alvin*. The crew removed the batteries and—sure enough—found that the connector plates had loosened, letting water leak in. They opened every battery case, then drained and cleaned each battery.

When it came to mechanical matters, Marvin J. McCamis, known universally as "Mac," almost always guessed right. In 1966, Mac was in his forties but still wiry and strong as a teenager, his eyes bright and intense beneath his flat-top buzz cut. He never exercised but could crank out one-arm pull-ups without breaking a sweat. According to *Alvin* lore, he had once gotten into an argument with an Air Force officer in a bar and the two had agreed to fight it out. The officer had grabbed Mac in a martial arts hold, threatening to break his finger unless he gave in. Mac had simply stared the officer down until his finger finally snapped.

As a teenager, Mac had dropped out of high school, enlisted in the Navy, and trained as an electrician. He spent twenty years in Navy submarines and developed a deep, innate understanding of underwater mechanics. But despite his long service and experience he remained prickly and temperamental. He had little respect for, or patience with, people who lacked mechanical skill and who failed to see things his way. "He was totally uneducated and unpolished," said Chuck Porembski, an electronics engineer who worked with McCamis. "That's why he often got into trouble."

The Office of Naval Research, which owned *Alvin*, had called Mac's group on January 22, asking them to join the search in Spain. By that point, the Navy knew that the fourth bomb might have fallen into the Mediterranean. The water at Simó's sighting was just over 2,000 feet deep, unreachable to divers. Minesweepers had scored plenty of sonar hits in the area but couldn't identify them further. The Navy hoped that *Alvin* could dive deep and investigate the sonar contacts.

At the time of the call, the *Alvin* crew had been finishing its annual "teardown," taking every last bit of the little sub apart, checking and cleaning every component, and screwing it all back together. The group was based in Cape Cod, Massachusetts, at the Woods Hole Oceanographic Institute, called WHOI (pronounced "who-ee") for short. But that winter, they worked in an empty airplane hangar at nearby Otis Air Force Base, which offered more space than WHOI. They had been tearing *Alvin* apart since November, freezing their tails off in the cavernous hangar. An adjoining building, which housed the bathrooms, had the only running water. The *Alvin* crew ran hoses from that building, across the frozen ground, to get water into the hangar. Often the hoses would split and leak, the spurting water freezing into fantastic ice formations. The crew kept warm, or tried to, with sweaters and space heaters.

Earl Hays, the senior scientist of the *Alvin* group, called the crew together and told them about the situation in Palomares. The Navy wanted *Alvin* in Spain, he said, but this was strictly a volunteer mission. Anyone could back out if he wished.

This was not an idle question. *Alvin* was an experimental sub. It had first submerged to its test depth—6,000 feet—the previous summer, under the critical watch of Navy observers. On that dive, all three of *Alvin*'s propellers had failed, leaving the sub deep in the ocean with no propulsion. But *Alvin* could float even if she couldn't be steered, and she had made it to the surface safely. Prior to the test, Earl Hays had wisely created a set of code words so he and the pilots could discuss mechanical problems without the Navy brass understanding. The *Alvin* crew had played it cool, and the Navy was impressed. The next month, the sub had had her first (and only) real mission, inspecting a secret array of Navy hydrophones near Bermuda. But Hurricane Betsey had stormed through, allowing *Alvin* to make only three dives. When she had actually managed to get below 3,000 feet, her propellers had stopped without warning, then inexplicably started, then stopped again. Before heading home, the crew had managed one additional dive, to 6,000 feet. This time, the propellers had worked but the underwater telephone had not. The sub was a work in progress.

Diving in *Alvin* was a risky endeavor, and now Earl Hays was asking the group to fly to Spain, to find—of all things—a hydrogen bomb. He asked if anyone wanted to back out. Nobody did.

"We knew the country had a big problem and had to clean it up," said McCamis. "*Alvin* had never done a project like this before. And we had no idea what we was getting into, but we was willing to try." McCamis also hoped the mission would allow *Alvin* to strut her stuff in front of skeptics. "It hadn't proven itself to the scientific parties or the military," he said. "No one was really paying any attention to it." Art Bartlett, another electronics engineer on *Alvin,* agreed. He thought, "This is it. If we can go pull this off, we're in good shape."

Bartlett had another reason to volunteer for the trip to Spain—he wanted to get off Cape Cod and out of the freezing airplane hangar.

The crew scrambled to prepare *Alvin* and pack their gear. On February 1, a cargo plane carrying seven *Alvin* crew members and 35,346 pounds of gear took off from cold, windy Otis Air Force Base and headed toward Spain. The next day, the plane carrying McCamis, Wilson, and *Alvin* followed. Bartlett stepped off the plane at Rota and smiled up at the blue, 70-degree sky and the shining sun. Woods Hole had given him $500 spending money, and the young engineer felt as if he had hit the lottery. His colleague Chuck Porembski had brought a half bottle of scotch along for the mission. He said later that he should have brought more.

When the Navy created Task Force 65, it shouldered the responsibility of finding bomb number four if it had fallen into the water. This was no small burden, and the Navy threw everything it had into the effort. On the day it established the task force, it also formed a small committee in Washington called the Technical Advisory Group (TAG). The five men on the TAG, each with expertise in salvage, oceanography, or deep-ocean work, were supposed to find technology, people, and resources that might be useful to Admiral Guest and then swipe them from other missions and send them to Spain.

Looking around for deepwater gear, the TAG found that there wasn't much on offer. The Navy, along with civilian scientists, had long struggled to explore the deep ocean. But its work, never well funded, had always lurched forward in fits and starts. By the time of the Palomares accident, *Alvin*, the experimental, temperamental minisubmarine, represented some of the most advanced deep-ocean technology in the world.

The idea of *Alvin* had been born years before, in the mind of a geophysicist named Allyn Vine. When the United States dropped nuclear weapons on Hiroshima and Nagasaki, Vine, perhaps alone in the world, saw underwater implications. Someday, he thought, submarines might carry nuclear weapons. And someday, one of these submarines might become marooned or lose one of those deadly weapons on the ocean floor. If that happened, the Navy would need a deep-diving ship for rescue and salvage.

After the war, while Vine worked on underwater acoustics for the Navy at WHOI, the idea of a maneuverable, deep-diving submersible continued to grow in his mind. Vine thought that such a vessel could complement oceanographic research. And soon he saw another military justification for such a sub. By the 1950s, the Navy had built a secret underwater listening system called SOSUS (Sound Surveillance System) to detect Soviet submarines. During the Cold War, SOSUS involved a network of underwater hydrophones, positioned on continental slopes and seamounts, listening for enemy subs. Miles of undersea cable connected the hydrophones to listening stations on land. With all those hydrophones and snaking cables, Vine saw an opportunity. A deep-diving minisub would be perfect for inspecting and repairing the system. "Manned submersibles are badly needed," Vine wrote in 1960, "to carry out on the job survey, supervision of equipment, and trouble shooting." The Office of Naval Research, swayed by Vine's arguments, signed a contract in 1962 for the sub that would become *Alvin. Alvin*'s curious name caused some consternation. Many suspected it was named for the irksome Alvin and the Chipmunks and considered it too frivolous for such a technological wonder. But the truth is that *"Alvin"* was a contraction of "Allyn Vine," the name of the man who had first imagined the sub and had had the persistence to bring it to life. A year later, a national tragedy—one with direct bearing on the events in Spain—would prove him prescient.

On the morning of April 9, 1963, the USS *Thresher* slipped from its berth at Portsmouth Naval Yard and sailed into the Atlantic. The *Thresher* rendezvoused with the USS *Skylark,* a submarine rescue ship, and together they sailed toward an operating area off the coast of Boston. The *Thresher* was the lead ship in a new class of nuclear submarines that would dive deeper, faster, and more quietly than any before and carry a more formidable payload. The ship had completed various sea trials in 1961 and 1962, and then spent nearly nine months in Portsmouth for inspection, repairs, and alterations. Now she was ready for a round of deep-diving trials.

On the morning of April 10, the *Thresher,* sailing about 220 miles off the coast of Cape Cod, dove to four hundred feet and reported to *Skylark* that it was proceeding to test depth. (A nuclear submarine's "test depth" is the depth at which she is designed to operate and fight; in this case, 1,300 feet.) The sea was calm; no other ships sailed nearby. Ten minutes later, at 9:13 a.m., the *Thresher* sent another message: "Experiencing minor difficulties, have positive up angle, attempting to blow." At 9:17 a.m., *Skylark* received a garbled message, which seemed to include the words "test depth." One minute later, *Skylark* heard the words "nine hundred north." That was the last message *Skylark* received from *Thresher.*

By that evening, rescue ships had discovered an oil slick, as well as floating cork and heavy yellow plastic, all common materials on nuclear submarines. Searchers knew that the *Thresher* couldn't survive much below her test depth, and the floating debris signaled a catastrophic failure. Within a day, the Navy knew the grim truth: *Thresher* was gone and all 129 men aboard had died, the worst death toll for a submarine accident in history. The Navy couldn't save the men, but it had to find the wreckage. The *Thresher* was the first in a new class of sub, and three more like it were already sailing at sea. The Navy had to learn why the *Thresher* had sunk, to keep the other ships out of danger. They also wanted to ensure that the *Thresher*'s nuclear reactor hadn't leaked and contaminated the ocean and to dispel Soviet propaganda on the subject.

The Navy quickly organized a task force to find the wreckage, and put Captain Frank Andrews in charge. During the search, Captain Andrews had several Navy ships and submarines at his disposal, including a deep-diving vessel called the *Trieste,* purchased from the Swiss physicist Auguste Piccard several years before. But because few tools existed for deep-ocean work, the search was slow, frustrating, and improvised. (At one point, the crew of the *Atlantis II,* a WHOI vessel helping with the search, built a small dredge from baling wire and coat hangers and dragged it from their underwater camera rig.) It took two summers for the task force to locate the debris, photograph it, and bring back a definitive piece of the sub. "One of the many lessons learned from this tragedy," Andrews wrote later, "was the U.S. Navy's inability to locate and study any object which was bottomed in the deep ocean."

Frank Andrews was not the only person to come to this conclusion. In April 1963, soon after the accident, the secretary of the Navy formed a committee called the Deep Submergence Systems Review Group. The group's mission was to examine the Navy's capabilities for deep-ocean search and rescue and recommend changes. The group, chaired by Rear Admiral Edward C. Stephan, the oceanographer of the Navy, became known as the Stephan Committee.

The Stephan Committee released its report in 1964, advising the Navy to focus research in several key areas. The Navy should be able to locate and recover both large objects, such as a nuclear submarine, and small objects, such as a missile nose cone. It should train divers to assist in salvage and recovery operations anywhere on the continental shelf. Finally and most urgently, concluded the Stephan Committee, the Navy must develop a Deep Submergence Rescue Vehicle (DSRV) to rescue submariners trapped in sunken ships. To make the Stephan Committee's recommendations a reality, the Navy created a group called the Deep Submergence Systems Project, or DSSP.

The Deep Submergence Systems Project landed on the desk of John Craven, chief scientist of the Navy's Special Projects Office, which had overseen the development of the Polaris nuclear submarine. Craven knew that the DSSP was supposed to advance ocean search and recovery operations, not military intelligence or combat. But according to Craven, the intelligence community soon saw a role for the DSSP far beyond what the Stephan Committee had envisioned. Instead of just search, rescue, and recovery, the new technology created for DSSP could be used to gather information on the Soviets, investigating their lost submarines and missiles. Craven considered this a fine idea, though it ran counter to the original spirit of the mission.

To staff the DSSP, Craven inherited a jumble of existing projects, such as SEALAB, a Navy program to build an underwater habitat where divers could live and work for months. Craven also inherited the *Trieste* and its crew. Because of the DSSP's newfound intelligence-gathering role, much of its work was quickly classified, so that money seemed to disappear down a black hole. Senator William Proxmire awarded the project a "Golden Fleece" award for its monumental cost overruns, most of which, according to Craven, were simply being diverted to secret projects.

Nearly three years after the *Thresher* disaster, on January 11 and 12, 1966, a conference called "Man's Extension into the Sea" convened in Washington, D.C., to review the progress of the DSSP. In his keynote address, Under Secretary of the Navy Robert H. B. Baldwin said that this program, while chiefly serving the needs of the Navy, would also advance civilian science, engineering, and shipbuilding, and the general understanding of the ocean. Furthermore, he emphasized, DSSP was not just another money-sinking bureaucracy. Rather, it stood ready for action:

I want to stress that we have no intention of building a paper organization with empty boxes and unfilled billets. Over 2,000 years ago, Petronius Arbiter stated:

"I was to learn later in life that we tend to meet any new situation by reorganizing; and a wonderful method it can be for creating the illusion of progress while producing confusion, inefficiency and demoralization."

The Deep Submergence Systems Program is a viable organization. It is here—*today*—to serve both the Navy and the national interest.

Less than a week after Baldwin's speech, two planes crashed over Spain and four bombs fell toward Palomares. In contrast to Baldwin's rousing speech, the DSSP was not exactly ready to leap in with both feet. The DSSP had moved forward in some areas but had postponed or neglected others. The program called Object Location and Small Object Recovery, which could have come in quite handy in Spain, was scheduled for "accomplishment" in 1968 and later estimated for completion in 1970. The Deep Submergence Rescue Vehicle, which could have swum down to search for the bomb, had not yet been built. The DSSP did have the *Trieste,* but at the time of the accident, it was undergoing a major overhaul, sitting in bits and pieces in San Diego, and couldn't be readied for a mission.

The DSSP, created in 1964 for something exactly like the Palomares accident, simply was not ready. We had "almost nothing," said Craven. "No assignments had gone on, nothing," said Brad Mooney, a thirty-five-year-old Navy lieutenant who had piloted the *Trieste* during the exploration of the *Thresher* wreckage and remained with the *Trieste* group afterward. "Then, before DSSP really gets its act together, the bomb goes down. So all that they could do was get a pickup team to go over there. And it was a ragtag pickup team." Brad Mooney and other veterans of the *Thresher* search were sent to Spain, along with a handful of SEALAB divers. But if people expected the DSSP to provide a detailed recovery plan, a crack team of searchers, and lots of shiny new gear, they would be sorely disappointed. "The Navy had achieved no interim readiness for search and recovery," said the Navy's final report on Palomares. "The entire operation, from its initial inception to its termination, was improvised."

9.

The Fisherman's Clue

Back on dry land, the Air Force continued its tedious search for bomb number four. Joe Ramirez spent his days talking to locals, collecting data for damage claims, and listening for clues about the bomb. Conflicting information, possible leads, and various complaints whizzed around the young lawyer with dizzying speed. To keep track, he started jotting notes in a narrow notebook.

FOR FEB 2 '66

1. ~~Tomatoes to Viuda de Conetero~~
2. Buyers
3. Mayor of Villaricos
4. Maj. Geir Oranges
5. Lady w/ injured arm
6. ~~Shredder~~
7. ~~Judge Advocate—will report to us at 4 p.m.~~
8. ~~La torre~~

Other pages held more interesting notes. One page read, "Antonio Alarcon Alarcon—House is next one over to south of La Torre. Have been moved out. Pig with litter of pigs—litter has to be fed. Why can't they move the pigs?" Another page listed two names already well known to many searchers: Roldán Martínez and Simó Orts.

One person who hadn't yet heard of the two fishermen was Randy Maydew, the Sandia engineer who had overseen the computer calculations suggesting that bomb number four might have landed in the sea. At the request of General Wilson, Maydew had flown to Spain to help narrow down the search area. He was surprised by how much the Almería desert resembled Albuquerque, "except for that blue, blue Mediterranean out there." But when he walked into Camp Wilson, he found that Air Force staffers didn't have much regard for eggheads like him. This changed when General Wilson discovered that Maydew had also served in the Pacific during World War II. As a navigator in a B-29 bomber, Maydew had flown thirty bombing missions, including LeMay's famous firebombing of Tokyo. The missions did more to establish Maydew's credibility with General Wilson than his engineering degrees or his years of research on bombs and parachutes.

Though Maydew had won over General Wilson, by early February he was little closer to pinpointing bomb number four. Then, one morning, Joe Ramirez stopped by Maydew's tent and told him about his interview with the Spanish fishermen. Ramirez knew that Roldán and Simó had seen something significant. Perhaps Maydew, with his engineering expertise, could put the pieces together. The engineer agreed to talk to Simó.

On the evening of February 2, Maydew and Ramirez drove to Aguilas and interviewed Simó in the mayor's office. Simó told the men his story. He told them about the small parachute carrying a half man with his insides trailing. And he told them about the dead man, floating from a bigger chute, who had sunk before he could reach him. Maydew asked the fisherman how much the objects hanging from the chutes had swung in the sky. Moving his hand in the air, Simó indicated that the "half man" below the small chute hadn't swung much, maybe about 10 degrees. But the "dead man" under the larger chute had oscillated about 30 degrees.

The information made sense: Maydew knew that the big sixty-four-foot chute would oscillate about 30 degrees as it fell, while the sixteen-foot chute would hardly sway at all. The engineer picked up a sheet of paper and roughly sketched the two parachutes, then asked

Simó if they looked right. Simó examined the drawings and shook his head. Then he grabbed the pen and sketched his own, with greater detail. The engineer was astonished.

Looking at the fisherman's drawings, it was obvious that Simó's "dead man" was a bomb, or part of a bomb, falling into the sea underneath the sixty-four-foot parachute. And the "half man"? That was clearly the empty canvas bag of the large parachute, hanging from the sixteen-foot ribbon chute and trailing its "entrails"—the packing lines—behind. Simó had sketched it with uncanny accuracy. "Before I left the mayor's office," Maydew said later, "I was convinced absolutely that he had seen number 4 go into the sea."

By the time Maydew reported his findings to General Wilson and Admiral Guest a few days later, however, he had decided to hedge his bets. In their calculations, Maydew's team took all information into account: Simó's report; the testimony of the B-52 airmen who had seen parachutes after the crash; the location of the other bombs; the tailplate from bomb number four; and other important pieces of wreckage. They also noted another new piece of information regarding the B-52's tail section: someone had found four scratches on the upper surface of the tail, which appeared to have been made by a radioactive object.

On February 5, Maydew's team briefed General Wilson and Admiral Guest on their findings. It was certainly possible, they said, that Simó had seen the intact weapon fall into the ocean. But the more likely scenario was this: After the explosion, weapon number four had collided with falling debris (possibly scratching and contaminating the B-52 tail section) and broken up in midair. The heavy nuclear warhead had probably fallen onto land and buried itself five to twenty feet below the surface. The bomb casing had drifted out to sea, where Simó had seen it fall.

Maydew's team advised the Navy to center its search on the area pinpointed by Simó. The Air Force, meanwhile, should continue its search on land, centering their efforts on a 10,000-foot-diameter circle calculated by the engineers. Air Force searchers had already combed this area, but this time they should look for a shallow depression about three to eight feet in diameter. The nuclear warhead would likely be buried below. Maydew's team printed copies of their report and distributed them on February 7. Then they returned to America, leaving a handful of replacements to continue the work.

It is unclear whether Admiral Guest didn't like Maydew's team or didn't trust their calculations, but he didn't entirely buy their conclusions. Over the next few days, as more Navy men interviewed Simó, Guest became more convinced that the fisherman had seen the whole bomb fall into the sea. On February 7, the USS *Pinnacle* again carried Roldán and Simó out to sea, where they again showed the Navy where the parachutes had hit the water. This time, Simó placed the chutes about five hundred yards west of his previous position, but the Navy men were still impressed by his story and navigation skills.

A few days later, Red Moody, who now berthed aboard the admiral's flagship, went ashore to visit Simó himself. Red spent the afternoon with Simó reviewing the story, then joined him for a late dinner. Moody, already inclined to trust the instincts of locals, found the fisherman credible. By the end of the evening, Moody thought that Simó might have seen the bomb, but he couldn't be sure. "What does a weapon look like to a person that's never seen one, when it's coming down and you're kind of busy?" wondered Moody. "Everybody on the scene was questioning: Is it intact? Is it not intact? If it's not intact, how much? If it came apart, what would happen?"

Moody drove back to Camp Wilson that evening, mulling over these questions. When he arrived at camp, he found that a storm was brewing and all boat traffic had been canceled. Marooned onshore, Red spent a miserable night in a wind-whipped tent. He tried to sleep, but his cot had no sheets or blankets. Blowing sand scoured his face all night. It was the worst birthday he'd ever had.

On the night of the big storm, Red Moody had it bad, but Mac McCamis had it far worse. First of all, he was stuck inside *Alvin* with Val Wilson, or "Slick Willie," as Mac liked to call him. Wilson, another *Alvin* pilot, always rubbed Mac the wrong way. Both men had served on Navy submarines, but Mac had spent his time with tools in hand, wrenching machinery into submission. Wilson had worked as a quartermaster, managing a submarine's operations and handling copious paperwork. On the *Alvin* team, Wilson was known for his ability to push paper through Washington, an important skill but one of little interest to Mac. McCamis called him the "clock winder." That was Wilson's greatest mechanical skill, he said—winding clocks on a ship.

Being stuck inside *Alvin* with Slick Willie the Clock Winder was bad enough, but even worse, *Alvin* was trapped on the water's surface off the coast of Palomares, moored to a buoy and rocking on the high waves. The previous day, the USS *Plymouth Rock* had arrived in Rota to pick up *Alvin* and her crew. The *Plymouth Rock* was a type of vessel called a landing ship dock, designed to transport marines and their amphibious landing craft to battle. The center of the ship contained a well deck, a cavernous compartment the size of a warehouse that flooded with water, allowing small boats to sail in and out. After the *Alvin* crew patched the sub together at Rota, they putted the craft into the *Plymouth Rock*'s well deck, parked it next to another submersible named *Aluminaut,* and set sail for Palomares. They arrived the following day.

The *Plymouth Rock* had to leave for other duties, so they prepared to transfer the *Alvin* and *Aluminaut* to another landing ship dock, the *Fort Snelling*. Wilson and McCamis sailed *Alvin* out of the well deck and tied the sub to a buoy. Nearby, the *Aluminaut* crew did the same. They planned to wait there for a couple of hours as the *Fort Snelling* moved into position and prepared to take them on. It was about 2 p.m., bright and sunny. For a while, the subs rocked placidly on the waves. Then, around 5:30 p.m., the wind began to blow.

The Navy captain Lewis Melson was sitting down to supper on the admiral's flagship with Cliff Page, Admiral Guest's chief of staff, when Page, whose seat faced out the door, suddenly stiffened and said, "Good gosh, look at that." Melson turned to see a wall of flying sand bearing down on the ship. What happened next was so dramatic that Melson recorded it in a letter home:

> We rushed out onto the main deck and were greeted with a blast of wind that almost knocked us down. Later on, we found out the gust recorded 63 knots. We couldn't see more than a few feet to seawards and the other ships had disappeared from sight. Out of the gloom came a small boat that was bearing down on our side and obviously out of control. As the boat neared us, we could see the coxswain struggling with his helm, then the canopy blew off and began to batter the passengers in the boat. The slight shelter from the side of the cruiser was enough to allow the coxswain to regain control and the boat slammed into our sides but did not capsize.

The thick cloud finally lifted and we could see the submersibles were still riding at their moorings. With the wind howling above

50 knots, all we could do was sit back and wait. We knew there were men on the subs.

When the wind picked up, Wilson and McCamis closed the hatch and hunkered down inside the tiny sub. Underwater, *Alvin* swam so smoothly that passengers could barely tell they were moving. But on the surface, especially in rough seas, it rocked and bobbed like a toy boat in a tempest. With no windows and no fresh air, it was a nauseating ride.

Wilson and McCamis spent the night in the sub, rolling in the waves and undoubtedly grating on each other's nerves. The next day, after twenty-one hours at sea, they managed to sail *Alvin* back into the *Plymouth Rock,* despite forty-knot winds and heavy seas. The two men emerged exhausted, as the crew inspected the tiny sub. Luckily, *Alvin* had suffered only minor damage, but it would still take days to repair.

Admiral Guest and the members of his staff had high expectations for *Alvin* when it arrived in Spain. Guest was eager to investigate the promising sonar hits around the area of Simó's sighting, and *Alvin* was one of the few tools he could use in such deep water. But the little sub wasn't the admiral's only hope. In addition to *Alvin,* the Technical Advisory Group in Washington had sent a few other gadgets. One was an unmanned device called the Westinghouse Ocean Bottom Scanning Sonar, or OBSS.

The OBSS, about the size of a sofa and weighing more than a thousand pounds, was a box of electronics with a propeller on one end. It was what Navy people call a "fish": a device designed to be dragged underwater at the end of a long cable. A minesweeper towed the OBSS near the bottom, and the device scanned a lane about 200 yards wide. (The device did not, however, scan directly below itself. Once the OBSS swept a lane, the minesweeper had to drag it back to overlap this blind spot.) The OBSS could work as deep as 20,000 feet, but in Spain it generally operated with a cable about 3,000 feet long.

A problem immediately emerged: the OBSS often got snagged on the rugged seafloor contours. When the OBSS sensed an undersea outcrop ahead, operators could winch it in or ask the minesweeper to speed up, either of which would raise the fish and hopefully spare it from harm. But both these tactics had a lag time, and by the time a minesweeper tried to raise the OBSS, it could be snagged, trapped, or lost. The Westinghouse technical representative in charge of the system decreed that operators could not tow the fish closer than 100 feet from the sea floor. Unfortunately, the device worked best at 20 to 30 feet off the bottom. The Navy eventually obtained three OBSS devices, so operators had some choices: they could tow low and accept a certain number of casualties, or they could tow higher and accept that the OBSS wasn't going to work very well. Or they could attempt to fix a high-speed winch to the back of a minesweeper. They needed to figure out something, because the OBSS was the only deep-water unmanned system the task force had.

The Washington group also sent Guest a handful of manned submersibles. The first to arrive was *Deep Jeep,* a two-man Navy sub that could dive to 2,000 feet but had dim underwater lights and insufficient power to fight the currents. After a few days, one of its electric motors failed.

Another sub, called *Cubmarine,* was twenty-two feet long, six feet high, and painted a bright banana yellow. It looked almost cartoonish, resembling the Beatles' vessel in *Yellow Submarine,* but was reliable and maneuvered well. The little sub held two people and could stay underwater for up to eight hours. But it could dive to only 600 feet, putting the fisherman's tantalizing search area out of its reach.

The Navy's hope therefore rested on the only deep-diving submersibles cleared for classified work and immediately available: *Alvin* and *Aluminaut.* Both vehicles were odd ducks. "*Alvin* was decidedly mongrel," wrote Victoria Kaharl in her book *Water Baby,* "a cross between aircraft, spacecraft and submarine." With its white, bulbous body, it reminded people of a fishing lure, a pregnant guppy, a washing machine, or a bottle of Clorox bleach. "When people see it for the first time, they're sort of let down," said the longtime *Alvin* mechanic George Broderson. "They have this feeling it should a long black sleek thing. Instead they see what looks like a big white toilet."

At *Alvin*'s core sat the personnel sphere, 6 feet, 10 inches in diameter, just big enough to squish three people inside and built of a new steel alloy that made the sphere thin and light enough to float on its own. The sphere rested in a metal frame that held batteries, ballast tanks, electric motors, and hydraulics. To make the contraption float, engineers designed a streamlined fiberglass hull and packed every nook and cranny with syntactic foam, a buoyant material made of microscopic glass bubbles embedded in an epoxy resin. Altogether, *Alvin* measured twenty-two feet long from nose to tail, its body only eight feet wide at the waist. *Alvin*'s batteries drove one big forty-eight-inch propeller on its tail and two fourteen-inch props on its back. The big prop could turn 50 degrees to either side, and the little ones could turn a full 360 degrees, allowing pilots to "fly" the sub like a helicopter. *Alvin* could glide along at about 2.5 knots or sprint at 6 knots in short bursts. She could stay underwater for ten hours, maybe twenty-four if the pilots conserved power, and swim down to 6,000 feet.

The only other sub in Spain that could dive that deep was *Aluminaut*, owned and operated by Reynolds Metal Company. (Company Vice President J. Louis Reynolds was a submarine buff and deep-ocean enthusiast.) *Aluminaut* was much bigger than *Alvin*, 50 feet, 11 inches long, and had greater endurance. Builders had assembled it from a series of huge aluminum doughnuts, shaped from the largest ingots of aluminum ever cast. Each massive doughnut stood eight feet tall; the builders had aligned them into a cylinder and bolted them together, capping each end with a bowl to create what looked like a giant aluminum Tylenol capsule. They had then painted the outside a bright orangey red. With three propellers the sub could cruise underwater at 3.8 knots, but its large size made it difficult to maneuver. If *Alvin* was a guppy, *Aluminaut* was a whale.

The sub could carry up to nine people, depending on the amount of gear they brought along. This is not to say that the sub was roomy. Rather, the inside felt like a subway car that had been shrunk to one-quarter scale and stacked high with luggage along the walls. The sub held two bunks that the crew usually pressed into service as work-tables. There was also a toilet, which the crew tried to use judiciously. With five to nine men in a cramped space for up to seventy-two hours with no fresh air, the sub already smelled like a sweaty locker room. No one wanted to add another smell to the already heavy air.

At the front end of the ship, a semicircular bench, padded and covered with green imitation leather, fit snugly to the inside of the hull. Sitting on the bench allowed one to see out of three of *Aluminaut*'s four viewports. The fourth viewport was under the bench, facing down toward the seafloor. If *Aluminaut* turned on its underwater lights, 1,500 candlepower of brightness would push into the gloom, allowing visibility of 100 feet.

Promotional artwork of the sub showed an otherworldly creature, armed with two grasping claws like a praying mantis, using high-powered lights to illuminate the ocean depths. Future applications for the new sub were enormous, according to press releases. It could cultivate undersea fish farms, dredge manganese modules from the seafloor, carry vacationers to underwater cities. "The Old Testament promises man 'dominion over the sea,' " said one slick brochure. "The *Aluminaut* is the first step toward the realization of that prediction."

Despite the heady propaganda, *Aluminaut* had limited prospects. During 1965, it completed diving trials and made demonstrations for scientists at the University of Miami and the Department of the Interior. Eventually it received a contract from the Navy Special Projects Office to test Doppler navigation equipment for submarine rescue. But with no other work on the horizon, the *Aluminaut* crew was eager to prove their worth, perhaps even more so than the *Alvin* group.

Despite his initial high hopes for *Alvin* and *Aluminaut,* Guest was quickly disillusioned. The admiral came from a different world than the submersibles. On his aircraft carriers, crack teams of young pilots flew the best equipment in the world. Guest expected both men and machines to perform at the top of their games. One can only imagine his thoughts when this odd-looking band of untested submersibles, bobbing in the waves like a pack of oversized bathtub toys, arrived off the coast of Spain. The subs were nothing like the high-performance jets streaking over Vietnam. They were delicate and temperamental. Even worse, each sub came with a ragtag crew of civilian operators and—in the case of *Alvin*—research scientists. Though many of the submersibles' crew members had served in the military, they had left that spit-and-polish world behind them. And the scientists had no use whatsoever for barking authority figures. Earl Hays wrote that Guest was "no great shakes." The feeling was mutual.

When the subs finally arrived, Guest planned to have them investigate promising sonar contacts, but their limited navigation made that impossible, at least at first. *Alvin* used a crude and rather unreliable method to navigate, sending pings and voice messages to a surface ship via underwater telephone. On a good day, the system could direct *Alvin* to within 400 yards of a desired point. When *Alvin* first arrived on scene, however, not even that primitive system was operating. The sub's underwater telephone worked erratically. Even worse, none of the surface ships on the scene could vector *Alvin* (or *Aluminaut*) below 2,000 feet. This situation would improve once the scientific support ship USNS *Mizar* arrived, housing gear that could navigate the submersibles with more accuracy. But all Guest knew at this stage of the game was that *Alvin* was basically blind. In addition, *Alvin*'s mechanical arm had not yet arrived. Even if the sub somehow stumbled upon the missing bomb, she would have no way to attach a line, a transponder, or anything else.

In short, Admiral Guest had no idea what to do with the subs. At one point, he suggested they drop a large concrete clump in the center of the search area, tether *Alvin* to the clump with nylon line, and let the sub swim around in circles like a dog chained to a tree. The plan would have left *Alvin* hopelessly tangled, but Guest didn't understand the subs or the deep sea. "What did he ever have to do with deep-ocean technology? Almost nothing," said John Craven of the Technical Advisory Group in Washington. "He expects another unit of the Navy to come in with bright, shining uniforms." Guest got nothing of the sort. "He was very displeased with the equipment," added Craven. "That I knew."

10.

Guest Charts a Course

In mid-February, Brad Mooney, the thirty-five-year-old Navy lieutenant who had helped search for the *Thresher,* arrived in Spain to join Admiral Guest's task force. Mooney reported to the USS *Boston,* which had replaced *Macdonough* as the flagship, and tracked down Guest in the admiral's stateroom. The young lieutenant entered the room and took a good look at the admiral. Clearly exhausted and ill, Guest sat bundled in a blue flannel shirt and leather flight jacket, with a white scarf wrapped around his neck. Every so often, a medical corpsman bustled into the room, took the admiral's temperature, and tried to feed him medicine.

Guest had slept little since he had arrived on the scene. He now understood the enormity of the task before him. His determination had turned to despair, and he poured out his heart to Mooney. He told Mooney an odd story, one that stuck with the young man for decades. Two years earlier, said Guest, he had been in the Tonkin Gulf during a questionable exchange of fire between U.S. and Vietnamese boats. This incident had led, shortly thereafter, to the rapid escalation of the Vietnam War. Now, he said, someone in the Navy was out to get him. "They sent me here to fail," he told Mooney. "I don't know anything about deep-ocean search and recovery. I'm an aviator."

Guest's remarks were curious. At the time of the Tonkin Gulf incident, Guest commanded an aircraft carrier, the USS *Constellation*, near the area. On August 2 and August 4, 1964, U.S. Navy destroyers in the gulf reported that Vietnamese torpedo boats had attacked them. Admiral Guest, as commanded, sent fighter planes to retaliate. Years later, evidence emerged that the August 4 attack most likely had not happened; sailors, confused by rain and radar ghosts, had mistakenly thought they were under fire. Guest, however, was barely involved with the initial incident, except for retaliating as ordered. And by February 1966, questions about Tonkin Gulf had not yet reached the public. According to the historian Edwin Moïse, Guest's involvement was peripheral; no one could legitimately have blamed him for anything. Moïse guesses that some in the Navy might have faulted him for not controlling the situation better, but this was hardly a major error.

Guest's stepson Doug Kingsbery also finds it unlikely that the Navy sent Admiral Guest to Palomares as punishment. The bomb search "was an extremely important mission at that time in the Cold War," said Kingsbery. "I can't imagine that the president and the high military people would not have selected the best person available they thought could do the job."

Regardless of his exact role in the Gulf of Tonkin, Guest was deeply affected by his tour in Vietnam. When he came home, his stepson Robert remembers him sleeping only two to four hours a night and smoking a carton of cigarettes a day. Faced with a seemingly impossible task in Palomares, it is not surprising that Guest grew despondent. It was not an easy assignment, even if he had not been set up to fail.

Brad Mooney listened to the admiral's story and did his best to cheer him up. He told Guest that few people in the world knew anything about finding lost objects in the deep ocean. Mooney had some experience from his time with the *Thresher* and the *Trieste* and also knew a bit about *Alvin* and *Aluminaut*. He promised Admiral Guest that he would do his best.

Soon afterward, Admiral Guest reported that Brad Mooney's arrival had been "like a ray of sunshine." Finally he had someone who understood the deep ocean and knew what to do with these ridiculous submersibles. Red Moody was also impressed with the new lieutenant, even though their similar names caused confusion when read over the ship's crackling intercom. "When Brad came aboard, he was a mover and a shaker," said Moody. "I just said, 'Here's a guy who can get things done.' " When the accident happened, Mooney had orders to report to Pearl Harbor and then take command of a submarine. During the mission in Spain, the Navy twice attempted to send Lieutenant Mooney to his original duties. Both times, Admiral Guest arranged to keep him on.

With Red Moody overseeing the divers, Brad Mooney tackling the submersibles, and the rest of his team and gear in place, Guest hunkered down and made a plan. On February 17, 1966, he laid it out in a long letter to the chief of naval operations.

First, Guest reviewed the current situation, which was not stellar. The Decca navigation system, which was supposed to have been up and running twenty-four hours after it arrived, still wasn't fully functional. The Ocean Bottom Scanning Sonar was scanning hundreds of contacts but couldn't tell if any particular contact was a lost bomb or a school of fish. (The ships of Task Force 65 didn't help matters by regularly dumping their garbage overboard in the search area, adding paint cans, soup cans, and machine shop shavings to the sonar contacts.) *Deep Jeep* was useless and had been sent back to the United States. *Aluminaut* had battery trouble, *Alvin* had sonar problems, and neither could navigate easily. *Cubmarine* was great, but only down to 600 feet. All in all, summarized Guest, "We enter this phase with equipment largely R&D and of marginal reliability and ruggedness."

Then Guest laid out his four search areas. Two were top priority: Alfa 1 and Alfa 2. One, a semicircle adjacent to the beach, extended the aircraft debris pattern into the ocean. For the other, Guest located the point where Simó had seen the "dead man" and his parachute hit the ocean, then noted eleven sonar contacts nearby. He averaged those sonar hits, noted that point on the chart, and drew a one-mile-radius circle around it. Guest also identified two other areas based on Sandia calculations. These, large rectangles stretching into the sea, were named Bravo and Charlie. Altogether, the four search areas encompassed about twenty-seven square miles of ocean. Guest had narrowed down the search area from two Manhattans to just over one. His task force would now have to sweep every inch of it for the missing bomb.

To divide these four large areas into searchable zones, Guest's team created a 132-square-mile grid system that they could lay over his charts. They first divided the area into lettered two-by-four-mile rectangles, then divided each of those into thirty-two numbered squares, each measuring 1,000 by 1,000 yards.

Guest depended on divers, sonar, and *Cubmarine* to handle the areas close to shore. Then, with Brad Mooney's advice, he made a plan for the submersibles. The more maneuverable *Alvin* got the deeper areas near Simó's sighting, where the underwater terrain rose and fell with rugged ridges and trenches. *Aluminaut* was sent to cover shallower, smoother areas, a plan that irritated her crew. Like almost everyone else, they thought that Simó Orts had seen the bomb fall and wanted to search there.

Mooney understood the crew's feelings, but he had reservations about *Aluminaut*. Aluminum, if exposed to salt water, can suffer catastrophic failures. So, for protection, builders coated *Aluminaut* with several layers of colored paint. After almost every dive, the submersible's support crew checked the hull for scratches or scars that might expose the aluminum to salt water. This vulnerability "probably scared a lot of people from using her very much," said Mooney. "Did me."

Such concerns annoyed the *Aluminaut* crew to no end. Art Markel, the manager of the *Aluminaut* team, thought his ship was far more capable than the Navy gave it credit for, and certainly more adept at deepwater searching than *Alvin*. *Aluminaut* was outfitted with search sonars that could read out to 800 feet, as well as a sweeping sonar that could see 2,000 feet. *Alvin* had nothing so elaborate. "They were using eyeballs," said Markel. "When you used an eyeball, you could see about fifty feet at the most. Fifty feet, that's all. The rest of it's black."

On one of their first dives, the *Aluminaut* sonars picked up a sunken Spanish ship, which appeared to be quite old. Markel suggested that his bosses at Reynolds contact the Spanish government regarding salvage rights. Perhaps *Aluminaut* could retrieve a cannon from the "ship of antiquity," as he called it, or even a treasure chest full of gold. He also suggested to Guest that they go back into the area and use the sunken ship as a target for calibrating *Aluminaut*'s sonar. Markel's request irked the admiral. Stop fooling around with Spanish galleons, he told Markel. We're looking for a hydrogen bomb.

Guest had little time to worry about the *Aluminaut* crew's bruised feelings. The Soviets had just cranked the international tension up a notch, putting the lost bomb into the middle of the fray. On February 16, the Soviet foreign minister handed a memorandum to the American ambassador to Moscow, charging the United States with violating the 1963 Limited Test Ban Treaty by dropping bombs on Palomares and contaminating the atmosphere. The following day, the same day that Guest laid out his search plans for the chief of naval operations, the Soviets upped the ante. At a disarmament conference in Geneva, the Soviet delegate, Semyon Tsarapkin, took the floor and read the accusatory memo to the entire assembly. Washington, said Tsarapkin, was endangering foreign lands and people with its B-52 missions. Only "a fortunate stroke of luck" had prevented an atomic catastrophe in Spain; America must end the nuclear flights without delay.

U.S. diplomats dismissed these charges as ridiculous, but they made international news and refocused attention on the missing bomb. And the Soviets weren't the United States' only diplomatic headache. A week later, President Charles de Gaulle of France announced that, by 1969, all military bases on French soil would be taken under French control. The United States, at the time, had several large Air Force bases in France, as well as a Navy headquarters and a number of Army supply and communication centers. If de Gaulle kicked the Americans out of France, it would likely heighten the importance of the U.S. bases in Spain. Ambassador Duke received assurances that the Spanish government would not take "Machiavellian advantage" of the situation, but every day the bomb stayed lost, the Spanish government gained more diplomatic clout.

Though not directly involved in any of these incidents, Admiral Guest surely felt pressure from all of them. His daily situation reports were often read by the chief of naval operations and sometimes by the secretary of defense and the president of the United States. Having to report no progress, day after day, was tremendously demoralizing. Red Moody said that he had never—even in combat—seen a flag officer under such pressure as Guest.

The admiral soon faced a problem closer to home: a Soviet spy ship, the *Lotsman,* cruising near the search areas. Guest, with permission from the Spanish, had established a large restricted zone in the Mediterranean encompassing the Alfa and Bravo search areas. He had then sent a Navy destroyer to patrol the boundaries. On February 17, the destroyer reported the arrival of the *Lotsman.* The Soviet ship was well known to the Americans—she usually cruised near Rota Naval

Air Station—and she didn't try to hide. For about two weeks Guest sent the Navy destroyer USS *Wallace L. Lind* to shadow the Soviets, just in case they tried any funny business.

The *Lotsman* sat low in the water, covered with rust. If anything happened, she was no match for the *Lind*. The Navy destroyer, about twice the size of the *Lotsman,* was built for antisubmarine warfare and armed with torpedoes, bombs, and guns. But occasionally the Soviets pushed their luck. On at least one night, the *Lotsman* steamed toward the *Lind,* trying to intimidate the American ship and force it to give way. The *Lind* held its ground. Anthony Colucci, the twenty-five-year-old lieutenant deck officer, recalled the *Lotsman* coming within twenty-five yards of the *Lind*. Colucci, who had served on an amphibious ship during the Cuban Missile Crisis, knew a few things about Cold War tension. But this was personal. "There were certainly more important strategic concerns," he said. But "when the captain is asleep and the *Lotsman* is coming in closer and closer to me, what was I thinking? I was thinking 'Oh crap, there's gonna be a collision.' "

News of the *Lotsman*'s snooping rippled through the task force, inviting speculation on what the Russians might try next. At the time, the Soviets had two advanced submersibles that could dive to 6,500 feet. Supposed they pulled a *Thunderball,* dove down, and picked up the bomb themselves? Or, even worse, suppose a Soviet submarine slipped into the search area and released a timed nuclear device? The bomb would explode, and everyone would point fingers at the Americans.

The *Lotsman* stayed on scene until early March, usually cruising between five and eleven miles away from Alfa 1. Then she vanished. Nobody knew what she had learned during her stay.

From Washington, Guest's Technical Advisory Group kept a close eye on the developments in Spain. Even if the bomb had fallen into the sea, Guest might never find it. If the admiral came up empty-handed, the Navy would have to stand before Congress—and the secretary of defense—and explain why it had spent so much money on an unsuccessful search. Heads would roll.

The TAG understood this clearly. The advisers were not only sending gear to Spain, they were also thinking about the endgame. If the search failed and the Navy brass were hauled before Congress, they would need proof that Guest had done everything possible to find the bomb. Or at least they would need something that seemed like proof—some fancy numbers to wave in front of the politicians. What they needed, they decided, was math.

John Craven of the Technical Advisory Group called Captain Frank Andrews, who had overseen the search for the USS *Thresher,* and asked for assistance. Andrews had retired from the Navy but was happy to help. He suggested that Craven call Wagner Associates, a small consulting firm outside Philadelphia. Soon Dan Wagner, the owner of the company, was flying to Washington with a member of his staff, a probability expert named Tony Richardson.

In Washington, Craven briefed the two mathematicians on the situation and gave Richardson a rough "probability map" that he had sketched. The map, which showed the area off the coast of Palomares, resembled a contour map. However, the contours on Craven's map showed not the height of a mountain ridge or the depth of an ocean trench but the probability that the bomb had fallen into certain points in the sea. Craven hadn't had much information when he had drawn the map, so his initial stab basically outlined what everyone already thought: that the bomb lay either right off the beach or somewhere near the fishermen's sighting. Craven gave Tony Richardson a copy and sent him and Frank Andrews to Spain.

On the plane to Madrid, Richardson sat next to Andrews and discussed his strategy, sketching out ideas on graph paper. He knew basically how to run a systematic search—mathematicians had been working on search theory since at least World War II. First he had to develop a probability map laying out where the bomb might be hiding. Second—this was the tough part—he had to find a way to evaluate the search as the Navy carried it out. And not just say "good" or "bad" but quantify the search, evaluate it mathematically. Then, as the search continued and new information came in, he would update the probability map, hopefully narrowing down the search area. Richardson could keep the analysis going until the Navy found the bomb or gave up the search.

On the plane, Richardson explained his system to Andrews. He thought he could call it "search failure probability." In other words, after the Navy had searched a given area, this was the probability that the bomb was there but the Navy had failed to find it. Andrews shook his head. Tony, he explained, you have it all backwards. You are dealing with the Navy. You can't talk about failure! You need to talk about *success*. Richardson objected, showing Andrews a sample probability he had plotted on his graph paper. Andrews looked at it and frowned. The line that Richardson had drawn sloped downward toward the bottom of the page. It looked like a business with a bad quarter or a stock market crash. No, no, no, Andrews explained. In the Navy, graphs need to point *up*.

Richardson and Andrews reported to Admiral Guest on February 22. Richardson's reputation had preceded him. The ship had prepared for the arrival of the distinguished mathematician, assigning him a generous stateroom with a private sink and stewards. So Guest was a bit taken aback to discover that Dr. Richardson was a baby-faced twenty-seven-year-old who looked even younger than his age.

Eyeballing this new member of his team, Guest asked Dr. Richardson what he could do for the mission. Richardson launched into a description of his plan—now called search *effectiveness* probability—and an explanation of Gaussian probability distributions. As Guest's eyes glazed over, Andrews stepped in and cut Richardson off. After the admiral escaped, Andrews turned to Richardson. Would this kid ever learn? "Tony," he said, "don't talk about Gaussian distributions to an admiral!" Later, Guest pulled Frank Andrews aside. "Where the hell did you get this high school kid?"

Soon, however, Guest began to see the value of his new addition. Richardson, working with the grid overlay of the search area, assigned each square a "search effectiveness probability" (or "SEP") number between 0 and 1. A low number, close to 0, meant that if the bomb lay in that square, searchers probably wouldn't have found it yet, either because they hadn't searched there or because they hadn't used the proper tools. A higher number, such as .95 or .98, meant that if the bomb rested in that area, the searchers probably would have found it by now. The goal was to get each square on the grid from a low number to a higher one.

Some on the task force had doubts about Richardson's system. After all, the information he used to make calculations was vague. Nobody could say for sure when *Alvin* or *Aluminaut* or OBSS had "covered" a particular area, because their navigation accuracy and the underwater terrain remained largely unknown. But Richardson had equations to cover these uncertainties. Every night, he crunched numbers using a

Frieden calculator—a mechanical adding machine the size of a cash register—in the *Boston*'s accounting office. Because the office was busy during the day, Richardson made all his calculations from about 11 p.m. to 3 a.m., the chug-chug-chug of the calculator keeping him company. At eight every morning, he presented his new chart to Guest at the admiral's daily briefing.

Guest grew to love Richardson's search effectiveness probability chart. Like all salvage missions, the search for the missing bomb was a succession of failures, one day after another of hard work, with nothing to show for it. Richardson's ever-changing numbers were the only tangible sign of progress. "It's important psychologically to have something that shows that you're actually achieving something. And SEP served that purpose," said Richardson. "It was kind of like the thermometer on the United Fund chart. It keeps going up and up."

That is to say, the numbers in certain squares kept going up and up; namely, those searched by Red Moody's inshore divers—probably the only searchers on Task Force 65 properly trained and equipped to do their job. By February 17, they had thoroughly scanned the water from the beach out to eighty feet deep. "He had guys swimming along the shore that were actually looking at the bottom with their eyes," recalled Richardson. "So I'd always have these very high numbers for Red, like over ninety percent." The numbers cheered Admiral Guest, not only because they showed progress but because he could then tease Red Moody, the towering, muscular diver, about intimidating the skinny mathematician into fixing his stats.

Deep water, however, was another story. With *Alvin, Aluminaut,* and OBSS struggling, the numbers in the deepwater boxes remained stubbornly close to zero. At times, Guest moved the submersibles inshore, probably to be able to check off a few more boxes on Richardson's chart. The submersible crews, with no understanding of the admiral's motivations, were greatly annoyed by these seemingly arbitrary moves. But the admiral didn't care, because he was greatly annoyed by the submersibles.

By the time *Alvin* and *Aluminaut* had been in Spain for a few weeks, specific grievances began to emerge. During a dive on level terrain, *Aluminaut* veered off her back-and-forth sweep pattern to examine what appeared to be a piece of airplane wreckage. The crew took photos and presented them to Guest at a meeting on the flagship. Instead of being congratulated on the find, as he expected, Art Markel received a rebuke. "What are you doing, going out of the area?" demanded Guest. "I think I'll have to send you back to the States, because you don't know how to take orders." Markel, proud of his work and his ship, was furious.

The *Alvin* crew had its own problems with the admiral. The high seas had led to several close calls for the little sub. On February 23, the waves rose too high for the crew to maneuver *Alvin* into the well deck of the *Fort Snelling,* so the Navy ship used its crane to lift *Alvin* over the side. It was a risky maneuver, dangling the fragile sub close to the side of the ship, and Earl Hays did not want to repeat it. He would not risk *Alvin* or her crew by diving in rough weather again and sent a message to the flagship stating so.

Soon after, Hays attended a briefing on the flagship. Guest told the scientist that he wanted *Alvin* to dive by 2 p.m. the following day. Knowing *Alvin* would dive only if the weather permitted, Hays replied, "Maybe I will, maybe I won't." Guest, taken aback by the scientist's insolence, asked what he meant. Hays, equally insulted by Guest's demand, replied, "If you're going to give me orders like that, Admiral, I'm going to take *Alvin* and go home." With that, Guest threw Hays out of the room. Then he turned to Brad Mooney, who had witnessed the exchange, and said, "What the hell do you do with a guy like that?"

Mooney, used to dealing with both admirals and scientists, knew that the two men came from vastly different cultures, one that demanded obedience and one that questioned authority. But Mooney also knew that no matter what their differences, these people had to work together to find the bomb. He said to Guest, "Admiral, he's a researcher. Why don't you not talk to him anymore and let me talk to him?" From that day on, says Mooney, Guest never spoke to Earl Hays. Such events soured the already strained relationship between Guest and the *Alvin* crew. Some of the crew understood the admiral, but many, according to Mooney, just "locked into their minds what a bastard Guest was."

By the end of February, Guest had all the deep-search tools he was going to get. Despite the personnel difficulties, *Aluminaut* and *Alvin* were diving and searching. The USNS *Mizar* had arrived, with hydrophones that could navigate *Alvin* more effectively. *Mizar* also brought a deep-towed camera sled to photograph the bottom. Often, the *Mizar* spent its days tracking *Alvin* and its nights taking photographs. The Ocean Bottom Scanning Sonar was up and running, at least for now. One Navy captain estimated that if all the deep-ocean gear worked well every day, they could cut the search time from three years to two.

Catching glimpses of divers, minisubs, and high-tech gear, the press played up the James Bond angle. *Life* magazine reported, "At first the *Thunderball* aspects of the great search were not discernible. But gradually the search force took on the familiar trappings: squads of frogmen emerged on the beaches, and tiny two- and three-man subs prowled the waters. Now the spirit of James Bond is all over this tiny coastal area of southern Spain." Admiral Guest would probably have disagreed. He was working with temperamental gadgets, experimental subs, and disrespectful scientists. He had nothing like the custom gear designed by James Bond's Q.

11.

The Fisherman's Catch

One Sunday morning in February, Joe Ramirez sat in the claims tent at Camp Wilson, poring over legal documents. Ramirez plunged deep into the villagers' claims, trying to place a value on each farmer's patch of alfalfa, peas, or tomatoes. As Ramirez worked, the phone rang. General Wilson wanted to see him.

Ramirez scampered to Wilson's tent to find an irritated general. "Your friend the fisherman," Wilson said, looking at Ramirez with annoyance, "has run the blockade."

Early that morning, Simó had sailed his fishing boat into the Navy's restricted area (which, as it happened, covered some prime fishing grounds). Simó had lowered his nets and caught something heavy, which he believed was the bomb. He had dragged the object to a small cove in nearby Terreros and tried to haul it up, but it had proved too heavy to reel in. Simó had radioed the Air Force with the news. I have your bomb, he said. If you want it, come get it.

Ramirez's first thought was "Damn, we finally found this bomb!" General Wilson gave the orders: Ramirez and two EOD divers should fly to Terreros and check out the situation. If Simó had the bomb, Ramirez should secure the area and report back to him.

So, at about 11:30 in the morning, Ramirez climbed into a helicopter with Red Moody and Oliver Andersen and headed up the coast.

By this point, Air Force searchers had accepted that bomb number four was probably not lying intact in an open crater. Many assumed that the bomb had fallen into the sea. But as the sea search dragged on, several other possibilities arose.

A Palomares schoolteacher said that he had seen something on the day of the accident: a large cloud of dust near the B-52 tail impact point. Perhaps, thought investigators, the bomb had buried itself in the desert sand. Searchers were ordered to mark any sort of crater, depression, or patch of earth that looked disturbed. The problem was, nobody knew what the crater above a buried bomb might look like. General Wilson asked the Sandia engineers to arrange some drop tests. They contacted their colleagues in Albuquerque, and they quickly organized a test at White Sands Missile Range in New Mexico, in a stretch of desert that resembled the land around Palomares.

The engineers at Sandia assumed that if the bomb had stayed intact before hitting the ground, the searchers would have found scattered debris on the surface. Since that hadn't happened, the engineers assumed that the bomb had broken apart in midair and that only the heavy primary or secondary sections had buried themselves underground. (These sections—top secret and possibly radioactive—were the parts of most interest to the military anyway.) They asked the scientists at Los Alamos to build some test shapes with the same weight and shape as the Mark 28 nuclear components. On Sunday, February 13, a handful of technicians and engineers gathered in the desert at dawn and watched as a helicopter hovered in the sky and dropped the shapes onto the sand.

Operation Sunday, as the exercise was called, discovered a couple of things. One was that the dummy bomb parts buried themselves about two feet underground when they landed. On the surface, they left elliptical craters about seven feet long and nearly two feet deep. Each crater and its rays, formed from moist soil, were darker than the surrounding ground, easily visible to an untrained observer. However, after a few hours, the soil dried out. Within a day, the crater and its rays were exactly the same color as the surrounding earth. The only telltale sign remaining was the shallow crater itself.

The engineer who compiled the test results recommended that all vehicular and food traffic in the search area should be "severely restricted," since it would easily destroy shallow craters. "Above all," he added, "no defoliation at all should be done until the areas have been cleared by ground-impact teams: it is probable that normal craters would be destroyed or filled in by the defoliating crews."

But trucks and buses had been swarming the area for weeks, with airmen tromping over miles of terrain and tearing up hundreds of tomato plants. If their work had damaged a crater, there was nothing to be done about it now. Sandia gave the Air Force some guidance for the next step: searchers should use long poles to probe any suspect hole, crater, divot, or ditch down to five feet. The Air Force also asked a representative from the Bureau of Mines to examine mine shafts and Oliver Andersen's divers to inspect open wells. Over the next few weeks, searchers would explore close to two hundred craters, mines, and wells.

Maydew's airburst theory was also looking more probable to everyone. In mid-February, the four B-52 airmen who had survived the explosion had urine samples tested for radiation. Only Larry Messinger showed a positive result. While his radiation level was not dangerous, it was puzzling. Messinger, like the others, had descended without an oxygen mask. Perhaps he had inhaled radioactive particles from the shattered bombs on the ground below. Or, perhaps bomb number four had broken apart in the air, and Messinger had encountered radioactive particles as he fell.

As the weeks went by, other witnesses kept emerging who had seen parachutes fall into the sea. The Spanish vessel *Juan de la Cosa* noted a parachute in its log on the day of the accident. Joe Ramirez also found a pharmacist in Garrucha, the fishing port just south of Palomares, who usually drank his morning coffee on a patio overlooking the Mediterranean. On the day of the accident, the pharmacist had had a perfect view of a handful of parachutes falling into the sea. He told Ramirez how many he had seen and pointed out where they had fallen.

As the possibilities proliferated, the searchers' morale drooped. Sweeping the fields for the sixth, seventh, or eighth time, a sense of futility grew. "This could only be considered as normal," said SAC's final report on the accident. "Even the most sincere dedication to a cause falters when nothing appears that promises to end a frustrating situation."

The helicopter carrying Ramirez, Moody, and Andersen spotted Simó's boat in a small cove a few hundred yards from the shore. Ramirez could see Simó's net resting on the bottom and something large tangled in it. He asked the pilot to circle low over Simó's boat. Catching the fisherman's eye, Ramirez signaled for him to send his small rowboat to shore. Then the helicopter settled down on the beach, and the three men stepped out onto the sand.

Simó's rowboat arrived shortly. The weather was cold and blustery. Once on board the fishing boat, Ramirez spoke to Simó while Andersen and Moody looked at the net. Something was tangled in there, but they couldn't tell what. For the sake of speed and because they didn't know if Simó had actually caught anything, they hadn't brought scuba gear. But as they studied the net, the weather began to pick up. The waves rose higher, rocking the boat and clouding the bottom with silt. Moody and Andersen soon realized that they couldn't identify the object from the boat. They would have to fly back to Camp Wilson to pick up scuba gear. Joe Ramirez decided to stay with Simó. Before the divers left, Ramirez asked them what they thought. One said he couldn't be sure, but it looked as if Simó might have snagged the bomb.

After about an hour, the divers returned with their gear. Andersen, now with two new divers, dove to look at the net. They came to the surface and yelled to Ramirez, but the wind and seas swelled so high that he couldn't hear them. Finally they delivered the news: the fisherman had caught a concrete clump. Because of the rough seas, the divers decided it was too dangerous to clear the net. They buoyed it off with flotation markers, and Simó dropped the rig from his boat.

A couple of days later, when the weather settled down, Andersen and the divers returned to the cove and untangled the net from the four-thousand-pound clump. It had anchored one of the Navy's scientific buoys, used to measure current speed. The divers cleared the clump and delivered the tangled, torn net back to Simó.

12.

Radioactividad

While the search for bomb number four slogged on, Bud White got busy. Colonel White, the man in charge of decontaminating Palomares, didn't know much about alpha radiation. But, having grown up on a farm in Texas, he knew how to run a tractor. It would prove a valuable skill in his difficult task.

Bud White did not have to clean up Palomares on his own. Spanish scientists from the Junta de Energía Nuclear (JEN) had rushed to the area soon after the accident. A week later, Dr. Wright Langham, a plutonium expert from Los Alamos, also arrived with a team. Langham was well known in the world of radioactive contamination. He had joined the Manhattan Project fresh out of graduate school and stayed at Los Alamos afterward, cultivating his knowledge of plutonium, the key ingredient in the "Fat Man" bomb dropped over Nagasaki. Plutonium exists in nature, but only in minute quantities. To get more than a few micrograms, scientists had to make their own, a feat they first accomplished in 1940. For years afterward, scientists had handled the warm, heavy metal, not knowing how dangerous it was. Everyone knew plutonium was radioactive, but nobody knew what would happen if you got some on your skin or breathed in a bit of dust. To keep workers safe, scientists began to study the effects of plutonium ingestion. Langham was involved from the start. By the time of the Palomares accident, he was the world's foremost expert on the subject, widely known as "Mr. Plutonium."

Many people involved with Palomares regarded Langham as a heroic figure, and he did much to calm the budding fears over radioactive contamination in the village. When the JEN scientists had arrived in Palomares, for example, they had taken a number of urine samples from villagers and Air Force men. Some of the urine samples had come back alarmingly high, sending the team into a panic. Langham quickly determined that the samples must have been contaminated during collection; anyone with readings that high would already be dead or close to it. Langham suggested that the scientists collect samples again under more sterile conditions. When they did, the results settled into the safe range. Langham next tackled crop and animal worries, assuring the villagers that they could eat livestock that had eaten contaminated vegetation, since animals take up little plutonium through their guts. He also told the farmers that once the Americans had cleaned up the contamination, even if a little was left behind, future crops would be safe, since plant roots could not absorb plutonium.

To Langham, the scene in Palomares was uncannily familiar. In 1962, the U.S. and British governments had cosponsored a series of four nuclear tests in the Nevada desert. The tests, called Operation Roller Coaster, examined what happened when the high explosive in a hydrogen bomb accidentally blew up, scattering uranium and plutonium without a nuclear detonation—in other words, an accident just like the one at Palomares.

Operation Roller Coaster, together with similar studies done in the 1950s, taught the scientists a lot. They learned, much to their surprise, that the greatest danger came from the immediate plutonium cloud and that the concentration of plutonium decreased rapidly with time. In Palomares, Langham said, the major plutonium hazard had vanished before anyone knew what had happened.

At the time of the accident, Langham also knew how much plutonium a human could ingest without danger. (He had used himself as a guinea pig, placing a bit of plutonium on his skin to measure absorption and also drinking a tiny amount in a glass of water.) At the time, the "maximum permissible body burden," the total amount of plutonium that a person can carry safely in his or her body, was judged to be six tenths of one millionth of a gram, about the weight of a dust particle. (Current limits, based on annual uptake, are more restrictive.) The maximum permissible air concentration was .00003 millionth of a gram per cubic meter of air, an amount akin to a grain of salt in four cubic yards of soil.

Plutonium-239, the material used in the Mark 28 weapon, has a half-life of 24,360 years. So if the Americans left any traces in Palomares, the villagers would have to live with it for a long, long time. Operation Roller Coaster was designed to study the long-term effects of plutonium ingestion, as well as the problem of resuspension—what happens when the heavy plutonium settles in the soil but then wind, weather, or people send it back into the air. But the tests had been conducted only four years before. Despite Langham's confidence, nobody in 1966 knew what the effects of such an accident would be in twenty or thirty years. But Langham, together with a team of Spanish and American scientists, plus military and government officials, had to invent a decontamination plan for Palomares now.

Studying Bud White's maps of the contaminated land, Langham calculated how much soil and vegetation the Air Force would have to remove in order to clean up the plutonium. Then, to be absolutely safe, he applied the standard "factor of ten," setting the safe levels ten times below his calculations, and created a proposal for cleanup. The Spanish officials looked at his numbers and shook their heads. They wanted more assurance that the area would be safe—that tourists would keep coming to Spain's sunny coasts, that real estate values would keep climbing, and that the farmers of Palomares could sell their next tomato crop. The Spanish drew up a counterproposal and gave it to Langham's team. They wanted the Americans to remove topsoil from more than one hundred acres of land, replacing it with uncontaminated dirt.

The Air Force considered this excessive. If the accident had happened on American soil, it would never agree to this level of decontamination. Eventually the two sides reached a compromise. The Air Force would remove any topsoil reading above 400 micrograms of plutonium per square meter. Areas with less contamination would be watered and/or plowed under to a depth of ten inches, diluting the plutonium to a safe level. This meant that Bud White's team would have to remove topsoil from only 5.5 acres of land. They would have to plow or water more than five hundred acres more.

The area around the site of bomb number two posed its own set of problems. The ground there was too steep and rocky to plow, but it was also the most contaminated. The Air Force agreed to turn the area by hand, with picks and shovels, until the radiation count dropped below the level of detection. They also agreed to work with the Spanish government to create a long-term monitoring program of Palomares and its people.

The Strategic Air Command had actually been through similar situations before. According to the U.S. Departments of Defense and Energy, there had been at least twenty-eight nuclear accidents before the one in Spain. Here are a few examples, paraphrased from official DOD/DOE records:

March 11, 1958: A B-47 left Hunter Air Force Base, Georgia, en route to an overseas base. After leveling off at 15,000 feet, the plane accidentally jettisoned an unarmed nuclear weapon, which landed in a sparsely populated area 6½ miles east of Florence, South Carolina. The bomb's high explosive detonated on impact, causing property damage and several injuries on the ground.

October 15, 1959: A B-52 bomber and a KC-135 tanker were refueling in the air, 32,000 feet over Hardinsburg, Kentucky. Shortly after the B-52 began refueling, the two planes collided. Four members of the B-52 crew ejected from the plane, but four did not. All four men aboard the KC-135 tanker were killed. The B-52's two unarmed nuclear weapons were recovered intact. One had been partially burned but did not disperse any nuclear material.

January 24, 1961: During an airborne alert mission, a B-52 suffered a structural failure of the right wing. The B-52 broke up in the air, dropping two weapons near Goldsboro, North Carolina. Five of the eight crew members survived. One bomb's parachute deployed, and the weapon received little damage. The other bomb fell free and broke apart upon impact. No explosion occurred, but a portion of one bomb containing uranium landed in a waterlogged field. Despite excavation to fifty feet, the bomb section was not recovered. The Air Force purchased an easement, requiring permission for anyone to dig there. There is no detectable radiation in the area.

These accidents were public knowledge. And many Americans, accepting the logic of deterrence, also accepted that accidents could and would happen. But they assumed that the people in control of nuclear weapons were, in fact, in control. Others were not so sure.

By the early 1960s, a public debate began to take shape, as Americans started to wonder whether they were more likely to be killed, injured, or contaminated by *American* nuclear weapons, set off by accident, rather than a Soviet attack. As the United States' nuclear arsenal continued to grow, this possibility seemed increasingly likely. With thousands of warheads stuffed into silos, trundled onto planes, and exploded in countless tests, it seemed inevitable that someday something would go terribly wrong.

Even President Kennedy grew worried. Reportedly he found the 1961 Goldsboro accident, which occurred four days after his inauguration, especially alarming. Although the Air Force never admitted this publicly, a nuclear physicist named Ralph Lapp later claimed that the bomb jettisoned over Goldsboro had been equipped with six interlocking safety mechanisms, all of which had to be triggered in sequence to detonate the bomb. "When Air Force experts rushed to the North Carolina farm to examine the weapon after the accident," wrote Lapp, "they found that five of the six interlocks had been set off by the fall." President Kennedy, shocked by this close call (and reportedly by his limited control of SAC planes during the Cuban Missile Crisis), ordered that nuclear weapons safeguards be reexamined to reduce the possibility of an accident. His order led weapon designers to equip bombs with electronic locks called permissive action links, or PALs, ensuring that only the president could launch a nuclear attack.

Yet public fears remained, played out in popular books and films of the early 1960s such as the drama *Fail-Safe* and the dark comedy *Dr. Strangelove*. *Dr. Strangelove*, in particular, openly parodied the Strategic Air Command. In the 1964 film, Colonel Jack D. Ripper (widely rumored to be based on Curtis LeMay) is a SAC wing commander at the fictional Burpleson Air Force Base. Ripper goes bonkers, overrides presidential authority, and sends an armada of B-52s on airborne alert toward the USSR. The president orders the Army to seize control of Burpleson and take Colonel Ripper into custody. This leads to several ironic battle scenes, as soldiers exchange heavy gunfire near billboards bearing SAC's motto: "Peace is our profession." Eventually, one B-52 makes it to a Soviet target and is able to drop one nuclear bomb. This is enough to trigger war.

Within the military, however, SAC was widely considered one of the strictest and safest commands. Safety was almost a religion in SAC, and its straitlaced in-house magazine, *Combat Crew,* reflected this zeal. *Combat Crew* was notable for its utter lack of levity. One regular feature was "Pilot Error," a grim comic strip demonstrating how sloppy flying technique led to deadly accidents. Another regular item, "Safety Bird Is Watching," contained a "gotcha" photograph of an airman engaged in unsafe behavior, such as wearing a wedding ring while working on a plane. The "Safety Bird" photos, most of which seemed to be taken with a telephoto lens, gave the impression that any slip would be noted and punished. Some airmen thrived in this rigid environment, but others found it oppressive. One pilot, who eventually left SAC to fly fighter planes in another command, described SAC as uptight. "You needed a checklist to take a shit" was how he put it. In many officers' clubs, pilots replaced the SAC insignia, which featured an armored fist gripping lightning bolts and a laurel of peace, with a caricature: an armored fist crushing a man's genitals.

Both those who feared and those who lauded nuclear weapons used the Palomares accident to bolster their arguments. Some said that Palomares proved how dangerous the nuclear arms race had become, endangering lives even in peacetime. Others pointed out that, until the accident in Palomares, 18,340 KC-135 tankers had safely launched to refuel 8,209 airborne-alert B-52s over Spain. One accident, out of all those refuelings, was a pretty good record. Furthermore, some boasted that the Palomares accident had actually proved how *safe* nuclear weapons were, because the bombs had endured such stress but still had not detonated.

Still, everyone could agree that losing a nuke in another country— and doing it publicly, over civilian territory—complicated matters. Operation Roller Coaster and similar tests in the late 1950s had led the U.S. Air Force to create a cleanup plan called "Moist Mop." The plan called for radiation teams to enter the area first, accompanied by EOD teams. The radiation teams would check for contamination while the EOD men tended to fragments of high explosive. Everyone except emergency personnel should stay 1,500 feet away from the accident; everyone entering the area should wear full face masks for protection. But Moist Mop assumed that the accident would take place somewhere under U.S. government control, such as an Air Force base. It didn't account for sheep, goats, tomato fields, and curious Spanish villagers. Nothing in the plan mentioned that one bomb would be found by an Air Force lawyer, another by a Spanish shopkeeper.

Thus, the early days of the Palomares cleanup were decidedly ad hoc. Any men plowing, scraping, or removing vegetation were supposed to wear gloves, surgical caps, and masks. Anyone working in a dusty area was supposed to wear a half-face respirator. Men were ordered to tape their shirtsleeves and gloves together with masking tape to keep dust out; the same with their pant cuffs and boots. At the end of every day, each man and his gear were to be checked for contamination and washed down. Some adhered to these guidelines, and enforcement certainly got more strict as the operation progressed. But many airmen recall spotty safeguards and monitoring in the beginning.

Robert Finkel, who spent many long days chopping tomato plants, says his men wore fatigues and T-shirts. Their only protective gear was hats for the sun. At the end of each day, they would decontaminate themselves by walking, fully clothed, into the Mediterranean. "Ultimately we got showers, and things improved dramatically," recalled Finkel. "But initially it was pretty tough."

Soon after Red Moody arrived in Palomares, he suggested that the Navy begin testing for contamination. The Navy regularly sampled the water and also swiped dew off ships' decks to test for airborne alpha. To the best of Moody's memory, the Navy never found any contamination, but the divers weren't entirely out of harm's way. One day, Gaylord White, one of the divers who had come to Palomares from Rota, traded a diver's knife for a warm Air Force jacket. White, happy with the swap, took his new jacket back to the EOD tent. When he arrived, one of the other divers told him to leave the jacket outside while he ran to get an alpha monitor. Sure enough, the jacket was contaminated. White, undeterred, came up with a plan. He ran a line up one sleeve and out the other, then staked the jacket on the beach below the high-tide line. After a few days of ocean washing, White let the jacket dry in the sun.

Some contamination stories had more dramatic endings. Henry Engelhardt, the commander of an Army EOD detachment in Mannheim, Germany, answered a call for assistance and sent a small EOD team to Palomares shortly after the accident. When Engelhardt's unit commander arrived on the scene, an Air Force colonel told the men not to wear protective clothing "because it might scare the locals." The Army commander refused the order and appealed to a higher command. According to Engelhardt, the Air Force colonel was finally relieved over the dispute, and the Army men were allowed to wear protective gear. However, Engelhardt, worried about the primitive safety conditions in Palomares, had a decontamination team waiting when the team returned to Germany. As suspected, the men were hot—their clothing and gear tested four times as high as permissible levels. Three men also had high counts on their fingernails, probably from putting their hands in their pockets. The decon team ordered the men to undress on the spot, bagged their clothes and gear, and sent the men to the showers. Luckily, says Engelhardt, they didn't have to decontaminate the plane.

Despite such mishaps, "Don't scare the locals" became the overriding theme regarding radiation in Palomares. When Bud White's team first mapped out the contaminated areas, for example, they marked the boundaries with red flags. This color choice "proved to be unacceptable due to psychological factors," according to the SAC final report. The Air Force ordered the red flags changed to green. Furthermore, the guardias civiles and U.S. air police who controlled access into the contaminated areas were forbidden to post signs prohibiting entry or noting the radiation hazard.

In any emergency situation, authorities want to prevent undue panic, a logical and even admirable goal. But in Palomares, it is unclear whether the Air Force crossed a line, choosing public relations over public health. When they decided not to post warning signs, they undoubtedly prevented unnecessary worry, but they also avoided embarrassing photographs being published in the international papers. It is difficult to determine which goal was more important.

This much is certain: the broken bombs certainly emitted enough alpha radiation to cause harm. And at the start of the operation, safety measures were haphazard at best. Some men, such as Gaylord White and the Army EOD team, left Palomares with high radiation readings and were monitored for months afterward. The Air Force maintains that the radiation exposures were not significant, but military health records from Palomares remain classified or heavily redacted.

After Spanish and American officials decided how much soil and vegetation to remove, another question arose: where to put it. The vegetation problem was quickly solved. Spanish officials said the Americans could burn the less contaminated vegetation in the dry bed of the Almanzora River, as long as the smoke blew out to sea.

Burning the vegetation was an operation in itself. On an average day, Bud White's team hauled 140 truckloads of vegetation to a temporary pit or the burn site, located near the former resting place of the B-52 tail section. In late February, the Air Force built a new road to the burn site so they wouldn't have to drive their radioactive haul through an inhabited area. In the end, the team hauled 3,728 truckloads of vegetation to the riverbed, and burned it all.

This left the question of what to do with the more contaminated dirt and vegetation. At first, it was generally assumed that the Americans would bury it in Spain. But to hold all the contaminated soil, they would have to dig a pit about the size of the Empire State Building lying on its side. To complicate matters, the Spanish government wanted the pit in a mountainous, uninhabited area about three miles west of Palomares.

As ideas bounced between Washington and Madrid, with Ambassador Duke, the State Department, and the Department of Defense weighing in, opinion quickly turned against a burial pit in Spain. Jack Howard, the assistant secretary of defense for atomic energy who oversaw Palomares for the Pentagon, worried about a permanent monument to the accident. A burial site could become a stark reminder of nuclear danger for decades to come, perhaps even a gathering point for annual anti-American protests. Nobody wanted that.

Spanish and American officials had already worked through this problem with regard to the aircraft debris. Neither the United States nor Spain wanted to leave the wreckage (some of which was slightly contaminated) lying around Spain, possibly leading to "lingering recriminations against the United States." Spain, with an eye toward the tourist and fishing trades, also didn't want the debris dumped in the Mediterranean. Both sides eventually agreed to dump the wreckage in the Atlantic Ocean. The Navy built a fifty-foot pier off the beach at Palomares and used a twelve-ton crane to load two barges full of debris. The USS *Luiseno* hooked the barges and pulled them through the Strait of Gibraltar into the Atlantic. By February 27, the *Luiseno* had dumped the debris into the deep ocean, in international waters about 170 miles west of Portugal.

Officials discussed whether to dump the dirt in the ocean as well or move it to the United States. Eventually, the Americans agreed to haul it to the Savannah River Facility, a nuclear processing center in Aiken, South Carolina.

To prepare the dirt and vegetation for shipment, the Americans decided to excavate a temporary burial pit at the site where bomb number two had been found. This area was already contaminated, relatively barren, and some distance from the village. The Americans dug a trench measuring approximately one thousand cubic yards and started to haul in contaminated dirt and mulched vegetation.

Once the U.S. government started stripping contaminated crops and topsoil from the land, the farmers had to be paid. By late February, the Air Force had a full-blown claims office, with lawyers interviewing about twenty people a day to assess damages to crops, homes, livestock, and livelihoods.

The claims work was as complicated as the radiation cleanup, if not more so. Lawyers had to sort out which odd-shaped plot of land belonged to whom, how big it was exactly, what had been growing there, and how much that crop had been worth. This might have been easy in Oklahoma, but in Palomares, farmers often marked property lines with buried rocks or nothing at all. Formal records didn't help: when lawyers consulted the owners' registry at Cuevas de Almanzora, they found that the entries were as much as six years behind. Furthermore, boundaries had been shifted and parcels had changed hands without being recorded. It didn't help that many people in Palomares had similar—or identical—names. Four claimants, for instance, were named Francisco Sabiote Flores; *twelve* were named Navarro Flores.

Joe Ramirez sympathized with the villagers. He did his best to be fair with their claims and give them their due, and he says the Air Force supported him. He was troubled, however, that it never made any allowance for fear, anguish, or general disruption of life. The Air Force had procedures for foreign claims and in some Eastern countries it allowed a "salve" payment for mental hardship. But there was no such plan in place for Spain. Ramirez felt that the United States had upset these people's lives and they should be compensated. It was not an easy situation, recalled Ramirez. "How do you value anxiety?"

MARCH

13.

Spin Control

Ambassador Duke stood on a rocky beach, dressed in nothing but swim trunks, loafers, a blue bathrobe, and a bathing cap. The morning air felt sharp and chilly; the blue waves, slithering on the shoreline, looked cold and forbidding. Behind the ambassador, up a slight incline, squatted a white modern building—a new parador, or government-run hotel—that seemed utterly out of place in the barren desert. The dapper ambassador, too, seemed out of place, half naked and shivering on this godforsaken strip of sand. But Duke was a man of duty, and he had a job to do. He slipped off his loafers and sank his toes into the cold, damp sand. He untied his bathrobe and tossed it aside on the beach. Then, as a swarm of news reporters watched, their cameras clicking, Duke shouted, "Okay, let's go!" With his children following gleefully behind, he ran down the beach and splashed into the 54-degree water.

A few minutes later, Duke emerged looking winded. The water was "thrilling," he told the gathered reporters. "Sensational!" As the ambassador dressed quickly, the questions peppered him: "Did you detect any radioactivity in the water?" asked one reporter. "If this is radioactivity," said the ebullient Duke, "I love it!" Another reporter questioned the ambassador: "When you were out there, did you happen to see the bomb?" Duke replied gamely, "I wish I had!"

On March 2, less than a week before the ambassador's swim, the U.S. government had finally admitted that it had lost an H-bomb in Spain. For weeks, the U.S. and Spanish governments, aware that the current press policy was neither controlling information nor calming fears, had been debating how to release more information. Duke had been pushing for a more liberal press policy since early February but could not get the two governments to agree on the particulars. The stalemate finally broke when Dr. Otero Navascuéz, president of Spain's Junta de Energía Nuclear, discussed the subject with the Spanish news agency CIFRA, which published lengthy articles on March 1. The Americans didn't know if Navascuéz had acted independently or in concert with the Spanish government, and the leak annoyed them. But it was also a relief. The Department of Defense used the opportunity to publish a formal press release. It read:

> Search is being pressed off the Spanish Coast for the recovery of material carried by the two planes involved in the recent air collision, and for fragments of wreckage which might furnish clues to the cause of the accident. Included aboard the B-52 which collided with the KC-135 tanker were several unarmed nuclear weapons, one of which has not yet been recovered.
>
> When this search and investigation have been concluded further announcement will be made of the results.
>
> The impact of the weapons on land resulted in a scattering of some plutonium (PU 239) and uranium (U 235) in the immediate vicinity of the point of impact. There was no nuclear explosion.
>
> Built-in safeguards perfected through years of extensive safety testing, have allowed the US to handle, store and transport nuclear weapons for more than two decades without a nuclear detonation. Thorough safety rules and practices also have been developed for dealing with any weapon accident which might result in the spilling of nuclear materials.
>
> Radiological surveys of the Palomares area and its human and animal populations have included detailed laboratory studies by leading Spanish and U.S. scientists throughout the 44 days since the accident.

They have obtained no evidence of a health hazard. These experts say there is no hazard from eating vegetables marketed from this area, from eating the meat or fish or drinking the milk of animals.

Steps have been taken to insure that the affected areas are thoroughly cleaned up, and some soil and vegetation are being removed.

These measures are part of a comprehensive program to eliminate the chance of hazard, to set at rest unfounded fears, and thus to restore normal life and livelihood to the people of Palomares.

Immediately, various government agencies began stumbling over one another, releasing press statements, talking points, and question-and-answer sheets in both Washington and Madrid. The Department of Defense, trying to control the situation, quickly ordered the embassy to coordinate all publicity but permitted General Wilson and Admiral Guest to handle routine public affairs matters on their own.

The press reacted to the sudden surge of information with a mixture of bemusement and sarcasm. Despite the official stonewalling, reporters had known the main points for weeks. "The news is now official. One of our H-bombs is missing," said an editorial in *The Boston Globe,* which then compared the searchers to basketball players looking for a lost contact lens. "One U.S. official insisted that the bomb was not actually lost," added *Newsweek.* " 'We just haven't found it,' he explained." *The Washington Post* and *The New York Times* ran a cartoon of a befuddled military man tipping his hat to two Spanish peasants. "Perdoneme," he asks, "ha visto un—uh—H-bomb?"

Duke was pleased with the new policy. But now that the radioactive contamination was public knowledge, he worried that Soviet propaganda could hurt Spain's largest industry: tourism. Together, Ambassador Duke and Manuel Fraga Iribarne, the Spanish minister of information and tourism, cooked up a publicity stunt to defuse any fears. Fraga was planning a trip to Almería to dedicate the new parador; Duke and his family would join him at the hotel and then swim in the Mediterranean to prove it wasn't radioactive. "If I could take my children there swimming, and go in myself, why, obviously it could not be all that dangerous," said Duke. The CBS reporter Bernard Kalb called the swim a Spanish-American effort at "aquatic diplomacy." "There are lots of things, like money," he said, "riding on this dip in the Med."

Something went awry on the morning of the swim, however, and Fraga never showed up. Duke made his chilly dip without the Spanish minister, chatted with newsmen, and posed for photos on the deck of the new parador. Then he changed clothes, threw his bathing suit into the trunk of a car, and headed a few miles down the road to Camp Wilson for a scheduled briefing.

At some point, Fraga and his entourage also arrived at Camp Wilson. Tim Towell, Ambassador Duke's aide, wondered what the Spanish officials were up to. Towell saw Fraga walking along the beach with a Spanish general and some members of the Spanish press. Curiously, the group seemed to be edging toward the water. Suddenly it dawned on him: Fraga was trying to pull a fast one. "He wants to swim *alone,*" said Towell. "He'll be dipped if he's going to share this with the American ambassador. This is *his* thing."

Towell and Duke both realized that Fraga was about to upstage the ambassador. The two men looked at each other and said, "Holy shit!" Towell tore down the beach and burst into a tent. There he found a handful of Navy divers on break, lying on their cots. Towell, huffing and puffing, asked for help. "The American ambassador needs a bathing suit," he said. "We gotta go swimming instantly, it's an emergency!" The divers said they had just come in from the water and their suits were dripping wet. Doesn't matter, said Towell—we'll take what you have.

Moments later, Duke stepped into the tent, peeled off his European clothes, and wriggled into a wet bathing suit that Towell described as a "little damp jock strap." Emerging from the tent, Duke jogged across the sand and caught up with Fraga just after he had entered the water. "Fraga's been had, so what's he to do?" asked Towell. "And in they go together."

Fraga, Duke, and a few others in the entourage splashed merrily in the sea for a few minutes, then returned to shore and chatted with reporters. Then the two men toured Palomares, greeted by cheering townspeople carrying neatly lettered signs—most likely not the handiwork of peasant farmers—praising America and General Wilson. "The humble of Palomares welcome the illustrious visitors," read one sign. "We have blind faith in the justice of your plans," said another. Afterward, Duke gave a short radio interview with Jay Rutherfurd of Mutual News Madrid:

Duke: It was with confidence and pleasure that my family and I enjoyed our swim here this morning. And soon thousands of visitors will follow our example and enjoy the beauties and the pleasures of this coast in Almería.

Rutherfurd: Mr. Ambassador, have our relations with Spain been affected?

Duke: Well, Mr. Rutherfurd, they were obviously put in jeopardy initially, to the extent that confusion and fears can always disturb relations. The Spanish government, quite understandably, was concerned as well by the possibly adverse effect on tourism, Spain's most lucrative source of income, as you know. But as the facts began to emerge and fears to fade away, a new spirit entered into our relationship. In effect, we were drawn together in our adversity.

The swim was a public relations masterpiece, making news in Europe, the United States, and Latin America. An Associated Press photo of Duke and Fraga waving to the cameras made page one of *The New York Times* and was reprinted around the globe. American papers praised the ambassador, calling the swim daring and imaginative, a stunt that had taken guts and courage. "We think of our diplomats as men who do not mind being in hot water," said *The Dallas Morning News*. "But Ambassador Duke may have been the first diplomat who had to prove the water wasn't hot." *Variety* summed up the enthusiasm with this headline: "Duke's 'Swim-in' for Spanish Tourism Best Water Show since Aquacade."

Letters poured in to the embassy from various luminaries:

THE WHITE HOUSE
WASHINGTON

March 9, 1966

Dear Angie:

I'm glad your bathing suit finally got wet. Seeing it splashed all over today's press reminded me that I can always count on you for the dramatic ideas. (Though it did look like you were more in danger of catching pneumonia than radioactive poisoning.) . . .

Jack Valenti
Special Assistant to the President

March 12, 1966

Dearest Angie—

How happy I was to see you coming out of the ocean—looking marvelous. That was such a wonderful thing of you to do—I was so proud of you. I hope you saw all the nice things that were written about you here. . . .

Mrs. John F. Kennedy

THE INSTITUTE FOR ADVANCED STUDY
PRINCETON, NEW JERSEY

March 15, 1966

Dear Angie:

. . . I trust that excessive swimming has not made you radioactive. My love to Robin.

Yours ever,
Arthur Schlesinger, Jr.

Some letters arrived from lesser-known parties. Nathan Arrow, a forty-eight-year-old Spanish translator in Flushing, New York, had this to say:

March 10, 1966

Dear Mr. Ambassador:

. . . I can understand our Government's desire to placate and assure the local residents of the area. I think, however, that it is completely ludicrous for you and Sr. Fraga Iribarne to go bathing in the freezing Mediterranean merely to prove that the waters are not radioactive. It is hardly likely that there will [be], or would have been, a great rush of Europeans and Americans to the bare and forbidding Almería coastline, particularly in the vicinity of Palomares and Mojácar. You and I both know, since we were there, that Palma, Formentor, Ibiza, Mahón, and many other points in the Balearics are far more conducive to tourism than is the barren and unappetizing coastline in Almería province. None of our protestations will assuage the worries of those poor tomato farmers in the Palomares area, so why should we make ourselves look ludicrous in trying to promote tourism, by the highest representative of the U.S. in Spain, no less, in that forsaken corner of the Iberian Peninsula. . . .

Some journalists also turned a more cynical eye to the event. "Feel safer already?" asked *Newsweek*. "Supposing a bomb is reported missing in Norway? In the winter?" asked a writer in *The Times* of London. "Perhaps in such cases the job could be suitably left to the Naval Attaché." The Moscow publication *Izvestia* also weighed in, saying that Ambassador Duke should receive the "Order of the Bath" for his feat.

At least one paper questioned the airborne alert program that had led to the accident in the first place. "For many years," read an editorial in *The Boston Globe,*

it has been part of this nation's defense setup to have bombers carrying nuclear weapons flying many hours, ready for nuclear war in case of attack. This may have been necessary in times of crisis, though it was already scary in 1961 to know that the world's stockpile of nuclear weapons contained the equivalent of 30 tons of T.N.T. for every person on the planet.

But today, when intercontinental missiles have better capability of delivery than airplanes, is it not time to call a halt to routine flights with nuclear weapons?

A few days later, Curtis LeMay added his two cents to the debate, taping an interview for CBS. LeMay had retired by this point and, dressed in a gray suit and a striped tie, looked more like a midwestern businessman than a fire-breathing general. But the old man could still shoot plenty of sparks.

First of all, said LeMay, this whole Palomares business had been "exaggerated all out of proportion." The newspapers were scaring people for no reason. The Air Force had had accidents before where a weapon had broken open and scattered a little radiation around. They had just gone in and cleaned it up, no big deal. "The chance of scattering radioactive material over a wide area," he said, "does not exist." And there was no danger of radioactive contamination at sea, even if they never found the fourth bomb.

The interviewer pressed LeMay. Is it really necessary, he asked, to have SAC bombers in the sky at all times, loaded with nuclear bombs and refueling in midair? Yes, replied LeMay, ticking off the reasons why. SAC's primary mission is to prevent war. We need to be strong, and our enemies must know this. In order to be ready for war, we have to train for war with usable weapons. Furthermore, SAC has been refueling in the air for years. "The fact that we had an accident means nothing," said LeMay.

The general ended with a warning and a plug for the airborne alert program. America's deterrent force is not as strong as it was a few years ago, he said. Our enemies are moving faster; the gap is narrowing. Cutting down the manned bomber force, depending too much on missiles, would be a mistake. With manned bombers, he argued, SAC could offer more choices to America's leaders. "A man can think and react and do things he never thought he'd have to." If war began, he wanted "a thinking man, a loyal man," at the controls. Not some mindless missile.

While the big shots handled public relations, Wilson's men started loading barrels with contaminated soil and vegetation.

The Navy requested that a radiological survey team accompany the barrels back to the United States. However, they offered to dispense with this formality if each barrel was numbered and painted with the words "Poison Radioactive Material" on the top, bottom, and sides. The Air Force balked at the request. Such alarming labels were not, they said, "in line with the spirit of the operation." After some discussion, the Navy agreed to carry the barrels with standard radiation warnings.

As the barrel loading continued, General Wilson and the Spanish military liaison, Brigadier General Arturo Montel Touzet, held a meeting for the townspeople of Palomares and Villaricos. Wilson apologized for causing any hardship and thanked the villagers for their patience and cooperation. "The payment of claims is now progressing satisfactorily and should proceed at a rapid pace," he said. "It gives me great satisfaction to see a return to normalcy for this area.

"Although my camp will disband in the near future and we will be returning to our bases, I want to assure you that our close ties will continue," he added. "We will be leaving with a great admiration for the people of this part of Spain, and I also hope that we will be leaving as your lasting friends."

On March 24, men moved the last barrel off the beach and onto the USNS *Lt. George W. G. Boyce* for shipment to Charleston. The ship left that day, carrying 4,810 barrels of Spanish soil. One chapter of the Palomares saga, it appeared, had closed.

There was still, of course, the matter of the missing bomb.

By early March, the land and sea searches were still plowing forward, but everyone was running out of ideas. A second team of ballistics experts had recrunched the numbers and come up with another high-probability area on land, which the Air Force duly searched. "By 1 March," said SAC's final report of the accident, "literally no stone had been left unturned, and no depths unplumbed. It was doubtful if any area of equivalent size, about ten square miles, was as well-known as this one."

With regard to the water search, the ballistics team interviewed the Garrucha pharmacist, took a second look at the contaminated debris, and ran the numbers again. They concluded that Messinger and the tail section could have been contaminated by dust rising from the broken weapons on the ground, rather than a midair breakup of bomb number four. Sandia engineer Bill Barton briefed Admiral Guest on March 1, concluding what the admiral already believed: that Simó Orts had probably seen bomb number four land in the water. Based on this new report, the secretary of defense authorized General Wilson to terminate the land search. The burden of finding bomb number four now fell squarely on Guest.

In Washington, officials in the Defense Department braced for a bad outcome. Guest's job seemed impossible, and Pentagon insiders began to accept that the Navy would probably not find the bomb. On March 9, Deputy Secretary of Defense Cyrus Vance created a "Search Evaluation Board" to evaluate Guest's task force, putting the physicist Robert Sproull in charge. Sproull had worked in the Pentagon for two years as the director of ARPA, the Advanced Research Projects Agency. He had recently returned to academia but still held high government clearances. Sproull was chosen for this job, he says, because he was "expendable." "It was pretty clear that if the fourth one was not found, there'd be a congressional investigation, and mud all over the face of everyone," said Sproull. "But if Congress made a monkey out of me, it wouldn't hurt the Defense Department."

The Search Evaluation Board, also known as the Vance Committee, included representatives from every agency involved: the State Department, the Atomic Energy Commission, Defense, Navy, Air Force, the Joint Chiefs of Staff, and the National Labs. Vance ordered the group to "examine all implications of the search." But its main job, everyone knew, was to figure out when, how, or *if* the Navy could safely abandon the search.

In early March, the group held a meeting that Sproull described as "very glum." The committee had two major concerns: Spain and the USSR. "We were always looking toward Capitol Hill," said Sproull, "how we would guarantee to the Congress that the Soviets would not pick it up and that it would not do any damage to the relations with Spain." The men went home that day having decided little. They planned to meet again on March 16.

In anticipation of the next meeting, Admiral Leroy Swanson, the head of the Technical Advisory Group and also a member of the Vance Committee, sent a list of questions to Guest. He wanted to know, among other things, what percentage of Alfa 1 and Alfa 2—the top-priority areas—had been searched and when the task force would finish Alfa 1. He also wanted to know the probability that the bomb could have buried itself in the bottom mud and what sort of protective screen had been placed around the area before the Navy arrived. Swanson wanted answers by Tuesday, March 15, in time for the board's next meeting. For Guest, the clock was ticking.

14.

The Photograph

On the morning of March 1, Mac McCamis stood in front of an instrument panel, manning *Alvin*'s surface controls. The day's search plan had put him in a rotten mood. *Alvin* had been searching the rough terrain of area B-29, a square inside Alfa 1, for a week, and it would dive there again today. Mac thought they had covered B-29 frontways and back and the time had come to move on. This decision, however, like so many others, was not his to make. The *Fort Snelling* maneuvered into position and opened its well deck, allowing *Alvin* to sail out into the waves. Mac directed the *Alvin* pilots to dive. As the sub disappeared beneath the surface, Mac hatched a plan.

Today, three weeks after their arrival in Spain, *Alvin* pilots Bill Rainnie and Val Wilson were piloting the sub, with Frank Andrews as a guest observer. Andrews had asked Earl Hays, the senior scientist for the *Alvin* group, for a ride in the sub. Hays, who didn't feel compelled to tell Admiral Guest who rode in *Alvin* or why, much less ask the admiral's permission, often gave the observer spot to old friends and VIPs. Andrews, being both, squeezed in for the ride.

To dive, Rainnie and Wilson vented *Alvin*'s ballast, blowing a froth of bubbles to the surface. The sub, now five hundred pounds negatively buoyant, sank slowly toward the bottom. As *Alvin* descended, the passengers felt no sense of falling. The three men sensed movement only by looking out the portholes and watching the "snow"— swirling clouds of tiny organisms—moving upward as the sea grew dark. When *Alvin* neared the bottom, the pilot flipped a switch and dropped two stacks of steel plates weighing a total of five hundred pounds. Now neutrally buoyant, the sub could cruise the area without floating up or down. (To make smaller adjustments in ballast— up to two hundred pounds positive or negative—the pilot could use *Alvin*'s variable ballast tanks, which pumped seawater in and out.) When the time came to surface, Rainnie and Wilson would drop another five hundred pounds of steel plates and float to the surface. The plates would remain on the ocean floor, a trail of breadcrumbs marking *Alvin*'s path.

The pilots and observer had their eyes glued to *Alvin*'s three viewports—one in the front center and one on either side. (A fourth viewport, on the sub's belly, was hidden by the floor and rarely used.) Each window was a Plexiglas cone twelve inches in diameter on the outside, tapering to five inches diameter on the inside. Observers peeking out these tiny windows could see only a narrow, V-shaped sliver of the world outside. Their fields of vision did not overlap; they could not see directly above, behind, or beneath the sub. Their view was further obscured by shadows, silt, and the distortion of water, which made outside objects appear closer than they were.

In Palomares, the visibility near the bottom was especially poor. On a good day, the crew could see about twenty feet. But if they accidentally brushed the bottom, the fine silt stirred into a dense cloud, an underwater sandstorm that could hang for fifteen to twenty minutes. And because the surface ship could position them within only a few hundred yards, pilots basically had to navigate on their own. In order to steer a straight line, a pilot had to look at his compass, peer out the tiny porthole, get a glance at the bottom, and look back at the compass. It was, said McCamis, like trying to walk "a straight line in a snowstorm." In much of the search area, the bottom stretched before them gray and featureless, with no vegetation or landmarks for guidance.

On March 1, as usual, *Alvin* was "flying a contour." The area loomed with steep slopes and deep gullies, mimicking the mountains alongside Palomares. The plan called for *Alvin* to stay at a consistent depth while flying along an undersea slope, looking for something lying on the hillside and snapping photos along the way. When they had finished searching the area at one depth, they could move deeper.

Mac McCamis, however, had lost patience with B-29. He noticed that *Alvin* was near an adjacent search area, C-4, closer to the actual point where Simó had seen the "dead man" hit the water. Mac asked the support ship's captain if he could "play stupid" and steer *Alvin* out of its assigned space. "You're the controller," said the captain. "Why not?"

McCamis seized the moment and sent the sub into the new area. Near the end of the dive, pilot Bill Rainnie spotted something on the bottom.

"Wait a minute, I see something," Rainnie said.

"What?" Wilson asked.

"I'm not sure, a little to the left, that's it, no, dammit, you went over it, to the right."

"What?"

"To the right, dammit! That's it, right on target."

"What is it?"

It's nothing, Rainnie said. Never mind.

The pilots saw nothing else of interest and surfaced soon afterward. Mac's gamble, it seemed, had been a bust.

When they arrived back on the *Fort Snelling,* the pilots handed off their film for developing. That night at their briefing, the *Alvin* crew gathered around the latest batch of photos. Mac, looking at the pictures, spotted something odd—a curious track in the sediment. It looked, he said, "like a barrel had been dragged over the bottom, end to end." Brad Mooney agreed with Mac. "To me, it looked like a torpedo had slid down," said Mooney. "It had a curved shape to it, all the way down."

The pilots were excited. What they were seeing, they hoped, was the track of bomb number four sliding down the undersea slope. The next day, this time with official permission, the *Alvin* crew returned to the area to look for the track. They couldn't find it. They returned on March 3, 4, and 7, combing the bottom, going over and over the area where they had photographed the track. Nothing.

On March 8, the day of Ambassador Duke's swim, the task force suddenly yanked *Alvin* off the trail and sent her to search a shallow inshore area. Near the beach, some undersea gullies plunged too deep for Navy divers to search. Most likely, Admiral Guest had sent *Alvin* to investigate these gullies so he could check another square off his chart. But whatever the admiral's intentions, the *Alvin* crew received no explanation for the sudden change and no information about when they could return to the promising track. The move, which seemed completely arbitrary, demoralized the crew and hardened their attitudes toward Guest. "My turn at surface control," grumbled Mac, "and we're still messing around in 800 feet of water."

By the third week in March, the mood of the searchers had settled into a mix of frustration, boredom, determination, and despair. *Alvin* moved back to deeper water but couldn't find the mysterious track. *Aluminaut,* likewise, was coming up empty-handed. The Ocean Bottom Scanning Sonar, Task Force 65's only unmanned deep search system, made nine runs over a dummy test shape and couldn't find it. On March 12, an OBSS towed by the USS *Notable* snagged a ridge, snapped its line, and never came up from the bottom.

The divers had wrapped up most of their inshore search, leaving Red Moody without much to do. Guest asked the long-faced Moody if he wanted to head home to Charleston. With little work left for him in Spain, Red agreed. On March 14, Red Moody flew to Rota Naval Air Station to catch a plane home.

Ambassador Duke, picking up on the mood in Palomares and catching wind of the shifting tone in Washington, sensed that the search might soon be called off. Trying to ensure his role in the endgame, Duke wrote to Jack Valenti, special assistant to Lyndon Johnson:

Madrid, March 14, 1966

CONFIDENTIAL

Dear Jack:

Word has reached me that Cy Vance is heading up an interdepartmental group to cover all aspects of the search and recovery operations in connection with the nuclear weapon problems here in the Palomares area of Spain.

This brings to mind the possibility that the search for the missing device might be called off. The Spanish Government, of course, is not unaware of this possibility, and I foresee no irreparable damage to our relationships if such a decision is handled extremely carefully and properly. Through other channels I am suggesting to the Department that thought be given to my being called back to go over in great detail how such a step should be handled. I have in mind recommendations such as a hand-carried letter from the President to the Chief of State here giving him personal reassurances in the matter.

I write you now (events happen so fast) in order to head off any possibility of premature announcements, either at the White House level or State Department level, before I would be given an opportunity to be heard and subsequently empowered to handle the matter at this end. The manner in which the Palomares incident is terminated will be of great importance not only in Spain but to every nation in the world where there are nuclear overflights or bases.

With every best wish,
Sincerely,
Angie

On the following day, Tuesday, March 15, Tony Richardson, the baby-faced mathematician analyzing the search for Admiral Guest, sat on a small boat skipping across the waves toward Camp Wilson. Along with a WHOI oceanographer named John Bruce, Richardson planned to pick up Simó Orts and revisit, once again, the area of his parachute sighting. The Navy searchers worried that they had misread Simó's point and were searching the wrong area. Perhaps another outing with Simó, now widely known as "Paco de la Bomba," could set their minds at ease.

Richardson arrived at Camp Wilson around 10 a.m. to meet Simó and the Navy men who had driven the fisherman from Aguilas. The group climbed back onto the boat and headed out to the minesweeper USS *Salute*. Over coffee, the men discussed the search. Simó told the group that he had taken a fathometer tracing on the day of the accident—perhaps it contained some clues. He also let the men in on a plan. By attaching some small lines and hooks to his trawling nets, he said, he could probably grab the bomb's parachute. If the Navy didn't find it soon—or abandoned the search—he just might go out there and snag it himself.

• • •

While Simó and his group chatted, Admiral Guest sat on the USS *Boston*. His response to the Cyrus Vance committee was due in Washington that day, and Guest and his team had been working on it for four days. The long memo answered all the committee's questions in comprehensive detail. In it, Guest explained Richardson's search effectiveness probability, estimating that he needed thirty more working days to bring Alfa 1 to 95 percent. For Alfa 2, he would need only twelve more days. There was, however, an undersea canyon stretching between the two search areas, its slopes and floor slimy with ooze. The weapon could be lying there, completely buried in the mud, invisible.

On that same morning, the *Alvin* crew prepared for their last dive in the area where they had seen the track. They were supposed to get a new transponder installed that morning to allow the *Mizar* to track them within about 130 feet. After that, they would be transferred to Bravo, a secondary search area. However, when the new gear arrived, it required two days of bench testing before installation in *Alvin*. Knowing that *Alvin* would be sitting idle, Brad Mooney nagged Admiral Guest for another day in C-4. Guest brushed him off. The area had already been searched to 98 percent. It was time to move on. But Mooney persisted. "All right, goddamn it," Guest told Mooney. "One more day, and that's all."

That day Mac McCamis and Val Wilson piloted the sub, with a WHOI technician, Art Bartlett, tagging along as the observer. As the sub descended, Mac spoke to Bill Rainnie, who was the surface controller that day. Mac told Rainnie to put them right on the elusive track, because today was his son's birthday.

Alvin drifted down, and almost as soon as the sub reached the bottom, Wilson saw the track. He snapped pictures and shouted directions to McCamis, as the pilot struggled to hover near the track without stirring up clouds of silt. Soon Mac could see the track out the front window—it seemed to head down a steep slope, about 70 degrees. Mac decided to follow the track by backing down the slope, so he could see it out the front window. Slowly, Mac edged down as Bartlett and Wilson called out directions. The sub reached about 2,500 feet. Then, the two men started shouting, "That's it!" "That's it!"

Outside, on the gray bottom, lay a massive parachute. Underneath, the men saw the shape of a bomb.

The task force had established code words for the search. If the *Alvin* pilots spotted the bomb, they were supposed to say the words "instrument panel." Wilson, in his excitement, forgot the code and shouted over the phone, "We found a parachute and we believe we have a fin of the bomb in sight! It's underneath the parachute!"

"Had a hell of a time shutting him up," said Mac.

That morning, the USS *Albany* had arrived to relieve the *Boston* as Task Force 65's flagship. Admiral Guest invited the *Albany*'s captain to lunch before the ceremonial transfer of the flag. During lunch, an aide burst into the room to hand Guest a slip of paper. The note read, "ALVIN reports INSTRUMENT PANEL." Guest read it, rose from the table, and hurried off without explanation. Someone else would have to handle the ceremony.

On board the minesweeper USS *Salute*, lunch was also under way. Tony Richardson, Simó Orts, and the others had just started eating when the commanding officer entered the wardroom to tell the group that *Alvin* had sighted the weapon. The Navy men rushed off, leaving Richardson and Bruce to escort Simó back to the beach. When the group arrived at Camp Wilson, an Air Force helicopter flew them to Aguilas. John Bruce, the oceanographer, arranged to visit Simó the next evening to look at the fathometer trace. After all, there was still a chance that the *Alvin* crew was wrong.

Deep below the surface, Val Wilson snapped pictures of *Alvin*'s prize. Then Mac eased *Alvin* away from the parachute to avoid tangling the submersible in the straps or shrouds. He wedged the sub into a crevice just below the chute, so they could keep an eye on it and not accidentally drift away in the current. Then he shut off the lights to conserve power and waited for instructions from the surface. One of the men reached into his pocket and pulled out a cigarette. Smoking was, of course, prohibited in the sub. But the three men, all heavy smokers, knew they might be down there for a while and decided to give it a go. Bartlett, the technician, knew the air system inside and out and figured he could pull this off without incinerating or suffocating the crew. He turned up the oxygen, gave the crew a good blast, then shut it off. They lit the cigarette and passed it around, inhaling deeply. Then Bartlett cranked up the CO_2 scrubber, hoping for the best. McCamis and Wilson, having both served on submarines, could sense when the CO_2 approached the danger zone. At least that's what they told Bartlett, who watched the gauges and hoped they were right.

While they waited, the men discussed what to do if they accidentally hooked the bomb or the chute. They all agreed that they could just drop a battery and surface, dragging the bomb with them. *Alvin*'s total battery weight, however, was only about 750 pounds. The bomb weighed more than two tons. There was no way they could pull it up. The military had never told the *Alvin* crew how much the secret weapon weighed. It was the mushroom theory, said Bartlett: "Feed them shit and keep them in the dark."

On the surface, Admiral Guest and Brad Mooney discussed options. *Alvin* could remain submerged for twenty-four hours—tops—if the pilots conserved power, meaning it had about twenty hours left. Mooney suggested sending *Aluminaut* down to rendezvous with *Alvin*. If the larger sub carried a transponder, the surface ship *Mizar* could fix her position when she got near the bomb. The rendezvous was a risky proposition, and Mooney knew it. At that depth, the silt and snow scattered light, allowing even powerful beams to pierce only about sixty feet. And depending on a sub's momentum, sixty feet might be too short to stop if the pilot suddenly saw trouble ahead. Generally, pilots avoided running two submersibles anywhere near each other under the sea. Mooney wanted to break this rule. What he proposed was much like sending two cars to meet in a midnight blizzard, on an icy road unfamiliar to both drivers. It would be dangerous, but it was their best option.

Guest readily agreed to the plan, liking the idea of keeping human eyes on the target. But he had difficulty comprehending the risk involved. "I can fly my F4s wingtip to wingtip at Mach speed and they don't hit each other," he told one staffer. "You guys can't even go in the same *area* and stay out of each other's way?"

Mooney summoned *Aluminaut*. The sub picked up a transponder, got a quick battery charge, and hustled over to the search area. Though disappointed that *Alvin* had found the bomb first, the crew was glad they had an important role to play. On the way down, Admiral Guest and his staff told the *Aluminaut* crew, more than once, not to touch the bomb or try to recover it. "He thought we were a bunch of wild cowboys down there," grumbled Art Markel.

The *Alvin* crew sat in the dark, on the bottom of the cold sea, for eight hours, waiting for *Aluminaut*. Finally, peeking through their windows, the crew saw the glow of lights in the distance. "It was beautiful, the most beautiful thing I ever saw," said McCamis. "A great silvery-pink monster, it looked like, with great green phosphorescent eyes coming up silent through the water." Mac flipped on *Alvin*'s lights, giving *Aluminaut* a clear target. *Aluminaut* approached slowly, cautiously parking herself about twenty-five yards behind *Alvin,* in clear sight of the parachute. The *Aluminaut* held steady as *Alvin* left her station and rose to the surface.

Alvin surfaced after ten hours and twenty-three minutes underwater, her longest dive of the mission. Mac sailed her to the *Fort Snelling* and entered the well deck at 8:12 p.m., just about the time that Guest and his staff arrived on board. The *Alvin* crew sent their photographs to be developed, then told the admiral what they had seen. The photographs were ready about midnight. The weary Guest gathered his key staff members to look at the pictures. They didn't see a bomb. They saw a parachute. Everyone agreed that the weapon probably lay shrouded underneath, but they couldn't tell for sure.

Mac McCamis was outraged. He knew it had to be the bomb. Guest asked him, "How do you know it's not a parachute full of mud?" To which McCamis replied impatiently, "What else is going to be down there with a parachute and a bomb rack hanging on to it?" McCamis went to bed that night discouraged. "In all my life," he said, "I'd never had my intelligence so insulted."

• • •

After the meeting, Admiral Guest wrote a situation report to his superiors, sending it at 2:50 a.m. on March 16. In it, Guest said that *Alvin* had photographed a large parachute covering an object. The contact was promising but not conclusive; positive identification was impossible. However, he was starting to plan the recovery. He planned to proceed as slowly and deliberately as possible, but if the object started to slide down the slope, he might have to take immediate action. He would use three ships, *Mizar, Privateer,* and *Petrel,* as the primary support vessels for the recovery, with two minesweepers on security patrol. All other ships would attend to business as usual. Guest didn't want the newsmen on shore to notice anything odd.

The other memo, the one for the Cyrus Vance committee that had taken four days to write, was never sent.

Early on the morning of March 16, Robert Sproull, the chair of the Cyrus Vance committee, went to the Pentagon for the group's second meeting. Sproull expected this gathering to be as gloomy as the first. He arrived around 4:30 a.m. to gather his thoughts and prepare for the meeting. He checked the message traffic, just in case there had been any developments in Spain, and found Admiral Guest's report. The second meeting, Sproull remembers, went off rather well.

That morning in Rota, a radioman found Red Moody at the Bachelor Officers Quarters. Moody had stayed out late the night before, drinking with an old friend. The messenger handed Moody a clipboard, the cover indicating that the note inside was classified. Red looked at the note and then at the messenger. "Tell them I'm coming back," he said. He asked for an early flight.

That afternoon in Spain, Tony Richardson and John Bruce, the mathematician and oceanographer who had escorted Simó out to sea the day before, visited the fisherman at his house. Simó found the fathometer trace and unraveled it on the dinner table. John Bruce looked at the trace and questioned Simó. He saw nothing resembling the falling weapon.

The Americans told Simó that he would be paid for the previous day's excursion—his boat had lost an entire day of fishing. Then Bruce, curious to see Simó's fathometer, asked if they could visit the *Manuela Orts*. Simó agreed. The men boarded the ship, took a look around, and were impressed with the sleek vessel and its modern gear. When they finished, Simó offered to buy the men a drink, and they headed to a nearby tavern.

At the bar, Tony Richardson sipped a beer and watched news of the Gemini 8 space shot. The ship had launched from Cape Kennedy that morning and was due to orbit earth for three days. During that time, Gemini pilots planned to link the nose of their capsule with a satellite called Agena. If they pulled it off, it would be the first time two crafts had docked in space, a key component in the plan for landing a man on the moon by the end of the decade.

After a flawless start to the flight, Gemini docked to the satellite successfully. But shortly thereafter, a thruster on the spacecraft stuck open and set the linked vehicles spinning crazily. The astronauts separated their capsule from the satellite and stabilized the craft, using rockets normally reserved for reentry. NASA ordered the crew to make an emergency landing in the Pacific. The astronauts were picked up after three hours at sea.

The outer-space drama received massive news coverage: a banner headline on the front page of *The New York Times,* with more than two full pages of stories. *Alvin* and *Aluminaut*'s deep-sea rendezvous, the first time two submersibles had ever accomplished such a feat, remained secret.

The same day that General Wilson received Guest's report, he sent three nuclear weapons experts to the *Fort Snelling* to look at the *Alvin* photographs. One man worked for the Atomic Energy Commission; the other two were EOD officers who had several years' experience with the Mark 28.

The weapons experts showed the *Alvin* crew photos of a Mark 28 bomb, and they recognized it immediately as the object they had seen. "That's it!" the crew said. The weapons team then examined the photos that Wilson had taken underwater. Although the parachute had wrapped itself around the object almost completely, the experts saw what appeared to be a lift lug. They also recognized the parachute as the right type for a Mark 28. Convinced that the *Alvin* crew had seen the bomb, the weapons experts took a boat to the flagship to tell Admiral Guest.

On board the USS *Albany,* the experts found Guest resistant to their news. "It is the opinion of my team that they had difficulties in convincing CTF-65 of similarities between the two sets of photographs," wrote General Wilson in a secret telegram to his Air Force superiors the next day. "Offers by my EOD team to assist in recovery operations and provide technical assistance met with cool reception." Wilson promised to keep his superiors in the loop as new developments arose.

In the same message, Wilson also mentioned that both he and Guest had received marching orders from the embassy in Madrid. The identification and recovery of the weapon must be handled secretly. Only the embassy, working with the government of Spain, could make public announcements on the matter.

In Madrid, Duke was determined to keep the rest of this story under his control. If he played his cards right, the weapon recovery could become a proud moment for the U.S. and Spanish governments, an example of how well the two countries had worked together to tackle a tough problem. In the upcoming base negotiations, Spanish officials would remember how well the Americans had handled the accident, scoring points for U.S. negotiators.

But on March 17, two days after *Alvin* found the parachute, Duke's phone rang, and his vision of a smooth ride to the finish was shattered. The man on the phone was Harry Stathos, the Madrid bureau chief for UPI, who had just returned from a trip to Germany. On the plane, he had struck up a conversation with a Pan Am pilot, who had been out drinking with an Air Force colonel the night before. The colonel had told the pilot, who told the reporter, that the bomb had been found. Now Stathos asked Duke: Had it? Duke said simply, "No comment." But the word was out.

Trying to nip this gossip in the bud, Duke decided to hold a press conference to announce the news officially. The ambassador was hosting a gala reception at the embassy that evening. He would talk to the press when the party ended. Staffers sent word to the press corps to assemble at the American Embassy at 1 a.m.

Meanwhile, Duke sent a telegram to the secretary of state. In light of the UPI news break, he said, he planned to make the following public statement:

> The undersea vessel, *Alvin,* made contact on March 16th with an object lying in 2,500 feet of water approximately five miles off shore near Palomares. Military experts have evaluated underwater photographs taken of the object and believe it to be the missing nuclear weapon. Actions are being taken to recover the device. The photographs show a parachute attached to an object with [*sic*] is similar in size and shape to the missing nuclear weapon. The parachute, however, is covering part of the object preventing positive identification. Experts who have examined the photographs indicate that the casing appears to be intact, thereby precluding any radioactive contamination in the water.

At 12:45 a.m., as reporters gathered in the embassy, Duke received a reply from the State Department, ordering him to cancel the press conference and say nothing. Instead, the embassy information officer, William Bell, read a telegram from Secretary of State Dean Rusk to the assembled reporters: "There have been hopeful developments but I cannot give you further information at this time. If we have a positive identification and recovery, we will so inform you." The reporters were furious. And the slight did not stop them from filing stories for the following day.

The articles were remarkably accurate. They reported that *Alvin* had found the bomb and parachute at 2,500 feet and that experts had seen photos and identified the weapon. A front-page article in *The Washington Post* also explained that the object rested precariously on an undersea slope a few miles off the coast of Palomares. "Recovery promises to be a delicate operation," the article added. "Not only is the parachute-shrouded object already in deep water, but apparently it is balanced on the slope in such a way that a wrong nudge could send it rolling into even deeper water."

A page-one story in *The New York Times* predicted a fast recovery. According to officials, claimed the article, it would take only up to three days to recover the weapon. "No pictures of the bomb or the recovery operations would be permitted," it added, "because of the highly secret nature of the material."

Duke may have been unhappy about the news break, but he shared the reporters' confidence. He was certain that *Alvin* had found the bomb but also felt, contrary to the *Times*' report, that to ensure credibility the Navy must display the recovered bomb to Spanish officials and the press.

The military thought that was a terrible idea. First, there was the problem of logistics: nobody had ever recovered a weapon from this depth. Guest didn't know how long the recovery might take or if it would go smoothly. He also had no idea if the weapon—if it *was* the weapon—was intact or broken and perhaps leaking radiation. As for the Air Force, it had no interest in showing a top secret H-bomb to the press. It had never displayed a nuclear weapon in public before. Why start now?

Confident that he could iron out these disagreements, Duke formed a committee to devise a plan for the public recovery and viewing. Looking ahead, he also drafted a press release, which he sent to the secretary of state on March 18 for review:

> The fourth and final weapon from the January 17 crash near Palomares Spain has been recovered today and is enroute to the United States at this time. The casing was intact and no release of radioactivity into the coastal waters has occurred. The weapon was located on March 16 in 2500 feet of water, approximately five miles off shore by the submersible *Alvin*. Photographs taken at that time tentatively identified the object as the missing weapon. The recovery of this weapon brings to a close the search phase of the operation. All wreckage fragments and associated aircraft material of interest to the US have now been located and recovered.

Duke's press release would prove extremely premature, his hope for a quick and easy recovery overly optimistic. The Navy might have found the bomb, but it had no way to lift it.

On March 16, McCamis and Wilson piloted *Alvin* back to the contact to relieve *Aluminaut*. *Alvin,* now outfitted with a transponder, could be guided by the *Mizar* almost directly to the target. *Aluminaut* had been down for twenty-two hours, babysitting the parachute-covered object. As they approached the larger sub, the *Alvin* pilots could see that it had parked itself at an angle, with its nose toward the bottom and its stern floating upward. The *Alvin* pilots approached the *Aluminaut* slowly, finally stopping just behind its elevated stern. At that moment, someone in the *Aluminaut* decided to walk to the back of the sub in order to use the urinal. As he did, the sub dipped its rear end toward *Alvin,* whose pilots squawked with alarm. McCamis grabbed the joystick and scooted *Alvin* off to the right. Then *Aluminaut* took off for the surface, showering *Alvin* with steel shot and mud from her underside.

After recovering from these indignities, the *Alvin* pilots settled in for another shift. They had returned to keep an eye on the object, not attempt a recovery. *Alvin* by now had a mechanical arm with a reach of six feet, a rotating wrist, and two pincers like a lobster claw. They used the arm to place a transponder near the bomb, so the *Mizar* could find the weapon when *Alvin* left. But the arm couldn't lift the bomb. Outstretched, the arm could carry twenty-five to fifty pounds. Or it could hang on to two hundred pounds in the crook of the elbow. (*Aluminaut* would eventually have two arms with similar lifting ability, but they hadn't arrived in Spain yet.) There was no way *Alvin* could lift a two-ton nuclear weapon.

Guest needed another way to raise the bomb. As McCamis and Wilson began their second vigil in the dark, the admiral's staff began to lay their plans.

15.

POODL versus the Bomb

On March 22, 1966, CBS News aired a thirty-minute special report called "Lost and Found, One H-Bomb." The show opened with the anchor, Charles Kuralt, seated before a two-color map of Spain indicating only two cities: Madrid and Palomares. "We live in a world in which it is possible to mislay a hydrogen bomb," intoned Kuralt. "That is the central fact of the drama in Spain." He continued:

With thousands of men and millions of dollars and a flotilla of fifteen ships and with luck, we have apparently also found it, lying on the bottom of the sea. With the concurrence of the dark Mediterranean, it now seems likely that it will even be recovered and put in a safe place. But for the sixty days that one of our H-bombs was missing, worried people in the village of Palomares and thoughtful people everywhere asked, "Could it explode?" "Could it leak poisonous radiation?" "Could somebody else find it and put it to use?" Those are awesome questions but, considering the nature of the loss, not unreasonable ones.

Later in the report, CBS showed a long scene from the movie *Thunderball*, then cut to a shot of *Deep Jeep* being hoisted from the water.

(The Navy had already sent *Deep Jeep* back to the United States, but the journalists were apparently unable to resist its photo-friendly bright yellow hull.) "This is not a search for a fictional missing H-bomb, this is a search for a real one," said Kuralt. "If it looks a little like *Thunderball,* that is a comment on how fantastic fact has become lately."

Kuralt wrapped up the program with a shot of the blue Mediterranean, the hills of Palomares rising in the distance. "The bomb has not yet been brought to the surface, but it must be," he said solemnly. "Because if we don't recover it, there remains the nagging, distant possibility that someone else will."

For about a week, Red Moody, now back on the task force, had been working on a plan. The key problem was getting a line down to the bottom, one heavy enough to support the weight of the bomb. *Alvin* or *Aluminaut* could carry a very light line. But if a submersible stretched a heavy line from a surface ship to the bomb, the force of the line in the current could overwhelm the sub's engines and sweep it off course.

Working with two consultants to the task force, Ray Pitts and Jon Lindbergh (a diving expert and son of the famed aviator), Moody designed and built a gangly contraption called POODL. The curious name, a contraction of Pitts, Moody, and Lindbergh, had nothing to do with POODL's appearance or duties. POODL looked nothing like a poodle; it was a seven-foot-tall steel frame shaped like a giant shuttlecock and mounted with a slew of items: several pingers and transponders so the *Mizar* could track the device, a strobe light, a bucket containing 190 feet of carefully coiled nylon line with a grapnel on the far end, and another 150 feet of coiled nylon line ending with a hook.

Aboard the *Mizar,* Moody and his team rigged up a length of 3½-inch nylon line with a breaking strength of 22,000 pounds. At the end they attached an anchor; thirty-eight feet above the anchor, they fastened POODL with a wire strap. In addition to the lines carried by POODL, they attached another 300-foot line, with a grapnel on the end, to the anchor itself. The plan was to lower the entire contraption—anchor, POODL, and all—into the water and, they hoped, land it near the bomb. Then *Alvin* could swim over, pick up the three lines, and dig the hook and grapnels into the parachute.

That was the plan, anyway. Lieutenant Commander Malcolm MacKinnon, a naval engineer on Guest's staff, took one look at the half-built POODL and winced. "Oh, my God," he thought. "It was really a kludge."

MacKinnon was not being overly critical. Even Moody admitted that they had "gypsy-engineered" the rig. But POODL was the best and quickest option they had. The weapon's position was precarious, and the Navy worried that the bomb could slip down the slope into deeper water or fall into an underwater crevice and disappear forever. That fear overshadowed everything.

So on March 23, the captain of the *Mizar* positioned the ship over the bomb. Red Moody and his team dropped the anchor, with POODL attached, off the *Mizar*. Soon, the anchor and POODL hit bottom, their line stretching to the surface. Sailors grabbed the line, hooked it to a buoy, and floated it on top of the water. Then they waited to see what *Alvin* could do.

POODL was not the Navy's first recovery plan. Soon after *Alvin* had found the bomb, it had carried a light line down to the bottom. The end of the line was tied to a fluke, which the *Alvin* pilots dug into the sediment near the bomb. The Navy planned to slide a heavier line down this messenger line, but when they tried, the fluke pulled out of the bottom. On March 19, the task force members tried another tactic: they coiled some lines on the *Mizar*'s instrument sled and tried to float the sled near the bomb. But the *Mizar* crew couldn't hold the sled steady, and they abandoned that plan, too. After this attempt, McCamis and Wilson visited the bomb in *Alvin* and reported that it had slid twenty feet downslope. That evening, Admiral Guest wrote a pessimistic situation report to his superiors. He faced bad weather, untested equipment, experimental techniques, a precarious target position, and submersibles that needed constant maintenance. He warned that the recovery might take a while.

Other ideas arose. Art Markel thought *Aluminaut* could lift the bomb and devised a plan. On its hull, *Aluminaut* carried a camera mount that could pan and tilt, and Markel proposed building a makeshift arm by attaching a wooden or metal pole to the camera mount. The pole would carry a metal hook, which the pilot could loop into the parachute. The hook would be attached, via cable, to *Aluminaut*'s emergency ballast, a 4,400-pound lead weight on its belly.

Then, with the bomb securely hooked to the ship, *Aluminaut* could blow its ballast tanks and rise to the surface, with enough buoyancy to pull the bomb with it.

Markel was excited about the plan, mentioning it in several letters to Reynolds. This was *Aluminaut*'s chance, he wrote, to share some of *Alvin*'s limelight. But Guest rejected the idea. If *Aluminaut* got into trouble, he reasoned, she might have to drop her emergency ballast, leaving him with a new problem: a two-ton bomb hooked to a 4,400-pound lead weight. Guest never explained his reasoning to the *Aluminaut* crew, however, and this brush-off—the latest in a string of them—left the crew bitterly disappointed. "It is quite apparent that CTF 65 does not want *Aluminaut* in the act if they can help it," Markel wrote. "I am quite disgusted over this whole mess." Markel had half a mind to take his lifting rig to the sunken ship of antiquity and hoist a cannon to the surface. That would show the world what *Aluminaut* could do.

As the recovery plan slogged forward, the press got antsy. On March 22, the *Los Angeles Times* ran a pessimistic front-page article that was reprinted in the *International Herald Tribune*. The headline read, "H-Bomb May Slip into Deep Sea Crevice, Balk Recovery." The article reported that the weapon was teetering on the edge of a steep undersea slope, in imminent danger of sliding into the abyss. "American officials here and at the scene are more pessimistic now about the situation than at any time since the search began," said the article. "They are depressed at having come so near only to face the possibility that a stray undersea current and the peculiar bottom topography may rob them of success."

Duke, disturbed by such gloomy press, asked permission to release regular progress reports without consulting the government of Spain. It is unclear whether he ever received a reply. But it is doubtful that Admiral Guest would have wanted to cooperate with such a plan; he had little interest in keeping the world press informed of his every move. In fact, he and his staff had become increasingly alarmed by the detailed information regularly appearing in the papers. There was a leak somewhere, and they didn't like it. The Air Force thought that someone in the Pentagon was talking to Washington reporters or that someone at Camp Wilson was chatting with the press. But Guest suspected the embassy in Madrid, perhaps even the ambassador himself. He didn't know Duke well, but he disliked the ambassador and didn't trust him. There is no evidence, however, that Duke passed illicit information to the press. Indeed, he seemed as mystified by the leaks as anyone.

On the morning of March 23, soon after Red Moody sent POODL to the bottom, McCamis and Wilson flew *Alvin* over to have a look. *Mizar* had landed the anchor and POODL about eighty feet from the bomb. When *Alvin* arrived at the site, the pilots saw that POODL had landed on the bottom and fallen over, spilling its lines into a tangle. *Alvin* tried to reach through the metal bars to grab the lines but couldn't. It then picked the remaining line off the anchor and tried to attach it to the billowing chute. With the pilots still getting used to the mechanical arm, the job proved difficult. Finally, they hooked the line into the parachute. But by that time, *Alvin*'s battery had run low and the sub had to surface. At the debriefing, the pilots reported that the bomb had moved about six feet and now rested in a small ravine.

The next day, Wilson and McCamis dove again. Again, they couldn't clear the tangled lines from POODL. They returned to the anchor line, which was already attached to the parachute, and tried to connect it more firmly. *Alvin* grabbed the grapnel and slowly, painstakingly twisted it into at least six parachute risers. Then the parachute billowed, and *Alvin* backed off. The pilots reported the news to the surface: they had snarled the grapnel in the chute. And, they added, the other two lines remained fouled on the POODL. The pilots couldn't possibly reach them.

Guest's staff met aboard the *Mizar*. The admiral did not want to lift the bomb with only one line, which seemed way too risky. But his staff pushed him to try. The breaking strength of the attached line, they argued, was ten times the weight of the weapon and rig combined. If they waited, the grapnel might work itself loose, or the line could tangle. Bad weather posed a constant threat. If the wind blew up, it could cancel operations for days. Washington and Madrid were losing patience. The sooner they recovered the bomb, the better.

Guest didn't like the idea. But eventually he was persuaded.

• • •

Guest's staff made a plan. *Mizar* would hover directly above the bomb, then winch it straight up through its center well, or moon pool. Once the bomb was safely off the seafloor, *Mizar* would pull it slowly toward shallow water, winching it up along the way. When the bomb was about 100 feet below the surface, EOD divers would attach two sturdy wire straps, and the bomb could be hoisted aboard a ship.

McCamis, still underwater in *Alvin,* heard that *Mizar* was going to attempt the lift. He asked if *Alvin* could stay submerged so the pilots could observe the operation. The answer came from the surface: No. It was too dangerous for *Alvin* to linger during the lift. The pilots were ordered to surface.

Meanwhile, Red Moody was having his own argument with the captain of the *Mizar.* Moody worried that the *Mizar* couldn't hold position directly above the weapon. He suggested that the captain place landing craft, known as Mike boats, on either side of the ship to hold the *Mizar* steady. The captain refused, saying he could maneuver his ship without help. Moody gave up, and the lift got under way.

The *Mizar*'s crew snagged the floating buoy tied to the anchor and the POODL. They jettisoned the buoy and attached the lift line to the ship's winch. Moody and Jon Lindbergh stood by the *Mizar*'s moon pool to watch the operation. Guest and members of his staff waited in the ship's laboratory, watching the instrument panels. At about 7:30 p.m., *Mizar*'s winch began to turn. Guest started to pray.

After about an hour, the instruments noted a slight strain as POODL rose off the seafloor. Fifteen minutes later, the rope took a heavy strain: the anchor had cleared the bottom. Slowly, the winch turned. The line grew steadily more taut, but the instruments showed that the strain was not severe. Ten minutes passed. Twenty. Thirty. The instruments showed another strain. The bomb had lifted off the bottom.

Three minutes later, the instruments jumped. Moody and Lindbergh, watching the line, saw it suddenly go slack. Staring at the loose line, Lindbergh felt a terrible sinking feeling. Moody thought, "Oh, shit."

The winch took another long hour to reel in the anchor. The line below the anchor—the one that had been attached to the bomb—ended in a frayed stump. The bomb itself was gone. Looking at the mangled rope, Lindbergh guessed that about three fourths of the strands had been cut cleanly on some sharp object. The rest had just split.

Moody later discovered that *Mizar* had, in fact, drifted off course while raising the bomb. The captain had cut power while the winch turned, sending the ship drifting toward shore and likely dragging the bomb upslope before lifting it. But it's not clear if *Mizar*'s drift snapped the line. The line could have fouled on the anchor flukes, rubbed on a sharp rock, or even cut itself on the POODL. Perhaps the nylon line was too prone to splitting or this particular line was defective. Nobody ever figured it out for sure.

McCamis and Wilson were eating dinner when they heard the bad news. "Oh, boy," said Mac. "Now we got to go find it again."

Alvin needed a battery charge and repairs to her ballast system and couldn't dive again for almost a full day. The admiral ordered *Aluminaut* to head down and look for the bomb. Several times, *Mizar* reported that the sub passed within 100 feet of the weapon's former position, but the *Aluminaut* crew saw no sign of it. After five hours of searching, they were ordered to surface to avoid disturbing the bottom further. When *Alvin* returned to the weapon site on the evening of March 25, the bottom was scored with deep gouges. "The slope looked [as] if it had been torn up by bulldozers," said Mac. The pilots found chunks of stone, clay, and mud, but no bomb.

The broken line seemed like a small mishap—an unlucky break rather than a tragedy. The recovery team hadn't moved the weapon far from its original resting place, and they knew where they had dropped it. How far could it have gone? Surely, the subs would soon find it again.

So, as Task Force 65 combed the ocean floor, the embassy staffers didn't panic. Instead, they continued to argue about how to display the bomb when Guest finally brought it up. Ever since word had leaked out that the bomb had been found, an international chorus had been offering suggestions and making demands. The Soviet newspaper *Izvestia* called for an international commission to verify the discovery, witness the bomb raising, and judge if the bomb had leaked any radiation. U.N. Secretary General U Thant privately suggested inviting the International Atomic Energy Commission (IAEC) to verify the recovery. American officials balked at both suggestions. The Soviet Union was a member of the IAEC, and the military certainly didn't want a mob of Communist scientists poking around its top secret weapon.

There was still the question of logistics, as well. The embassy wanted Duke, Spanish Vice President Muñoz Grandes, and other VIPs to witness the actual bomb raising. Wilson opposed this idea: the bomb might be dangerous and should be rendered safe before VIPs showed up. Should he keep Muñoz Grandes, the number two man in Spain, waiting in a tent, maybe for days? Guest agreed. Military officials hated the idea of displaying the bomb in public. If they had their way, they would raise the bomb in secret, pack it into a box, and ship it back to the United States under cover of darkness.

Duke knew this was impossible. Finding this slender bomb in the depths of the Mediterranean had been a nearly impossible task. If the Americans didn't show the bomb to the world, nobody would believe they had really found it. Rumors would linger for years; the story of the accident would never die. So when Duke reached an impasse with Wilson and Guest, he broke protocol and called Secretary of Defense Robert McNamara. A serious breach of diplomatic decorum, the call was the only time, Duke claims, that he directly crossed the divide between State and Defense. McNamara was a friend, and the ambassador was desperate. On the phone, Duke argued his position, and McNamara agreed that the find had to be verified. Together, the Departments of Defense and State ordered Wilson and Guest to come up with a plan that would satisfy everyone.

Developing a plan for public display soon seemed less urgent, however. As one day stretched into another with no sign of the bomb, Guest's hope faded. Days passed. Then a week. The bomb seemed to be hiding.

Among the members of Guest's staff, the tension ramped up a notch. Red Moody felt personally responsible. The dropped bomb had been an accident, but Moody had played a large part in the recovery operation and shouldered his share of the blame. The mood on the USS *Albany* was bleak. "Here we were in the ninth inning, and the score is zero to zero," said George Martin, a *Trieste* pilot who had been sent to Palomares to augment the task force. "And the fans—we'll call that the world opinion—was also at zero."

The crew of the USS *Albany,* already operating at a higher state of readiness than usual, responded to the heightened tension. The flagship carried long-range TALOS missiles, which could deliver either conventional or nuclear warheads. Usually, the crew armed the missiles with conventional warheads. But on March 29, the gun crews aboard the *Albany* made the switch. The flagship now bristled with nukes of her own. The task force was ready for anything.

At the end of March, Duke received a secret cable from the Departments of State and Defense regarding nuclear overflights of Spain. The tone was urgent:

> Because arrangements for overflights of Austria, Switzerland, France or Morocco with nuclear weapons for various reasons not feasible, resumption such overflights of Spain extremely important not only in maintaining our tactical alert and dispersal plans but also in providing nuclear logistics support to forces in Mediterranean area. Restoration US overflights could have favorable influence elsewhere in world where such flights involved. Early approach Spanish authorities is desirable to seek resumption such flights through Spain. . . . Would like views on timing such approach in light current request on three squadrons and in relation recovery B-52 weapon.

Duke responded in a secret cable to the secretary of state. His tone was patient but annoyed, like a father explaining, once again, why his son could not play baseball in the living room. He reminded Washington that the Department of Defense had just asked the Spanish government to station three fighter plane squadrons at Torrejón and had considered transferring France-based Air Force engine facilities to Spain. He pointed out that the United States soon faced the problem of extending, and probably renegotiating, its valuable base agreement with the Spanish government. And, in case anyone had forgotten, there was still a hydrogen bomb lost somewhere in the Mediterranean. "Timing of our demands, with an eye to international context, is important," he wrote. "It would be patently inopportune to raise subject of resuming overflights carrying nuclear weapons before lost weapon safely recovered and entire incident well behind us."

Guest assumed that the weapon now rested upslope from its former position. *Mizar,* he guessed, had probably been dragging the bomb uphill before it lifted off the bottom. Bolstering this theory, when *Alvin* went down to look, the crew found a track leading up the slope. Everyone hoped that this track, like the one before, would lead them to the bomb.

But it didn't. And after a few days of fruitless searching, the *Alvin* pilots began to imagine a different scenario. They suspected that the uphill track had been dredged by the dragging anchor, not the bomb. Maybe the bomb had dropped into its old track and skidded down the slippery slope. The *Alvin* pilots wanted permission to search downhill.

At a meeting with Guest, a member of the admiral's staff raised the idea of letting *Alvin* look downhill. They even sweetened the pot by encouraging Guest to ride along as an observer. Admiral Guest turned down the offer: there was no way he was diving in a submersible, especially one built by civilians. But just to get the *Alvin* pilots off his back, he agreed to let them search downslope. And he suggested that George Martin, who was standing nearby, take his place as observer.

On the morning of April 2, *Alvin* dove again, with Rainnie, McCamis, and George Martin inside. The sub had cruised down to about 2,800 feet when Mac spotted an anomaly—a clod of dirt that seemed out of place. Nearby, they saw some more dirt that looked oddly displaced. Then, suddenly, they saw a parachute, still tightly wrapped around an object that they knew was the bomb. They had been searching for just over a half hour.

The elated crew announced their find to the surface and settled in to wait for another rendezvous with *Aluminaut.* As they had suspected, the bomb and chute had slid downslope, landing about 120 yards south of its previous position. It was deeper now—resting at about 2,800 feet—but lying on a gently sloping plain that seemed far less precarious. George Martin marveled at the sight; this long-sought object, so far under the sea. To commemorate the occasion, he pulled a 100-peseta note out of his pocket and asked his companions to sign it. Then he sat back, ate the peanut butter and jelly sandwich he had packed for lunch, and wrote a letter to his wife.

Red Moody heard a buzz on ship and asked what was going on. He was told that *Alvin* had found the weapon but it was wrapped tightly in the parachute and nobody knew if it was the same bomb or not. Moody laughed. "How many bombs do we have down there?" he asked. "Let's just go get her, but do a better job this time."

APRIL

16.

Hooked

Soon after *Alvin* found the bomb, a diver named Herman Kunz flew from the United States to Spain and reported to Task Force 65. Kunz was an expert in deepwater rigging and explosive ordnance disposal. He was also the quintessential Navy diver: hard-living, hard-drinking, and tough.

Kunz arrived on the USS *Albany* and headed down to his quarters, a cramped room already bunking five ensigns. Malcolm MacKinnon, the naval engineer and an old friend of Kunz, showed him the way. Ignoring the lounging ensigns, Kunz began to unpack. MacKinnon watched, stunned, as Kunz opened an aluminum suitcase to display twelve neatly packed bottles of Gilbey's gin, lined up square like soldiers at attention. "Herman!" said MacKinnon. "What the hell are you doing?" Both men knew that liquor—especially *that much* liquor—was not allowed on a Navy ship. The ensigns looked over, undoubtedly with a mixture of interest and alarm. Kunz shrugged. "I thought I might have to spend time on the beach."

Before leaving for Spain, MacKinnon and Kunz had visited the Naval Ordnance Test Station (NOTS) in Pasadena. The supervisor of salvage had told MacKinnon about a torpedo recovery device called CURV, which might be useful in Palomares, and asked him to check it out. MacKinnon visited CURV and realized that the Navy might need this device in Spain. He told the technicians to prepare CURV for the mission and then headed to Palomares himself.

The engineers and technicians at NOTS had built CURV, which stood for Cable-controlled Underwater Research Vehicle, two years earlier because the Navy needed a better way to recover prototype torpedoes. To test a new torpedo, the Navy used a real weapon but removed the warhead and replaced it with an "exercise head" containing lead weights and pingers. Then it took the modified weapon to the test range off Long Beach and shot it at a target. If all went well, the torpedo completed its full run, using up all its fuel, and then dropped its lead weights. The loss of fuel and weights made the torpedo buoyant. Spent, it floated to the surface, where the Navy could recover it easily.

But test torpedoes didn't always work as planned. Often they sputtered before finishing their test run and, carrying their heavy load of fuel, sank to the bottom. With each sunken torpedo costing close to $100,000—and holding important information about the failure—the Navy couldn't just leave them there and so developed a crude way to recover them. It tracked the torpedo's pinger and, when it located its resting place, sailed a barge to the site. The barge had a moon pool in the center and four mooring winches, one on each corner. When the barge arrived at the torpedo, searchers moored the ship directly over it with three or four anchors. Then they lowered a rectangular frame containing lights, sonar, a wire noose, and a TV camera and looked for the lost torpedo. To move the dangling frame, the captain had to motor the entire barge back and forth. Eventually, if the searchers were in the right place, they would see the torpedo and try to snare it with the noose. The process was long, slow, and awkward; it could take days to recover one torpedo.

CURV resembled this old system in some ways. It consisted of a frame of aluminum tubing, which held sonar equipment, lights, cameras, and three propellers. On top rested four oblong buoyancy tanks, and off the front jutted an arm holding a metal hydraulic claw lined with rubber. The whole contraption measured about five feet high, six feet wide, and thirteen feet long.

To recover a torpedo, the Navy steered a ship to the site and lowered CURV into the water. But CURV didn't just dangle there as the barge swayed overhead. CURV was remote-controlled, attached to the surface ship with a thick umbilical cord. A surface operator, sitting at a console, could see the bottom through CURV's TV and sonar and direct its propellers with joysticks. The operator flew CURV to the lost torpedo, grasped it around the middle with CURV's claw, then carried it to the surface. If the torpedo was too heavy, the operator could jettison the claw and back away. The claw, attached to a lift line, could then be raised to the surface. Early in its career, CURV managed to recover an unheard-of four torpedoes in one day.

By the time the Air Force dropped four bombs over Palomares, CURV had been operating for about two years and had plucked up fifty-two torpedoes from as deep as 2,000 feet. The CURV team had mastered their job, but the device itself was still a work in progress, and the CURV group remained a small-scale, low-budget operation.

When the Navy requested CURV's services in Spain, the team welcomed another opportunity to show off their skills. If they were successful, it would mean more recognition and money for their project. An H-bomb, to them, was just a big torpedo, and they certainly knew how to recover those. There was only one problem—the tether was too short.

CURV's umbilical cord, an inch-and-a-half-diameter cable that fed power and commands to the device, was about 2,000 feet long. But by March 15, when *Alvin* found the bomb at 2,500 feet, the Navy knew that CURV would have to go deeper. So the CURV team embarked on a crash program to lengthen its lifeline by splicing in an additional 1,000 feet of cable.

The splicing was tedious work. The cable contained fifty-five separate conductors, each of which had to be spliced individually. The team staggered the splices over about four feet of cable, then covered the wounded area with a gray, pliable goo used for sealing air ducts. (The team dubbed the material "monkey shit.") Then they wrapped the area in black electrical tape, sealing the splices as well as they could. Larry Brady and George Stephenson, the CURV operators, spent several days on the splicing operation. When they finished, the splice was an ugly black blob. "It looked like a python had swallowed a dog," said Brady. "Or a couple of dogs."

Dragging the device to a NOTS range, the CURV team ran a few test dives. The ugly splice held. The cable now stretched 3,100 feet long—long enough for the job—but they couldn't go much below 2,800 feet and still maneuver. There were some other bugs as well: CURV's depth gauge didn't work well below 2,000 feet, and its altimeter, which measured CURV's distance from the bottom, didn't work at all. But on March 24, as soon as Task Force 65's first lift attempt failed and the bomb fell back into the Mediterranean, Admiral Swanson ordered CURV to Spain. On March 26, the team packed up the CURV system, loaded it onto a cargo plane, and headed to Palomares.

The CURV team set up shop on the USS *Petrel,* a submarine rescue ship, on March 29. The *Petrel* and her commanding officer, Lieutenant Commander Max Harrell, were old hands at Navy salvage, having worked on such operations for years, and the ship proved a good home for CURV. The CURV team set up their gear but had little to do; the bomb was still missing after the failed lift attempt. So for a couple of days, they ran tests. The Navy dropped a dummy bomb into the water with the same dimensions as the missing weapon and sent CURV off to find it.

The CURV team operated the device from a small control shack on the deck of the *Petrel.* It took two people to run the device: one to operate the sonar and read the compass, the other to move the switches and levers that spun CURV's three propellers and sent it swimming. When it came to "flying" CURV, Larry Brady was the undisputed master. He just imagined himself sitting on the device, sailing happily underwater, and the moves came naturally. Once he found the target, Brady grabbed it with the claw, like a kid in an arcade grabbing cheap toys from a bin.

A couple of days after his arrival on the *Petrel,* Brady dove CURV to 1,050 feet, found the dummy bomb, and recovered it with a special claw the team had built in California. The next day, CURV dove to 2,400 feet and recovered a pinger hidden inside a barrel. The team could have continued performing ever-more-elaborate circus tricks for weeks, but on April 2, *Alvin* found the bomb resting on the gray bottom 2,800 feet below the surface, just within CURV's reach. As the parachute had wrapped itself completely around the weapon, however, CURV couldn't grab it with its claw. The crew needed another way to snare the bomb.

Robert Pace, CURV's project engineer, came up with an idea.

Sketching a grapnel that would fit onto CURV's arm, Pace brought the drawing to the *Albany*'s tender and asked the men in the machine shop to build it. Pace envisioned a grapnel with softly curving spring-loaded tines that couldn't accidentally slice the parachute shrouds and wouldn't let go once they hooked in. The chief who ran the machine shop looked at the drawing skeptically. Another grapnel? They had already made a bunch of these things for *Alvin* and *Aluminaut,* all of which had never been used or had ended up somewhere on the bottom of the sea. And his crew had already been at sea ninety days longer than planned, with no end in sight. It was really too much. And now they wanted another grapnel? The chief complained until he ran out of steam. Then, realizing that Pace wasn't going anywhere without his grapnel, he ordered his men to get to work. In the end, they made him three.

On April 3, the day after relocating the bomb, *Alvin* rendezvoused with *Aluminaut,* and *Aluminaut* surfaced. *Alvin,* left alone with the bomb (now code-named "Robert" after Admiral Guest's stepson), tried to pull the parachute aside to examine the weapon. The parachute and bomb lay tightly tangled, however, and the *Alvin* crew couldn't get a good look at it. They attached two pingers to the parachute, placed a transponder nearby, and headed to the surface, leaving the bomb alone.

As *Alvin* worked beneath the sea, the CURV team prepared for their first dive on the bomb. With the weapon resting at 2,800 feet and CURV's cable just 300 feet longer, the device would practically be hanging on the end of the line, with little room to maneuver. CURV would literally be at the end of its tether.

To give CURV as much freedom as possible, the commander of the *Petrel,* Max Harrell, had to hold his ship almost directly over the bomb each time it dove. And he couldn't use the *Petrel*'s own power: the CURV lines dangled dangerously near the *Petrel*'s propeller, and Harrell couldn't risk turning it on. Instead, he decided to position the ship with two Mike boats, one attached to the bow and one to the stern. By directing them with walkie-talkies, he would try to keep his ship over the bomb, with only 50 yards of leeway in any direction. The first time they tried the maneuver, both Mike boats got tangled in their own tow lines and had to be untangled by divers and boat crews. Harrell would have to keep them untangled—and in position—for at least ten hours each dive.

While Harrell ironed out the positioning, the CURV team prepped their lift line. The machine shop had finished Bob Pace's grapnel, strength-tested it to 10,000 pounds, and found it could hold the weight. The grapnel was attached to one end of a braided nylon line that stretched 3,200 feet, well over half a mile. The other end of the line was hooked to a buoy. The rest of the lift line—the entire midsection—was attached to CURV's umbilical cable with masking tape at regular intervals. The tape would keep the line in place until CURV ejected the grapnel and pulled away.

On April 4, just before 9 a.m., CURV dropped into the water and headed down to the bomb. Air Force experts had told Larry Brady that the apex was the strongest point of the parachute; if Brady could hook the grapnel in there, he was home free.

Around noon, CURV reached the bomb, guided by the pingers that *Alvin* had left behind. Brady sailed CURV around the bomb, looking at the tangled chute through the video monitors. He found the apex and, with his usual dexterity, dug three tines of the grapnel in through the hole and out through the chute. Sure that the grapnel was firmly attached, Brady ejected it from CURV and backed away. The masking tape binding the nylon line to the cable snapped, piece by piece, and the lift line buoyed off. The operation had gone exactly as planned.

Larry Brady and the rest of the CURV crew had been cocky since their arrival in Spain. After all, they retrieved lost bombs for a living. They had heard about the first attempt to retrieve the bomb and thought that the men involved, while certainly earnest, had been amateurs. It was as if, said Brady, two guys flipped their car into a ditch, tried to tow it out on their own, and burned up the clutch before finally calling a tow truck. CURV, said Brady, was the tow truck. With one line solidly attached, Brady considered his job done. He was surprised to learn that it wasn't.

The CURV crew expected that the Navy would now lift the bomb. Instead, they learned that Admiral Guest wanted two more lines attached. Guest had been burned the first time around; it wouldn't happen again. Bob Pace tried to talk Guest out of it. "Admiral," he said, "you got that parachute ballooning in the water now. It's going to be difficult enough to get another grapnel into it without tangling it." Guest shook his head. "I can't help that," he said.

• • •

On April 5, Mac McCamis and Val Wilson dove *Alvin* down to the bomb to assess the situation with human eyes. When they arrived, they saw the chute, supported by the buoyed line, floating in the water column. The parachute danced in the water like a giant jelly-fish, the bomb still tangled in its tentacles. Dragged by the bobbing buoy on the surface, the bomb and chute had moved several hundred feet west and now rested a bit deeper, at about 2,850 feet. Trying to get a better look, McCamis carefully nudged the sub toward the dangling mess. "This sixty-four-foot cargo chute was billowing up like you was under a Barnum and Bailey circus tent," said Mac. "My biggest worry was getting tangled."

Approaching cautiously, Mac stopped just short of the parachute. But Wilson, looking out the side window, panicked. The curvature of the window made it appear that the parachute was reaching over them, threatening to engulf the sub. "Scared him dead," said McCamis. "So he yelled topside to Rainnie that we're in the parachute, which we weren't, and I couldn't shut him up quick enough. So I moved off to the side, to get him back in his seat." Worried by Wilson's report, Rainnie ordered the sub back to the surface.

Both Mac and Wilson had been spooked by the close call. If *Alvin* got trapped or tangled, the pilot could jettison various parts of the ship—the batteries, the mechanical arm—with explosive bolts, hope-fully allowing the sub to surface. If that didn't work, he could lift a panel on the floor, exposing a stout metal cylinder: the sphere release. If the pilot turned the cylinder 90 degrees, *Alvin* would release the personnel sphere, and it would rocket, spinning, to the surface. The sphere separation could save the inhabitants from death at the bottom of the sea, but it would be a rough and terrifying ride to safety.

Just before midnight on April 5, CURV dove to attach a second line. In the early-morning hours, Larry Brady twisted CURV's second grapnel into the parachute, snaring at least six lines. Then he ejected the grap-nel, and the line was buoyed off. *Alvin*, diving to check on CURV's progress (but now keeping a safe distance from the chute), reported that the bomb had shimmied farther downslope, dragged by the two buoyed lines. The news injected new urgency into the operation. Admiral Guest and his staff feared that the bomb might slip out of CURV's reach. They had to get that third line attached as soon as possible.

But just as the Navy got the second line to the surface on the morning of April 6, the weather turned sour. Twenty-two-knot winds whipped the sea into five-foot waves, conditions too dangerous to operate CURV. Admiral Guest looked at the recovery crews. Most of the men had been awake for more than thirty hours and looked like zombies. Since the seas were too rough to dive anyway, Guest stood them down until that evening.

Just before 9 p.m., sensing that a recovery attempt was near, Admiral Guest and his staff boarded the *Petrel*. Bad weather grounded CURV until after midnight. Around 1 a.m., CURV dove to attach the third and final line. The control shack was crowded. Members of Guest's staff, including the admiral himself, watched over Brady's shoulder as he flew CURV toward the target. Guest asked him to pull closer to the chute, to try to see the bomb. Since Admiral Guest was paying the bill, Brady indulged him. "We might get stuck," he told Guest, "but we'll sure give it a try."

Brady steered CURV back and forth around the dangling bomb, trying to give Admiral Guest a clear view of the weapon. Suddenly he noticed that a switch on the control panel had flipped. It was the circuit breaker for the starboard thruster. Brady reached up, flipped it on, and tried to run the thruster. The circuit breaker popped again. Brady panned the underwater TV camera around, looking back over CURV's shoulder. The parachute had tangled in the starboard thruster. CURV was stuck. Brady pointed at the TV and said, "We're fouled."

Guest and his staff stared at the image on the screen. Then they stood up and walked out. Guest thanked his lucky stars that CURV was an unmanned machine, rather than a manned sub. Then he climbed the steps to the wardroom and gathered his staff. He had to make a decision.

The CURV crew waited in the control shack, killing time by playing cards. Eventually, a member of the CURV team came down from the wardroom, looking grim. You're not going to believe this, he told his colleagues. The admiral wants to cut CURV's umbilical cord, tie it off to a buoy, and retrieve the bomb later. The men in the control shack were shocked. They had two lift lines solidly in place; why not just raise the bomb?

The same argument flew about the wardroom. The atmosphere grew so tense that Howard Tarkington, the CURV division head, fainted from the stress. Guest had vowed not to make another lift attempt without three lines attached. Yet if they strained to free CURV, the only vehicle that could attach a third line, the bomb might be dragged out of reach. Guest wanted to cut CURV loose. He turned to each member of his staff and asked his opinion. Red Moody and Brad Mooney argued against cutting CURV free. CURV, in a way, was the third line they were looking for. They should lift the bomb now.

Cliff Page, the admiral's chief of staff, agreed. Knowing that Mooney enjoyed a strong rapport with Admiral Guest and had excellent diplomatic skills—one Navy man called Mooney "the snake charmer"—Page took charge. He cleared out the wardroom, leaving the lieutenant and the admiral to slug it out. They stayed there, behind a closed door, for hours. "I tried to be as respectful as I could, but I was saying, 'Admiral, this is dumb as hell to cut this thing loose,' " recalled Mooney. " 'It's totally enmeshed in there, and they can't help but lift it now.' "

By early morning, Mooney had beaten the admiral down. At 5:02 a.m. on Thursday, April 7, Guest sent a message to General Wilson. The message said that Admiral Guest had a broken leg, code that the lift would soon begin.

Red Moody and Max Harrell, the commanding officer of the *Petrel,* had already started preparations. The two men went over every detail: they didn't want any lift lines snapping this time around. Harrell designed a system of blocks and pulleys that would haul the two lines up, distributing the load equally between them. He attached a dynamometer to measure the total lifting stress.

Both lines were wound around one capstan, ensuring that the ship would hoist both at the same speed. Moody made sure that the capstan was smooth, free from any imperfections that might cut the lines. A second capstan would wind CURV's umbilical cable. CURV, though hopelessly tangled in the chute, was slightly buoyant and didn't pose much of a lifting problem. But to keep it neutral during the lift, it had to be raised at the same speed as the weapon.

Harrell positioned the Mike boats that would hold *Petrel* steady for the lift. Looking at the weather, he knew that today would prove particularly difficult. April 7 dawned with little breeze and a calm sea, beautiful for a spring picnic but less than ideal for ship control. It was easiest to judge and hold position when a breeze or surface current offered a force to work against. With neither of these, Harrell's difficult job would be that much harder.

Guest and his staff gathered in the wardroom to watch the lift on CURV's video monitor. Meanwhile, Moody cleared all nonessential personnel—"tourists," he called them—off the *Petrel*'s stern, or fantail. The only people allowed on deck were those actually recovering CURV or the bomb. Moody wanted to give the recovery team space to work, not necessarily protect the men who hustled belowdecks. Moody was certain the bomb wouldn't explode. But if it somehow did, it wouldn't matter if a man were abovedecks or below. As one EOD diver put it, there'd be nothing left but a greasy stain.

At 5:50 a.m., the *Petrel* began to raise the weapon. Guest worried most about the bomb lifting off the bottom. He had been told that when the bomb was within 100 feet of the bottom and 100 feet of the surface, vibrations in the nylon line could reduce its strength by as much as 75 percent. The admiral was not the only man in the wardroom worried about this possibility; one scientist paced back and forth with such a scowl that Red Moody and Herman Kunz had to take him outside and tell him to cheer up. Guest, powerless to do anything but wait, looked sick to his stomach. He turned to the man next to him and said, "I'd prefer combat any day to this."

As it turned out, the weapon came up so smoothly that they hardly noticed it leaving the bottom. For an hour and forty-five minutes, the capstans turned slowly, gently raising the weapon. Finally, the top of the parachute broke the surface. Two of Red Moody's divers jumped into the water to inspect the bomb. The weapon, they found, wasn't dangling below the chute but remained tangled about a third of the way up. The fact that they saw the weapon was a huge relief; for the first time, Guest knew he really, truly had the bomb.

The divers attached metal straps and hoisting lines to the bomb. Boatswain mates rigged the lines to the cargo boom on the *Petrel*'s fantail. Then the divers cut CURV free from the chute, and the signal was given to lift. The *Petrel* hoisted the weapon clear of the water and swung it inboard. Immediately, the EOD team swarmed the waterlogged weapon with radiation monitors. The readings were negative. The boom swung the bomb over the back of the ship and set it down. It was 8:46 a.m.

Nobody breathed easy yet. The Navy EOD team, joined by Air Force and Sandia experts, inspected the bomb as it sat on a pair of wooden chocks. The rough ride had battered the weapon. The tail section was torn and jagged, the parachute twisted and fouled, the nose dented as if punched by a giant fist. But the rest had remained intact, with a portion of the bomb rack still attached and little corrosion from its stay in the salty sea.

The EOD team began to render the bomb safe, dismantling key components to make sure it couldn't explode or release radiation. Carefully, they removed covers and disconnected cables in a specific sequence. The job went smoothly until about 10 a.m., when they tried to remove the thermal battery. The pressure of the deep water had squeezed the battery into place, and it stuck stubbornly inside the bomb. The EOD diver in charge of the render-safe, Walter Funston, consulted the manual, which included instructions for this contingency. The manual said to drill a hole in the battery, insert a wood screw, and use the screw to yank the battery out. Funston turned to the Sandia expert standing nearby and asked if the battery configuration had changed. He was about to drill a hole into a hydrogen bomb and wanted to hit the mark. Getting the go-ahead, the team drilled a small hole in the center of the battery and inserted a three-inch wood screw. Several men tried to pull the battery clear, but it refused to budge. Funston had an idea. He hooked a short nylon strap to the wood screw and attached it to a shackle on the ship's bulwark. As he twisted the strap, the battery slowly eased out. At 10:15 a.m. the bomb was declared safe.

On the fantail, there were no shouts of joy, no claps on the back. Everyone was too tired. In the wardroom, the staff applauded, more with relief than excitement. Guest, nearly sick with exhaustion, said simply, "Thank God we finally did it."

Someone cut up the parachute, handing out small strips as souvenirs. For the next two hours, the members of the task force congratulated one another and autographed the little pieces of parachute. Then all those who could headed to their bunks.

As Brad Mooney walked toward his quarters, Herman Kunz leaned out of a doorway and beckoned to him. Mooney followed Kunz to his room and watched, goggle-eyed, as Kunz opened a folding desk and displayed his fine collection of alcohol. Kunz offered Mooney a drink, but the young lieutenant demurred. He told the diver that he had never drunk alcohol aboard a Navy ship before, and he wasn't about to start now. That's fine, said Kunz. You're tired. Go to bed.

A short time later, after Mooney was in bed, the ship's doctor paid him a visit. "Guest tells me you've been up for three days," said the doctor. "You really need to have some medication." He handed Mooney some clear liquid. "Here," he said. "This is yours. Take your time drinking it." Mooney took a couple of sips. It was pure gin. Somehow, Herman Kunz had convinced the doctor to give him a prescription for booze. Mooney, just following orders, found Kunz, joined him in a celebratory dose of medicine, then returned to his quarters and fell asleep.

The next day, April 8, was Good Friday. That morning, approximately a hundred newsmen and photographers, following the plan that the embassy, Navy, and Air Force had finally agreed upon, gathered at a dock in Garrucha and were ferried to the USS *Albany*. From the deck of the flagship, under a warm spring sun, they watched *Alvin, Aluminaut,* and *Cubmarine* sail by in a multicolor minisub review. They also watched the *Petrel* sail back and forth along the starboard side of the *Albany,* about thirty-five yards away. Ambassador Duke posed for photos with his wife and various Spanish and American officials. For about twenty minutes, the press had a clear view of bomb number four, still resting on its wooden chocks on the *Petrel*'s fantail.

It was the first time the United States had ever displayed a nuclear weapon in public, and pictures of the bomb appeared in television stories and on front pages around the globe. Bernard Kalb, reporting for CBS, noted how innocent the bomb seemed. It lay, he said, "under the Mediterranean sun as if it were a bathing beauty posing for photographers." "For a multimegaton monster," he added, "it looks extremely dull."

The embassy had drafted a press release to be given to reporters at this event. Part of the release stated that the weapon had been found "in 2,500 feet of water, approximately five miles off shore by the submersible *Alvin*." The Navy said this made it look as if *Alvin* had done all the work alone. It asked the embassy to change the sentence, and it complied. The statement released to the press read: "The weapon was located on March 15 in 2,500 feet of water, approximately five miles off shore by units of Task Force 65."

After the bomb display, Guest, flanked by Wilson, Duke, and Spanish dignitaries, held a press conference aboard the *Albany*. He gave a detailed explanation of the search and recovery operations, then opened the floor for questions. One reporter asked him how much the operation had cost. Guest refused to estimate. But regardless of the cost, he said, the Navy had learned more about deepwater operations from Task Force 65 than from any previous mission.

Guest had hardly slept in days, and, as the press conference wore on, he sounded steadily more testy and exhausted. He praised the *Alvin* crew but couldn't remember their names. At one point, he apologized for asking a reporter to repeat a question, saying "I'm just about out on my feet." Finally, before the admiral collapsed, Duke stepped in and commandeered the mike. "Admiral," he said, "you have the gratitude of grateful countrymen, a grateful host country, and in fact the gratitude of the world. Thank you very much." With that Guest thanked the crowd and signed off.

Palomares invites superlatives. It involved the greatest striking force in military history, the worst nuclear weapons accident, the largest sea search. The magnitude of the accident forced Americans to confront their country's nuclear policies as never before.

Throughout the Cold War, there had always been people who worried and complained about nuclear weapons. But most Americans managed to make peace with them, or at least accept them as a necessary evil. This uncomfortable peace existed only because Americans believed that their government had control over the weapons. The United States would launch the nuclear bombs only to respond to a Soviet attack or to offer a controlled display of American strength.

That is why Palomares proved so disconcerting. The United States not only lost control of four hydrogen bombs, it actually lost one of them. The accident upset the fragile peace that Americans had made with nuclear weapons, the deal they had made with their government. Palomares was "a nightmare of the nuclear age," as one writer said, not because of what happened, but because it opened people's minds to what could have happened. Despite America's best efforts, it seemed that nuclear weapons could not be easily controlled. Perhaps, in accepting this necessary evil, America had made a deal with the Devil.

Suddenly, the 32,193 warheads stashed around the country seemed less like a security blanket and more like a loaded gun with the potential to misfire. As the security expert Joel Larus wrote in 1968, Palomares "made millions of people aware of how threatened their lives had become—even in peacetime." In the years after the accident, the public increasingly questioned the need for such a massive, potentially dangerous nuclear arsenal. After 1966, amid growing concerns of nuclear accidents and neglect of conventional forces, America began to shrink its nuclear stockpile. The deal with the Devil, people decided, no longer seemed quite so worthwhile.

EPILOGUE

After the press and VIPs left the scene on April 8, the EOD team finished dismantling the weapon. That afternoon, they placed its parts into an aircraft engine container, packed sand around them, and sealed the lid. General Wilson had proposed that the bomb be taken ashore, trucked to San Javier, flown to Torrejón, and then shipped back to the United States. Spanish Vice President Agustín Muñoz Grandes nixed this idea, saying he didn't want the bomb to touch Spanish soil. So, after dismantling the bomb, the Navy loaded it onto the USS *Cascade,* which carried the weapon back to the United States and handed it over to the Air Force.

The Air Force sent bomb number four to join its three siblings at the Pantex Ordnance Plant in Amarillo, Texas. Weapons experts disassembled the bombs, buried the most contaminated parts, and salvaged the valuable nuclear material. Then they sent the fuses, firing sets, and weapon bodies from bombs one and four to Sandia for analysis. The plutonium pits went to Los Alamos.

The engineers learned some lessons from Palomares that prompted them to change the design of weapons. The accident proved that high explosive could detonate in an accident, as it had in bombs two and three, scattering dangerous plutonium. After Palomares, Los Alamos developed an insensitive nuclear explosive that would not detonate on impact. It eventually incorporated it into most nuclear weapons.

The USNS *Boyce* arrived in Charleston on April 5, carrying 4,810 barrels of contaminated Spanish soil. Under the watchful eyes of two AEC couriers and the JEN scientist Emilio Iranzo, workers lifted all the barrels, except two, off the *Boyce* and loaded them into twenty-six railroad cars. The two AEC couriers stayed with the barrels on their train ride to the Savannah River Site, traveling in the caboose, and Iranzo met them there. At Savannah River, Iranzo watched as 4,808 barrels were placed into a massive, muddy trench. Satisfied, he returned to Spain.

The other two barrels were shipped to Wright Langham, "Mr. Plutonium," at Los Alamos for tests. He said he planned to grow tomatoes with the soil.

For all its searching, bomb recovery, and soil transport, the Navy billed the Air Force $6.5 million. However, the Navy calculated that its total cost was actually much higher: $10,230,744, or $126,305 per day. It was the most expensive salvage operation in history.

On April 7, 1967, exactly one year after the recovery, George Martin, who had been in *Alvin* when they refound the bomb, held a Task Force 65 reunion at his home in Maryland. Tony Richardson composed a poem for the occasion:

> Robert, an H-bomb in Spain,
> Gave the Navy a great deal of pain.
>> He shouldn't have otter
>> Gone into the water.
> The Air Force should get all the blame.

> *Alvin,* a submarine nifty,
> Found the bomb in a search that was risky.
>> To recover she tried
>> But the bomb tried to hide.
> Finally CURV saved the day, and quite quickly.

After the *Boyce* sailed off, the remaining airmen at Camp Wilson tidied up Palomares the best they could: replacing topsoil, repairing ditches, and building new concrete fences to replace the cactus fencing they had destroyed. The legal staff drew up official "certificates of decontamination" to give to the villagers.

By the end of March, Camp Wilson had dwindled to 144 people. On March 20, a delegation consisting of the mayors of Palomares, Villaricos, and Cuevas de Almanzora, along with eighty townspeople, visited the camp for a ceremony to mark the near closing of operations. General Wilson gave a speech and handed $1,000 to the local priest for repairs to the church in Palomares and $200 for the people of Villaricos. Officers and airmen had donated the money in appreciation for the hospitality of the local citizens.

By early April, Camp Wilson was gone, but a skeleton crew of lawyers—including Joe Ramirez—lingered. By September 26, Ramirez and the legal team had interviewed more than five hundred claimants and paid $555,456.45 in damages. A few sticky claims remained, including that of Francisco Simó Orts.

For his help in rescuing the downed fliers and pinpointing the spot where bomb number four had hit the water, the U.S. military had given Simó $4,565.56—reimbursement for his time and expertise and the use of his boat. In April, in a ceremony in Madrid, Ambassador Duke presented Simó with a medallion and a scroll. The medallion carried a picture of Lyndon Johnson. The scroll read:

As testimony and admiration of the exceptional talents and profound knowledge of the sea of

DON FRANCISCO SIMO ORTS

which led to the finding of the nuclear bomb which fell into the sea on the coast of Palomares, and as a symbol of gratitude on behalf of my country, I make this document in Madrid, Today, April 15, 1966.

Simó, however, wanted more than plaudits. He wanted cash. In June, he presented his own claim to the U.S. Air Force, asking for $5 million. To most Americans (and some Spaniards), Simó's claim seemed outrageous. But, as he told CBS News, Simó guessed he had saved the military at least five days of searching, which he valued at about $1 million a day. He didn't want the money for himself, he added. He would use it to educate the children of fishermen and aid the local fishing industry.

The claim, too big for the Air Force lawyers in Torrejón, went to Washington, where the U.S. government rejected it. Simó hired a New York law firm to represent him, and the case was finally settled in Admiralty Court in 1971. He was awarded $10,000.

In the spring and summer of 1966, the Spanish government, through various meetings and public statements, made it clear that the upcoming base negotiations would not be easy. It refused to reinstate America's nuclear overflights and started to flex its newfound muscle in other ways. It wanted the United States to help it gain control of Gibraltar and push for Spain's membership in the EEC, and it planned to use the base negotiations as leverage. In May, *The New York Times* reported that Franco would not renew the thirteen-year-old defense agreement, at least not in its present form. "Now, with its economy and its political ties in Europe both steadily expanding, the Spanish Government is said to be tiring of its 'equal but separate role,' " reported the *Times.* Even more worrisome, there were reports that Franco might open the military bases—built largely by the United States—to multinational use.

The base negotiations got under way in late 1967, and Duke placed himself in the thick of them. Finally, he had a chance to shape U.S. foreign policy. He had been lobbying hard for a water desalinization plant for Palomares, a goodwill gift from America to soothe the psychological pain of the accident. If he could announce the gift as soon as possible, preferably before the two-year anniversary of the accident, it would improve the atmosphere for the base negotiations. The American diplomats had to remember, said Duke, that "The accident brought home to the Spanish, in a most dramatic way, that the American military presence in Spain was not without serious risks."

On January 6, 1968, Duke was dining at the embassy in Madrid when President Johnson called. Johnson handed Duke some surprising news: he wanted Angie to leave his post as ambassador and return to Washington. Johnson faced a tough reelection battle, and he wanted Angie at his side as his director of protocol. Dismayed, Duke saw his policy-making ambitions vanishing in a puff of presidential whimsy. He protested: he couldn't leave now. He was in the middle of touchy base negotiations with the Spanish, which wouldn't wrap up until September. But Johnson insisted; he needed Angie back in Washington before then.

Duke was bitterly disappointed. But if the president needed him, he had to obey. For the next few months, he sped around Spain, tying up loose ends and making farewell calls. On March 31, 1968, Duke and his family climbed onto a military airplane in Madrid and flew to the United States. They arrived in Washington exhausted. They checked into the Watergate Hotel, ordered room service, and turned on the television. President Johnson would be speaking at 8 p.m., and Duke, with his wife and children, gathered to watch the broadcast. President Johnson appeared on the screen and told the nation that he would not seek reelection.

Duke sat stunned in front of the television. He had been yanked away from Spain for nothing. Soon after, Duke was sworn in as director of protocol, a job that now seemed more frivolous than ever. The president did not attend the ceremony, sending Lady Bird instead. "He must have known," said Duke, "how disappointed I was."

During his famous swim, Duke predicted a bright future for the gritty beaches of Costa Bomba. Time eventually proved him right. Today, the once barren coast is crammed with beachfront condominiums and beet-faced British tourists. The Garrucha waterfront, once a working wharf packed with fishing boats, now sports a tony marina and a stylish promenade lined with palm trees. Two miles inland from Palomares sits a luxury golf resort called Desert Springs, its emerald links flanked by dramatic sculptures of rearing horses. The resort looks as if it had been carved out of Tucson, airlifted across the Atlantic, and plunked down in the Spanish desert. Closer to Palomares, Playa de Quitapellejos, the former site of Camp Wilson, remains much the same. The sand is rough and rocky, scattered with black slag. But there have been some changes. Two miles south, on what used to be a barren beach, is a thriving nudist colony.

In Palomares itself, there are few remnants of the dusty farming village that grabbed the world's attention in 1966. Palomares is now a modern, prosperous town, thanks to industrial agriculture and tourism. Modern greenhouses blanket the fields, and produce-processing centers the size of airplane hangars squat on the outskirts of town. The village square boasts a community center resembling a suburban library. The modern building faces a wide tiled plaza and new three-story condos, built for vacationing Europeans. The skyline of Palomares—the town now has a skyline—bristles with cranes lifting steel beams. The only memorial to the accident is a small street near the central plaza marked with a sign reading "Calle de 17 de enero de 1966"—January 17, 1966, Street.

Manolo and Dolores González still live in Palomares, in a small but comfortable apartment in the center of town. (They also own a gracious hacienda on the outskirts.) Like the rest of the town, Manolo and Dolores have prospered. Instead of a Citroën pickup truck, Manolo now drives a luxury-model silver Mercedes. As upbeat and enthusiastic as ever, Manolo says the town is no worse off from the accident. There is an endless supply of British tourists, with their bottomless, deep-seated craving for the Spanish sun. Plutonium or no plutonium, the building boom was inevitable.

As the town sprawls outward, however, the echoes of the past are making themselves heard. In 1966, during the initial cleanup, the Spanish and American governments created a program to monitor the air and soil of Palomares, as well as the health of its people. They named the program "Project Indalo" and put Emilio Iranzo, the JEN scientist, in charge. (The name "Indalo" comes from a petroglyph found in nearby caves, showing a stick figure of a man holding an arc over his head. Indalo is an omnipresent tourist symbol for Almería, visible on place mats, key chains, and shot glasses throughout the area.) From the beginning, the U.S. government has funded part of the program, though it refuses to say publicly how much it has contributed.

In 1966, JEN set up air monitors in and around the town and has regularly checked the contamination levels since then. It has also tested chickens, rabbits, tomatoes, and other crops. Every year, about 150 residents of Palomares travel to Madrid—all expenses paid—for complete physical examinations, including urine testing for plutonium. So far, at least 1,029 people have received more than 4,000 medical and dosimetric examinations. According to the U.S. Department of Energy, these tests show that about 5 percent of the people studied carry plutonium in their bodies. However, say the authorities, the increased plutonium causes no health risk. This is proven, they say, by the fact that the residents of Palomares have shown no increase in illnesses or deaths that might be caused by plutonium ingestion.

Unfortunately, neither CIEMAT—the successor to JEN—nor the DOE has made these medical results public. Villagers who visit Madrid for screenings are given detailed printouts listing their weight, blood pressure, and cholesterol but are never told anything about the plutonium that may or may not be in their bodies. Only one small study examining the villagers' long-term cancer rates has been published. It found that the cancer rates in Palomares were no higher than those in another Spanish town with a similar population.

Nevertheless, the accident continues to haunt the village. In the late 1970s, a large irrigation pool was built next to the area where bomb number two fell and cracked open. This area, which also served as the staging ground for loading the contaminated soil into barrels, remains the most contaminated zone. The heavy digging for the pool resuspended some of the buried plutonium, spiking contamination levels. Iranzo, who still ran the program at the time, insists that the levels, even at their highest, remained safe for the villagers.

In 2002, because of development encroaching on this same area, CIEMAT purchased about twenty-three acres of contaminated land in order to restrict use. It forbade farmers to plant in the area and eventually enclosed it with a ten-foot-high chain-link fence. ("*Now* they put a fence around it!" said Dolores González, rolling her eyes.) Around the same time, DOE and CIEMAT created a new program to survey, once again, the contaminated areas around Palomares.

Between November 21, 2006, and February 22, 2007, CIEMAT technicians swept 71 million square feet of land—the equivalent of 660 soccer fields—in and around Palomares with radiation meters, collecting 63,000 measurements. The preliminary results, released in the summer of 2007, surprised the scientists. The plutonium contamination was higher and more widespread than they had suspected, and several areas they had considered clean were contaminated with americium, a product of plutonium disintegration. In April 2008, CIEMAT announced another surprise: the discovery of two trenches, about ten yards long and thirty yards wide, containing radioactive debris. Little information on the trenches is available, though they appear to contain many "small radioactive metal objects" left by the Americans. Though the U.S. and Spanish governments had long known of the trenches' existence, they had not known their exact location.

The scientists insist that the radiation levels, though higher than expected, are still safe for residents. But as a result of the 2007 findings, they widened the "contaminated" zone from 107,000 square yards to almost 360,000. They have also restricted construction in and the sale of produce from the most contaminated areas. They have not yet established a plan for remediation.

The townspeople, who stand to gain or lose much from land use restrictions, are not happy with the increased attention. Manolo and Dolores González consider the new rules ridiculous. Manolo is not worried about the plutonium; after the accident, he says, he took a piece of the melted wreckage and used it for a paperweight, and he is healthy as a horse. "Everybody is healthy, no one is sick. The death rate in Palomares is below the national average," said Manolo. Everyone just needs to be *tranquilo*.

Alvin and *Aluminaut* met, one final time, in 1969.

After Palomares, both subs received their share of good press, and John Craven predicted a boom in miniature submersibles. "Minisubs," he told *The Washington Post,* "may some day be as common under the sea as planes streaking over it." But, much as space colonies failed to flourish and astronauts never made it to Mars, this imagined world of minisubs and undersea habitats never emerged.

However, *Alvin* and *Aluminaut* both kept busy after Palomares, though their jobs were decidedly odd. In 1967 and 1968, *Alvin* dove along the continental slope for geology and biology studies and also surveyed the tops of seamounts for a new acoustic test range. By late 1968, it had completed 307 successful dives. *Aluminaut,* meanwhile, took scientists on expeditions, salvaged lost gear, made a film with Jacques Cousteau, and sampled outflow from a Miami sewage treatment plant.

Then, on October 16, 1968, a freak accident seemed to change the future of both subs. On that day, *Alvin* was preparing for a routine dive about ninety miles southeast of Nantucket. Its task was to dive near a deep-moored buoy to inspect the line holding it. During the launch, two cables securing *Alvin*'s bow snapped, and the sub plunged forward. As its nose dunked under water, water poured into the open hatch. A few seconds later, someone yelled that the ballast tanks had ruptured. *Alvin*'s three crewmen scrambled for the hatch and barely had time to escape before the sub went under. It sank in about sixty seconds.

Immediately, everyone on board *Alvin*'s mother ship, *Lulu,* began to throw objects overboard—scrap metal, aluminum lawn chairs, a fifty-five-gallon barrel—to mark the spot. *Lulu* and her escort ship,

Gosnold, took bearings and swept the area with sonar, trying desperately to pinpoint the spot where *Alvin* had come to rest.

The ships left the area with a pretty good sense of where *Alvin* had landed. But because neither ship could photograph *Alvin* on the bottom, nobody knew if the sub had landed intact or broken to bits. WHOI eventually persuaded the Navy to send the USNS *Mizar* to sweep the ocean floor for *Alvin.* In June 1969, *Mizar* found and photographed *Alvin.* The little sub sat upright on the bottom, about 5,000 feet deep, slightly embedded in the soft mud. It was intact except for a broken aft propeller.

Alvin, fully flooded, was estimated to weigh about 8,800 pounds in water. WHOI wanted its sub back, but no object as big or heavy as *Alvin* had ever been recovered from such depths. The salvage operation would be difficult and costly, and the Navy wasn't sure if it wanted to bother. When a team at the Office of Naval Research met to decide whether or not to salvage *Alvin,* the chief of naval research reportedly grumbled, "Leave that damn toy on the bottom of the ocean." But eventually *Alvin*'s advocates persuaded the Navy to fund the recovery.

Salvage experts agreed that the best way to recover *Alvin* was to place a spring-loaded nine-foot toggle bar in its open hatch. The bar would then be hooked to a lift line, which *Mizar* could winch to the surface. Experts considered all the submersibles that could dive below five thousand feet and plant the toggle bar and then chose *Aluminaut* for the job. The assignment was a coup for the *Aluminaut* team. It got them a fat government contract and allowed them to rescue the sub that had upstaged them in Spain.

On August 27, 1969, *Aluminaut* submerged about three miles from *Alvin* and was guided to the sunken sub by *Mizar.* In addition to her crew, *Aluminaut* carried a Navy observer and Mac McCamis. Still part of the *Alvin* crew, Mac had helped design the toggle bar. Since he knew *Alvin* as well as anybody, he was a good man to have along.

The job proved difficult. *Aluminaut,* not especially maneuverable, faced a delicate job while fighting a steady current. Also, the toggle bar, which was slightly buoyant, was difficult to handle. Bob Canary, the *Aluminaut* pilot, said that getting the bar into *Alvin* was like trying to thread a wet noodle into a soda bottle in a half-knot current. Time after time, *Aluminaut* carefully climbed the side of *Alvin* and its crew tried to maneuver the toggle into the open hatch. Time after time, they failed. Mac McCamis, watching from the wings, grew increasingly frustrated. He wanted to grab the controls and do the job himself. (Some *Alvin* veterans say he did just that, an account flatly denied by the *Aluminaut* crew.) But finally *Aluminaut* managed to drop the toggle bar into *Alvin*'s hatch, trip the release, and back away.

The bar was connected to a twenty-five-foot length of line with a snap hook at its end. The *Aluminaut* grasped the snap hook in one of its claws, carried it to a ring at the end of the lift line, and snapped it in. *Mizar* raised *Alvin* and towed the crippled sub to a fishing ground off Martha's Vineyard, where a crane lifted *Alvin* onto a barge. *Alvin*, it turned out, was in remarkably good condition. Scientists and engineers flushed and cleaned every system, replaced the broken parts, and, by 1971, had her back on the job.

But just as *Alvin* got back to work, government funding for deep-sea exploration dried to a trickle. *Aluminaut*, despite its great success recovering *Alvin*, grew desperate for work, accepting projects that embarrassed the crew. The most famous, and perhaps the one for which *Aluminaut* is best remembered, was a television commercial for Simoniz Wax. Producers coated one side of a Ford Falcon with Simoniz, the other with Brand X, then tied the car to *Aluminaut* and submerged it under water. ("I don't even like to think about it," said one crew member.) But such exploits failed to cover *Aluminaut*'s operating costs, and in 1971 Reynolds canceled the *Aluminaut* program and put the sub into storage. It planned to put it back into the water when it would prove profitable. That day never came.

Alvin, on the other hand, managed to survive the lean years despite its saltwater dunking and went on to a long and prosperous career of scientific discovery. The sub is probably best known for exploring the wreck of the *Titanic* in 1986 and aiding the discovery of "black smokers," hydrothermal vents off the Galápagos Islands teeming with bizarre marine life. Over the years, WHOI has replaced individual parts of the sub in piecemeal fashion. All that remains of the original *Alvin* is three metal plates circling the entry hatch. The sub will retire by 2015, after nearly fifty years of service.

Palomares was not the last major nuclear weapons accident.

On January 21, 1968, almost exactly two years after the accident over Palomares, a SAC B-52 on airborne alert was circling 33,000 feet above Thule Air Base, Greenland. At around 3:30 p.m., the copilot, feeling chilly, cranked the cabin heater up to maximum. Shortly afterward, when other crew members complained about the heat, the copilot started to turn it down. A few minutes later, one crew member smelled burning rubber. As the fumes grew stronger, the aircraft commander told the crew to put on oxygen masks. The crew searched the plane and discovered a small fire in the lower cabin. The navigator fought the fire with two extinguishers, but the flames grew out of control, filling the plane with dense smoke. The pilot reported the fire to the ground, requested an emergency landing at Thule Air Base, and began his descent. Soon afterward, the electrical power on the plane blinked out. The pilot gave the order to eject. Six of the crew members bailed out into the darkness and landed safely in the snow. The seventh was killed.

The pilotless B-52, carrying four Mark 28 hydrogen bombs, continued its descent. The plane glided over the air base, banked left, then crashed into the ice seven miles away. When it hit, the plane was flying more than five hundred miles per hour. The jet fuel on board exploded into a massive fireball, detonating the high explosive in all four hydrogen bombs and spreading radioactive debris over miles of ice. U.S. personnel took four months to clean up the contamination, eventually removing 237,000 cubic feet of ice, snow, and aircraft parts.

By the time of the Thule accident, Secretary of Defense Robert McNamara had concluded that airborne alert was not necessary for national security. In 1966, using the Palomares accident for leverage, McNamara had proposed canceling the program. The Joint Chiefs of Staff and SAC objected to McNamara's plan. Eventually, the two sides compromised. In June 1966, President Johnson approved a curtailed program, allowing only four nuclear-armed bombers on airborne alert each day. It was one of these bombers that crashed in Greenland.

After the Thule accident, McNamara had had enough. He ordered SAC to stop carrying nuclear weapons on airborne alert. Within a day, the weapons had been removed. SAC continued to fly the missions with unarmed bombers, buying time as it continued to lobby for airborne alert. Its arguments, however, failed to persuade civilian authorities, who were tired of cleaning up diplomatic messes left by SAC's accidents. The program was canceled by the end of 1968.

The Strategic Air Command, the most powerful military force ever built, gradually diminished in power as the Navy and Army gained more nuclear weapons and the need for conventional weaponry increased. In 1992, after the fall of the Soviet Union, the U.S. government closed down SAC, divvying up its resources among other commands. Even then, with the USSR disintegrated into fifteen separate countries, SAC veterans were shocked by the decision. In their view, SAC remained the key deterrent of nuclear war; it was impossible to imagine the world without it. One pilot said he couldn't sleep for days, sure that the Russians were simply lying in wait to attack America the moment she let her guard down.

In 2007, Russian President Vladimir Putin announced that the Russian air force would begin regular long-range bomber patrols over the world's oceans. The Russian bombers are capable of carrying nuclear weapons, but Putin did not say whether the flights would be armed. In August of that year, Russian bombers flew so near the American military base on Guam that the United States scrambled fighter jets to shadow them. The American fighters flew so close to the Russians that the pilots could see one another's faces. According to Russian authorities, there was no altercation. The pilots smiled at one another and then went their separate ways.

ACKNOWLEDGMENTS

Writing this book has been like building Mount Everest with pebbles. Since 2002, I have gathered tidbits of information here and there as the story slowly took shape and the main characters emerged from the fog. Along the way, I interviewed close to a hundred people, read countless documents, and spent innumerable hours in libraries and archives. I received valuable support and advice from many people, both military and civilian, and would like to acknowledge some key players here.

Several characters in the book were also invaluable in my research. Joe Ramirez and his wife, Sylvia, sat for hours of interviews, shared personal notes and photographs, and told me where to stay in Madrid. Mike Rooney, Charlie Wendorf, and Larry Messinger, the three pilots who survived the crash, shared their stories during several interviews. Brad Mooney gave me time, stories, and good humor. Red Moody sat for hours of interviews, shared his life story, answered endless questions and e-mails, and wouldn't let me pay for lunch. Bill Barton answered countless questions over four years. Lewis Melson, one of the first people I interviewed, loaned me photos and personal letters. Art Markel kindly took the time for a long interview and a tour of the *Aluminaut*, despite his advanced illness.

Within the Navy, Lieutenant Lesley Lykins and Lieutenant Commander Leslie Hull-Ryde helped arrange research trips. Lieutenant Mike Morley at Rota floored me with his organizational abilities. Bobbi Petrillo at NAVSEA worked on my FOIA requests for years and sometimes sent informal notes with advice and encouragement. Ed Finney, Jr., was an enthusiastic and helpful photo archivist at the Naval Historical Center. Matt Staden, Gary Weir, and John Sherwood helped me find documents at the Naval Historical Center. Tom Lapuzza at SPAWAR illuminated the story of CURV. Lieutenant Commander Brad Andros, Master Diver Ron Ervin, Commander Miguel Gutierrez, and the divers of EOD 6 allowed me to observe their training and learn what makes divers tick.

In the Air Force, Sid Girardin at Pease Air Force Base arranged for me to fly on a KC-135, observe a midair refueling, and speak with SAC veterans. The staff at Minot Air Force Base allowed me to tour a B-52 and interview pilots. Joe Caver at AFHRA and Ann Webb at the Air University Library helped me find documents to flesh out the history of SAC.

On the civilian side, Shelley Dawicki, Rosemary Davis, and Lisa Raymond helped me find documents at WHOI. Liz Caporelli, Bob Brown, and Bruce Strickrott, also at WHOI, arranged my visit to *Alvin* and took time to give me an extensive tour. Zach Elder at Duke University was a great help with the Angier Biddle Duke papers, and Myra O'Canna was a great help with photos. Becky Kenny, David Hoover, and Sam Bono at the National Atomic Museum helped with archives and interview space, and were very gracious during my two visits. David Hahn and Nancy Tait at the Science Museum of Virginia helped me uncover a treasure trove of *Aluminaut* documents in a dusty storeroom.

The staff of the LBJ Library, the National Archives at College Park, Maryland, and the MIT Libraries were patient and knowledgeable. Randall Bergmann at DTIC tracked down the TF 65 final report. At Sandia and the NNSA, Terry Apodaca and Stefani Holinka helped push my FOIA requests through the system. Francis Smith shared stories of life on the *Albany* and the best brisket in Austin.

In Spain, Anouschka Orueta, my translator, gave me insights into her country. Her work went well beyond the call of duty. José Herrera Plaza generously opened his home and his files, gave me his time, and fed me well. And in Boston, the very patient Joe Federico tutored me in Spanish.

A number of scholars and historians took time to share their knowledge and research. Jerry Martin, the USSTRATCOM historian, gave insight on strategic bombing, the mighty hammer of SAC, and many other things. He kindly reviewed chapter 1 and offered comments. Scott

Sagan of Stanford University shared research gathered for his book *The Limits of Safety*. Edwin Moïse of Clemson shared his knowledge and insights into the Tonkin Gulf incidents. Richard Rhodes offered leads and SAC stories. Andy Karam, a health physicist at the Rochester Institute of Technology, explained nuclear fusion and alpha radiation and generously reviewed certain technical sections of this book.

I also owe a great debt to Flora Lewis and Tad Szulc, two newspaper reporters who published books about the accident in 1967. These two books, *One of Our H-Bombs Is Missing* (Lewis) and *The Bombs of Palomares* (Szulc), offer clear, straightforward reporting, with details of Palomares in 1966 and the immediate aftermath of the crash. These accounts were especially valuable because the town of Palomares today bears little resemblance to the town in this story and several key characters are deceased. Thus, occasionally I relied heavily on one of these two books. In those instances I either quoted them outright or cited their contribution in the endnotes.

Closer to home, I'd like to thank Doug Starr, who taught me well and saw promise in this story, and Ellen Ruppel Shell, who told me to swim at Mojácar. Johanna Kovitz, my transcriber, offered lots of enthusiasm and news tips. Karen Rowan and John Ost provided excellent research assistance. Carey Goldberg helped with the *Lotsman* and other things Russian. Jon Palfreman funded a research trip to Florida to interview Mac McCamis and Larry Messinger. Fred Schwarz, my editor at *Invention & Technology*, suggested I turn this story into a book. Jonathan Jao, my editor at Random House, gave me wonderful edits and made my first draft much better. Without his help, the book would have sunk under the weight of chapter 8. My agent, Michelle Tessler, offered encouragement and advice, and worked hard to get this story noticed. Shannon Densmore and my sister Patty were great friends throughout, especially after Finny was born. And my friend Steven Bedard read early drafts of this book for a measly payment of sardines. If I had the means, I would offer him a ride on the *Trieste*.

Finally, I want to thank my husband, Brian, who always believed in me and this story. Over the past six years, he has listened to endless stories of *Alvin* and H-bombs, read many drafts of this book, helped me drive in Spain, and offered other assistance, large and small. I owe him more than I can say.

BIBLIOGRAPHY

ABBREVIATIONS

AFHRA	Air Force Historical Research Agency
DOD	US Department of Defense
DOE	US Department of Energy
DOS	US Department of State
Duke	Duke University Rare Book, Manuscripts and Special Collections Library
FOIA	Freedom of Information Act (denotes a document obtained through a FOIA request)
LBJ	Lyndon B. Johnson Library
LANL	Los Alamos National Laboratory
NARA	National Archives and Records Administration
NHC	Naval Historical Center
NNSA	National Nuclear Security Agency
SMV	Science Museum of Virginia
SNL	Sandia National Laboratories
WHOI	Woods Hole Oceanographic Institute

PRINT MATERIAL

"Addendum to SAT Study of 7 February 1966." March 4, 1966. Document no. SAC200118190000. Secret. (NNSA, FOIA.)

Aircraft Salvage Operation Mediterranean (Aircraft Salvops Med). Lessons and Implications for the Navy. U.S. Department of the Navy, Office of the

Chief of Naval Operations. Washington, D.C.: Office of the Chief of Naval Operations, April 7, 1967. (FOIA.)

Aircraft Salvage Operation Mediterranean (Aircraft Salvops Med). Sea Search and Recovery of an Unarmed Nuclear Weapon by Task Force 65, Interim Report. U.S. Department of the Navy, Naval Ship Systems Command. Reston, Va.: Ocean Systems, July 15, 1966. (NHC, FOIA.)

Aircraft Salvage Operation Mediterranean (Aircraft Salvops Med). Sea Search and Recovery of an Unarmed Nuclear Weapon by Task Force 65, Sixth Fleet, 17 January–7 April, 1966, vols. 1–4. U.S. Department of the Navy, Naval Ship Systems Command. Reston, Va.: Ocean Systems, February 15, 1967. (NHC, FOIA.)

Allen, Everett S. "Research Submarine *Alvin.*" *U.S. Naval Institute Proceedings,* April 1964.

"The *Aluminaut* Story." March 6, 1986. (SMV.)

Anderton, David A. *Strategic Air Command: Two-Thirds of the Triad.* New York: Charles Scribner's Sons, 1951.

Andrews, Frank A. "Searching for the *Thresher.*" *U.S. Naval Institute Proceedings,* May 1964.

———. "Search Operations in the *Thresher* Area—1964, Section I." *Naval Engineers Journal,* August 1965.

———. "Search Operations in the *Thresher* Area—1964, Section II." *Naval Engineers Journal,* October 1965.

Arnold, H. H. *Third Report of the Commanding General of the Army Air Forces to the Secretary of War.* Washington, D.C.: Army Orientation Branch, Information and Education Division, War Department, November 12, 1945.

Asselin, S. V. *B-52/KC-135 Collision near Palomares, Spain.* SC-DR-66-397. Albuquerque, N.M.: Sandia Corporation, August 1966. Secret. (FOIA.)

———. *Notes on the EOD Render Safe Procedure of Weapon #4 (W28 #45345) near Palomares Spain,* March 15, 1966. Document no. SAC200118480000. Confidential. (NNSA, FOIA.)

"Background for War: Man in the First Plane." *Time,* September 4, 1950.

Baker, Russell. "Madrid Provides Warm 'Saludos.' " *The New York Times,* December 22, 1959.

Baldwin, Hanson W. "Ready or Not? President Upheld on Plan Not to Keep Bombers Constantly in Air on Alert." *The New York Times,* March 8, 1959.

———. "Strategy and Politics Shape Defense Debate: U.S. Concern over Soviet Bombers Gives Impetus to Congress' Study." *The New York Times,*
May 13, 1956.

Ballard, Robert D. *The Eternal Darkness: A Personal History of Deep-Sea
Exploration.* Princeton, N.J.: Princeton University Press, 2000.

Bartholomew, C. A. *Mud, Muscle and Miracles: Marine Salvage in the
United States Navy.* Washington, D.C.: Department of the Navy, 1990.

Biography: Major General Delmar Wilson. U.S. Department of the Air Force;
www.af.mil/bios.

Biography of Rear Admiral William S. Guest. Washington, D.C.: Naval Historical Center, U.S. Department of the Navy. Undated.

"Bison vs. B-52." *The New York Times,* Week in Review, May 6, 1956.

"The Bomb Is Found." *Time,* March 25, 1966.

Borowski, Harry R. *A Hollow Threat: Strategic Air Power and Containment
before Korea.* Westport, Conn.: Greenwood Press, 1982.

Boyne, Walter. *Boeing B-52: A Documentary History.* Washington, D.C.:
Smithsonian Institution Press, 1981.

Broad, William J. "New Sphere in Exploring the Abyss." *The New York
Times,* August 26, 2008.

Casey, Dennis, and Bud Baker. *Fuel Aloft: A Brief History of Aerial Refueling.* Undated. (AFHRA.)

Coffey, Thomas M. *Iron Eagle: The Turbulent Life of General Curtis LeMay.*
New York: Crown Publishers, 1986.

Cowley, Robert, ed. *The Cold War: A Military History.* New York: Random
House, 2005.

Craven, John Peña. *The Silent War: The Cold War Battle beneath the Sea.*
New York: Simon & Schuster, 2001.

Dallek, Robert. *Flawed Giant: Lyndon Johnson and His Times, 1961–1973.*
New York: Oxford University Press, 1998.

Deck Logs of the USS *Ability,* MSO-519. 1966. (NARA.)

Deck Logs of the USS *Albany,* CG-10. 1966. (NARA.)

Deck Logs of the USS *Boston,* CAG-1. 1966. (NARA.)

Deck Logs of the USS *Charles R. Ware,* DD-865. 1966. (NARA.)

Deck Logs of the USS *Fort Snelling,* LSD-30. 1966. (NARA.)

Deck Logs of the USS *Hoist,* ARS-40. 1966. (NARA.)

Deck Logs of the USS *Petrel,* ASR-14. 1966. (NARA.)

Deck Logs of the USS *Pinnacle,* MSO-462. 1966. (NARA.)

Deck Logs of the USS *Wallace L. Lind,* DD-703. 1966. (NARA.)

"Defense under Fire." *Time,* May 14, 1956.

Dennis, Jack, ed. *The Nuclear Almanac: Confronting the Atom in War and Peace.* Reading, Mass.: Addison-Wesley Publishing Company, 1984.

"Description of Normal Operation." Document no. SAC200118830000. (NNSA, FOIA.)

Dickson, Paul. *Sputnik: The Shock of the Century.* New York: Berkley Books, 2001.

Druckman, Daniel. *Negotiating Military Base-Rights with Spain, the Philippines, and Greece: Lessons Learned.* Arlington, Va.: George Mason University, Center for Conflict Analysis and Resolution, 1990.

Duke, Angier Biddle. *Address to American Management Association.* January 17, 1966. Angier Biddle Duke Papers, Box 18. (Duke.)

———. *Notes Taken After First Visit to the Palomares Site.* April 5, 1968. Angier Biddle Duke Papers, Box 64, Palomares folder. (Duke.)

———. "Remarks of Ambassador Angier Biddle Duke on 'CBS Special Report.' " March 16, 1966. Angier Biddle Duke Papers, Box 18. (Duke.)

"Duke, Angier Biddle." *Current Biography,* vol. 23, no. 2. New York: H. W. Wilson Co., February 1962. Angier Biddle Duke Papers, Box 1. (Duke.)

Finney, John W. "Research Submarine Will Hunt for Lost H-Bomb." *The New York Times,* January 28, 1966.

———. "U.S. Concedes Loss of H-Bomb in Spain." *The New York Times,* March 3, 1966.

Fletcher, Harry R. *Air Force Bases.* Vol. 2: *Air Bases outside the United States of America.* Washington, D.C.: U.S. Air Force, Center for Air Force History, 1993.

Ford, Corey, and James Perkins. "Our Key SAC Bases in Spain and How We Got Them." *Reader's Digest,* August 1958.

Furman, Necah. *Sandia National Laboratories: The Postwar Decade*. Albuquerque, N.M.: University of New Mexico Press, 1989.

Gaddis, John Lewis. *The Cold War: A New History*. New York: Penguin Press, 2005.

Geitner, Paul. "Spanish Town Struggles to Forget Its Moment on the Brink of a Nuclear Cataclysm." *The New York Times,* September 12, 2008.

Gentile, Gian P. *How Effective Is Strategic Bombing? Lessons Learned from World War II to Kosovo*. New York: New York University Press, 2001.

Gibson, James A. *Nuclear Weapons of the United States: An Illustrated History*. Atglen, Pa.: Schiffer Publishing, 1996.

Goode, Sanchez. "Postscript to Palomares." *U.S. Naval Institute Proceedings* 94, no. 12, December 1968, pp. 49–53.

Grenfell, E. W. "USS *Thresher* (SSN-593), 3 August 1961–10 April 1963." *U.S. Naval Institute Proceedings,* March 1964.

Grugel, Jean, and Tim Rees. *Franco's Spain*. London: Arnold Publishers, 1997.

Hansen, Chuck. *The Swords of Armageddon: U.S. Nuclear Weapons Development since 1945*. Sunnyvale, Calif.: Chukelea Publications, 1995.

———. *U.S. Nuclear Weapons: The Secret History*. New York: Crown Publishers, 1988.

"An H-Bomb Is Missing and the Hunt Goes On." *Newsweek,* March 7, 1966.

"H-Bomb Located in Sea off Spain." *The New York Times,* March 18, 1966.

Healion, James V. "Boom on 2-Man Subs Seen." *The Washington Post,* June 25, 1967.

Hearings before the Joint Committee on Atomic Energy, Congress of the United States, Eighty-eighth Congress, First and Second Sessions on the Loss of the USS Thresher. June 26, 27, July 23, 1963, and July 1, 1964. Washington, D.C.: Government Reprints Press, 2001.

Heller, Richard K. "Accomplishments of the Cable-Controlled Underwater Research Vehicle." Presentation to the AIAA Marine Sciences Symposium," April 21, 1966.

Higgins, Marguerite. "He Takes the Starch Out of Protocol." *The Saturday Evening Post,* September 29, 1962. Angier Biddle Duke Papers, Box 1. (Duke.)

Hopkins, J. C., and Sheldon A. Goldberg. *The Development of the Strategic Air Command, 1946–1986.* Offutt Air Force Base, Neb.: Office of the Historian, Headquarters Strategic Air Command, September 1, 1986.

Hubbell, John G. "The Case of the Missing H-Bomb." *Reader's Digest,* September 1966.

Iranzo, E., et al. "Air Concentrations of ^{239}Pu and ^{240}Pu and Potential Radiation Doses to Persons Living near Pu-Contaminated Areas in Palomares, Spain." *Health Physics* 52, no. 4, April 1987.

Iranzo, Emma, et al. "Resuspension in the Palomares Area of Spain: A Summary of Experimental Studies." *Journal of Aerosol Science* 25, no. 5, 1994.

"Is It or Isn't It?," *Newsweek,* March 28, 1966.

Johnson, Leland. *Sandia National Laboratories: A History of Exceptional Service in the National Interest.* Albuquerque, N.M.: Sandia National Laboratories, 1997.

"Johnson Rebuffs de Gaulle Quickly in Bases Dispute." *The New York Times,* March 9, 1966.

Kaharl, Victoria. *Water Baby: The Story of* Alvin. New York: Oxford University Press, 1990.

Kahn, E. J. "Good Manners and Common Sense." *The New Yorker,* August 15, 1964.

Kaplan, Fred. *The Wizards of Armageddon.* New York: Simon & Schuster, 1983.

Kohn, Richard H., and Joseph P. Harahan, eds. *Strategic Air Warfare: An Interview with Generals Curtis E. LeMay, Leon W. Johnson, David Burchinal, and Jack Catton.* Washington, D.C.: Office of Air Force History, 1988.

Kramer, Andrew E. "Recalling Cold War, Russia Resumes Long-Range Sorties." *The New York Times,* August 18, 2007.

Larus, Joel. *Nuclear Weapons Safety and the Common Defense.* Columbus: Ohio State University Press, 1967.

LeMay, Curtis, with MacKinlay Kantor. *Mission with LeMay: My Story.* New York: Doubleday and Company, 1965.

"LeMay Discusses Air War of Future." *The New York Times,* November 20, 1945.

"LeMay Says Flaw Has Delayed B-52; 31 of 78 Rejected." *The New York Times,* May 3, 1956.

"LeMay Sees Peril to Nation by 1959: Gives Senators 'Guess' That Soviet Surprise Attack Could Destroy U.S." *The New York Times,* May 27, 1956.

Leviero, Anthony. "Air Critics Omit Navy and B-47's, Eisenhower Says. Public Will Feel 'Lot Better' When Full Story Is Told, President Promises." *The New York Times,* May 5, 1956.

———. "Big Russian Jets Estimated at 100." *The New York Times,* May 4, 1956.

———. "General LeMay Fears Soviet Lead in Air by 1960." *The New York Times,* May 1, 1956.

———. "3.8 Billion More a Year Is Sought in Bomber Funds." *The New York Times,* June 12, 1956.

Lewis, Flora. *One of Our H-Bombs Is Missing.* New York: McGraw-Hill, 1967.

Lloyd, Alwyn T. *A Cold War Legacy: A Tribute to the Strategic Air Command, 1946–1992.* Missoula, Mont.: Pictorial Histories Publishing Company, 1999.

Man's Extension into the Sea. Symposium Proceedings, January 11–12, 1966. Washington, D.C.: Marine Technology Society, 1966.

Martin, George W. "Lasting Legacies of *Thresher.*" *The Submarine Review,* July 2003.

———. "The Search for *Thresher.*" *The Submarine Review,* April 2003.

May, Mike. "Gas Stations in the Sky." *Invention & Technology* 19, no. 4, Spring 2004.

Maydew, Randall C. *America's Lost H-Bomb! Palomares, Spain, 1966.* Manhattan, Kans.: Sunflower University Press, 1997.

Maydew, Randall C., ed. *A Kansas Farm Family.* Freeman, S. Dak.: Pine Hill Press, 1992.

McCamis, Marvin J. "Captain Hook's Hunt for the H-Bomb." *Oceanus* 31, no. 4, Winter 1988–89.

McDowell, Bart, and Albert Moldvay. "The Changing Face of Old Spain." *National Geographic,* March 1965.

Melson, Lewis B. "Contact 261." *U.S. Naval Institute Proceedings* 93, no. 6, June 1967.

Méndez, Rafael. "Detectada contaminación en Palomares fuera de las zonas expropiadas y valladas." *El País*, July 1, 2007.

———. "España halla las zanjas radiactivas que EEUU ocultó en Palomares." *El País*, April 4, 2008.

Miller, James E., ed. *Foreign Relations of the United States, 1964–1968.* Vol. 2: *Western Europe.* Washington, D.C.: U.S. Government Printing Office, 2001.

"The Missing H-Bomb." *The Boston Globe,* March 4, 1966.

Mitchell, Eugene B., and William I. Milwee. "Recovery of *Alvin*—A Practical Ocean Engineering Operation." *Naval Engineers Journal,* December 1969.

Moody, D. H. "40th Anniversary of Palomares." *Faceplate* 10, no. 2, September 2006.

Moody, Walton S. *Building a Strategic Air Force.* Washington, D.C.: Air Force History and Museums Program, 1996.

Moïse, Edwin E. *Tonkin Gulf and the Escalation of the Vietnam War.* Chapel Hill: University of North Carolina Press, 1996.

Morland, Howard. "The H-Bomb Secret." *The Progressive,* November 1979.

Morris, John D. "Soviet ICBM Held Able to Pinpoint 5,000-Mile Target." *The New York Times,* January 31, 1959.

Moscow, Warren. "Center of Tokyo Devastated by Firebombs." *The New York Times,* March 11, 1945.

Narducci, Henry M. *Strategic Air Command and the Alert Program: A Brief History.* Offutt Air Force Base, Neb.: Office of the Historian, Headquarters Strategic Air Command, April 1, 1988.

"Narrative Summaries of Accidents Involving U.S. Nuclear Weapons 1950–1980." Undated. (NNSA, FOIA.)

National Intelligence Estimate 11-4-61: Main Trends in Soviet Capabilities and Policies, 1961–1966. U.S. Director of Central Intelligence. RG 263, Box 16, Folder 9. (NARA.)

"Naval Forces under the Sea: A Look Back, a Look Ahead." Symposium Proceedings, March 27–29, 2001. Flagstaff, Ariz.: Best Publishing Company, 2002.

Naval Ordnance Test Station, Pasadena Annex. *AirsalopsMed/CURV Notes,* 1966.

"New Diplomatic Hand." *Newsweek*, January 11, 1965. Angier Biddle Duke Papers, Box 66. (Duke.)

Norris, John G. "Lessons Thresher Taught Didn't Help with H-Bomb." *The Washington Post*, March 27, 1966.

Norris, Robert S., William M. Arkin, and William Burr. *Nuclear Weapons Databook Working Paper 87-1 (Rev. 1): US-USSR Strategic Offensive Nuclear Forces 1946–1987*. Washington, D.C.: Natural Resources Defense Council, December 1987.

———. "Where They Were." *The Bulletin of the Atomic Scientists*, November–December 1999.

"Officials Take Cold Dip to Deny H-Bomb Hazard." *The Washington Post*, March 9, 1966.

Olid, Miguel. "Luz sobre Palomares." *El País*. Undated.

"On Arms and Aid." *The New York Times*, Week in Review, May 13, 1956.

"On Continuous Alert." *The New York Times Magazine*, December 8, 1957.

Oreskes, Naomi. "A Context of Motivation: U.S. Naval Oceanographic Research and the Discovery of Sea-Floor Hydrothermal Vents." *Social Studies of Science* 33, no. 5, October 2003.

Oulahan, Richard. "The Case of the Missing H-Bomb." *Life*, February 25, 1966.

Palomares Nuclear Weapons Accident: Revised Dose Evaluation Report. U.S. Department of the Air Force, Air Force Medical Service, April 2001. (FOIA.)

Pinilla, Pedro Martínez, et al. "Evolución de la mortalidad en Palomares antes y después del accidente nuclear de 1966." *El Médico* 16, no. 1, 1987.

Place, W. M., et al. *Palomares Summary Report*. Kirtland Air Force Base, N.M.: Field Command, Defense Nuclear Agency, Technology and Analysis Directorate, January 15, 1975.

Plaza, José Herrera, and Antonio Sánchez Picón. *Operación "Flecha Rota": Accidente nuclear en Palomares (Almería)*. Almería, Spain: Consejería de Cultura, Centro Andaluz de la Fotografía, 2003.

Podvig, Pavel, ed. *Russian Strategic Nuclear Forces*. Cambridge, Mass.: MIT Press, 2004.

Polmar, Norman. *The Death of the USS* Thresher: *The Story Behind History's Deadliest Submarine Disaster.* Guilford, Conn.: Lyons Press, 1964.

Polmar, Norman, and Timothy M. Laur, eds. *Strategic Air Command: People, Aircraft and Missiles.* 2nd ed. Baltimore, Md.: Nautical and Aviation Publishing Company of America, 1990.

Pothier, Richard. "Star of Deep for Six Years, She's to Be a Sub on Bench." *The Miami Herald,* undated.

"Power Airs SAC Deterrent Capability." *Aviation Week,* April 20, 1959.

Rae, Bruce. "300 B-29's Fire 15 Square Miles of Tokyo." *The New York Times,* March 10, 1945.

Rainnie, William O. "*Alvin* . . . and the Bomb." *Oceanus* 12, no., August 1966.

———. "Equipment and Instrumentation for the Navigation of Submersibles." Undated. DSV Alvin Records, 1949–1998 AC 18, Box 17, Folder 23: Navigation, General. (WHOI.)

———. "How We Found the Missing H-Bomb." *Popular Mechanics,* August 1966.

Rainnie, William O., and William I. Milwee. "How We Raised the *Alvin* from 5000 Feet." *Popular Mechanics,* January 1970.

Raymond, Jack. "President Sees Dangers in Full Mobilization Now." *The New York Times,* March 5, 1959.

Recollections for Tomorrow. Albuquerque, N.M.: Sandia National Laboratories, 1989.

Recovery of Deep Research Vehicle Alvin. NAVSHIPS 0994-004-5010. U.S. Department of the Navy, Naval Ship Systems Command. Washington, D.C.: Naval Ship Systems Command, December 1969.

Reed, Thomas C. *At the Abyss: An Insider's History of the Cold War.* New York: Ballantine Books, 2004.

Report of Major Aircraft Accident, KC-135A, 61-0273, B-52G, 58-256. Directorate of Safety, Sixteenth Air Force, U.S. Department of the Air Force. January 31, 1966. (FOIA.)

Reynolds Aluminum. Aluminaut: *The Deep Diving Aluminum Submarine.* Brochure, undated. (SMV.)

Rhodes, Richard. *Dark Sun: The Making of the Hydrogen Bomb.* New York: Simon & Schuster, 1995.

——. *The Making of the Atomic Bomb.* New York: Simon & Schuster, 1986.

Richardson, Henry. Diary, March 15 to April 7, 1966. Author's collection.

Richmond, C. R. "Remarks on Palomares—Seven Years Later," March 9, 1973. (NNSA, FOIA.)

Rosenberg, David Alan. " 'A Smoking Radiating Ruin at the End of Two Hours': Documents on American Plans for Nuclear War with the Soviet Union, 1954–1955." *International Security* 6, no. 3, Winter 1981–82.

Rubottom, R. Richard, and J. Carter Murphy. *Spain and the United States since World War II.* New York: Praeger Publishers, 1984.

"Russians Accuse U.S. in B-52 Crash." *The New York Times,* February 18, 1966.

Rutherfurd, Jay. "Duke's 'Swim-in' for Spanish Tourism Best Water Show since Aquacade." *Variety,* March 16, 1966.

SAC Historical Study #109: Sixteenth Air Force Operation Recovery, 17 January–7 April, 1966, vols. 1 and 1A. History and Research Division, Headquarters Strategic Air Command, U.S. Department of the Air Force, April 1968. (FOIA.)

"SAC's Deadly Daily Dozen." *Time,* March 17, 1961.

Sagan, Scott D. *The Limits of Safety: Organizations, Accidents and Nuclear Weapons.* Princeton, N.J.: Princeton Studies in International History and Politics, 1993.

Salisbury, Karen. "Defense: Bombers at the Ready." *Newsweek,* April 18, 1949.

Shapley, Deborah. *Promise and Power: The Life and Times of Robert McNamara.* Boston: Little, Brown and Company, 1993.

Simons, Howard. "Intensive, Expensive Hunt under Way to Locate H-Bomb Lost over Spain." *The Washington Post,* February 24, 1966.

——. "Lost H-Bomb Is Recovered by U.S. Ship." *The Washington Post,* April 8, 1966.

——. "Some Experts Fear Strategic Loss if Curbs Are Put on Nuclear Routes." *The Washington Post,* February 27, 1966.

——. "U.S. Faces an Unending Cleanup Task." *The Washington Post,* February 25, 1966.

——. "U.S. Finally Admits Loss of H-Bomb over Spain." *The Washington Post,* March 3, 1966.

——. "U.S. to Hunt Weapon until Certain It Can't Be Found—by Friend or Foe." *The Washington Post,* February 26, 1966.

"600 Spanish March in Anti-U.S. Protest." *The New York Times,* February 5, 1966.

"Some B-52's in Air around the Clock: S.A.C. Begins Training for Possible Establishment of an Airborne Alert." *The New York Times,* January 19, 1961.

"Soviet Asks World Check on U.S. H-Bomb off Spain." *The New York Times,* March 19, 1966.

Spaatz, Carl. "Strategic Air Power: Fulfillment of a Concept." *Foreign Affairs,* April 1946.

"Spain: the Awakening Land." *Time,* January 21, 1966.

Springer, Roy M., et al. "Palomares/Navy." *Combat Readiness,* October–December 1966.

"Staff Study by Systems Analysis Team of Search Operations," February 7, 1966. Document no. SAC200118390000. Secret. (NNSA, FOIA.)

Stannard, J. Newell. *Radioactivity and Health, A History,* vol. 2: *Environmental Aspects.* Richland, Wash.: Pacific Northwest Laboratory, 1988.

Stiles, David. "A Fusion Bomb over Andalucía: U.S. Information Policy and the 1966 Palomares Incident." *Journal of Cold War Studies* 8, no. 1, Winter 2006.

Storms, Barbara. "When the Sky Fell." *The Atom,* May 1966. (LANL, FOIA.)

The Strategic Air Command Alert Force: History and Philosophy (Briefing). Offutt Air Force Base, Neb.: Office of the Historian, Headquarters Strategic Air Command, September 1, 1988.

Streeter, Michael. *Franco.* London: Haus Publishing, 2005.

Stuart, John. "Army Air Leaders Want U.S. on Guard for Sudden Attack." *The New York Times,* October 2, 1945.

"Sub Finds H-Bomb off Spain: Weapon Reported Intact in Water 2500 Feet Deep." *The Washington Post,* March 18, 1966.

"Swimming Party." *Newsweek,* March 14, 1966.

Szulc, Tad. *The Bombs of Palomares.* London: Victor Gollancz, 1967.

———. "Dented H-Bomb Is Displayed on Recovery Ship." *The New York Times,* April 9, 1966.

———. "H-Bomb Is Recovered Intact after 80 Days." *The New York Times,* April 8, 1966.

———. "H-Bomb Searchers Fail Again as Sea Cable Snaps." *The New York Times,* March 26, 1966.

———. "Palomares Learns to Love the Bomb." *The New York Times Magazine,* February 20, 1966.

———. "U.S. Envoy Swims Where H-Bomb Fell." *The New York Times,* March 9, 1966.

Tanner, Henry. "De Gaulle Insists on Rule of Bases of NATO in France." *The New York Times,* February 22, 1966.

"Texts of Franco and Eisenhower Talks." *The New York Times,* December 22, 1959.

Thomas, Hugh. *The Spanish Civil War.* New York: Harper & Row, 1961.

"Tossing a Curv." *Business Week,* April 16, 1966.

Toth, Robert C. "H-Bomb May Slip into Deep Sea Crevice, Balk Recovery." *Los Angeles Times,* March 22, 1966.

———. "New Bomb Recovery Try Slated." *Los Angeles Times,* March 23, 1966.

———. "Recovery Operations to Raise H-Bomb Begin in Rough Seas." *Los Angeles Times,* March 19, 1966.

———. "Soviet Spy Ship Watches U.S. Hunt Bomb." *Los Angeles Times,* March 8, 1966.

———. "Spanish Town Could Have Been a Hiroshima." *Los Angeles Times,* March 13, 1966.

———. "Submarine Tows Lost H-Bomb up Sea Slope toward Recovery." *Los Angeles Times,* March 20, 1966.

USAF Nuclear Safety, Special Edition: Project Crested Ice 65 (part 2), no. 1, U.S. Department of the Air Force, Jan–Feb–Mar 1970.

"U.S. Bars H-Bombs in Airborne Alert." *The New York Times,* February 29, 1968.

"Vital Contributions Made by Sandia in Locating Lost Nuclear Weapon." *Sandia Lab News,* April 22, 1966. (SNL.)

Weart, Spencer R. *Nuclear Fear: A History of Images.* Cambridge, Mass.: Harvard University Press, 1988.

Welles, Benjamin. "Eisenhower Gets Franco's Support." *The New York Times,* December 23, 1959.

———. "Eisenhower Is Hailed in Madrid." *The New York Times,* December 22, 1959.

———. "Franco Aide's Visit to Highlight Improving U.S. Ties with Spain." *The New York Times,* December 30, 1959.

———. "Franco's Prestige High as He Awaits Eisenhower's Visit." *The New York Times,* December 19, 1959.

———. "Spain Offers 3 Proposals on Gibraltar." *The New York Times,* May 27, 1966.

Whitaker, Arthur P. *Spain and the Defense of the West: Ally and Liability.* New York: Harper & Brothers, 1961.

Wilford, John Noble. "Gemini 8 Crew Is Forced Down in Pacific after Successful Linkup with Satellite; Spacemen Picked Up after 3 Hours in Sea." *The New York Times,* March 17, 1966.

———. "Gemini Is Fueled for Link-up Today." *The New York Times,* March 16, 1966.

Wilson, Delmar E. *Speech to Residents of Palomares and Villaricos.* March 20, 1966. (USAF, FOIA.)

Winkler, Allan M. *Life under a Cloud: American Anxiety about the Atom.* New York: Oxford University Press, 1993.

Witkin, Richard. "S.A.C. Operating New Alert Program: Aims to Get Third of Bomber Force Airborne within 15 Minutes after Attack." *The New York Times,* November 11, 1957.

Wolk, Herman S. *Toward Independence: The Emergence of the U.S. Air Force 1945–1947.* Washington, D.C.: Air Force History and Museums Program, 1996.

Worden, Mike. *Rise of the Fighter Generals: The Problem of Air Force Leadership, 1945–1982.* Maxwell Air Force Base, Ala.: Air University Press, March 1998.

LETTERS, CABLES, AND MEMOS

Airgram, Embassy in Madrid to Department of State, "U.S. Policy Assessment," May 7, 1966. National Security File, Country File, Spain, Spain memos vol. 1, Box 204. Confidential. (LBJ.)

Airgram, Embassy in Madrid to Department of State, "Undersecretary Rostow's Conversation with Joaquín Ruiz-Giménez," December 24, 1966. National Security File, Country File, Spain, Spain Cables vol. 1, Box 204. Confidential. (LBJ.)

Cable, from 16th AF Torrejón AB Spain to RUEKDA/Secretary of Defense, January, 1966, #61642. National Security File, Country File, Spain 1/17/66, TS/RD B-52/KC-135 Accident, Box 204. Secret. (LBJ.)

Cable, from CINCLANTFLT, undated, #70834. National Security File, Country File, Spain 1/17/66, TS/RD B-52/KC-135 Accident, Box 204. Secret. (LBJ.)

Cable, CSAF to Joint Chiefs of Staff et al., January 19, 1966, #53337. National Security File, Country File, Spain 1/17/66, TS/RD B-52/KC-135 Accident, Box 204. Secret. (LBJ.)

Cable, CSAF to Joint Chiefs of Staff et al., January 19, 1966, #59032. National Security File, Country File, Spain 1/17/66, TS/RD B-52/KC-135 Accident, Box 204. Secret. (LBJ.)

Cable, CTF Sixty-five to REUCW/CNO, "Sitrep Seventy-nine," March 16, 1966. National Security File, Country File, Spain 1/17/66, TS/RD B-52/KC-135 Accident, Box 204. Confidential. (LBJ.)

Cable, DASA to RUECW/CNO, January 21, 1966, #51711. National Security File, Country File, Spain 1/17/66, TS/RD B-52/KC-135 Accident, Box 204. Secret. (LBJ.)

Cable, Department of Defense, January 23, 1966, #65908. National Security File, Country File, Spain 1/17/66, TS/RD B-52/KC-135 Accident, Box 204. Secret. (LBJ.)

Cable, Department of State to Embassy in Madrid, January 17, 1966, Deptel 08319. National Security File, Country File, Spain 1/17/66, TS/RD B-52/KC-135 Accident, Box 204. Confidential. (LBJ.)

Cable, Department of State to Embassy in Madrid, January 22, 1966, Deptel 12217. National Security File, Country File, Spain 1/17/66, TS/RD B-52/KC-135 Accident, Box 204. Secret. (LBJ.)

Cable, Department of State to Embassy in Madrid, February 12, 1966, Deptel 06998. National Security File, Country File, Spain 1/17/66, TS/RD B-52/KC-135 Accident, Box 204. Secret. (LBJ.)

Cable, Department of State to Embassy in Madrid, February 17, 1966. RG 59, Central Files 1964–66, DEF 17 US. Secret. (NARA.)

Cable, Department of State to Embassy in Madrid, May 6, 1966. RG 59, Central Files 1964–66, POL 17-5 SP-US. Confidential. (NARA.)

Cable, Department of the Air Force, January 21, 1966, #61510. National Security File, Country File, Spain 1/17/66, TS/RD B-52/KC-135 Accident, Box 204. Secret. (LBJ.)

Cable, Dir Nuclear Safety Kirtland AFB NMEX to RUTQBN/16AF Torrejón AB Spain, undated. National Security File, Country File, Spain 1/17/66, TS/RD B-52/KC 135 Accident, Box 204. Secret. (LBJ.)

Cable, Embassy in Madrid to SECSTATE, March 18, 1966, #1226. National Security File, Country File, Spain 1/17/66, TS/RD B-52/KC-135 Accident, Box 204. Confidential. (LBJ.)

Cable, Embassy in Madrid to SECSTATE, December 10, 1966, #9187. National Security File, Country File, Spain, Spain Cables vol. 1, Box 204. Confidential. (LBJ.)

Cable, Embassy in Madrid to SECSTATE WASHDC, March 1, 1966. National Security File, Country File, Spain 1/17/66, TS/RD B-52/KC-135 Accident, Box 204. (LBJ.)

Cable, Embassy in Madrid to SECSTATE WASHDC, March 22, 1966, Deptel 1185. National Security File, Country File, Spain, Spain Cables vol. 1, Box 204. Confidential. (LBJ.)

Cable, Embassy in Madrid to SECSTATE WASHDC IMMEDIATE, March 17, 1966, #1219. National Security File, Country File, Spain, Spain Cables vol. 1, Box 204. Confidential. (LBJ.)

Cable, Embassy in Madrid to SECSTATE WASHDC PRIORITY, March 25, 1966, #23577. National Security File, Country File, Spain, Spain Cables vol. 1, Box 204. Secret. (LBJ.)

Cable, Embassy in Madrid to SECSTATE WASHDC PRIORITY, March 25, 1966, #24270. National Security File, Country File, Spain, Spain Cables vol. 1, Box 204. Secret. (LBJ.)

Cable, Embassy in Madrid to SECSTATE WASHDC PRIORITY, April 1, 1966, #849. National Security File, Country File, Spain, Spain Cables vol. 1, Box 204. Secret. (LBJ.)

Cable, from Embassy in Madrid, February 14, 1964, #1552. National Security File, Subject File, Nuclear Weapons, Spain, vol. 1, Box 34. Secret. (LBJ.)

Cable, Embassy in Madrid to the Department of State, January 19, 1966, #855. National Security File, Country File, Spain, vol 1. Secret. (LBJ.)

Cable, Embassy in Madrid to the Department of State, January 19, 1966, #856. National Security File, Country File, Spain 1/17/66, TS/RD B-52/KC-135 Accident, Box 204. Confidential. (LBJ.)

Cable, Embassy in Madrid to the Department of State, January 19, 1966, #857. National Security File, Country File, Spain 1/17/66, TS/RD B-52/KC-135 Accident, Box 204. Secret. (LBJ.)

Cable, Embassy in Madrid to the Department of State, January 21, 1966, #867. National Security File, Country File, Spain 1/17/66, TS/RD B-52/KC-135 Accident, Box 204. Confidential. (LBJ.)

Cable, Embassy in Madrid to the Department of State, January 21, 1966, #869. National Security File, Country File, Spain 1/17/66, TS/RD B-52/KC-135 Accident, Box 204. Confidential. (LBJ.)

Cable, Embassy in Madrid to the Department of State, January 22, 1966, #871. National Security File, Country File, Spain 1/17/66, TS/RD B-52/KC-135 Accident, Box 204. Secret. (LBJ.)

Cable, Embassy in Madrid to the Department of State, January 26, 1966, #896. National Security File, Country File, Spain 1/17/66, TS/RD B-52/KC-135 Accident, Box 204. Confidential. (LBJ.)

Cable, Embassy in Madrid to the Department of State, January 27, 1966, #903. National Security File, Country File, Spain 1/17/66, TS/RD B-52/KC-135 Accident, Box 204. Confidential. (LBJ.)

Cable, Embassy in Madrid to the Department of State, February 21, 1966. Madrid Post Files: Lot 71 A 2420, Def 17. Secret. (DOS.)

Cable, Embassy in Madrid to the Department of State, February 25, 1966, #1054. National Security File, Country File, Spain 1/17/66, TS/RD B-52/KC-135 Accident, Box 204. Confidential. (LBJ.)

Cable, SAC Comm. Ctr. Offutt AFB to Air Staff OASD-DA, January 19, 1966. National Security File, Country File, Spain 1/17/66, TS/RD B-52/KC-135 Accident, Box 204. (LBJ.)

Cable, SAC to RUEAHQ/CSAF, undated, #67467. National Security File, Country File, Spain 1/17/66, TS/RD B-52/KC-135 Accident, Box 204. Secret. (LBJ.)

Cable, SAC to White House Lt. Col. Cross Armed Forces Aide to the President, January, 1966, #00527. National Security File, Country File, Spain, vol 1. Secret. (LBJ.)

Cable, SECDEF to SAC, February 12, 1966. National Security File, Country File, Spain 1/17/66, TS/RD B-52/KC-135 Accident, Box 204. Confidential. (LBJ.)

Cable, SECDEF to 16ADVON Spain and CTF 65, "Observation of Weapon During and Immediately Post Recovery," March 23, 1966. National Security File, Country File, Spain 1/17/66, TS/RD B-52/KC-135 Accident, Box 204. Confidential. (LBJ.)

Cable, SECSTATE WASHDC to DOD WASHDC, January 25, 1966, Deptel 888. National Security File, Country File, Spain 1/17/66, TS/RD B-52/KC-135 Accident, Box 204. Confidential. (LBJ.)

Cable, SECSTATE WASHDC to RUEHEX/White House Immediate, January 20, 1966, #341. National Security File, Country File, Spain 1/17/66, TS/RD B-52/KC-135 Accident, Box 204. Secret. (LBJ.)

Cable, from 16ADVON Spain to RUCSC/SAC, March 17, 1966, #71560. National Security File, Country File, Spain 1/17/66, TS/RD B-52/KC-135 Accident, Box 204. Secret. (LBJ.)

Cable, from 16AF ADVON to RUEKDA/SECDEFWASH, undated, #67589. National Security File, Country File, Spain 1/17/66, TS/RD B-52/KC-135 Accident, Box 204. Secret. (LBJ.)

Cable, from 16AF ADVON Spain to SEC of DEF, undated, #71088. National Security File, Country File, Spain 1/17/66, TS/RD B-52/KC-135 Accident, Box 204. Secret. (LBJ.)

Cable, from 16th AF Torrejón AB Spain, January 19, 1966, #41960. National Security File, Country File, Spain 1/17/66, TS/RD B-52/KC-135 Accident, Box 204. Secret. (LBJ.)

Cable, from 16th AF Torrejón AB Spain, January 19, 1966, #49311. National Security File, Country File, Spain 1/17/66, TS/RD B-52/KC-135 Accident, Box 204. Secret. (LBJ.)

Cable, from 16th AF Torrejón AB Spain, January 19, 1966, #57879. National Security File, Country File, Spain 1/17/66, TS/RD B-52/KC-135 Accident, Box 204. Secret. (LBJ.)

Cable, from 16th AF Torrejón AB Spain, January, 1966, #59141. National Security File, Country File, Spain 1/17/66, TS/RD B-52/KC-135 Accident, Box 204. Secret. (LBJ.)

Cable, State and Defense to Embassy in Madrid, March 30, 1966, Deptel 1240. National Security File, Country File, Spain 1/17/66, TS/RD B-52/KC-135 Accident, Box 204. Secret. (LBJ.)

Letter, Nathan Arrow to Angier Biddle Duke, March 11, 1966. Angier Biddle Duke Papers, Box 5. (Duke.)

Letter, John Bruce to Paul Fye, February 28, 1966. Directors Collection, P. Fye. Folder, Vessels: *Alvin,* "Adventures in Spain," 1966. (WHOI.)

Letter, John Bruce to Paul Fye, March 9, 1966. Directors Collection, P. Fye. Folder, Vessels: *Alvin,* "Adventures in Spain," 1966. (WHOI.)

Letter, Angier Biddle Duke to Jack Valenti, March 14, 1966. Confidential File, CO 272 Spain, Box 11. Confidential. (LBJ.)

Letter, Earl Hays to Paul Fye, March 8, 1966. Directors Collection, P. Fye. Folder, Vessels: *Alvin,* "Adventures in Spain," 1966. (WHOI.)

Letter, Jacqueline Kennedy to Angier Biddle Duke, March 12, 1966. Angier Biddle Duke Papers, Box 5. (Duke.)

Letter, Flora Lewis to Bill Moyers, August 3, 1966. National Security File, Country File, Spain 1/17/66, TS/RD B-52/KC-135 Accident, Box 204. (LBJ.)

Letter, Art Markel to Carrie, February 18, 1966. (SMV.)

Letter, Art Markel to Carrie, March 28, 1966. (SMV.)

Letter, Art Markel to Carrie, April 6, 1966. (SMV.)

Letter, Art Markel to Louis Reynolds, February 23, 1966. (SMV.)

Letter, Lewis Melson to Folks, February 12, 1966. Author's collection.

Letter, Lewis Melson to Adm. Leyton, February 15, 1966. Author's collection.

Letter, Lewis Melson to Adm. Leyton, February 25, 1966. Author's collection.

Letter, Bill Moyers to Flora Lewis, August 11, 1966. National Security File, Defense, Gen ND 21, 6/9/66–6/30/67, Box 425. (LBJ.)

Letter, Arthur Schlesinger, Jr., to Angier Biddle Duke, March 15, 1966. Angier Biddle Duke Papers, Box 5. (Duke.)

Letter, Jack Valenti to Angier Biddle Duke, March 9, 1966. White House Central Files, Name File, Duke, Angier Biddle. (LBJ.)

Memo, S.V. Asselin to S. A. Moore. "Trip to Pantex, April 27 and 28, 1966," undated. Document #SAC200118240000. Confidential. (NNSA, FOIA.)

Memo, ATSD (AE) to Secretary of Defense et al. "Situation report, B-52/KC-135 Accident, 17 January 1966," January 18, 1966. National Security File, Country File, Spain 1/17/66, TS/RD B-52/KC-135 Accident, Box 204. Secret. (LBJ.)

Memo, William Barton. "The Missing Bomb," undated. Randall Maydew files. (SNL.)

Memo, "B-52/KC-135 Mid-Air Collision." Undated. National Security File, Country File, Spain 1/17/66, TS/RD B-52/KC-135 Accident, Box 204. Secret. (LBJ.)

Memo, Commander Task Group 65.3 to Commander Task Force 65. "Report of Inshore Search, Identification and Recovery Unit," March 13, 1966. EOD U2, Post 46, Command Files, Operational Archives. Confidential. (NHC.)

Memo, Barrett Fountos to Tom Bell et al. "Trip Report to Spain with Accomplishments Related to Palomares Program Review," September 23, 1998. Author's collection.

Memo, Bill Hoagland to Jack Howard. "Summary Prepared by Stu Asselin," document #SAC200118490000. Undated. (NNSA, FOIA.)

Memo, Art Markel to office, "Tape 3," recorded March 19, 1966. (SMV.)

Memo, Art Markel to office, "Tape 4," recorded March 20, 1966. (SMV.)

Memo, Art Markel to office, "Tape 5," recorded March 22, 1966. (SMV.)

Memo, Art Markel to office, "Tape 6," recorded March 23, 1966. (SMV.)

Memo, Art Markel to office, "Tape 17," recorded April 11, 1966. (SMV.)

Memo, R. C. Maydew and W. R. Barton to G. A. Fowler. "Chronological Summary of Significant Events in the 9300 Participation in Broken Arrow Operation," March 29, 1966. Randall Maydew files. (SNL.)

Memo, Art McCafferty to Bromley Smith, January 17, 1966. National Security File, Country File, Spain 1/17/66, TS/RD B-52/KC-135 Accident, Box 204. Top Secret. (LBJ.)

Memo, Robert L. McNeill to William N. Caudle. "Field Observation Operation Sunday," February 15, 1966. Document #SAC200118670000. Secret. (NNSA, FOIA.)

Memo from Lewis Melson. "WHOI's OCEANUS WINTER 1988/1989 Issue Extract for 1 March 1966," undated. Author's collection.

Memo, Dewitt H. Moody to Commander, Naval Ordnance Systems Command. "Report of Explosive Ordnance Disposal Operation (OPNAV REPORT 3571-1)," May 10, 1966. EOD U2, Post 46, Command Files, Operational Archives. Secret. (NHC.)

Memo from National Military Command Center. "Special Situation Report for the White House: B-52/KC-135 Accident in Southeastern Spain," January 19, 1966. National Security File, Country File, Spain 1/17/66, TS/RD B-52/KC-135 Accident, Box 204. Top Secret. (LBJ.)

Memo, W. O. Rainnie to Files. "Weekly Progress Report of ALVIN Field Operations, Week of January 23 to January 30, 1966," March 4, 1966. Directors Collection, P. Fye. Folder, Vessels: *Alvin,* "Adventures in Spain," 1966. (WHOI.)

Memo, W. O. Rainnie to Files. "Weekly Progress Report of ALVIN Field Operations, Week of January 31 through February 7, 1966," March 4, 1966. Directors Collection, P. Fye. Folder, Vessels: *Alvin,* "Adventures in Spain," 1966. (WHOI.)

Memo, W. O. Rainnie to Files. "Weekly Progress Report of ALVIN Field Operations, Week of February 8 through February 14, 1966," March 4, 1966. Directors Collection, P. Fye. Folder, Vessels: *Alvin,* "Adventures in Spain," 1966. (WHOI.)

Memo, W. O. Rainnie to Files. "Weekly Progress Report of ALVIN Field Operations, Week of February 15 through February 21, 1966," March 4, 1966. Directors Collection, P. Fye. Folder, Vessels: *Alvin,* "Adventures in Spain," 1966. (WHOI.)

Memo, W. O. Rainnie to Files. "Weekly Progress Report of ALVIN Field Operations, Week of February 22 through February 28, 1966," March 7, 1966. *Alvin* Ops, DSV *Alvin* Records AC18, Box 3, Folder 7. (WHOI.)

Memo, W. O. Rainnie to Files. "Weekly Progress Report of ALVIN Field Operations, Week of March 1 through March 7, 1966," March 29, 1966. Directors Collection, P. Fye. Folder, Vessels: *Alvin,* "Adventures in Spain," 1966. (WHOI.)

Memo, W. O. Rainnie to Files. "Weekly Report of Field Activity of ALVIN, March 8 through March 14, 1966," March 29, 1966. Directors Collection, P. Fye. Folder, Vessels: *Alvin,* "Adventures in Spain," 1966. (WHOI.)

Memo, W. O. Rainnie to Office of Naval Research. "Quarterly Informal

Letter Status Report of Contract Nonr 3834(00), Deep Submergence Research Vehicle Project, January 1, 1966 through April 9, 1966," June 10, 1966. Alvin Ops, DSV *Alvin* Records AC18, Box 17, Folder 3: Quarterly Reports. (WHOI.)

Memo, 16AF Torrejón AB Spain to US Embassy Spain and JUSMG Madrid Spain. February 2, 1966. (USAF, FOIA.)

Memo, Bromley Smith to Bill Moyers, January 19, 1966. National Security File, Country File, Spain 1/17/66, TS/RD B-52/KC-135 Accident, Box 204. (LBJ.)

Memo, U.S. Information Agency to All Principal USIS Posts. "Talking Paper No. 28—'The Bomb in Spain,' " March 4, 1966. Limited Official Use. (LBJ.)

Memo, Allyn C. Vine to Paul Fye, "ASW," October 10, 1960. ODR 26/35 Folder: Personnel, Allyn C. Vine, 1960–61. (WHOI.)

Memo, White House Situation Room to President Johnson, January 17, 1966, 7:05 A.M. National Security File, Country File, Spain 1/17/66, TS/RD B-52/KC-135 Accident, Box 204. Top Secret. (LBJ.)

Memo, White House Situation Room to President Johnson, January 17, 1966, 9:00 P.M. National Security File, Country File, Spain 1/17/66, TS/RD B-52/KC-135 Accident, Box 204. (LBJ.)

Memo, White House Situation Room to President Johnson, January 18, 1966, 7:00 A.M. National Security File, Country File, Spain, vol 1. Secret. (LBJ.)

Memo, White House Situation Room to President Johnson, January 18, 1966, 9:05 P.M. National Security File, Country File, Spain, vol 1. Secret. (LBJ.)

Memo, White House Situation Room to President Johnson, January 22, 1966, 7:15 A.M. National Security File, Country File, Spain, vol 1. Secret. (LBJ.)

Memo, White House Situation Room to President Johnson, January 23, 1966, 7:00 A.M. National Security File, Country File, Spain, vol 1. Secret. (LBJ.)

Memo, White House Situation Room to President Johnson. "Report on Nuclear Weapon in Spain," March 17, 1966. National Security File, Country File, Spain, vol 1. Confidential. (LBJ.)

Memo, Delmar E. Wilson to SAC (Gen. John D. Ryan). "Search Operations, Palomares, Spain," February 13, 1966. (DOD, FOIA.)

Memorandum of Conversation, January 25, 1966. "Spanish Government Position on Overflights of Spain by Military Aircraft of NATO Countries Bound for or Going to Gibraltar." RG 59, Central Files 1964–66, POL 19 GIB. Confidential. (NARA.)

Memorandum of Conversation, January 28, 1966. "Gibraltar." RG 59, Central Files 1964–66, POL 19 GIB. Confidential. (NARA.)

Memorandum of Conversation, November 13, 1967. "Base Negotiations." RG 59, Central Files 1967–69, DEF 15-4 SP-US. Confidential. (NARA.)

Memorandum for the Files, December 5, 1967. "Spanish Base Negotiations and Palomares." RG 59, Central Files 1967–69, DEF 15-4 SP-US. Secret. (NARA.)

AUDIOVISUAL

"Air Force Gen. Curtis LeMay on Missing Bomb." CBS News, March 12, 1966.

"American Experience: Victory in the Pacific." Directed by Austin Hoyt. Documentary, 2005.

"Angier Biddle Duke radio interview with Jay Rutherfurd." Audio recording, 1966. Angier Biddle Duke Papers, Box 65. (Duke.)

"Cold War." Television documentary, CNN, 1998.

A Gathering of Eagles. Directed by Delbert Mann. Feature film, Universal Pictures, 1963.

"H-Bomb Lost in Spain." CBS News, January 23, 1966.

"H-Bomb Recovered." CBS News, April 8, 1966.

"The Mission of SAC: SAC Film Report No. 2." U.S. Air Force, January 1961.

"Navy on Search for Bomb." CBS News, March 10, 1966.

"Noticias NO-DO 1210 B" (Manuel Fraga Iribane visit to Palomares). Newsreel, Filmoteca Española, undated.

"Noticias NO-DO 1253 C" (Simó Orts receives award). Newsreel, Filmoteca Española, undated.

"Operación Flecha Rota: Accidente nuclear de Palomares (Almería)." Directed by José Herrera Plaza. Documentary, 2007.

"Palomares Recovery Operations." CBS News, March 25, 1966.

"Palomares Revisited re: Atom Bomb." CBS News, December 20, 1966.

"Search for H-Bomb." CBS News, March 14, 1966.

"Search for Missing Bomb." CBS News, March 7, 1966.

"Special Report: Lost and Found, One H-Bomb." CBS News, March 22, 1966.

Strategic Air Command. Directed by Anthony Mann. Feature film, Paramount Pictures Corp., 1955.

Thunderball. Directed by Terence Young. Feature film, United Artists, 1965.

"US Envoy Swims in Mediterranean." CBS News, March 9, 1966.

"William S. Guest Press Conference." Audio recording, April 8, 1966.

INTERVIEWS AND ORAL HISTORIES

All interviews were conducted by author unless otherwise noted. Most interviews were taped and transcribed, and many were followed up with additional interviews and/or correspondence.

Allsopp, Steven. Personal interview. August 17, 2006.

Andersen, Oliver. Telephone interview. January 22, 2007. Personal interview. March 31, 2007.

Andrews, Frank. Telephone interview. November 10, 2006.

Andros, Brad. Personal interviews. March 20–21, 2007.

Bartlett, Arthur C. Telephone interview. February 5, 2007.

Barton, William. Personal interviews. January 22, 2004, and October 23, 2006.

Bender, Harry. Personal interview. August 23, 2005.

Boykin, Rhodes. Telephone interview. March 16, 2007.

Brady, Larry. Telephone interviews. January 18 and 31, 2007.

Breuer, Glynn. Personal interview. August 23, 2005.

Broderson, Eva. Personal interview. October 4, 2006.

Brown, Robert. Personal interview. July 2, 2007.

Bruce, John. Personal interview. August 17, 2006.

Bruner, Gordon. Interview by Flora Lewis. AFHRA, K416.051-64 (tapes 1 and 2). Undated.

Burchinal, David K. U.S. Air Force Oral History interview by John B. Schmidt. AFHRA, K239.0512-837. April 11, 1975.

Cammack, Colonel (no first name listed). Interview by Flora Lewis. AFHRA. July 11, 1966.

Canary, Robert. Telephone interview. November 14, 2006.

Caudle, William. Personal interview. January 22, 2004.

Chase, Donald. Personal interview. August 25, 2005.

Colucci, Anthony. Telephone interview. July 31, 2007.

Craven, John. Telephone interview. April 19, 2007.

DePriest, Eric. Personal interview. August 23, 2005.

Detmer, Charles. Telephone interview. December 13, 2006.

Duke, Angier Biddle and Robin. Duke Living History interview by James David Barber, John TePaske, and Taylor Cole, October 24, 1990. Duke Living History Program, Box 1. Duke.

Duke, Robin. Telephone interview. June 7, 2007.

Durbin, Phil. Telephone interview. March 15, 2007.

Eliason, Andrew. Personal interview. October 4, 2006.

Engelhardt, Henry "Bud." Telephone interview. May 17, 2006.

Ervin, Ron. Personal interview. March 21, 2007.

Finkel, Robert. Telephone interview. April 4, 2007.

Foster, Dudley. Personal interview. July 25, 2006.

Fraga Iribarne, Manuel. Personal interview. February 15, 2007.

González, Manolo and Dolores. Personal interview. February 24, 2007.

Herb, Michael. Personal interview. January 8, 2007.

Herrera Plaza, José. Personal interview. February 25, 2007.

Holt, Ira. Telephone interview. November 9, 2006.

Hooper, Rich. Personal interview. January 8, 2007.

Howard, Jack. Telephone interview. April 3, 2007.

Iranzo, Emilio. Personal interview. February 16, 2007.

Jeffords, Ed. Telephone interview. November 27, 2006.

Jenkins, Ralph. Telephone interview. March 14, 2007.

Kennedy, Max. Personal interview. August 25, 2005.

Kingsbery, Douglas. Telephone interview. July 27, 2007.

Kingsbery, Robert. Telephone interview. July 19, 2007.

Landau, George. Telephone interviews. January 22, 2007, and August 9, 2007.

LeMay, Curtis. U.S. Air Force Oral History interview. AFHRA, K239.0512-714. January 1965.

———. U.S. Air Force Oral History interview by Bill Peck. AFHRA, K239.0512-785. March 1965.

———. U.S. Air Force Oral History interview by John T. Bohn. AFHRA, K239.0512-736. March 9, 1971.

———. U.S. Air Force Oral History interview by Thomas Belden. AFHRA, K239.0512-593. March 29, 1972.

———. U.S. Air Force Oral History interview by Robert Futrell, Thomas Belden, and J. Van Staaveren. AFHRA, K239.0512-592. June 8, 1972.

Ligon, Tom. Telephone interview. November 30, 2006.

Lindbergh, Jon. Telephone interview. July 11, 2007.

MacKinnon, Malcolm. Personal interview. December 4, 2006.

Markcum, Glenn. Personal interview. March 27, 2007.

Martin, George. Telephone interview. May 9, 2007.

Martin, Jerome. Personal interview. August 26, 2005.

Maydew, Jean and Barbara. Personal interview. October 21, 2006.

Maydew, Randall. Oral history. Randall Maydew files, SNL. August 22, 1985.

———. Interview by Necah Furman. SNL. December 1991.

Markel, Art. Personal interview. September 25, 2006.

McAlees, Sam. Personal interview. October 23, 2006.

McCamis, Marvin. Personal interview. January 31, 2003.

Melson, Lewis. Personal interview. August 23, 2006.

Messinger, Larry. Personal interview. January 31, 2003. Telephone interview. October 19, 2004.

Miracle, Stephen. Personal interview. August 23, 2005.

Moïse, Edwin. Telephone interview. August 16, 2007.

Montalbine, Gary. Telephone interview. August 16, 2007.

Moncrief, "Monty." Personal interview. August 23, 2005.

Montgomery, John B. U.S. Air Force Oral History interview by Mark C. Cleary. AFHRA, K239.0512-1586. April 30–May 1, 1984.

Moody, Dewitt "Red." Personal interview. November 7, 2006. Telephone interview. July 17, 2007.

Mooney, J. Bradford "Brad." Personal interview. March 30, 2007.

Morris, Chuck. Telephone interview. November 14, 2006.

Pace, Robert. Telephone interview. February 6, 2007.

Page, Horace C. Telephone interview. April 3, 2007.

Pepper, William. Personal interview. October 21, 2006.

Porembski, Chester. Personal interview. November 17, 2006.

Porteous, John. Personal interview. September 6, 2006.

Ramirez, Joe. Personal interviews. January 27, 2007, and April 27, 2007.

Ramirez, Sylvia. Telephone interview. May 25, 2007.

Richardson, Henry "Tony." Telephone interviews. October 31 and November 9, 2006. Personal interview. October 31, 2007.

Rooney, Michael. Telephone interviews. January 14, 2005, April 14, 2005, and June 27, 2005.

Sass, Rick. Personal interview. January 8, 2007.

Singleton, Robert. Telephone interview. November 27, 2006.

Smith, Francis. Personal interview. March 28, 2007.

Smith, Joseph. Telephone interviews. January 23, 2007, and August 9, 2007.

Sproull, Robert. Telephone interview. May 11, 2007.

Starkweather, Glen. Personal interview. July 29, 2005.

Stevens, Denford. Telephone interview. November 30, 2006.

Strickrott, Bruce. Personal interview. July 2, 2007.

Towell, Timothy. Telephone interview. January 5, 2007. Personal interview. January 8, 2007.

Tyler, George. Personal interview. September 26, 2006.

Tyndale, Clyde. Personal interview. November 3, 2006.

Ulrich, Rebecca. Personal interview. October 24, 2006.

Vornbrock, Walter. Telephone interview. April 23, 2007.

Walden, Barrie. Personal interview. July 25, 2006.

Wendorf, Charles. Interview by Flora Lewis. AFHRA, KWG-68-5U-PE (tapes 1 and 2). Undated.

———. Telephone interviews. October 16, 2004, and July 30, 2005.

White, Alton "Bud." Interview by Flora Lewis. AFHRA, K416.051-63 (tapes 1 and 2) and K416.051-64 (tape 3). Undated.

White, Gaylord. Personal interview. March 3, 2007.

Wiley, Mo. Personal interview. August 23, 2005.

Winkler, Allan. Telephone interview. January 14, 2005.

Wolk, Herman. Telephone interview. November 21, 2005.

Zablocki, Robert. Telephone interview. December 11, 2006.

NOTES

ABBREVIATIONS

AFHRA   Air Force Historical Research Agency
DOD   U.S. Department of Defense
DOE   U.S. Department of Energy
DOS   U.S. Department of State
Duke   Duke University Rare Book, Manuscripts and Special Collections Library
FOIA   Freedom of Information Act
LANL   Los Alamos National Laboratory
LBJ   Lyndon B. Johnson Library
NARA   National Archives and Records Administration
NHC   Naval Historical Center
NNSA   National Nuclear Security Agency
SMV   Science Museum of Virginia
SNL   Sandia National Laboratories
WHOI   Woods Hole Oceanographic Institute

PROLOGUE

ix   **Francisco Simó Orts stood:** Simó's actions on the day of the accident come from several sources, most notably Flora Lewis, *One of Our H-Bombs Is Missing* (New York: McGraw-Hill, 1967), pp. 37–41; Tad Szulc, *The Bombs of Palomares* (London: Victor Gollancz, 1967), pp. 38–40; U.S. Department of the Navy, Naval Ship Systems Command, *Aircraft Salvage Operation Mediterranean (Aircraft Salvops Med). Sea Search and Recovery of an*

Unarmed Nuclear Weapon by Task Force 65, Sixth Fleet, 17 January–7 April 1966 (Reston, Va.: Ocean Systems, 1967) (henceforth *Aircraft Salvops Med*), vol. 1, p. 9; and author's interviews with Joe Ramirez, January 27, 2007, and April 27, 2007.

ix **Like a bronzed Kirk Douglas:** The quote is from Lewis, *One of Our H-Bombs,* p. 40.

x **And two splashed down:** Some sources list the distances in meters, others in yards. The sources agree that Simó saw six parachutes, but to avoid confusion, the author mentions only those that the fisherman saw landing in the water.

JANUARY

CHAPTER 1: MIGHTY SAC

3 **Twenty-four hours earlier:** Wendorf's personal history and his account of the day of the accident come from two major sources: author's interviews with Wendorf on October 16, 2004, and July 30, 2005, and U.S. Department of the Air Force, *Report of Major Aircraft Accident, KC-135A, 61-0273, B-52G, 58-256* (Directorate of Safety, Sixteenth Air Force, 1966).

4 **logging 2,100 flying hours:** Lewis, *One of Our H-Bombs,* p. 5.

4 **His copilot:** Rooney's personal history and his account of the day of the accident come from two major sources: author's interviews with Rooney on January 14, 2005, April 14, 2005, and June 27, 2005, and *Report of Major Aircraft Accident.*

4 **One writer described the pilot:** Rooney enjoyed "the charms of nurses, daughters of senior officers, and belles of nearby Raleigh." Lewis, *One of Our H-Bombs,* p. 7.

5 **The third pilot that day:** Messinger's personal history and his account of the day of the accident come from two major sources: author's interviews with Messinger on January 31, 2003, and October 19, 2004, and *Report of Major Aircraft Accident.*

6 **The big news stories:** *The New York Times,* January 16, 1966, p. 1.

6 **And 35,000 feet above it all:** Author's interview with Charles Wendorf, October 16, 2004.

6 **32,193 nuclear warheads:** www.brookings.edu/projects/archive/nucweapons/50.aspx.

6 674 bombers, 968 missiles, and 196,887 people: Alwyn T. Lloyd, *A Cold War Legacy: A Tribute to the Strategic Air Command, 1946–1992* (Missoula, Mont.: Pictorial Histories Publishing Company, 1999), pp. 676–677.

6 The commander of SAC directed: SAC, in conjunction with the Joint Strategic Target Planning Staff (JSTPS), was legally responsible for selecting targets for Air Force and Navy strikes, but the commander of SAC was also the director of the JSTPS. Jerome Martin, e-mail to author, March 10, 2008.

6 SAC supplied much of the military intelligence: An excellent overview of SAC's dominance comes from Mike Worden, *Rise of the Fighter Generals: The Problem of Air Force Leadership, 1945–1982* (Maxwell Air Force Base, Ala.: Air University Press, 1998), especially chaps. 3 and 4.

7 At dusk on March 9, 1945: Information on the bombing of Tokyo comes from Thomas M. Coffey, *Iron Eagle: The Turbulent Life of General Curtis LeMay* (New York: Crown Publishers, 1986), pp. 155–165; Bruce Rae, "300 B-29's Fire 15 Square Miles of Tokyo," *The New York Times,* March 10, 1945, p. 1; Warren Moscow, "Center of Tokyo Devastated by Firebombs," *The New York Times,* March 11, 1945, p. 1. See also "American Experience: Victory in the Pacific," directed by Austin Hoyt, 2005, transcript at www.pbs.org/wgbh/amex/pacific/filmmore/pt.html.

7 LeMay had been running the show: The background on LeMay in Guam is from Curtis LeMay with MacKinlay Kantor, *Mission with LeMay: My Story* (New York: Doubleday and Company, 1965), pp. 342–347, and Coffey, *Iron Eagle,* pp. 146–147.

8 Sensing impatience from Washington: Coffey, *Iron Eagle,* pp. 155–156.

8 At about 2 a.m.: Ibid., p. 163.

8 When World War II began: Background on the AAF and long-range strategic bombing comes from many sources, including Worden, *Rise of the Fighter Generals,* chap. 1; author's interview with Jerome Martin, August 26, 2005; Walton S. Moody, *Building a Strategic Air Force* (Washington, D.C.: Air Force History and Museums Program, 1996), chap. 1; Richard H. Kohn and Joseph P. Harahan, eds., *Strategic Air Warfare: An Interview with Generals Curtis E. LeMay, Leon W. Johnson, David Burchinal, and Jack Catton* (Washington, D.C.: Office of Air Force History, 1988).

9 an assignment to a bomber crew: The dangers of flying in a World War II bomber are covered in Worden, *Rise of the Fighter Generals,* chap. 1, and Coffey, *Iron Eagle,* chaps. 5 and 6.

9   the 100th Bomber Group lost seven planes: Coffey, *Iron Eagle,* pp. 99–100.

9   Bomber crews were more likely: Worden, *Rise of the Fighter Generals,* p. 8.

10 A stricken B-17:   Coffey, *Iron Eagle,* p. 86.

10 LeMay, head of the 4th Bombardment Wing: The background on LeMay in England comes from Coffey, *Iron Eagle,* chaps. 5 and 6, and Kohn and Harahan, *Strategic Air Warfare,* pp. 19–47.

11 The Navy brass, riding high: Coffey, *Iron Eagle,* p. 145.

11 In a city like Tokyo: The details on the firebombing of Tokyo come from Coffey, *Iron Eagle,* pp. 164–165; Bruce Rae, "300 B-29's Fire 15 Square Miles of Tokyo," *The New York Times,* March 10, 1945, p. 1; Warren Moscow, "Center of Tokyo Devastated by Firebombs," *The New York Times,* March 11, 1945, p. 1. See also "American Experience: Victory in the Pacific" and Richard Rhodes, *Dark Sun: The Making of the Hydrogen Bomb* (New York: Simon & Schuster, 1995), pp. 17–24.

12 "When you kill 100,000 people":   Drea, quoted in "American Experience: Victory in the Pacific."

12 "No matter how you slice it":   LeMay, *Mission with LeMay,* p. 352.

12 When the B-29s returned from Tokyo: Coffey, *Iron Eagle,* pp. 166–172.

12 By summer, LeMay announced: Ibid., p. 174.

13 "I think it's more immoral":   LeMay, *Mission with LeMay,* p. 382.

13 It was far more humane: Ibid., p. 384.

13 LeMay attended the Japanese surrender ceremonies: Ibid., p. 390.

13 the atomic bombs had been impressive but anticlimactic: Curtis LeMay, U.S. Air Force Oral History, January 1965 (AFHRA). See also Coffey, *Iron Eagle,* p. 179; Worden, *Rise of the Fighter Generals,* p. 25; Richard Rhodes, *Dark Sun,* pp. 17–24.

13 In the months after VJ Day: Background on the AAF drive for independence comes from Worden, *Rise of the Fighter Generals,* pp. 27–34; "LeMay Discusses Air War of Future," *The New York Times,* November 20, 1945, p. 3; John Stuart, "Army Air Leaders Want U.S. on Guard for Sudden Attack," *The New York Times,* October 2, 1945, p. 1; and author's interview with Jerome Martin, August 26, 2005.

13 The famed pilot Jimmy Doolittle: Worden, *Rise of the Fighter Generals,* pp. 30–31.

14 "Being peace-loving and weak": Stuart, "Army Air Leaders Want U.S. on Guard for Sudden Attack."

14 With the Army's blessing: Worden, *Rise of the Fighter Generals,* p. 31.

14 The Air Force started life: E-mail, Jerome Martin to author, March 10, 2008.

14 they saw SAC as the key: Worden, *Rise of the Fighter Generals,* pp. 30–33.

14 Not that there was much to grab: Worden, *Rise of the Fighter Generals,* pp. 27–29; author's interview with Jerome Martin, August 26, 2005; Kohn and Harahan, *Strategic Air Warfare,* pp. 73–75, 82.

14 "We just walked away": Kohn and Harahan, *Strategic Air Warfare,* p. 74.

14 "We started from nothing": Ibid., p. 82.

14 SAC floundered: Ibid., pp. 73–78; and Jerome Martin interview, August 26, 2005. For a deeper discussion of SAC's postwar troubles, see Harry R. Borowski, *A Hollow Threat: Strategic Air Power and Containment before Korea* (Westport, Conn.: Greenwood Press, 1982).

14 But by 1948: A good introduction to the Berlin Crisis and the early Cold War can be found in John Lewis Gaddis, *The Cold War: A New History* (New York: Penguin Press, 2005), chap. 3.

15 On October 19, 1948: Lloyd, *A Cold War Legacy,* p. 666.

15 The situation shocked him: Curtis LeMay, U.S. Air Force Oral History Interview, March 9, 1971 (AFHRA); Kohn and Harahan, *Strategic Air Warfare,* pp. 78–84; Coffey, *Iron Eagle,* pp. 271–276; LeMay, *Mission with LeMay,* pp. 429–447; Worden, *Rise of the Fighter Generals,* pp. 58–63.

15 "We had to be ready": Curtis LeMay, U.S. Air Force Oral History Interview, March 9, 1971, p. 29 (AFHRA).

15 LeMay sprang into action: LeMay's transformation of SAC is discussed in Worden, *Rise of the Fighter Generals,* pp. 59–63; Kohn and Harahan, *Strategic Air Warfare,* pp. 78–84; Karen Salisbury, "Defense: Bombers at the Ready," *Newsweek,* April 18, 1949, pp. 24–26.

15 Power was not well liked: Coffey, *Iron Eagle,* p. 276; Worden, *Rise of the Fighter Generals,* pp. 81–82.

16 "My goal": Kohn and Harahan, *Strategic Air Warfare,* p. 84.

16 he had created a religion: LeMay explains his theories on deterrence in

his autobiography, *Mission with LeMay,* as well the oral histories he recorded for the Air Force. In *Strategic Air Warfare,* p. 97, Kohn and Harahan recorded a telling exchange between LeMay and Kohn:

> KOHN: Was it difficult because it was peacetime, or was there no sense of peacetime in SAC . . .
>
> LEMAY: It was wartime.

17 The year 1952 began the golden age: A detailed discussion of SAC's rise to power can be found in Worden, *Rise of the Fighter Generals,* chaps. 3 and 4. For Eisenhower's views on nuclear war, see Gaddis, *The Cold War,* pp. 66–68. For an overview of Americans' attitudes toward nuclear weapons in the 1950s, see Allan M. Winkler, *Life under a Cloud: American Anxiety about the Atom* (New York: Oxford University Press, 1993), chap. 3.

17 Eisenhower's philosophy led to a windfall: Statistics in this paragraph come from Worden, *Rise of the Fighter Generals,* p. 67, and Lloyd, *Cold War Legacy,* pp. 676, 677, 681.

17 "SAC was still the big daddy": Jerome Martin interview, August 26, 2005.

18 SAC hosted a classified briefing: Moore's memo is in David Alan Rosenberg, " 'A Smoking Radiating Ruin at the End of Two Hours': Documents on American Plans for Nuclear War with the Soviet Union, 1954–1955," *International Security* 6, no. 3 (Winter 1981–82), pp. 25–28. The Sunday Punch is described in Fred Kaplan, *The Wizards of Armageddon* (New York: Simon & Schuster, 1983), p. 204, and Worden, *Rise of the Fighter Generals,* p. 108.

18 The concept of alert time: Kaplan, *Wizards of Armageddon,* pp. 97–110.

19 LeMay had flown to Washington: Information on the 1956 "bomber gap" hearings comes from Kaplan, *Wizards of Armageddon,* pp. 156–160; Worden, *Rise of the Fighter Generals,* pp. 78–79; and *The New York Times'* coverage of the hearings.

19 Worrisome intelligence had trickled in: Information on the 1955 Soviet airshow comes from Kaplan, *Wizards of Armageddon,* p. 156; Worden, *Rise of the Fighter Generals,* p. 78; and "Bison vs. B-52," *The New York Times,* May 6, 1956, The Week in Review, p. 1.

20 The Soviets had only ten Bisons: Pavel Podvig, ed., *Russian Strategic Nuclear Forces* (Cambridge, Mass.: MIT Press, 2004), p. 375.

20 The budget already included $16.9 billion: "On Arms and Aid," *The New York Times,* Week in Review, May 13, 1956, p. 1.

21 **"Curt LeMay thinks only of SAC":** "Defense under Fire," *Time,* May 14, 1956.

21 **To counter the threat:** Henry M. Narducci, *Strategic Air Command and the Alert Program: A Brief History* (Offutt Air Force Base, Neb.: Office of the Historian, Headquarters Strategic Air Command, 1988), pp. 1–4; Lloyd, *Cold War Legacy,* pp. 244–245; J. C. Hopkins and Sheldon A. Goldberg, *The Development of the Strategic Air Command, 1946–1986* (Offutt Air Force Base, Neb.: Office of the Historian, Headquarters Strategic Air Command, 1986), p. 65. An earlier alert operation occurred in February 1955, but the first true proof-of-concept test for ground alert was Operation TRY OUT, from November 1956 to March 1957. A description of life on ground alert can be found in "On Continuous Alert," *The New York Times Magazine,* December 8, 1957, pp. 10–11.

21 **the Soviets launched *Sputnik*:** Paul Dickson, *Sputnik: The Shock of the Century* (New York: Berkley Books, 2001). The Johnson quote appears on p. 117. See also Kaplan, *Wizards of Armageddon,* pp. 135–136. An example of press reaction to ground alert in the wake of *Sputnik* is Richard Witkin, "S.A.C. Operating New Alert Program: Aims to Get Third of Bomber Force Airborne within 15 Minutes after Attack," *The New York Times,* November 11, 1957, p. 12.

22 **SAC began testing another program:** Hopkins and Goldberg, *Development of the Strategic Air Command, 1946–1986,* p. 74.

22 **"Any Soviet surprise attack":** Hanson W. Baldwin, "Ready or Not? President Upheld on Plan Not to Keep Bombers Constantly in Air on Alert," *The New York Times,* March 8, 1959.

22 **Airborne alert was ready to go:** John D. Morris, "Soviet ICBM Held Able to Pinpoint 5,000-Mile Target," *The New York Times,* January 31, 1959, p. 1; Power, quoted in Hopkins and Goldberg, *Development of the Strategic Air Command,* p. 83.

22 **"futile and disastrous":** Jack Raymond, "President Sees Dangers in Full Mobilization Now," *The New York Times,* March 5, 1959, p. 1.

22 **Eventually the two sides reached a compromise:** "Some B-52's in Air around the Clock: S.A.C. Begins Training for Possible Establishment of an Airborne Alert," *The New York Times,* January 19, 1961, p. 12; Hopkins and Goldberg, *Development of the Strategic Air Command,* p. 101; Narducci, *Strategic Air Command and the Alert Program,* pp. 4–6; "SAC's Deadly Daily Dozen," *Time,* March 17, 1961, p. 19.

22 the exact number remained classified: Airborne alert rates can now be found in Lloyd, *Cold War Legacy,* p. 681.

22 SAC named the program "Chrome Dome": A map of the Chrome Dome routes in 1966 appears in Scott D. Sagan, *The Limits of Safety: Organizations, Accidents and Nuclear Weapons* (Princeton, N.J.: Princeton Studies in International History and Politics, 1993), p. 194. Despite many interviews with SAC airmen, the author never discovered a definitive genesis of the name.

22 Power refused to confirm or deny: "Some B-52's in Air around the Clock," *The New York Times,* January 19, 1961, p. 12; *The Strategic Air Command Alert Force: History and Philosophy (Briefing)* (Offutt Air Force Base, Neb.: Office of the Historian, Headquarters Strategic Air Command, 1988), p. 10.

23 LeMay had moved on: Lloyd, *Cold War Legacy,* pp. 666–667. Stats on SAC in 1957 come from ibid., pp. 676–677, 681.

23 Power carried the torch: A good overview of Power's views can be found in "Power Airs SAC Deterrent Capability," *Aviation Week,* April 20, 1959, pp. 66 ff.

23 But as missiles grew more sophisticated: Hopkins and Goldberg, *Development of the Strategic Air Command,* pp. 104–105. For further reading on McNamara's relations with SAC, see Deborah Shapley, *Promise and Power: The Life and Times of Robert McNamara* (Boston: Little, Brown and Company, 1993), chaps. 6–9.

23 "backbone of SAC's deterrent strength": *The Mission of SAC: SAC Film Report no. 2* (U.S. Air Force, 1961).

CHAPTER 2: THE ACCIDENT

24 At midmorning on January 17, 1966: The account of the accident comes from two major sources: author's interviews with Wendorf, Rooney, and Messinger; and *Report of Major Aircraft Accident.*

24 The lower compartment, where Rooney sat: The author toured a B-52 at Minot Air Force Base on August 23, 2005, and interviewed six airmen with B-52 experience: Mo Wiley, "Monty" Moncrief, Eric DePriest, Stephen Miracle, Harry Bender, and Glynn Breuer. Bender also demonstrated a midair refueling in a B-52 simulator. Additional details of B-52 culture came from retired airmen Max Kennedy and Donald Chase, interviewed by the author on August 25, 2005.

25 **Messinger was about to attempt:** Background on midair refueling comes from Mike May, "Gas Stations in the Sky," *Invention & Technology* 19, no. 4 (Spring 2004), pp. 10–19, and Dennis Casey and Bud Baker, *Fuel Aloft: A Brief History of Aerial Refueling,* undated (AFHRA). For additional information on the importance of midair refueling to SAC, see Kohn and Harahan, *Strategic Air Warfare,* pp. 104–108.

26 **and they remain so today:** In 2008, the Air Force awarded a contract for the next generation of aerial refueling tankers to the European Aeronautic Defence and Space Company (EADS) and the U.S.-based Northrop Grumman. Boeing and the U.S. Government Accountability Office challenged the decision, and the Pentagon decided to recompete the $35 billion contract. As of this writing, the KC-135 and its flying boom remain the state of the art, though some planes use a probe-and-drogue system.

26 **The boom is an aluminum tube:** The description of a KC-135 refueling a B-52 comes from two sources: author's visit to Minot Air Force Base on August 23, 2005, and author's flight on a KC-135 refueling mission on July 29, 2005. During the refueling flight, boom operator Glen Starkweather answered many questions about the process; the boomer jokes come from him.

28 **"It was a dog":** Larry Messinger interview, October 19, 2004.

28 **"First you tell the plane to turn":** Harry Bender interview, August 23, 2005.

29 **Pilots usually refer to the B-52:** The background on the B-52 comes from the author's visit to Minot Air Force Base on August 23, 2005; author's visit to the Strategic Air and Space Museum on August 25, 2005; and interviews with airmen with B-52 experience. Statistics on the number of B-52s in SAC's inventory can be found in Lloyd, *Cold War Legacy,* p. 677.

29 **The G model:** Information on the B-52G can be found at www .globalsecurity.org/wmd/systems/b-52g.

29 **B-52 pilots injected 10,000 pounds of water:** The background on water augmentation comes from the author's visit to Minot Air Force Base on August 23, 2005.

30 **Rooney and Wendorf suspect that fatigue failure:** In one famous example, the horizontal stabilizer snapped off a B-52 during severe turbulence. The plane landed successfully. See "Something Missing," *Aerospace Safety,* April 1964, pp. 4–7. The fatigue failure problem is also discussed at www.globalsecurity.org/wmd/systems/b-52g.

31 The one surviving member: To the best of the author's knowledge, Ross C. Cox is the only living member of the accident investigation board. He refused several requests for an interview.

31 Buchanan, in the lower compartment: Buchanan's story comes from author's interviews with Mike Rooney and *SAC Historical Study #109: Sixteenth Air Force Operation Recovery, 17 January–7 April, 1966* (History and Research Division, Headquarters Strategic Air Command, U.S. Department of the Air Force, 1968), vol. 1, pp. 13–14.

34 about eight miles from land: Different accounts place Messinger between five and fifteen miles from shore. "Eight miles" comes from *SAC Historical Study #109*, p. 15.

35 The survivors stayed: The chronology of the survivors' movements is from *SAC Historical Study #109*, pp. 14–16.

35 At 7:05 a.m. Washington time: Letter, Bill Moyers to Flora Lewis, August 11, 1966 (LBJ).

CHAPTER 3: THE FIRST TWENTY-FOUR HOURS

37 Manolo González Navarro believed in fate: Manolo González's story comes from author's interview with Manolo and Dolores González, February 24, 2007, and "Operación Flecha Rota: Accidente nuclear de Palomares (Almería)," directed by José Herrera Plaza, 2007. Some additional information about Manolo and Dolores is in Lewis, *One of Our H-Bombs,* pp. 26–29.

38 Fiery debris rained onto Palomares: Additional information about the debris shower can be found in Szulc, *The Bombs of Palomares,* pp. 41–42, and Lewis, *One of Our H-Bombs,* pp. 22–28.

38 Palomares sat on the southeastern coast: The description of Palomares in 1966 comes from author's interview with Manolo and Dolores González, February 24, 2007; Szulc, *The Bombs of Palomares,* pp. 14–22; author's visit to the area, February 24–27, 2007.

40 Wendorf's bomber had not been alone: *SAC Historical Study #109,* pp. 5–10.

40 The two planes had planned to switch: *Report of Major Aircraft Accident,* Wendorf's statement, p. 2.

41 the Morón Command Post radioed: *SAC Historical Study #109,* pp. 8–10.

41 The tanker, after finishing the refueling: Ibid., p. 20.

41 **Morón reported the incident to SAC:** Ibid., p. 9.

42 **the phone rang on the desk:** Joe Ramirez's recollections of the first twenty-four hours and his personal background are from author's interviews with Ramirez, January 27, 2007, and April 27, 2007.

44 **About twenty minutes before 2 p.m.:** *SAC Historical Study #109,* pp. 67–69. The times noted in the SAC Historical Study are "Zulu" time, or Greenwich Mean Time. The local time in Palomares was Zulu plus 1 hour.

44 **He was a steady, capable leader:** The characterization of Wilson comes from author's interviews with several men who served under him, including Walter Vornbrock on April 23, 2007, and Ralph Jenkins on March 14, 2007.

44 **Wilson also had a unique link:** Coffey, *Iron Eagle,* pp. 148–149.

45 **he learned that three:** Szulc, *The Bombs of Palomares,* p. 71; Lewis, *One of Our H-Bombs,* pp. 79–81.

46 **"This miracle is too big":** Quoted in "An H-bomb Is Missing and the Hunt Goes On," *Newsweek,* March 7, 1966, p. 57.

46 **Night had fallen by then:** Additional details on the first night's fruitless search can be found in Lewis, *One of Our H-Bombs,* pp. 75–76.

46 **A sergeant named Raymond Howe:** The story of finding bomb number one comes from Lewis, *One of Our H-Bombs,* pp. 78–79, and Szulc, *The Bombs of Palomares,* pp. 74–75.

47 **The bomb was torpedo-shaped:** The description of the Mark 28 comes from Chuck Hansen, *U.S. Nuclear Weapons: The Secret History* (New York: Crown Publishers, 1988), pp. 149–154, and James A. Gibson, *Nuclear Weapons of the United States: An Illustrated History* (Atglen, Pa.: Schiffer Publishing, 1996), pp. 99–100. Additional information can be found in Chuck Hansen, *Swords of Armageddon,* vol. 6: *Gravity Bomb Histories* (Sunnyvale, Calif.: Chukelea Publications). The Palomares weapons were Mark 28RI (Retarded Internal). There is disagreement as to whether the bomb was eleven or twelve feet long, perhaps because the bomb could be configured in different ways.

47 **It had a nine-inch gash:** The condition of bomb number one is from *SAC Historical Study #109,* pp. 32–33, and Cable, DASA to RUECW/CNO, January 21, 1966, #51711 (LBJ).

47 **The "H" in "H-bomb":** The background on nuclear bombs comes from Richard Rhodes, *Dark Sun,* pp. 116–117 and pp. 247–248; Chuck Hansen,

U.S. Nuclear Weapons, pp. 11–25; Jack Dennis, ed., *The Nuclear Almanac: Confronting the Atom in War and Peace* (Reading, Mass.: Addison-Wesley Publishing Company, 1984), chap. 10. The author has converted metric weights and measures to English units.

49   "without splattering the beer":   Quoted in Rhodes, *Dark Sun,* p. 117.

50   "Fission bombs":   Ibid., p. 511.

50   The exact inner workings: The explanation of a fusion bomb comes from Chuck Hansen, *U.S. Nuclear Weapons,* pp. 21–25, and Howard Morland, "The H-Bomb Secret," *The Progressive,* November 1979, pp. 3–12. Andy Karam provided additional comments in his e-mail to the author, September 9, 2007.

51   The charred remains: *SAC Historical Study #109,* pp. 18–19; Lewis, *One of Our H-Bombs,* pp. 81–82; Szulc, *The Bombs of Palomares,* p. 76.

52   General Wilson and his entourage: Lewis, *One of Our H-Bombs,* p. 82; author's interview with Joe Ramirez, January 27, 2007.

52   thirty-eight guardias civiles: *SAC Historical Study #109,* pp. 18, 71.

52   Wilson had sent a message: Ibid., pp. 76, 81; Szulc, *The Bombs of Palomares,* p. 75; Lewis, *One of Our H-Bombs,* p. 82.

53   When Wilson's message arrived in Torrejón: *SAC Historical Study #109,* p. 81; author's interviews with Robert Finkel, April 4, 2007, and Phil Durbin, March 15, 2007.

53   Ramirez and a handful of others: Lewis, *One of Our H-Bombs,* p. 83; Joe Ramirez interview, January 27, 2007.

53   By 7:30 a.m.:   *SAC Historical Study #109,* p. 75.

53   The small teams moved out: Szulc, *The Bombs of Palomares,* p. 82.

54   helicopters arrived from Morón: Ibid., pp. 82, 84; *SAC Historical Study #109,* p. 22.

54   Ramirez and others went to look: Szulc, *The Bombs of Palomares,* p. 84; Lewis, *One of Our H-Bombs,* pp. 85–86; author's interview with Joe Ramirez, January 27, 2007.

54   Bomb number two was in bad shape: The condition of bomb number two is from *SAC Historical Study #109,* pp. 33–34; Cable, DASA to RUECW/CNO, January 21, 1966, #51711; and a photograph of the bomb obtained from NNSA through FOIA.

55   If he had looked up: Lewis, *One of Our H-Bombs,* p. 89.

55 Bomb number three lay in a plowed field: The story of the discovery of bomb number three is in Lewis, *One of Our H-Bombs,* pp. 88–89; Szulc, *The Bombs of Palomares,* pp. 50–51, 84–85; "Special Report: Lost and Found, One H-Bomb," CBS News, March 22, 1966.

56 "I knew it was a bomb": "Special Report: Lost and Found, One H-Bomb."

56 According to some accounts: "An H-Bomb Is Missing and the Hunt Goes On," p. 57.

56 The bomb lay in its crater: The condition of bomb number three is from *SAC Historical Study #109,* pp. 34–35; Cable, DASA to RUECW/CNO, January 21, 1966, #51711; and a photograph of the bomb obtained from NNSA through FOIA.

56 A situation report was sent: Memo, ATSD (AE) to Secretary of Defense et al. "Situation Report, B-52/KC-135 Accident, 17 January 1966," January 18, 1966.

CHAPTER 4: THE AMBASSADOR

58 On the morning of the accident: Duke's actions on the morning of the accident come from author's interview with Joseph Smith, January 23, 2007, and Szulc, *The Bombs of Palomares,* pp. 60–63. See also Angier Biddle Duke, "Address to American Management Association," January 17, 1966, and Angier Biddle Duke, "Remarks of Ambassador Angier Biddle Duke on 'CBS Special Report,' " March 16, 1966 (both in Angier Biddle Duke Papers, Box 18, Duke).

59 If America had to choose: The background on Duke comes from author's interviews with Robin Duke, June 7, 2007; George Landau, January 22, 2007; and Joseph Smith, January 23, 2007. Print sources include *Current Biography* 23, no. 2 (February 1962), p. 7; Marguerite Higgins, "He Takes the Starch Out of Protocol," *The Saturday Evening Post,* September 29, 1962, pp. 24–25; E. J. Kahn, "Good Manners and Common Sense," *The New Yorker,* August 15, 1964, pp. 34 ff.; "New Diplomatic Hand," *Newsweek,* January 11, 1965, pp. 27–28. Also see Angier Biddle Duke, Living History interview, conducted by James David Barber, John TePaske, and Taylor Cole, October 24, 1990 (Duke Living History Program, Box 1, Duke). A Duke family genealogy can be found at http://library.duke.edu/uarchives/history/duke_familyndx.html.

62 "tobacco-rich playboy": "New Diplomatic Hand," *Newsweek,* January 11, 1965, p. 27.

62 **"He has dedicated more sewers"**: Quoted in *Current Biography* 23, no. 2 (February 1962), p. 8.

62 **"I'm lost"**: E. J. Kahn, "Good Manners and Common Sense," *The New Yorker*, August 15, 1964, p. 35.

63 **"When I got there"**: Angier Biddle Duke, Living History interview, October 24, 1990, part II, p. 7.

63 **There was only one reason**: The background on the importance of the Spanish bases comes from author's interviews with George Landau, January 22, 2007, and Joseph Smith, January 23, 2007. Cable #1552 from the Embassy in Madrid, February 14, 1964 (LBJ), notes, "GOS attributes great importance to military relationship with US and would be most reluctant to liquidate present arrangements. However . . . It is psychologically very important to Spain that they stand up against us on some issue."

63 **The Air Force operated three bases**: Information on the U.S. military presence in Spain comes from Harry R. Fletcher, *Air Force Bases*, vol. 2: *Air Bases outside the United States of America* (Washington, D.C.: U.S. Air Force, Center for Air Force History, 1993), pp. 187 ff.; and Arthur P. Whitaker, *Spain and the Defense of the West: Ally and Liability* (New York: Harper & Brothers, 1961), pp. 56–64.

63 **Zaragosa in northeastern Spain**: Zaragosa was reduced to "modified caretaker status" on January 1, 1966, and reassigned to USAFE on April 15, 1966. It returned to active status on February 19, 1970, when Wheelus Air Base in Libya closed. Fletcher, *Air Force Bases*, p. 201.

64 **Generalissimo Francisco Franco**: The description of Franco comes from Michael Streeter, *Franco* (London: Haus Publishing, 2005), and Jean Grugel and Tim Rees, *Franco's Spain* (London: Arnold Publishers, 1997). For further reading on the Spanish Civil War, see Hugh Thomas's classic text *The Spanish Civil War* (New York: Harper & Row, 1961).

64 **"the most uncharismatic dictator"**: Angier Biddle Duke, Living History interview, October 24, 1990, part II, p. 10.

65 **The Allies worked hard**: Spain's relations with the West during World War II and in the postwar years is described in detail in Whitaker, *Spain and the Defense of the West*, chaps. 1 and 2. See also R. Richard Rubottom and J. Carter Murphy, *Spain and the United States since World War II* (New York: Praeger Publishers, 1984).

65 **"Henceforth" said one historian**: Whitaker, *Spain and the Defense of the West*, p. 11.

66 "more weight was given": Ibid., p. 32.

66 In July 1947, he told a reporter: Paraphrased in ibid., pp. 35–36.

66 "I don't like Franco": Quoted in Streeter, *Franco*, p. 106.

66 "The strategic advantages": Quoted in Whitaker, *Spain and the Defense of the West*, p. 40.

67 American military officials: In *Spain and the Defense of the West*, p. 39, Whitaker argues that the push for Spanish bases came from the U.S. Navy. But Corey Ford and James Perkins, in "Our Key SAC Bases in Spain and How We Got Them," *Reader's Digest*, August 1958, pp. 23–26, say the impetus came from SAC.

67 "a bitter pill": Quoted in Whitaker, *Spain and the Defense of the West*, p. 50.

67 President Eisenhower visited Madrid: The description of Eisenhower's visit to Madrid comes from ibid., pp. 80–82. Also see *The New York Times'* coverage of the visit: Benjamin Welles, "Franco's Prestige High as He Awaits Eisenhower's Visit," December 19, 1959, p. 3; Russell Baker, "Madrid Provides Warm 'Saludos,' " December 22, 1959, p. 8; "Texts of Franco and Eisenhower Talks," December 22, 1959, p. 8; Benjamin Welles, "Eisenhower Is Hailed in Madrid," December 22, 1959, p. 1; Benjamin Welles, "Eisenhower Gets Franco's Support," December 23, 1959, p. 11; Benjamin Welles, "Franco Aide's Visit to Highlight Improving U.S. Ties with Spain," December 30, 1959, p. 3.

68 Spain slowly began to climb: Details on Spain's economic recovery come from "Spain: The Awakening Land," *Time*, January 21, 1966, pp. 26–39; Bart McDowell and Albert Moldvay, "The Changing Face of Old Spain," *National Geographic*, March 1965, pp. 291–341.

68 The Spanish magazine ¡Hola!: Author's reading of ¡Hola! magazine.

69 keeping a lid on the press: Bill Moyers, letter to Flora Lewis, August 11, 1966: The Spanish government "was acutely sensitive to any public statements made about the incident and the presence of nuclear weapons."

69 On the day of the accident: The first few days of press coverage are detailed in Cable, CSAF to Joint Chiefs of Staff et al., January 19, 1966, #59032 (LBJ); *SAC Historical Study #109*, pp. 311–312; Cable, Embassy in Madrid to the Department of State, January 19, 1966, #855 (LBJ); Cable, Embassy in Madrid to the Department of State, January 19, 1966, #856 (LBJ).

70 Duke sat down to discuss: Cable, Embassy in Madrid to the Depart-

ment of State, January 21, 1966, #869 (LBJ); Cable, Embassy in Madrid to the Department of State, January 19, 1966, #855 (LBJ).

70 Although the U.S. military had stored nuclear weapons: To the best of the author's knowledge, the United States has never publicly admitted storing nuclear weapons in Spain. However, the fact of their existence has long been accepted. See Robert S. Norris, William M. Arkin, and William Burr, "Where They Were," *The Bulletin of the Atomic Scientists,* November–December 1999, pp. 26 ff.

70 "The subject was still very touchy": Joseph Smith interview, August 9, 2007.

71 On January 19, a secret cable: Cable, CSAF to Joint Chiefs of Staff et al., January 19, 1966, #59032 (LBJ).

71 A young reporter: Andró del Amo's story is told in Szulc, *The Bombs of Palomares,* pp. 107–116, and *SAC Historical Study #109,* pp. 314–315.

73 Duke got wind of del Amo's dispatch: Cable, Embassy in Madrid to the Department of State, January 19, 1966, #857 (LBJ).

73 Exercising its iron grip: Cable, Embassy in Madrid to the Department of State, January 21, 1966, #869 (LBJ).

74 the UPI article landed on Franco's desk: The fallout over the UPI article is detailed in Cable, Embassy in Madrid to the Department of State, January 22, 1966, #871 (LBJ).

75 "the only friend we really had": George Landau interview, August 9, 2007.

75 Muñoz Grandes's decree: Author's interviews with George Landau, August 9, 2007, and Joseph Smith, January 23, 2007. See also Lewis, *One of Our H-Bombs,* pp. 98–99, and Howard Simons, "Some Experts Fear Strategic Loss if Curbs Are Put on Nuclear Routes," *The Washington Post,* February 27, 1966, p. A1.

76 Believe we must be prepared: Cable, Embassy in Madrid to the Department of State, January 22, 1966, #871 (LBJ).

CHAPTER 5: PARACHUTES

77 Joe Ramirez pushed aside: Joe Ramirez interview, January 27, 2007.

79 had found the combat mission folder: *SAC Historical Study #109,* pp. 39–40.

79 General Wilson realized: Ibid., p. 75.

79 "Until every avenue of search": Ibid.

79 Hundreds of searchers: Ibid., pp. 81–82, 89–90; author's interviews with Robert Finkel, April 4, 2007, and Phil Durbin, March 15, 2007.

80 Wilson's men got organized: The ground search is described in *SAC Historical Study #109*, pp. 95–98; see also author's interviews with Walter Vornbrock, April 23, 2008, and Phil Durbin, March 15, 2007.

80 a reservoir—a piece of a bomb: *SAC Historical Study #109*, pp. 42–43.

80 a searcher found a round metal plate: Ibid., pp. 40–42; Cable, from 16th AF Torrejón AB Spain to RUEKDA/Secretary of Defense, January, 1966, #61642 (LBJ); Randall C. Maydew, *America's Lost H-Bomb! Palomares, Spain, 1966* (Manhattan, Kans.: Sunflower University Press, 1997), p. 54.

81 The engineers at Sandia: The background on Sandia comes from author's interviews with William Barton, January 22, 2004, and October 23, 2006; William Caudle, January 22, 2004; Sam McAlees, October 23, 2006; William Pepper, October 21, 2006; and Rebecca Ulrich, October 24, 2006. For additional information on the history of Sandia National Laboratories, see Necah Furman, *Sandia National Laboratories: The Postwar Decade* (Albuquerque, N.M.: University of New Mexico Press, 1989), and Leland Johnson, *Sandia National Laboratories: A History of Exceptional Service in the National Interest* (Albuquerque, N.M.: Sandia National Laboratories, 1997).

81 he called Secretary of Defense Robert McNamara: Letter, Bill Moyers to Flora Lewis, August 11, 1966. The author found no record of this conversation in the Johnson telephone archive, but not all telephone calls were recorded.

81 Word was passed to Jack Howard: Author's interview with Jack Howard, April 3, 2007; Memo, R. C. Maydew and W. R. Barton to G. A. Fowler, "Chronological Summary of Significant Events in the 9300 Participation in Broken Arrow Operation," March 29, 1966 (Randall Maydew files, SNL).

81 Pope called Randy Maydew: Randall Maydew, oral history, conducted by Necah Furman, December 1991, p. 5 (SNL).

82 High-energy and hyperactive: The background on Randy Maydew comes primarily from author's interview with Jean and Barbara Maydew, October 21, 2006. Additional information is from interviews with William Barton, January 22, 2004, and October 23, 2006; William Caudle, January 22, 2004; and Sam McAlees, October 23, 2006.

82 when he got the call: Maydew, *America's Lost H-Bomb,* pp. x, 43–44, 54; Randall Maydew, oral history, conducted by Necah Furman, December 1991, p. 5 (SNL).

82 The parachute question was critical: The explanation of the Mark 28 parachute system comes from Maydew, *America's Lost H-Bomb,* pp. 21–24; "Description of Normal Operation," document #SAC200118830000 (NNSA, FOIA); Randall Maydew, oral history, conducted by Necah Furman, December 1991, pp. 2–3 (SNL); Gibson, *Nuclear Weapons of the United States,* pp. 99–100.

82 Sandia had developed this "laydown system": Furman, *Sandia National Laboratories,* pp. 648–660; Johnson, *Sandia National Laboratories,* pp. 63–69; Randall Maydew, oral history, August 22, 1985 (SNL).

82 According to intelligence experts: *National Intelligence Estimate 11-4-61: Main Trends in Soviet Capabilities and Policies, 1961–1966,* U.S. Director of Central Intelligence (RG 263, Box 16, Folder 9, NARA).

83 The three bombs found on land: There are some minor disagreements about the speed at which bombs numbers one to three hit the ground. These numbers come from Randall Maydew, oral history, conducted by Necah Furman, December 1991, p. 3 (SNL).

84 Since bomb number four's tail plate: Randall Maydew, oral history, August 22, 1985, pp. 11–12 (SNL); Maydew, *America's Lost H-Bomb,* pp. 53–54. Maydew's chronology is somewhat jumbled; the tail plate was found by January 20, well before Maydew left for Spain.

84 37° 13.9′ N, 01° 42.3′ W: *SAC Historical Study #109,* p. 48. The author typed these coordinates into http://atlas.mapquest.com/maps/latlong.adp to verify that they were in the Mediterranean, closer to Africa than to Spain.

84 On January 27, General Wilson requested: Memo, Maydew and Barton to Fowler, March 29, 1966 (SNL).

84 "furnishing data to unseeing computers": *SAC Historical Study #109,* p. 49.

84 ultimately generating a three-foot stack: "Vital Contributions Made by Sandia in Locating Lost Nuclear Weapon," *Sandia Lab News,* April 22, 1966, pp. 4–5.

84 a forked stick: Maydew, *America's Lost H-Bomb,* p. 52.

84   **Ramirez had another lead:**   Ramirez's first meeting with Simó comes from author's interview with Joe Ramirez, January 27, 2007.

86   **he found himself on the USS *Pinnacle*:**   *SAC Historical Study #109*, pp. 45–46; Department of the Navy, Naval Ship Systems Command, *Aircraft Salvage Operation Mediterranean (Aircraft Salvops Med). Sea Search and Recovery of an Unarmed Nuclear Weapon by Task Force 65, Interim Report* (Reston, Va.: Ocean Systems, 1966), pp. 7, C2; Joe Ramirez interview, January 27, 2007.

86   **The water was just over two thousand feet:**   The water depth was 340 fathoms, which converts to 2,041 feet. *Aircraft Salvops Med,* Interim Report, p. 7.

86   **"sharp and hazy":**   *SAC Historical Study #109,* p. 46.

86   **President Johnson sat down:**   President's daily diary, January 22, 1966 (Box 5, LBJ).

87   **In the film:**   The description of *Thunderball* comes from the author's viewing of the film.

87   **When Jack Howard called Alan Pope:**   Maydew, *America's Lost H-Bomb,* ix.

87   **And early reports noted that real Soviets:**   Cable, Embassy in Madrid to the Department of State, January 21, 1966, #869 (LBJ).

CHAPTER 6: CALL IN THE NAVY

88   **Red Moody sat in the cockpit:**   Author's interview with DeWitt (henceforth "Red") Moody, November 7, 2006; D. H. Moody, "40th Anniversary of Palomares," *Faceplate* 10, no. 2 (September 2006), p. 15. The arrival of the divers in Spain and the early days of the search are chronicled in Memo, Commander Task Group 65.3 to Commander Task Force 65, "Report of Inshore Search, Identification and Recovery Unit," March 13, 1966 (NHC).

88   **On January 22:**   Maydew, *America's Lost H-Bomb,* pp. ix–x.

88   **the CNO had established a task force:**   *Aircraft Salvops Med,* Interim Report, 1966, p. C2.

89   **Four U.S. Navy minesweepers:**   The ships were the USS *Sagacity* (MSO-469), USS *Pinnacle* (MSO-462), USS *Skill* (MSO-471), USS *Nimble* (MSO-459), USNS *Dutton* (T-AGS-22), and USS *Macdonough* (DLG-8). *Aircraft Salvops Med,* Interim Report, pp. C1–C2.

89   **A small team of EOD divers:**   Author's interviews with Oliver Ander-

sen, January 22, 2007, and March 31, 2007, and Red Moody, November 7, 2006. Also Memo, Commander Task Group 65.3 to Commander Task Force 65, "Report of Inshore Search," March 13, 1966 (NHC).

89 "His sole purpose in life": Oliver Andersen interview, January 22, 2007.

90 Then Moody made an announcement: The story of Red Moody's first visit to the *Macdonough* is from Red Moody interview, November 7, 2006.

90 DeWitt "Red" Moody: Red Moody's personal history comes from author's interviews with Moody, November 7, 2006, and July 17, 2007.

91 Admiral Guest paid a visit: Author's interview with Red Moody, November 7, 2006; Memo, Commander Task Group 65.3 to Commander Task Force 65, "Report of Inshore Search," March 13, 1966 (NHC).

92 He had been thrown: Admiral Guest arrived in Palomares on January 24, 1966. *Aircraft Salvops Med,* Interim Report, p. C2.

92 Guest was a no-nonsense man: The description of Guest comes primarily from author's interviews with Douglas Kingsbery, July 27, 2007, and Robert Kingsbery, July 19, 2007. Additional information is from U.S. Department of the Navy, *Biography of Rear Admiral William S. Guest* (Washington, D.C.: Naval Historical Center, undated), and author's interviews with Red Moody, November 7, 2006, and July 17, 2007; Horace Page, April 3, 2007; and J. Bradford Mooney, March 30, 2007.

93 Guest hit the ground running: *Aircraft Salvops Med,* Interim Report, pp. 9, 11.

93 The wedge measured: Using the map shown in *Aircraft Salvops Med,* Interim Report, p. 9, the author calculated the area of the initial search area to be 51.03 square miles. Manhattan is 22.7 square miles.

93 Oliver Andersen, left in charge: The description of the inshore searching comes primarily from author's interviews with Oliver Andersen, January 22, 2007, and March 31, 2007.

93 The divers found a lot of debris: Memo, Commander Task Group 65.3 to Commander Task Force 65, "Report of Inshore Search," March 13, 1966 (NHC).

94 Underwater searching is complicated: The description of a jackstay search and other EOD diving background comes from the author's visit with the divers of EOD 6 on March 20–21, 2007, and interviews with Brad Andros and Ron Ervin during that time.

95 and there were no decent charts: *Aircraft Salvops Med,* pp. 17, 75.

95 One Navy captain named Lewis Melson: Author's interview with Lewis Melson, August 23, 2006.

95 On January 27, the USS *Kiowa* arrived: The background on the Decca hi-fix and its installation problems are from *Aircraft Salvops Med,* Interim Report, p. 18; *Aircraft Salvops Med,* Final Report, vol. 1, p. 24; *Aircraft Salvops Med,* Final Report, February 15, 1967, vol. 4, appendix B, pp. 3–11; and *SAC Historical Study #109,* pp. 295, 304.

96 "like going up here in the hills": "William S. Guest Press Conference," April 8, 1966.

96 "throwing a needle": Author's interview with Gaylord White, March 3, 2007.

96 "finding a needle in a haystack": "The Bomb Is Found," *Time,* March 25, 1966, p. 77.

96 "This must be the devil's": Szulc, *The Bombs of Palomares,* p. 172.

FEBRUARY

CHAPTER 7: VILLA JARAPA

99 "The once-deserted Mediterranean coast": Richard Oulahan, "The Case of the Missing H-Bomb," *Life,* February 25, 1966, p. 106B.

99 Wilson decided that the barren: *SAC Historical Study #109,* p. 82.

99 Camp Wilson served as home and office: Details on Camp Wilson can be found in *SAC Historical Study #109,* pp. 83–93. General Wilson's reports to SAC and the "Red-Eye Special" are discussed on pp. 72–74.

100 Robert Finkel, the squadron commander: Robert Finkel interview, April 4, 2007.

100 Joe Ramirez, also rooming happily: Joe Ramirez interviews, January 27, 2007, and April 27, 2007.

101 they called Camp Wilson "Villa Jarapa": Miguel Olid, "Luz sobre Palomares," *El País* (Sunday supplement), April 22, 2007, p. 32.

101 the military remained tight-lipped: *SAC Historical Study #109,* pp. 321–323; Szulc, *The Bombs of Palomares,* pp. 200–204.

101 The Navy was ordered: *Aircraft Salvops Med,* Final Report, vol. 1, part I, chap. 2, p. 7.

101 **"There are no denials":** "H-Bomb Lost in Spain," CBS News, January 23, 1966.

101 **A rumor circulated:** Author's interview with Malcolm MacKinnon, December 4, 2006.

101 **"So stringent is the official secrecy":** "An H-Bomb Is Missing and the Hunt Goes On," *Newsweek,* March 7, 1966, p. 55.

101 **Press briefings were maddening:** Szulc, *The Bombs of Palomares,* p. 202.

102 **Even the Spanish reporters:** Lewis, *One of Our H-Bombs,* p. 165.

102 **London papers reported:** *SAC Historical Study #109,* p. 365.

102 **The *Sydney Sun*:** Ibid., p. 366.

102 **Radio España Independiente:** Ibid., p. 301; Szulc, *The Bombs of Palomares,* pp. 157–158. The transcripts of REI broadcasts are located at the PCE Archive in Madrid. The author read a selection of them at the archive in February 2007.

103 **"It was a long":** *SAC Historical Study #109,* p. 80.

103 **estimated that searchers covered:** Walter Vornbrock interview, April 23, 2007.

103 **"found they liked the outdoor life":** *SAC Historical Study #109,* p. 92.

103 **Colonel Alton "Bud" White:** White's description of the cleanup operation comes from Flora Lewis, interview with Alton "Bud" White, undated (AFHRA).

103 **they cleared about 150 tons:** Ibid. says 150 tons; *SAC Historical Study #109,* p. 133, says 100 tons.

104 **Wilson and Montel spoke to a crowd:** *SAC Historical Study #109,* pp. 292–293; Szulc, *The Bombs of Palomares,* p. 161.

104 **Speaking through a translator:** The text of Wilson's speech can be found in Memo, 16AF Torrejón AB Spain to US Embassy Spain and JUSMG Madrid Spain, February 2, 1966 (USAF, FOIA).

104 **he was surprised—and a bit shocked:** Flora Lewis, interview with Alton White, undated (AFHRA).

104 **A team of scientists:** Emilio Iranzo interview, February 16, 2007.

105 **Starting at each bomb's impact point:** White's description of the radiation mapping comes from Flora Lewis, interview with Alton White, undated (AFHRA), and *SAC Historical Study #109,* pp. 141–146.

105　But the PAC-1S:　The problems with the PAC-1S are detailed in *SAC Historical Study #109,* pp. 271–277.

106　"The only way you could treat that land":　Flora Lewis, interview with Alton White, undated (AFHRA).

106　The job of chief tomato plant chopper:　Robert Finkel interview, April 4, 2007, and Szulc, *The Bombs of Palomares,* p. 125.

106　"the Boston Tomato Party":　Robert C. Toth, "Soviet Spy Ship Watches U.S. Hunt Bomb," *Los Angeles Times,* March 8, 1966, p. 1.

106　As a gesture of goodwill:　*SAC Historical Study #109,* p. 156; Flora Lewis, interview with Alton White, undated (AFHRA).

106　"Anywhere you turned around":　Walter Vornbrock interview, April 23, 2007.

106　A bit farther down the beach:　The description of the Navy EOD camp comes from author's interviews with Red Moody, November 7, 2006; Denford Stevens, November 30, 2006; Gaylord White, March 3, 2007; Robert Singleton, November 27, 2006; Oliver Andersen, January 22, 2007, and March 31, 2007; Charles Detmer, December 13, 2006; Tom Ligon, November 30, 2006; and Ed Jeffords, November 27, 2006. Stevens and Singleton also supplied personal photographs. Footage of Camp Wilson can be found at NARA, 342-USAF-40730A, reel 7.

106　"The Air Force is okay":　Gaylord White interview, March 3, 2007.

107　"Leave it to divers":　Ibid.

107　On the afternoon of February 2:　*SAC Historical Study #109,* p. 196; and Angier Biddle Duke, "Notes Taken after First Visit to the Palomares Site," April 5, 1968 (Duke). Duke's notes on the trip come from this document. The April 5, 1968, date is written on a cover sheet that appears to have been attached to the notes when Duke gave them to Duke University. The notes themselves appear to have been written by Duke during the February 1966 visit or very soon afterward. The visit is also mentioned in Szulc, *The Bombs of Palomares,* pp. 165–166.

107　Right after the accident:　The account of Smith and Towell's first visit to Palomares comes from author's interviews with Joseph Smith, January 23, 2007, and Timothy Towell, January 5 and 8, 2007. Their visit is also discussed in Szulc, *The Bombs of Palomares,* pp. 162–163.

107　"Just go in":　Joseph Smith interview, January 23, 2007.

107　"General Wilson was totally dismissive":　Timothy Towell interview, January 5, 2007.

107 **"If you take care of sovereign people":** Timothy Towell interview, January 8, 2007.

108 **Duke had already complained:** Cable, Embassy in Madrid to the Department of State, January 27, 1966, #903 (LBJ). Duke's views on openness with the press also come from the author's interview with Robin Duke, June 7, 2007.

109 **he called a press conference:** *SAC Historical Study #109*, pp. 320–321; Szulc, *The Bombs of Palomares*, p. 166.

109 **approximately six hundred people gathered:** *SAC Historical Study #109*, pp. 299–300 (a copy of the handbill is on p. 300); Szulc, *The Bombs of Palomares*, pp. 166–167; "600 Spanish March in Anti-U.S. Protest," *The New York Times*, February 5, 1966, p. 8; Simons, "Some Experts Fear Strategic Loss," p. 11.

CHAPTER 8: *ALVIN* AND THE DEEP, DARK SEA

110 *Alvin* **and her crew had arrived:** *Alvin*'s trip to Rota and the mechanical problems discovered there are discussed in *Aircraft Salvops Med,* Final Report, vol. 1, part I, chap. 2, p. 21; Memo, W. O. Rainnie to Office of Naval Research, "Quarterly Informal Letter Status Report of Contract Nonr 3834(00), Deep Submergence Research Vehicle Project, January 1, 1966 through April 9, 1966," June 10, 1966 (WHOI). Also, author's interviews with Arthur Bartlett, February 5, 2007, and Chester Porembski, November 17, 2006. Additional information about working at Otis Air Force Base is from author's interview with Clyde Tyndale, November 3, 2006. Footage of *Alvin* at Rota can be found at NARA, 342-USAF-40730A.

111 **Marvin J. McCamis, known universally as "Mac":** Personal background on McCamis comes from author's interviews with Marvin McCamis, January 31, 2003; Arthur Bartlett, February 5, 2007; Chester Porembski, November 17, 2006; Andrew Eliason, October 4, 2006; Barrie Walden, July 25, 2006; and John Porteous, September 6, 2006. See also Victoria Kaharl, *Water Baby: The Story of* Alvin (New York: Oxford University Press, 1990), p. 57.

112 **called the crew together:** Marvin McCamis interview, January 31, 2003.

112 *Alvin* **was an experimental sub:** Kaharl, *Water Baby,* pp. 59–62.

112 **"We knew the country had a big problem":** Marvin McCamis interview, January 31, 2003.

113 **it also formed a small committee:** The background on TAG comes from

Aircraft Salvops Med, Final Report, vol. 1, part I, chap. 2, pp. 8–9; *Aircraft Salvops Med,* Interim Report, pp. 5, B1, B4, B15.

113   **The idea of** *Alvin*:   The background on Allyn Vine comes from Naomi Oreskes, "A Context of Motivation: U.S. Naval Oceanographic Research and the Discovery of Sea-Floor Hydrothermal Vents," *Social Studies of Science* 33, no. 5 (October 2003), p. 701, and Kaharl, *Water Baby,* pp. 10–11, 19.

114   **By the 1950s:**   The background on SOSUS comes from Oreskes, "A Context of Motivation," p. 702.

114   **"Manned submersibles are badly needed":**   Memo, Allyn C. Vine to Paul Fye, "ASW," October 10, 1960 (WHOI).

114   **signed a contract in 1962:**   *Alvin,* originally called *Seapup,* was contracted from General Mills in 1962. General Mills had a Mechanical Division to build and repair the machines that mixed and cooked cereal. In 1940, the firm began building torpedo and gun parts to support the U.S. war effort. After the war, "the government contracts kept coming," as one historian put it. For more on the complicated history of *Alvin*'s purchase and construction, see Kaharl, *Water Baby,* chaps. 1–6.

114   *Alvin*'**s curious name:**   Kaharl, *Water Baby,* pp. 32–33.

114   **On the morning of April 9, 1963:**   The background on the *Thresher* comes from the following sources: George W. Martin, "Lasting Legacies of *Thresher,*" *The Submarine Review,* July 2003, pp. 77–88; George W. Martin, "The Search for *Thresher,*" *The Submarine Review,* April 2003, pp. 48–58; Frank A. Andrews, "Search Operations in the *Thresher* Area—1964, Section I," *Naval Engineers Journal,* August 1965, pp. 549–561; Frank A. Andrews, "Search Operations in the *Thresher* Area—1964, Section II," *Naval Engineers Journal,* October 1965, pp. 769–779; Frank A. Andrews, "Searching for the *Thresher,*" *U.S. Naval Institute Proceedings,* May 1964, pp. 69–77; E. W. Grenfell, "USS Thresher (SSN-593), 3 August 1961–10 April 1963," *U.S. Naval Institute Proceedings,* March 1964, pp. 37–47; and Norman Polmar, *The Death of the USS* Thresher: *The Story behind History's Deadliest Submarine Disaster* (Guilford, Conn.: Lyons Press, 1964).

115   **"One of the many lessons":**   Andrews, "Search Operations in the *Thresher* Area," p. 550.

115   **the secretary of the Navy formed a committee:**   *Hearings before the Joint Committee on Atomic Energy, Congress of the United States, Eighty-eighth Congress, First and Second Sessions on the Loss of the USS* Thresher. *June 26, 27, July 23, 1963, and July 1, 1964* (Washington, D.C.: Government Reprints Press, 2001), p. 50; author's interview with John Craven, April 19, 2007.

115 The Stephan Committee released its report: John Peña Craven, *The Silent War: The Cold War Battle beneath the Sea* (New York: Simon & Schuster, 2001), p. 109; Martin, "Lasting Legacies of *Thresher*," pp. 85–86.

116 The Deep Submergence Systems Project: Craven, *Silent War*, pp. 109–111; author's interview with John Craven, April 19, 2007.

116 Senator William Proxmire: Craven, *Silent War*, p. 125.

116 a conference called "Man's Extension": "Man's Extension into the Sea," Symposium Proceedings, January 11–12, 1966 (Washington, D.C.: Marine Technology Society, 1966). The Baldwin quote comes from p. 3.

117 The program called Object Location: U.S. Department of the Navy, Office of the Chief of Naval Operations, *Aircraft Salvage Operation Mediterranean (Aircraft Salvops Med), Lessons and Implications for the Navy* (Washington, D.C.: Office of the Chief of Naval Operations, April 7, 1967), p. 2.

117 We had "almost nothing": John Craven interview, April 19, 2007.

117 "No assignments had gone on": J. Bradford (henceforth "Brad") Mooney interview, March 30, 2007.

117 "The Navy had achieved": *Aircraft Salvops Med, Lessons and Implications for the Navy*, p. 2.

CHAPTER 9: THE FISHERMAN'S CLUE

118 he started jotting notes: Notebook shown to author during interview with Joe Ramirez.

119 Maydew had flown to Spain: Maydew arrived in Palomares on January 29. Memo, R. C. Maydew and W. R. Burton to G. A. Fowler, "Chronological Summary of Significant Events in the 9300 Participation in Broken Arrow Operation," March 29, 1966, Randall Maydew files (SNL).

119 "except for that blue, blue Mediterranean": Randall Maydew, oral history, conducted by Necah Furman, December 1991, p. 7.

119 he found that Air Force staffers: Randall C. Maydew, *America's Lost H-Bomb, Palomares, Spain, 1966* (Manhattan, Kans.: Sunflower University Press, 1997), p. 58.

119 As a navigator in a B-29: Randall C. Maydew, ed., *A Kansas Farm Family* (Freeman, S.Dak.: Pine Hill Press, 1992), pp. 128–129.

119 one morning, Joe Ramirez stopped by: The story of Maydew's meeting with Simó comes from Maydew, *America's Lost H-Bomb*, pp. 55–58, and au-

thor's interview with Joe Ramirez, January 27, 2007. See also *SAC Historical Study #109*, p. 45; and "Staff Study by Systems Analysis Team of Search Operations," February 7, 1966 (document no. SAC200118390000, Secret, NNSA, FOIA), pp. 11–14. "Staff Study" says the meeting took place on February 2, not February 3, as Maydew states in his book.

120 **"Before I left the mayor's office":** Randall Maydew, oral history, conducted by Necah Furman, December 1991, p. 10.

120 **By the time Maydew reported:** Maydew was part of a Systems Analysis Team that included experts from Sandia, Wright-Patterson Air Force Base, and Elgin Air Force Base, and was assisted by U.S. Air Force, Atomic Energy Commission, and Los Alamos personnel. Maydew left numerous descriptions of his role in Palomares, making it possible to tell the Systems Analysis Team's story from his point of view. The author refers to the team as "Maydew's team" or "the ballistics experts" to avoid confusion with TAG and the other groups mentioned in the book.

120 **In their calculations:** The Maydew team's conclusions are from "Staff Study of Systems Analysis Team," February 7, 1966 (NNSA); Memo, Delmar E. Wilson to SAC (Gen. John D. Ryan), "Search Operations, Palomares, Spain," February 13, 1966 (DOD, FOIA); *SAC Historical Study #109*, p. 49.

121 **It is unclear whether Admiral Guest:** Guest's reaction to the Systems Analysis Team report is in *Aircraft Salvops Med*, Final Report, vol. 1, part I, chap. 2, pp. 36–38. On page 37 it states, "Commander Task Force 65 was skeptical of the conclusions of this Sandia group and did not entirely accept their recommendations."

121 **On February 7, the USS *Pinnacle* again:** *Aircraft Salvops Med*, Final Report, vol. 1, part I, chap. 2, pp. 38–39.

121 **A few days later, Red Moody:** Red Moody interview, November 7, 2006.

121 **"Slick Willie":** The description of Mac's relationship with Val Wilson comes chiefly from the author's interviews with Chester Porembski, November 17, 2006, and John Porteous, September 6, 2006.

122 ***Alvin* was trapped on the water's surface:** *Alvin*'s arrival in Palomares and the storm are discussed in *Aircraft Salvops Med*, Interim Report, p. C5; Memo, W. O. Rainnie to Office of Naval Research, "Quarterly Informal Letter," June 10, 1966, p. 3; and Letter, Lewis Melson to Folks, February 12, 1966 (author's collection).

122 **The *Plymouth Rock* was a type of vessel:** The description of a landing ship dock comes from the author's visit to the USS *Ashland* (LSD 48) on September 29, 2006.

122 "We rushed out onto the main deck": Letter, Lewis Melson to Folks, February 12, 1966 (author's collection).

123 The OBSS: The description of the OBSS comes from *Aircraft Salvops Med,* Final Report, vol. 1, part I, chap. 2, pp. 42–43; *Aircraft Salvops Med,* Final Report, vol. 4, appendix B, pp. 57–62; *SAC Historical Study #109,* pp. 119–120; and Red Moody interview, July 17, 2007.

124 The first to arrive was *Deep Jeep*: *Aircraft Salvops Med,* Final Report, vol. 4, appendix B, pp. 30–34; *Aircraft Salvops Med,* Final Report, vol. 1, part I, chap. 2, p. 29; W. M. Place et al., *Palomares Summary Report* (Kirtland Air Force Base, N.M.: Field Command, Defense Nuclear Agency, Technology and Analysis Directorate, 1975), p. 106.

124 Another sub, called *Cubmarine*: *Aircraft Salvops Med,* Final Report, vol. 4, appendix B, pp. 25–29.

124 "*Alvin* was decidedly mongrel": Kaharl, *Water Baby,* p. 42.

124 it reminded people of a fishing lure: Ibid., p. 46.

124 "When people see it": Ibid., p. 83.

124 At *Alvin*'s core: The description of *Alvin* comes from ibid., pp. 42–43; *Aircraft Salvops Med,* Final Report, vol. 4, appendix B, pp. 12–18; Everett S. Allen, "Research Submarine *Alvin,*" *U.S. Naval Institute Proceedings,* April 1964, pp. 138–140. The author toured *Alvin* on July 2, 2007.

125 The only other sub: The description of *Aluminaut* comes from *Aircraft Salvops Med,* Final Report, vol. 4, appendix B, pp. 19–24; "The Aluminaut Story," March 6, 1986; Reynolds Aluminum, "Aluminaut: The Deep Diving Aluminum Submarine," undated. The *Aluminaut* is now housed at the Science Museum of Virginia in Richmond. The author toured the vessel with Art Markel on September 25, 2006.

126 "The Old Testament promises": Reynolds Aluminum, "*Aluminaut:* The Deep Diving Aluminum Submarine," p. 11.

126 During 1965, it completed diving trials: "The *Aluminaut* Story," March 6, 1986, pp. 3–4 (SMV).

126 the *Aluminaut* crew was eager: Author's interview with Art Markel, September 25, 2006. Markel's opinions about *Aluminaut*'s status are clear in his many letters to Reynolds headquarters during the mission in Spain. The letters are stored at the SMV.

126 Guest was quickly disillusioned: Author's interviews with John Craven,

April 19, 2007; George Martin, May 9, 2007; and Brad Mooney, March 30, 2007.

126 **"no great shakes":** Letter, Earl Hays to Paul Fye, March 8, 1966 (WHOI). Hays's full quote: "The Admiral here is no great shakes—sort of a scream and holler man. I think we have him convinced that we are reasonable people and are interested in doing all we can, but that we are not in the Navy and not likely to be."

126 **but their limited navigation:** *Aircraft Salvops Med,* Final Report, vol. 1, part I, chap. 2, p. 29; *Aircraft Salvops Med,* Interim Report, pp. 76–77.

126 *Alvin* **used a crude:** William O. Rainnie, "Equipment and Instrumentation for the Navigation of Submersibles," undated (DSV Alvin Records, 1949–1998 AC 18, Box 17, Folder 23: Navigation, General, WHOI), pp. 6–7.

126 **the system could direct** *Alvin* **to within four hundred yards:** Ibid. and *Aircraft Salvops Med,* Final Report, vol. 2, part I, chap. 8, p. V4.

126 **none of the surface ships on the scene:** Letter, Lewis Melson to Adm. Leyton, February 15, 1966 (author's collection).

127 *Alvin***'s mechanical arm:** Ibid.

127 **he suggested they drop:** Ibid.

127 **"What did he ever have to do":** John Craven interview, April 19, 2007.

CHAPTER 10: GUEST CHARTS A COURSE

128 **Mooney reported to the USS** *Boston:* Mooney's encounter with Admiral Guest comes from Brad Mooney interview, March 30, 2007.

129 **At the time of the Tonkin Gulf:** The explanation of Guest's role in the Tonkin Gulf incident comes from author's interview with Edwin Moïse, August 16, 2007. Admiral Guest was more involved with a third, lesser-known incident on September 18, which didn't result in any retaliation and had little bearing on the escalation of the war. For more on the incident, see Moïse, *Tonkin Gulf and the Escalation of the Vietnam War* (Chapel Hill: University of North Carolina Press, 1996).

129 **"was an extremely important mission":** Author's interview with Douglas Kingsbery, July 27, 2007.

129 **Guest was deeply affected:** Robert Kingsbery interview, July 19, 2007.

129 **"like a ray of sunshine":** *Aircraft Salvops Med,* Final Report, vol. 1, part I, chap. 2, p. 35.

129 **Red Moody was also impressed:** Red Moody interview, November 7, 2006.

130 **Mooney had orders to report:** E-mail from Brad Mooney to author, June 20, 2008.

130 **On February 17, 1966, he laid it out:** Guest's letter to the CNO is discussed at length in *Aircraft Salvops Med,* Final Report, vol. 1, part I, chap. 2, pp. 28–36.

130 **adding paint cans, soup cans:** Author's interview with Jon Lindbergh, July 11, 2007.

130 **"We enter this phase":** Quoted in *Aircraft Salvops Med,* Final Report, vol. 1, part I, chap. 2, p. 29.

130 **Guest laid out his four search areas:** Ibid., pp. 32–34.

130 **the four search areas encompassed:** Lewis, *One of Our H-Bombs,* p. 159.

130 **Guest's team created a 132-square-mile grid:** *Aircraft Salvops Med,* Interim Report, p. 23.

131 **he made a plan for the submersibles:** Author's interviews with Brad Mooney, March 30, 2007, and Art Markel, September 25, 2006.

131 **the *Aluminaut* sonars picked up:** Art Markel interview, September 25, 2006. Markel also discusses the "ship of antiquity" in Memo, Art Markel to office, "Tape 17," recorded April 11, 1966 (SMV); Letter, Art Markel to Carrie, February 18, 1966 (SMV); and Letter, Art Markel to Louis Reynolds, February 23, 1966 (SMV).

131 **He also suggested to Guest:** Art Markel interview, September 25, 2006.

132 **On February 16, the Soviet foreign minister:** "Russians Accuse U.S. in B-52 Crash," *The New York Times,* February 18, 1966, p. 4; Howard Simons, "Some Experts Fear Strategic Loss if Curbs Are Put on Nuclear Routes," *The Washington Post,* February 27, 1966, p. A1; *SAC Historical Study #109,* pp. 297–298.

132 **A week later, President Charles de Gaulle:** Henry Tanner, "De Gaulle Insists on Rule of Bases of NATO in France," *The New York Times,* February 22, 1966, p. 1; "Johnson Rebuffs de Gaulle Quickly in Bases Dispute," *The New York Times,* March 9, 1966, p. 1.

132 **Ambassador Duke received assurances:** Cable, Embassy in Madrid to SECSTATE WASHDC PRIORITY, March 25, 1966, #23577 (LBJ); Cable,

Embassy in Madrid to SECSTATE WASHDC PRIORITY, March 25, 1966, #24270 (LBJ).

132   a Soviet spy ship, the Lotsman: *Aircraft Salvops Med,* Final Report, vol. 1, part I, chap. 2, pp. 46–49; Toth, "Soviet Spy Ship Watches U.S. Hunt Bomb," *Los Angeles Times,* March 8, 1966, p. 1; author's interviews with Gary Montalbine, August 16, 2007, and Anthony Colucci, July 31, 2007.

133   the Soviets had two advanced submersibles: In an e-mail to the author on May 25, 2007, Anatoly Sagalevitch, who ran the Soviet submersible program, wrote that Russia had two "Sever-2" submersibles that could dive to two thousand meters, but that they were used for scientific purposes only. He doesn't recall the Soviets sending any submersibles to Palomares during the hunt for the bomb.

133   Heads would roll: In more bureaucratic language: "Overshadowing all efforts was the apprehension that the weapon might not be located at all and the Navy would be called upon to justify both the cost and its methods in the unsuccessful search." *Aircraft Salvops Med,* Final Report, vol. 1, part I, chap. 2, p. 3.

133   they would need proof: Author's interview with Henry (hereafter "Tony") Richardson, October 31, 2006.

134   In Washington, Craven briefed the two: Author's interviews with Tony Richardson, October 31, 2006, and Frank Andrews, November 10, 2006. Also see Craven, *The Silent War,* p. 169.

134   On the plane: The story of Richardson's trip to Spain and his first meeting with Guest comes from author's interviews with Tony Richardson, October 31, 2006, and Frank Andrews, November 10, 2006.

135   Richardson, working with the grid overlay: Author's interviews with Tony Richardson, and e-mail, Richardson to author, September 9, 2008. Also see Red Moody interview, November 11, 2006. A detailed explanation of the mathematics behind SEP can be found in *Aircraft Salvops Med,* Final Report, vol. 2, annex I, part II, chap. 5.

135   Some on the task force had doubts: George Martin interview May 9, 2007; and Letter, John Bruce to Paul Fye, March 9, 1966 (WHOI).

136   "It's important psychologically":   Tony Richardson interview, October 31, 2006.

136   By February 17, they had thoroughly scanned: *Aircraft Salvops Med,* Final Report, vol. 1, part I, chap. 2, p. 20.

136 **At times, Guest moved the submersibles:** Author's interviews with Rhodes Boykin, March 16, 2007, and Tony Richardson, October 31, 2007; Memo, W. O. Rainnie to Office of Naval Research, "Quarterly Informal Letter," June 10, 1966, p. 8.

136 **specific grievances began to emerge:** Guest's rebuke of Markel comes from Art Markel interview, September 25, 2006.

137 **The *Alvin* crew had its own problems:** Brad Mooney interview, March 30, 2007; Kaharl, *Water Baby,* pp. 67–69.

138 **One Navy captain estimated:** Letter, Lewis Melson to Adm. Leyton, February 25, 1966 (author's collection).

138 **"At first the *Thunderball* aspects":** Richard Oulahan, "The Case of the Missing H-Bomb," *Life,* February 25, 1966, p. 106A.

CHAPTER 11: THE FISHERMAN'S CATCH

139 **One Sunday morning in February:** The story of Simó's catch comes from author's interviews with Joe Ramirez, January 27, 2007, Red Moody, November 7, 2006, and Oliver Andersen, March 31, 2007; and from Commander Task Group 65.3, memo to Commander Task Force 65, "Report of Inshore Search, Identification and Recovery Unit," March 13, 1966 (NHC), p. 26. There is some slight disagreement on the date of this incident, but sources agree that it happened sometime around February 10, 1966.

140 **A Palomares schoolteacher:** *SAC Historical Study #109,* p. 47.

140 **Searchers were ordered to mark:** Ibid., p. 99.

140 **General Wilson asked the Sandia engineers:** Information on the Sandia drop tests ("Operation Sunday") comes from ibid., pp. 102–105; author's interview with William Caudle, January 22, 2004; and Memo, Robert L. McNeill to William N. Caudle, "Field Observation Operation Sunday," February 15, 1966 (NNSA).

141 **"severely restricted":** Memo, McNeill to Caudle, "Field Observation," p. 5.

141 **Maydew's airburst theory:** *SAC Historical Study #109,* pp. 43–44.

141 **Only Larry Messinger showed a positive result:** Ibid., p. 44.

141 **The Spanish vessel *Juan de la Cosa:*** Ibid., p. 47.

141 **Joe Ramirez also found a pharmacist:** Joe Ramirez interview, January 27, 2007.

141 "This could only be considered as normal": *SAC Historical Study #109*, p. 93.

CHAPTER 12: *RADIOACTIVIDAD*

143 Colonel White, the man in charge: Flora Lewis interview with Alton "Bud" White, undated (AFHRA), and Szulc, *The Bombs of Palomares*, pp. 147–149.

143 Dr. Wright Langham, a plutonium expert: The background on Langham is from Szulc, *The Bombs of Palomares*, pp. 145–147, and Lewis, *One of Our H-Bombs*, pp. 106–111.

144 Some of the urine samples: *The Bombs of Palomares*, pp. 153–154; Lewis, *One of Our H-Bombs*, pp. 109–111; *SAC Historical Study #109*, pp. 146–148.

144 Langham next tackled crop and animal worries: *SAC Historical Study #109*, pp. 155–156.

144 The tests, called Operation Roller Coaster: J. Newell Stannard, *Radioactivity and Health, A History*. Vol. 2: *Environmental Aspects* (Richland, Wash.: Pacific Northwest Laboratory, 1988), pp. 1193–1197, 1203–1207.

144 the major plutonium hazard had vanished: Paraphrased from Lewis, *One of Our H-Bombs*, p. 115.

144 He had used himself: Lewis, *One of Our H-Bombs*, p. 109.

144 "maximum permissible body burden": Ibid., p. 110.

145 Current limits: E-mail, Andy Karam to author, December 10, 2007.

145 The maximum permissible air concentration: Lewis, *One of Our H-Bombs*, p. 110.

145 an amount akin to a grain of salt: E-mail, Andy Karam to author, December 10, 2007.

145 has a half-life of 24,360 years: *SAC Historical Study #109*, p. 137.

145 Langham calculated how much soil: The soil remediation plan is discussed in Lewis, *One of Our H-Bombs*, pp. 115–120; Flora Lewis interview with Alton "Bud" White, undated (AFHRA); *SAC Historical Study #109*, pp. 160, 165–167, 171–173; and Place et al., *Palomares Summary Report* (Kirtland Air Force Base, N.M.: Field Command, Defense Nuclear Agency, Technology and Analysis Directorate, January 15, 1975), pp. 64–65. Unfortunately, official records list the contamination levels in counts per minute (CPM), a measurement that varies depending on the sensitivity of the instrument.

146 there had been at least twenty-eight nuclear accidents: "Narrative Summaries of Accidents Involving U.S. Nuclear Weapons 1950–1980," undated (NNSA, FOIA). Accident summaries are paraphrased from this document.

147 a public debate: For a historical discussion of the nuclear weapons safety issue, see Joel Larus, *Nuclear Weapons Safety and the Common Defense* (Columbus: Ohio State University Press, 1967).

147 Even President Kennedy grew worried: Larus, *Nuclear Weapons Safety,* pp. 32–33.

147 "When Air Force experts rushed": Quoted in ibid., pp. 93–94.

148 *Combat Crew,* reflected this zeal: Examples come from the author's reading of *Combat Crew.*

148 18,340 KC-135 tankers: *SAC Historical Study #109,* p. 288.

148 a cleanup plan called "Moist Mop": Ibid., pp. 138–139.

149 Any men plowing, scraping: Ibid., pp. 156–157.

149 Robert Finkel, who spent: Robert Finkel interview, April 4, 2007.

149 The Navy regularly sampled the water: Red Moody interview, November 7, 2006; Commander Task Group 65.3, memo to Commander Task Force 65, "Report of Inshore Search," March 13, 1966, p. 9.

149 Gaylord White, one of the divers: Gaylord White interview, March 3, 2007.

149 Henry Engelhardt, the commander: Author's interview with Henry "Bud" Engelhardt, May 17, 2006. Also see *SAC Historical Study* #109, pp. 163 and 165.

150 When Bud White's team first mapped: *SAC Historical Study #109,* p. 141.

150 The Air Force maintains: *Palomares Nuclear Weapons Accident: Revised Dose Evaluation Report,* U.S. Department of the Air Force, Air Force Medical Service, April 2001 (FOIA). This report states that some doses measured "unreasonably high" and suggests that more study would be needed to reconcile the data. A press release accompanying this report said that exposures were "not significant."

150 The vegetation problem: Flora Lewis, interview with Alton "Bud" White, undated (AFHRA); *SAC Historical Study #109,* pp. 170, 174.

151 This left the question: The soil problem is discussed in Flora Lewis,

interview with Alton "Bud" White, undated (AFHRA); author's interview with Jack Howard, April 3, 2007; *SAC Historical Study #109*, pp. 179–186.

151 **Spanish and American officials:** The disposal of the aircraft wreckage is discussed in *SAC Historical Study #109*, pp. 134–136; *Aircraft Salvops Med*, Interim Report, pp. C6–C7.

151 **"lingering recriminations":** *SAC Historical Study #109*, p. 134.

152 **To prepare the dirt:** Ibid., p. 173.

152 **with lawyers interviewing about twenty people:** Ibid., p. 391.

152 **The claims work was as complicated:** The background on claims comes from Joe Ramirez interviews, January 27, 2007, and April 27, 2007; and *SAC Historical Study #109*, chapter 7.

152 **when lawyers consulted the owners' registry:** *SAC Historical Study #109*, p. 397.

152 **Four claimants:** Ibid., p. 389, footnote.

MARCH

CHAPTER 13: SPIN CONTROL

155 **Ambassador Duke stood:** The description of Duke's solo swim and the quotes are from "US Envoy Swims in Mediterranean," CBS News, March 9, 1966.

156 **the U.S. government had finally admitted:** *SAC Historical Study #109*, pp. 327–329; the text of the DOD press release is on p. 328. See also John W. Finney, "U.S. Concedes Loss of H-Bomb in Spain," *The New York Times*, March 3, 1966, p. 1.

156 **For weeks, the U.S. and Spanish governments:** Arguments over the release of information are discussed in *SAC Historical Study #109*, pp. 324–326, and Szulc, *The Bombs of Palomares*, pp. 202–204.

157 **various government agencies began stumbling:** *SAC Historical Study #109*, p. 329.

157 **"The news is now official":** "The Missing H-Bomb," *The Boston Globe*, March 4, 1966, p. 14.

157 **"One U.S. official insisted":** "Swimming Party," *Newsweek*, March 14, 1966, p. 59.

157 Together, Ambassador Duke and Manuel Fraga Iribarne: Sources differ over who actually came up with the idea for the swim. In an oral history, Duke said the idea was his and Fraga agreed to the plan reluctantly, thinking it undignified for a government official to splash around in bathing trunks. General Spanish opinion holds that the idea was Fraga's and Duke finally agreed only to avoid being shown up. In recent interviews, Fraga and Robin Duke say the idea was mutual. They also said that it was mutually agreed that Robin Duke *not* swim, to avoid the spectacle of an ambassador's wife in a bikini. Interestingly, a famous Spanish newsreel of the event shows only Fraga, with a brief appearance by Ambassador Duke at the very end. (This newsreel forms most Spaniards' collective memory of the entire Palomares saga.) American papers discussed mainly Duke, with only rare mentions of Fraga. Sources: Angier Biddle Duke, Living History interview, October 24, 1990 (Duke), pp. 18–20; author's interviews with Manuel Fraga Iribarne, February 15, 2007, and Robin Duke, June 7, 2007; and *Noticias NO-DO 1210 B,* (Filmoteca Española), undated.

157 "If I could take my children": Angier Biddle Duke, Living History interview, October 24, 1990, p. 18.

157 "aquatic diplomacy": The Kalb quotes come from "US Envoy Swims in Mediterranean," CBS News, March 9, 1966.

157 Something went awry: The story of the second swim comes primarily from author's interview with Timothy Towell, January 8, 2007, and Szulc, *The Bombs of Palomares,* p. 204. Fraga denies this version of events, though without much vigor (interview, February 15, 2007). He says that everything went off as planned and that the two men swam together. However, Towell's story is corroborated by Red Moody as well as footage of the second swim, which shows Duke entering the water after Fraga.

158 "The humble of Palomares": Signs quoted in "Officials Take Cold Dip to Deny H-Bomb Hazard," *The Washington Post,* March 9, 1966.

158 "It was with confidence and pleasure": Angier Biddle Duke, radio interview with Jay Rutherfurd (Duke).

159 An Associated Press photo: Tad Szulc, "U.S. Envoy Swims Where H-Bomb Fell," *The New York Times,* March 9, 1966, p. 1.

159 "We think of our diplomats": *The Dallas Morning News,* March 12, 1966 (Angier Biddle Duke Papers, Palomares Scrapbook, Duke).

159 "Duke's 'Swim-in' ": Jay Rutherfurd, "Duke's 'Swim-in' for Spanish Tourism Best Water Show since Aquacade," *Variety,* March 16, 1966, p. 2.

159 **"I'm glad your bathing suit"**: Letter, Jack Valenti to Angier Biddle Duke, March 9, 1966 (LBJ).

160 **"How happy I was"**: Letter, Jacqueline Kennedy to Angier Biddle Duke, March 12, 1966 (Duke).

160 **"I trust that excessive swimming"**: Letter, Arthur Schlesinger, Jr., to Angier Biddle Duke, March 15, 1966 (Duke).

160 **"I can understand our Government's desire"**: Letter, Nathan Arrow to Angier Biddle Duke, March 11, 1966 (Duke).

161 **"Feel safer already?"**: "Swimming Party," p. 59.

161 **"Supposing a bomb is reported missing"**: Quoted in Szulc, *The Bombs of Palomares,* p. 212.

161 **The Moscow publication *Izvestia***: *SAC Historical Study #109,* p. 361.

161 **"For many years"**: "The Missing H-Bomb," *The Boston Globe,* March 4, 1966, p. 14.

161 **Curtis LeMay added his two cents**: "Air Force Gen. Curtis LeMay on Missing Bomb," CBS News, March 12, 1966.

162 **The Navy requested**: *SAC Historical Study #109,* pp. 184–185.

162 **"in line with the spirit"**: Ibid., p. 185.

162 **Wilson apologized**: Delmar E. Wilson, speech to residents of Palomares and Villaricos, March 20, 1966 (USAF, FOIA).

163 **On March 24, men moved**: *SAC Historical Study #109,* p. 188.

163 **A second team of ballistics experts**: Ibid., p. 50.

163 **"By 1 March"**: Ibid.

163 **With regard to the water search**: "Addendum to SAT Study of 7 February 1966," March 4, 1966 (NNSA); *SAC Historical Study #109,* pp. 51–53.

163 **The Sandia engineer Bill Barton**: Memo, Maydew and Barton to Fowler, "Chronological Summary," March 29, 1966, p. 3.

163 **the secretary of defense authorized**: *Aircraft Salvops Med,* Final Report, vol. 1, part I, chap. 2, p. 55.

163 **Cyrus Vance created a "Search Evaluation Board"**: The background on the Search Evaluation Board is from ibid., pp. 55–56, and author's interview with Robert Sproull, May 11, 2007. The Sproull quotes are from this interview.

164 In anticipation of the next meeting: *Aircraft Salvops Med,* Final Report, vol. 1, part I, chap. 2, p. 56.

CHAPTER 14: THE PHOTOGRAPH

165 On the morning of March 1: The story of *Alvin*'s move to search area C4 is from Marvin J. McCamis, " 'Captain Hook's' Hunt for the H-Bomb," *Oceanus* 31, no. 4 (Winter 1988–89), p. 24. There is some dispute about whether McCamis sneaked *Alvin* into C4, as he contends, or was assigned to dive there. Navy Captain Lewis Melson said that he and others met with Guest on February 28 and proposed sending *Alvin* into C4, and Guest agreed to the plan (see memo from Lewis Melson, "WHOI's OCEANUS WINTER 1988/1989 issue extract for 1 March 1966" [author's collection]). However, the deck logs of the *Fort Snelling* for March 1 say that *Alvin* was launched to search area B29, lending credence to McCamis's version of events. Also, such an antiauthoritarian scheme seems in character for McCamis. Long-time *Alvin* pilot Barrie Walden said, "McCamis, in my opinion, would be more likely to try something that was a little more outrageous than another pilot, in order to get the job done during the dive." (Author's interview with Barrie Walden, July 25, 2006.)

165 Bill Rainnie and Val Wilson: *Alvin* dive log, Dive 119, March 1, 1966. *Alvin*'s dive logs are available at www.whoi.edu/page.do?pid=11039.

165 Andrews had asked Earl Hays: Frank Andrews interview, November 10, 2006.

166 Rainnie and Wilson vented *Alvin*'s ballast: The description of *Alvin* diving comes from the author's visit to *Alvin* and interviews with Robert Brown and Bruce Strickrott, July 2, 2007.

166 the visibility near the bottom: Victoria Kaharl, *Water Baby: The Story of Alvin* (New York: Oxford University Press, 1990), p. 66; William O. Rainnie, "How We Found the Missing H-Bomb," *Popular Mechanics,* August 1966, pp. 75–76.

166 In order to steer a straight line: Marvin McCamis interview, January 31, 2003.

166 "a straight line in a snowstorm": Ibid.

166 the bottom stretched before them: Rainnie, "How We Found the Missing H-Bomb," p. 76.

166 *Alvin* was "flying a contour": Frank Andrews interview, November 10, 2006.

167   Mac McCamis, however, had lost patience: McCamis, " 'Captain Hook's' Hunt," p. 24.

167   "Wait a minute, I see something":   Rainnie and Wilson's dialogue is quoted in Kaharl, *Water Baby*, p. 69. The *Alvin* pilots regularly recorded their dives on reel-to-reel audiotape. However, the tapes of certain critical dives, including this one, are missing from the WHOI archives.

167   the pilots handed off their film: McCamis, " 'Captain Hook's' Hunt," p. 24.

167   "like a barrel had been dragged":   Marvin McCamis interview, January 31, 2003.

167   "To me, it looked like":   Brad Mooney interview, March 30, 2007.

167   the *Alvin* crew returned: McCamis, " 'Captain Hook's' Hunt," p. 24; deck logs of the USS *Fort Snelling*, March 3–7, 1966 (NARA).

167   the task force suddenly yanked: McCamis, " 'Captain Hook's' Hunt," p. 24; Tony Richardson interview, October 31, 2007; Memo, W. O. Rainnie to Office of Naval Research, "Quarterly Informal Letter," June 10, 1966, p. 8; *Alvin* dive logs, Dive 124, March 8, 1966, and Dive 125, March 9, 1966; Deck Logs of the USS *Fort Snelling*, March 8–9, 1966 (NARA).

168   "My turn at surface control":   McCamis, " 'Captain Hook's' Hunt," p. 24.

168   made nine runs over a dummy: *Aircraft Salvops Med,* Final Report, vol. 1, part I, chap. 2, p. 44.

168   On March 12, an OBSS: Ibid.

168   The divers had wrapped up: Red Moody interview, November 7, 2006; e-mail, Moody to author, December 19, 2007.

168   Duke wrote to Jack Valenti: Letter, Angier Biddle Duke to Jack Valenti, March 14, 1966 (LBJ).

169   Tony Richardson, the baby-faced mathematician: The details of Richardson's actions on March 15, 1966, come from Tony Richardson, diary, March 15 to April 7, 1966 (author's collection), and Tony Richardson interview, October 31, 2007.

169   "Paco de la Bomba":   Lewis, *One of Our H-Bombs,* p. 194.

170   His response to the Cyrus Vance committee: *Aircraft Salvops Med,* Final Report, February 15, 1967, vol. 1, part I, chap. 2, pp. 56–59.

170   They were supposed to get a new transponder: Ibid., pp. 53–54; author's interview with Brad Mooney, March 30, 2007.

170 That day Mac McCamis: McCamis, " 'Captain Hook's' Hunt," p. 25.

170 because today was his son's birthday: Ibid.

170 Wilson saw the track: *Alvin*'s discovery of the parachute on March 15 is detailed in ibid.; author's interviews with Marvin McCamis, January 31, 2003, and Art Bartlett, February 5, 2007; *Aircraft Salvops Med,* Final Report, vol. 1, part I, chap. 2, pp. 59–60. In his interview, McCamis said the code word was "bent nail," but Navy sources say it was "instrument panel."

171 "We found a parachute": Kaharl, *Water Baby,* p. 74. The reel-to-reel audiotape for the March 15, 1966, dive (Dive 128) is missing from the WHOI archives. However, the author viewed photographs taken by the pilots on this dive.

171 "Had a hell of a time": Marvin McCamis interview, January 31, 2003.

171 the USS *Albany* had arrived: Lewis, *One of Our H-Bombs,* p. 209; *Aircraft Salvops Med,* Final Report, vol. 1, part I, chap. 2, pp. 59–60.

171 Deep below the surface: Marvin McCamis interview, January 31, 2003; Art Bartlett interview, February 5, 2007; Kaharl, *Water Baby,* p. 76.

172 the men discussed what to do: Art Bartlett interview, February 5, 2007.

172 *Alvin* could remain submerged for twenty-four hours: Everett S. Allen, "Research Submarine *Alvin,*" *U.S. Naval Institute Proceedings,* April 1964, p. 138.

172 Mooney suggested sending *Aluminaut* down: Brad Mooney interview, March 30, 2007.

173 "I can fly my F4s": George Martin interview, May 9, 2007.

173 The sub picked up a transponder: E-mail, Red Moody to author, December 14, 2007.

173 got a quick battery charge: Art Markel interview, September 25, 2006.

173 "He thought we were a bunch": Ibid.

173 The *Alvin* crew sat in the dark: McCamis, " 'Captain Hook's' Hunt," p. 25.

173 "It was beautiful": Quoted in Lewis, *One of Our H-Bombs,* p. 208.

173 cautiously parking herself about twenty-five yards: *Aircraft Salvops Med,* Final Report, vol. 1, part I, chap. 2, p. 66.

173 *Alvin* surfaced after ten hours: Ibid.

173   entered the well deck at 8:12:   Deck logs of the USS *Fort Snelling,* March 15, 1966 (NARA).

173   The *Alvin* crew sent their photographs: *Aircraft Salvops Med,* Final Report, vol. 1, part I, chap. 2, pp. 66, 69–70.

173   Mac McCamis was outraged: McCamis, " 'Captain Hook's' Hunt," p. 25.

173   "How do you know":   Quoted in Kaharl, *Water Baby,* p. 77.

173   "What else":   Ibid.

173   "In all my life":   McCamis, " 'Captain Hook's' Hunt," p. 25.

174   Admiral Guest wrote a situation report: Cable, CTF Sixty-five to REUCW/CNO, "Sitrep Seventy-nine," March 16, 1966 (LBJ).

174   The other memo: *Aircraft Salvops Med,* Final Report, vol. 1, part I, chap. 2, p. 67.

174   Robert Sproull, the chair of the Cyrus Vance committee: Robert Sproull interview, May 11, 2007.

174   That morning in Rota: E-mail, Red Moody to author, December 19, 2007.

174   That afternoon in Spain: Tony Richardson, diary, March 15 to April 7, 1966 (author's collection); author's interviews with Tony Richardson, October 31, 2007, and John Bruce, August 17, 2006.

175   news of the Gemini 8 space shot: John Noble Wilford, "Gemini Is Fueled for Link-up Today," *The New York Times,* March 16, 1966, p. 1; John Noble Wilford, "Gemini 8 Crew Is Forced Down in Pacific after Successful Linkup with Satellite; Spacemen Picked Up after 3 Hours in Sea," *The New York Times,* March 17, 1966, p. 1.

175   he sent three nuclear weapons experts: Cable, from 16ADVON Spain to RUCSC/SAC, March 17, 1966, #71560 (LBJ).

176   The man on the phone was Harry Stathos: Lewis, *One of Our H-Bombs,* pp. 212–213; *SAC Historical Study #109,* pp. 331–332.

177   "The undersea vessel, *Alvin,* made contact":   Cable, Embassy in Madrid to SECSTATE WASHDC IMMEDIATE, March 17, 1966, #1219 (LBJ).

177   At 12:45 a.m., as reporters gathered: *SAC Historical Study #109,* pp. 331–332.

177   "Recovery promises to be":   "Sub Finds H-Bomb off Spain: Weapon

Reported Intact in Water 2500 Feet Deep," *The Washington Post,* March 18, 1966, p. 1.

177 **"No pictures of the bomb":** "H-Bomb Located in Sea off Spain," *The New York Times,* March 18, 1966, p. 1.

178 **to ensure credibility:** Angier Biddle Duke, Living History interview, October 24, 1990, pp. 23–24 (Duke).

178 **Duke formed a committee:** *SAC Historical Study #109,* p. 336.

178 **"The fourth and final weapon":** Cable, Embassy in Madrid to SEC-STATE, March 18, 1966, #1226 (LBJ).

178 **On March 16, McCamis and Wilson:** " 'Captain Hook's' Hunt," p. 25; William O. Rainnie, "Alvin . . . and the Bomb," *Oceanus* 12, no. 4 (August 1966), p. 19.

179 *Alvin* **by now had a mechanical arm:** Allen, "Research Submarine *Alvin,*" p. 140.

CHAPTER 15: POODL VERSUS THE BOMB

180 **On March 22, 1966, CBS News:** "Special Report: Lost and Found, One H-Bomb," CBS News, March 22, 1966.

181 *Alvin* **or** *Aluminaut* **could carry:** Red Moody interview, November 7, 2006; Brad Mooney, e-mail to author, September 17, 2008. Mooney pointed out another problem: the weight of the line should not be heavier than the positive buoyancy of the sub.

181 **Working with two consultants:** The description of POODL comes from author's interview with Red Moody, November 7, 2006; D. H. Moody, "40th Anniversary of Palomares," *Faceplate* 10, no. 2 (September 2006), p. 18; *Aircraft Salvops Med,* Final Report, vol. 4, appendix B, pp. 42–44; *Aircraft Salvops Med,* Interim Report, pp. 39, D59, D61. POODL was rebuilt several times during the bomb recovery effort, so it is difficult to determine its exact specifications at the time of the first recovery attempt. When there was a discrepancy in the records, author relied on *Aircraft Salvops Med,* Final Report, vol. 4, appendix B. The height of POODL (seven feet) comes from e-mail, Red Moody to author, September 17, 2008.

182 **"Oh, my God":** Author's interview with Malcolm MacKinnon, December 4, 2006.

182 **"gypsy-engineered":** Red Moody interview, November 7, 2006.

182 That fear overshadowed everything: *Aircraft Salvops Med,* Final Report, vol. 1, part I, chap. 2, p. 69.

182 the captain of the *Mizar:* *Aircraft Salvops Med,* Interim Report, pp. C12–C13.

182 it had carried a light line: Even this light polypropylene line, hand-tended from the surface, was a struggle for *Alvin* to carry down to the bottom. *Aircraft Salvops Med,* Final Report, vol. 1, part I, chap. 2, p. 73; Memo, W.O. Rainnie to Office of Naval Research, "Quarterly Informal Letter," June 10, 1966, p. 9; Rainnie, "How We Found the Missing H-Bomb," *Popular Mechanics,* August 1966, p. 78. According to Red Moody (e-mail to author, September 17, 2008) the sub crews had never attempted such a risky maneuver before and were understandably reluctant to try.

182 the task force members tried another tactic: *Aircraft Salvops Med,* Final Report, vol. 1, part I, chap. 2, p. 75.

182 That evening, Admiral Guest wrote: Ibid.

182 Art Markel thought *Aluminaut:* Art Markel interview, September 25, 2006; Memo, Art Markel to office, "Tape 3," recorded March 19, 1966 (SMV); *Aircraft Salvops Med,* Final Report, vol. 1, part I, chap. 2, p. 76.

183 Markel was excited: For example: Memo, Art Markel to office, "Tape 4," recorded March 20, 1966; Memo, Art Markel to office, "Tape 5," recorded March 22, 1966; Memo, Art Markel to office, "Tape 6," recorded March 23, 1966, all at SMV.

183 to share some of *Alvin*'s limelight: Memo, Art Markel to office, "Tape 3," recorded March 19, 1966 (SMV).

183 "It is quite apparent": Letter, Art Markel to Carrie, March 28, 1966 (SMV).

183 Markel had half a mind: Letter, Art Markel to Carrie, April 6, 1966 (SMV).

183 On March 22, the *Los Angeles Times:* Robert C. Toth, "H-Bomb May Slip into Deep Sea Crevice, Balk Recovery," *Los Angeles Times,* March 22, 1966, p. 1.

183 Duke, disturbed by such gloomy press: Cable, Embassy in Madrid to SECSTATE WASHDC, March 22, 1966, Deptel 1185 (LBJ).

183 The Air Force thought: *SAC Historical Study #109,* pp. 320, 334–335.

183 **But Guest suspected the embassy:** Author's interviews with Brad Mooney, March 30, 2007, and Robert Kingsbery, July 19, 2007.

184 **he seemed as mystified:** Author's interviews with Robin Duke, June 7, 2007, and Tim Towell, January 8, 2007. See also *SAC Historical Study #109,* p. 335.

184 *Mizar* **had landed the anchor and POODL:** *Aircraft Salvops Med,* Final Report, vol. 1, part I, chap. 2, pp. 78–79; *Aircraft Salvops Med,* Interim Report, p. C13. See also Tad Szulc, "H-Bomb Searchers Fail Again as Sea Cable Snaps," *The New York Times,* March 26, 1966, p. 9. March 23 was also the day that the diver Carl Brashear was injured in an accident aboard the USS *Hoist,* nearly severing his left lower leg. Brashear's story was dramatized in the feature film *Men of Honor.*

184 **Guest's staff met aboard the** *Mizar:* *Aircraft Salvops Med,* Final Report, vol. 1, part I, chap. 2, pp. 79–80; Jon Lindbergh interview, July 11, 2007.

184 *Mizar* **would hover directly above:** E-mail, Red Moody to author, December 19, 2007.

185 **McCamis, still underwater in** *Alvin:* Marvin McCamis interview, January 31, 2003.

185 **Red Moody was having his own argument:** Red Moody interview, November 7, 2006; e-mail, Red Moody to author, December 19, 2007.

185 **The** *Mizar***'s crew snagged the floating buoy:** The description of the lift attempt comes from *Aircraft Salvops Med,* Final Report, vol. 1, part I, chap. 2, pp. 80–81, and author's interviews with Jon Lindbergh, July 11, 2007, and Red Moody, November 7, 2006. There are some small (fifteen-minute) discrepancies in the timeline of events.

186 **"Oh, boy":** Marvin McCamis interview, January 31, 2003.

186 *Alvin* **needed a battery charge:** *Aircraft Salvops Med,* Final Report, vol. 1, part I, chap. 2, pp. 81–82.

186 **"The slope looked":** McCamis, " 'Captain Hook's' Hunt," p. 27.

186 **The pilots found:** Ibid.

186 **The broken line seemed:** *Aircraft Salvops Med,* Final Report, vol. 1, part I, chap. 2, p. 81.

186 **The Soviet newspaper** *Izvestia:* "Soviet Asks World Check on U.S. H-Bomb off Spain," *The New York Times,* March 19, 1966, p. 7.

186 U.N. Secretary General: Lewis, *One of Our H-Bombs,* p. 222.

187 There was still the question of logistics: *Aircraft Salvops Med,* Final Report, vol. 1, part I, chap. 2, pp. 84–85; *SAC Historical Study #109,* pp. 337–339.

187 Military officials hated the idea: Joseph Smith interview, January 23, 2007; Angier Biddle Duke, Living History interview, October 24, 1990, pp. 23–24.

187 he broke protocol and called: Angier Biddle Duke, Living History interview, October 24, 1990, pp. 23–24.

187 "Here we were in the ninth inning":   George Martin interview, May 9, 2007.

188 The crew of the USS *Albany*:   Deck logs of the USS *Albany,* March 29, 1966; Francis Smith, e-mails to author, February 2 and 4, 2008. Smith was a gunner's mate on the USS *Albany* during the bomb search. The deck logs for the morning of March 29 say, "Commenced handling TALOS missile warheads." TALOS was a long-range naval surface-to-air missile. It could be equipped with either a conventional or a nuclear warhead. To the best of the author's knowledge, this is the only mention of TALOS in the *Albany* deck logs during the Palomares mission.

188 "Because arrangements for overflights":   Cable, State and Defense to Embassy in Madrid, March 30, 1966, Deptel 1240 (LBJ).

188 Duke responded in a secret cable: Cable, Embassy in Madrid to SEC-STATE WASHDC PRIORITY, April 1, 1966, #849 (LBJ).

189 Guest assumed that the weapon: *Aircraft Salvops Med,* Final Report, vol. 1, part I, chap. 2, p. 82.

189 the crew found a track leading up: Ibid. and Rainnie, "How We Found the Missing H-Bomb," p. 78.

189 the *Alvin* pilots began to imagine: George Martin interview, May 9, 2007; Lewis, *One of Our H-Bombs,* pp. 223–224; *Aircraft Salvops Med,* Final Report, vol. 1, part I, chap. 2, p. 82; Rainnie, "How We Found the Missing H-Bomb," p. 78.

189 On the morning of April 2, *Alvin* dove: The description of this dive comes from author's interview with George Martin, May 9, 2007; *Aircraft Salvops Med,* Final Report, vol. 1, part I, chap. 2, p. 86; and McCamis, " 'Captain Hook's' Hunt," p. 27.

190 Red Moody heard a buzz: Red Moody interview, November 7, 2006.

APRIL

CHAPTER 16: HOOKED

193 **a diver named Herman Kunz:** Malcolm MacKinnon interview, December 4, 2006.

193 **MacKinnon and Kunz had visited:** Ibid.

194 **The engineers and technicians at NOTS:** The background on CURV comes mainly from author's interviews with Robert Pace, February 6, 2007, and Larry Brady, January 18 and 31, 2007; and e-mail, Larry Brady to author, September 18, 2008. See also *Aircraft Salvops Med,* Final Report, vol. 4, appendix B, pp. 45–52; and *Aircraft Salvops Med,* Final Report, vol. 1, part I, chap. 2, p. 86.

195 **"It looked like a python":** Larry Brady interview, January 31, 2007.

196 **The CURV team set up shop:** The background on the *Petrel* and Max Harrell is from Sanchez Goode, "Postscript to Palomares," *U.S. Naval Institute Proceedings* 94, no. 12 (December 1968), pp. 49–53.

196 **The Navy dropped a dummy bomb:** *Aircraft Salvops Med,* Final Report, vol. 1, part I, chap. 2, p. 86; *Aircraft Salvops Med,* Final Report, vol. 1, annex I, part I, chap. 2, p. 7.

196 **The CURV team operated the device:** Details on the CURV operations come mainly from author's interviews with Robert Pace, February 6, 2007, and Larry Brady, January 18 and 31, 2007, and e-mail, Larry Brady to author, September 18, 2008.

196 **CURV dove to 2,400 feet:** Naval Ordnance Test Station, Pasadena Annex [NOTS Pasadena], *AirsalopsMed/CURV Notes,* 1966 (author's collection).

197 **Sketching a grapnel:** Robert Pace interview, February 6, 2007; Larry Brady interview, January 31, 2007.

197 **Alvin, left alone with the bomb:** *Aircraft Salvops Med,* Interim Report, pp. C14–C15; deck logs of the USS *Fort Snelling,* April 3, 1966.

197 **now code-named "Robert":** Tony Richardson, diary, April 4, 1966; author's interview with Doug Kingsbery, July 27, 2007. Brad Mooney says that additional code words were used for underwater communications. Mooney recalls using codes based on the characters from "Peanuts" and the colors of the rainbow, so that "Lucy Red" might mean that a pilot had spotted something. (Brad Mooney interview, March 30, 2007.)

197   To give CURV as much freedom: Goode, "Postscript to Palomares," p. 52; Malcolm MacKinnon interview, December 4, 2006.

198   The machine shop had finished: Robert Pace interview, February 6, 2007.

198   The grapnel was attached: Larry Brady interview, January 31, 2007; *Aircraft Salvops Med,* Interim Report, p. 40.

198   On April 4, just before 9 a.m.:   Deck logs of the USS *Petrel,* April 4, 1966.

198   Air Force experts had told: Larry Brady interview, January 18, 2007.

198   Around noon, CURV reached the bomb: Deck logs of the USS *Petrel,* April 4, 1966; NOTS Pasadena, *AirsalopsMed/CURV Notes.*

198   dug three tines of the grapnel: Brady says four tines; the final Navy report says three. The photographs are unclear. Larry Brady interview, January 18, 2007; *Aircraft Salvops Med,* Interim Report, p. 40.

198   Sure that the grapnel: Larry Brady interview, January 31, 2007; *Aircraft Salvops Med,* Interim Report, p. 40.

198   two guys flipped their car: Larry Brady interview, January 31, 2007.

198   "you got that parachute":   Robert Pace interview, February 6, 2007.

199   On April 5, Mac McCamis: Marvin J. McCamis, " 'Captain Hook's' Hunt for the H-Bomb," *Oceanus,* 31, no. 4 (Winter 1988–89), p. 27; *Aircraft Salvops Med,* Interim Report, p. C15.

199   "This sixty-four-foot cargo chute":   Marvin McCamis, interview, January 31, 2003.

199   "Scared him dead":   Ibid.

199   If *Alvin* got trapped or tangled: The description of the *Alvin* emergency measures comes from the author's visit to *Alvin* and interviews with Bob Brown and Bruce Strickrott on July 2, 2007.

199   Just before midnight on April 5:   Deck logs of the USS *Petrel,* April 5, 1966; NOTS Pasadena, *AirsalopsMed/CURV Notes.*

199   Larry Brady twisted CURV's second grapnel: *Aircraft Salvops Med,* Interim Report, pp. 40, C15.

200   the weather turned sour: "William S. Guest Press Conference," April 8, 1966.

200 **Admiral Guest looked:** Ibid.

200 **Just before 9 p.m.:** Deck logs of the USS *Petrel,* April 6, 1966.

200 **Bad weather grounded CURV:** *Aircraft Salvops Med,* Final Report, vol. 1, part I, chap. 2, p. 94.

200 **Around 1 a.m., CURV dove:** Deck logs of the USS *Petrel,* April 7, 1966.

200 **The control shack was crowded:** The main source for this scene is Larry Brady interview, January 31, 2007. Other sources disagree on several points in this scene. Some say that Guest and his staff were in the wardroom, watching the underwater drama on closed-circuit TV, when CURV became fouled; Brady, however, remembers the scene in the CURV control shack in detail. In addition, some accounts say that the CURV team drove the vehicle into the parachute on purpose, but Brady and Robert Pace say it was an accident.

200 **Guest thanked his lucky stars:** "William S. Guest Press Conference," April 8, 1966.

200 **The CURV crew waited:** Larry Brady interview, January 31, 2007, and Robert Pace interview, February 6, 2007.

201 **The same argument flew:** Sources differ slightly on how Mooney and Guest ended up in the wardroom together, but all agree that it was Mooney who convinced Guest to raise the bomb. Author's interviews with Brad Mooney, March 30, 2007, and Red Moody, November 7, 2006; Kaharl, *Water Baby,* p. 79; George Martin, e-mail to author, September 18, 2008.

201 **fainted from the stress:** D. H. Moody, "40th Anniversary of Palomares," *Faceplate* 10, no. 2 (September 2006), p. 19; e-mail, Red Moody to author, September 19, 2008.

201 **"the snake charmer":** George Martin interview, May 9, 2007.

201 **"I tried to be":** Brad Mooney interview, March 30, 2007.

201 **Guest sent a message:** *Aircraft Salvops Med,* Final Report, vol. 1, part I, chap. 2, p. 95.

201 **The two men went over:** Red Moody interview, November 7, 2006; Goode, "Postscript to Palomares," pp. 51–52.

201 **Harrell designed a system:** Goode, "Postscript to Palomares," p. 51. This article also contains a diagram of Harrell's novel rigging and control system.

201 **Both lines were wound:** Ibid. Also, Red Moody, e-mails to author, September 19 and 21, 2008.

201 Looking at the weather, he knew: Goode, "Postscript to Palomares," p. 53.

202 Guest and his staff gathered: Red Moody interview, November 7, 2006.

202 "tourists": Ibid.

202 there'd be nothing left: Author's interview with Robert Singleton, November 27, 2006.

202 At 5:50 a.m., the *Petrel* began to raise: Deck logs of the USS *Petrel*, April 7, 1966.

202 Guest worried most: "William S. Guest Press Conference," April 8, 1966.

202 one scientist paced: Red Moody interview, November 7, 2006.

202 looked sick to his stomach: Ibid.

202 "I'd prefer combat": "William S. Guest Press Conference," April 8, 1966.

202 the weapon came up so smoothly: Ibid.

202 Two of Red Moody's divers: Ibid.; Red Moody interview, November 7, 2006; *Aircraft Salvops Med*, Final Report, vol. 1, part I, chap. 2, p. 95.

202 Boatswain mates rigged the lines: Goode, "Postscript to Palomares," pp. 51–52; author's interview with Red Moody, November 7, 2006.

202 Immediately, the EOD team: Dewitt H. Moody, memo to Commander, Naval Ordnance Systems Command, "Report of Explosive Ordnance Disposal Operation (OPNAV REPORT 3571-1)," May 10, 1966 (EOD U2, Post 46, Command Files, Operational Archives, Secret, NHC), p. 2.

202 It was 8:46 a.m.: Deck logs of the USS *Petrel*, April 7, 1966. The entry reads, "Weapon on deck with parachute."

203 The rough ride: The condition of weapon number four comes from Moody, memo to Commander, "Report of Explosive Ordnance Disposal," May 10, 1966, p. 4. The author also viewed photographs of the recovered weapon at Operational Archives, NHC. The weapon casings of bombs number one and four are now housed at the National Atomic Museum in Albuquerque, New Mexico.

203 The EOD team began to render: Ibid. and S. V. Asselin, "Notes on the EOD Render Safe Procedure of Weapon #4 (W28 #45345) Near Palomares Spain March 15, 1966" (Document no. SAC200118480000, Confidential,

NNSA, FOIA). See also author's interviews with Oliver Andersen, January 22, 2007, and Red Moody, November 7, 2006, and Moody, e-mails to author, September 23 and 28, 2008. Funston's rig is called, appropriately, a Spanish windlass.

203 **there were no shouts:** Author's interviews with Oliver Andersen, January 22, 2007, and Larry Brady, January 31, 2007.

203 **In the wardroom, the staff applauded:** Red Moody interview, November 7, 2006.

203 **"Thank God we finally did it":** *Aircraft Salvops Med,* Final Report, vol. 1, part I, chap. 2, p. 96.

203 **Someone cut up the parachute:** Author's interviews with Oliver Andersen, January 22, 2007, and Red Moody, November 7, 2006.

203 **As Brad Mooney walked:** Brad Mooney interview, March 30, 2007.

204 **approximately a hundred newsmen:** *SAC Historical Study #109,* pp. 344–345.

204 **"under the Mediterranean sun":** "H-Bomb Recovered," CBS News, April 8, 1966.

204 **The embassy had drafted:** *SAC Historical Study #109,* pp. 343–344.

205 **held a press conference:** "William S. Guest Press Conference," April 8, 1966.

205 **"a nightmare of the nuclear age":** Szulc, *Bombs of Palomares,* p. 253.

206 **"made millions of people aware":** Joel Larus, *Nuclear Weapons Safety and the Common Defense* (Columbus: Ohio State University Press, 1967), p. vii.

EPILOGUE

207 **After the press and VIPs left:** *Aircraft Salvops Med,* Interim Report, July 15, 1966, p. C16; Memo, Moody to Commander, "Report of Explosive Ordnance Disposal," May 10, 1966 (NHC), pp. 3–4; *SAC Historical Study #109,* pp. 60–61.

207 **General Wilson had proposed:** *SAC Historical Study #109,* p. 61.

207 **the Navy loaded it:** Deck logs of the USS *Petrel,* April 8, 1966.

207 **The Air Force sent bomb number four:** S. V. Asselin, memo to S. A.

Moore, "Trip to Pantex, April 27 and 28, 1966," undated (Document no. SAC200118240000, Confidential, NNSA, FOIA).

207 **The engineers learned some lessons:** Randall Maydew, oral history, conducted by Necah Furman, December 1991, p. 12.

208 **The USNS *Boyce* arrived:** *SAC Historical Study #109,* p. 188; Emilio Iranzo interview, February 16, 2007.

208 **The other two barrels:** *SAC Historical Study #109,* p. 189.

208 **He said he planned:** Lewis, *One of Our H-Bombs,* p. 236.

208 **the Navy billed the Air Force:** *SAC Historical Study #109,* p. 111.

208 **$10,230,744, or $126,305 per day:** W. M. Place et al., *Palomares Summary Report* (Kirtland Air Force Base, N.M.: Field Command, Defense Nuclear Agency, Technology and Analysis Directorate, January 15, 1975), p. 141. Pp. 142–144 contain a detailed cost breakdown.

208 **On April 7, 1967, exactly one year:** George Martin, e-mail to author, September 24, 2008.

208 **Tony Richardson composed a poem:** Tony Richardson interview, October 31, 2007.

208 **replacing topsoil, repairing ditches:** *SAC Historical Study #109,* pp. 189–190.

209 **The legal staff drew up:** Ibid.

209 **By the end of March:** Ibid., p. 86.

209 **On March 20:** Ibid., p. 302.

209 **but a skeleton crew of lawyers:** Joe Ramirez interview, April 27, 2007.

209 **By September 26:** *SAC Historical Study #109,* pp. 391, 492.

209 **For his help:** Place et al., *Palomares Summary Report,* p. 176.

209 **"As testimony and admiration":** Ibid.

209 **In June, he presented his own claim:** Details on the Orts claim can be found in Place et al., *Palomares Summary Report,* pp. 176–178.

209 **Simó guessed he had saved the military:** "Palomares Revisited re: Atom Bomb," CBS News, December 20, 1966.

210 **In the spring and summer of 1966:** The background of the diplomatic climate leading up to the base negotiations can be found in James E. Miller,

ed., *Foreign Relations of the United States, 1964–1968,* vol. 12, *Western Europe* (Washington, D.C.: U.S. Government Printing Office, 2001), and Airgram, Embassy in Madrid to Department of State, "U.S. Policy Assessment," May 7, 1966 (LBJ).

210 It refused: As of December 1966, the nuclear overflights were still under discussion. See Cable, Embassy in Madrid to SECSTATE, December 10, 1966, #9187 (LBJ).

210 It wanted the United States: Cable, Department of State to Embassy in Madrid, May 6, 1966 (NARA).

210 In May, *The New York Times* reported: Benjamin Welles, "Spain Offers 3 Proposals on Gibraltar," *The New York Times,* May 27, 1966, p. 19.

210 The base negotiations got under way: Memorandum of Conversation, November 13, 1967, "Base Negotiations" (NARA). This document is the earliest record found by the author that lists American and Spanish officials meeting for the express purpose of discussing the bases.

210 He had been lobbying hard: Memorandum for the Files, December 5, 1967, "Spanish Base Negotiations and Palomares" (NARA).

210 "The accident brought home": Ibid.

210 On January 6, 1968, Duke was dining: The story of Duke's return to Washington is from Angier Biddle Duke, Living History interview, October 24, 1990, pp. 20–21, and author's interview with Robin Duke, June 7, 2007.

211 Today, the once barren coast: The description of modern Palomares comes from the author's visit to the area, February 24–28, 2007.

212 Manolo says the town: Manolo and Dolores González interview, February 24, 2007.

212 though it refuses to say: On occasion, the U.S. government has released information about funding for a specific part of Project Indalo. For instance, a 1973 document obtained by the author states that the United States had provided approximately $250,000 in technical equipment and $25,000 a year in operating funds. (See C. R. Richmond, "Remarks on Palomares—Seven Years Later," March 9, 1973 [NNSA, FOIA].) However, the full cost of the project has never been disclosed. The author made numerous requests for interviews with Mohandas Bhat, the DOE project officer for Palomares, and CIEMAT representatives, all of which were refused.

212 It has also tested chickens: Emilio Iranzo interview, February 16, 2007.

212 **Every year, about 150 residents:** The testing numbers come from the DOE Web site on Project Indalo: www.hss.energy.gov/HealthSafety/IIPP/hservices/ps_msurv.html.

212 **these tests show that about 5 percent:** This statistic also comes from the Project Indalo Web site (see previous reference). However, the information on plutonium ingestion was removed from the Web site when it was updated. The author has a printout of the earlier Web page in her files.

212 **This is proven, they say:** Ibid. and Emilio Iranzo interview, February 16, 2007.

212 **Villagers who visit Madrid:** *Operación Flecha Rota: Accidente nucleár de Palomares (Almería),* directed by José Herrera, 2007.

213 **Only one small study:** Pedro Martínez Pinilla et al., "Evolución de la mortalidad en Palomares antes y después del accidente nuclear de 1966," *El Médico* 16, no. 1 (1987). An electronic copy of this article was given to the author by José Herrera Plaza, a documentary filmmaker in Spain, along with an English translation done for Oak Ridge National Laboratories. Herrera downloaded hundreds of Indalo documents from the DOE Web site to his home in Spain, which he generously shared with the author. The author, despite numerous attempts, was never able to download the same documents from the DOE Web site to her home in the United States.

213 **the accident continues to haunt:** See, e.g., Paul Geitner, "Spanish Town Struggles to Forget Its Moment on the Brink of a Nuclear Cataclysm," *The New York Times,* September 12, 2008.

213 **a large irrigation pool:** Emilio Iranzo interview, February 16, 2007; and E. Iranzo et al., "Air Concentrations of ^{239}Pu and ^{240}Pu and Potential Radiation Doses to Persons Living near Pu-Contaminated Areas in Palomares, Spain," *Health Physics,* April 1987, p. 460.

213 **CIEMAT purchased about twenty-three acres:** www.hss.energy.gov/HealthSafety/IIPP/hservices/ps_msurv.html.

213 **It forbade farmers:** Manolo and Dolores González interview, February 24, 2007.

213 **"Now they put a fence":** Ibid.

213 **Between November 21, 2006:** Rafael Méndez, "Detectada contaminación en Palomares fuera de las zonas expropiadas y valladas," *El País,* July 1, 2007.

213 **In April 2008, CIEMAT announced:** Rafael Méndez, "España halla las zanjas radiactivas que EEUU ocultó en Palomares," *El País,* April 4, 2008.

213 **"small radioactive metal objects":** Ibid.

213 **Though the U.S. and Spanish:** See, e.g., Memo, Barrett Fountos to Tom Bell et al., "Trip Report to Spain with Accomplishments Related to Palomares Program Review," September 23, 1998 (author's collection). In this memo, provided to the author by José Herrera Plaza, Emilio Iranzo is noted to have said, "Important to recognize that Pu was left at the site. There were not enough drums to take all the Pu away." Chet Richmond, an American scientist, added, "There were more drums brought in than were taken away. . . . Still need to clarify location of pits." Herrera has long suspected that radioactive material was secretly buried in Spain, an assertion that seems to be supported by this memo and the recent discoveries in Palomares.

213 **they widened the "contaminated" zone:** Méndez, "Detectada contaminación en Palomares," July 1, 2007. The zone was widened from 90,000 to 300,000 square meters, converted into square yards by the author.

214 **Manolo is not worried:** Manolo and Dolores González interview, February 24, 2007.

214 **"Minisubs":** James V. Healion, "Boom on 2-Man Subs Seen," *The Washington Post,* June 25, 1967.

214 **In 1967 and 1968, *Alvin* dove:** *Alvin* history is from WHOI Web site: www.whoi.edu/page.do?pid=10737.

214 **By late 1968, it had completed 307:** William O. Rainnie and William I. Milwee, "How We Raised the *Alvin* from 5000 Feet," *Popular Mechanics,* January 1970, p. 93.

214 *Aluminaut,* **meanwhile, took scientists:** Author's interview with George Tyler, September 26, 2006.

214 **a freak accident:** The description of *Alvin*'s sinking comes from Department of the Navy, Naval Ship Systems Command, *Recovery of Deep Research Vehicle* Alvin (Washington, D.C.: Naval Ship Systems Command, December 1969); Rainnie and Milwee, "How We Raised the *Alvin*"; and Kaharl, *Water Baby,* pp. 115–119.

215 **was estimated to weigh about 8,800:** Department of the Navy, Naval Ship Systems Command, *Recovery of Deep Research Vehicle* Alvin, p. 6.

215 **"Leave that damn toy":** Kaharl, *Water Baby,* p. 122.

215 **Salvage experts agreed:** The description of *Alvin*'s recovery comes from Department of the Navy, Naval Ship Systems Command, *Recovery of*

Deep Research Vehicle Alvin; Eugene B. Mitchell and William I. Milwee, "Recovery of *Alvin*—A Practical Ocean Engineering Operation," *Naval Engineers Journal,* December 1969, pp. 13–22; Rainnie and Milwee, "How We Raised the *Alvin*"; and Kaharl, *Water Baby,* pp. 121–124.

215 **The assignment was a coup:** George Tyler interview, September 26, 2006.

215 **On August 27, 1969,** *Aluminaut* **submerged:** Department of the Navy, Naval Ship Systems Command, *Recovery of Deep Research Vehicle* Alvin, p. 28.

215 **Bob Canary, the** *Aluminaut* **pilot:** The "wet noodle" quote is from Kaharl, *Water Baby,* p. 123.

216 **He wanted to grab the controls:** Ibid.

216 **an account flatly denied:** George Tyler interview, September 26, 2006. Tyler describes this story as "bullshit."

216 **was in remarkably good condition:** Mitchell and Milwee, "Recovery of *Alvin,*" pp. 21–22. Interestingly, a bologna sandwich salvaged from the sub showed no deterioration from bacteria. This accidental discovery that near-freezing temperatures and lack of oxygen aided preservation opened up new areas of scientific research. (See WHOI Web site, www.whoi.edu/page.do?pid=10737.)

216 **Scientists and engineers flushed:** Kaharl, *Water Baby,* pp. 126–127.

216 **government funding for deep-sea exploration:** Ibid., pp. 127–128; "The *Aluminaut* Story," March 6, 1986, p. 10.

216 **accepting projects that embarrassed:** George Tyler interview, September 26, 2006.

216 **in 1971, Reynolds canceled:** "The *Aluminaut* Story," March 6, 1986, p. 10; Richard Pothier, "Star of Deep for Six Years, She's to Be a Sub on Bench," *The Miami Herald,* undated. The records are not entirely clear, but it appears that the sub was semiretired in 1970 and mothballed in 1971.

216 **The sub is probably best known:** The *Alvin* history is from WHOI Web site: www.whoi.edu/page.do?pid=10737.

216 **All that remains of the original:** Author's visit to *Alvin* and interviews with Bob Brown and Bruce Strickrott, July 2, 2007.

216 **The sub will retire by 2015:** William J. Broad, "New Sphere in Exploring the Abyss," *The New York Times,* August 26, 2008, p. D1.

216   On January 21, 1968:   The details of the Thule accident come from Scott D. Sagan, *The Limits of Safety: Organizations, Accidents and Nuclear Weapons* (Princeton, N.J.: Princeton Studies in International History and Politics, 1993), pp. 156–157; "Narrative Summaries of Accidents Involving U.S. Nuclear Weapons 1950–1980," undated (NNSA, FOIA); Department of the Air Force, *USAF Nuclear Safety, Special Edition: Project Crested Ice,* 65 (part 2), no. 1, Jan–Feb–Mar 1970. In November 2008, the BBC revealed that the United States had secretly left nuclear components buried in the ice. See Gordon Corera, "Mystery of Lost U.S. Nuclear Bomb," http://news.bbc.co.uk/2/hi/europe/7720049.stm, posted November 10, 2008.

217   McNamara had proposed canceling: Sagan, *Limits of Safety,* pp. 178–179.

217   He ordered SAC to stop: "U.S. Bars H-Bombs in Airborne Alert," *The New York Times,* February 29, 1968, p. 1; Sagan, *Limits of Safety,* pp. 193–196.

217   who were tired of cleaning up: Sagan, *Limits of Safety,* p. 196. Sagan includes this relevant footnote: "Civilian authorities grew increasingly exasperated with the Strategic Air Command after these accidents. For example, in one press report, an unidentified civilian official recalls that Ambassador Angier Biddle Duke found it necessary to go for a swim in the ocean at Palomares to assure the Spaniards that there was no danger and says, 'Next time we ought to make the whole SAC command go swimming.' "

218   SAC veterans were shocked: Author's interviews with SAC veterans, August 23 and 25, 2005.

218   In 2007, Russian President Vladimir Putin: Andrew E. Kramer, "Recalling Cold War, Russia Resumes Long-Range Sorties," *The New York Times,* August 18, 2007.

INDEX

ABOUT THE AUTHOR

BARBARA MORAN is an award-winning science journalist whose work has appeared in *New Scientist, Invention & Technology, Technology Review,* and *The Boston Globe.* Her television documentary credits include the PBS series *Frontline, The American Experience,* and *NOVA,* as well as the History and Discovery Channels. Research for this book began when she was a Knight Fellow at MIT. A graduate of the University of Notre Dame and Boston University's Center for Science and Medical Journalism, she lives in Boston with her husband and son.

www.WrittenByBarbaraMoran.com